Lecture Notes in Computer Science 10910

Commenced Publication in 1973
Founding and Former Series Editors:
Gerhard Goos, Juris Hartmanis, and Jan van Leeuwen

More information about this series at http://www.springer.com/series/7409

Jessie Y. C. Chen · Gino Fragomeni (Eds.)

Virtual, Augmented and Mixed Reality

Applications in Health, Cultural Heritage, and Industry

10th International Conference, VAMR 2018
Held as Part of HCI International 2018
Las Vegas, NV, USA, July 15–20, 2018
Proceedings, Part II

 Springer

Editors
Jessie Y. C. Chen
US Army Research Laboratory
Aberdeen Proving Ground, MD
USA

Gino Fragomeni
US Army Research Laboratory
Orlando, FL
USA

ISSN 0302-9743   ISSN 1611-3349   (electronic)
Lecture Notes in Computer Science
ISBN 978-3-319-91583-8   ISBN 978-3-319-91584-5   (eBook)
https://doi.org/10.1007/978-3-319-91584-5

Library of Congress Control Number: 2018944282

LNCS Sublibrary: SL3 – Information Systems and Applications, incl. Internet/Web, and HCI

Printed on acid-free paper

This Springer imprint is published by the registered company Springer International Publishing AG
part of Springer Nature
The registered company address is: Gewerbestrasse 11, 6330 Cham, Switzerland

Foreword

The 20th International Conference on Human-Computer Interaction, HCI International 2018, was held in Las Vegas, NV, USA, during July 15–20, 2018. The event incorporated the 14 conferences/thematic areas listed on the following page.

A total of 4,373 individuals from academia, research institutes, industry, and governmental agencies from 76 countries submitted contributions, and 1,170 papers and 195 posters have been included in the proceedings. These contributions address the latest research and development efforts and highlight the human aspects of design and use of computing systems. The contributions thoroughly cover the entire field of human-computer interaction, addressing major advances in knowledge and effective use of computers in a variety of application areas. The volumes constituting the full set of the conference proceedings are listed in the following pages.

I would like to thank the program board chairs and the members of the program boards of all thematic areas and affiliated conferences for their contribution to the highest scientific quality and the overall success of the HCI International 2018 conference.

This conference would not have been possible without the continuous and unwavering support and advice of the founder, Conference General Chair Emeritus and Conference Scientific Advisor Prof. Gavriel Salvendy. For his outstanding efforts, I would like to express my appreciation to the communications chair and editor of *HCI International News*, Dr. Abbas Moallem.

July 2018   Constantine Stephanidis

HCI International 2018 Thematic Areas and Affiliated Conferences

Thematic areas:

- Human-Computer Interaction (HCI 2018)
- Human Interface and the Management of Information (HIMI 2018)

Affiliated conferences:

- 15th International Conference on Engineering Psychology and Cognitive Ergonomics (EPCE 2018)
- 12th International Conference on Universal Access in Human-Computer Interaction (UAHCI 2018)
- 10th International Conference on Virtual, Augmented, and Mixed Reality (VAMR 2018)
- 10th International Conference on Cross-Cultural Design (CCD 2018)
- 10th International Conference on Social Computing and Social Media (SCSM 2018)
- 12th International Conference on Augmented Cognition (AC 2018)
- 9th International Conference on Digital Human Modeling and Applications in Health, Safety, Ergonomics, and Risk Management (DHM 2018)
- 7th International Conference on Design, User Experience, and Usability (DUXU 2018)
- 6th International Conference on Distributed, Ambient, and Pervasive Interactions (DAPI 2018)
- 5th International Conference on HCI in Business, Government, and Organizations (HCIBGO)
- 5th International Conference on Learning and Collaboration Technologies (LCT 2018)
- 4th International Conference on Human Aspects of IT for the Aged Population (ITAP 2018)

Conference Proceedings Volumes Full List

1. LNCS 10901, Human-Computer Interaction: Theories, Methods, and Human Issues (Part I), edited by Masaaki Kurosu
2. LNCS 10902, Human-Computer Interaction: Interaction in Context (Part II), edited by Masaaki Kurosu
3. LNCS 10903, Human-Computer Interaction: Interaction Technologies (Part III), edited by Masaaki Kurosu
4. LNCS 10904, Human Interface and the Management of Information: Interaction, Visualization, and Analytics (Part I), edited by Sakae Yamamoto and Hirohiko Mori
5. LNCS 10905, Human Interface and the Management of Information: Information in Applications and Services (Part II), edited by Sakae Yamamoto and Hirohiko Mori
6. LNAI 10906, Engineering Psychology and Cognitive Ergonomics, edited by Don Harris
7. LNCS 10907, Universal Access in Human-Computer Interaction: Methods, Technologies, and Users (Part I), edited by Margherita Antona and Constantine Stephanidis
8. LNCS 10908, Universal Access in Human-Computer Interaction: Virtual, Augmented, and Intelligent Environments (Part II), edited by Margherita Antona and Constantine Stephanidis
9. LNCS 10909, Virtual, Augmented and Mixed Reality: Interaction, Navigation, Visualization, Embodiment, and Simulation (Part I), edited by Jessie Y. C. Chen and Gino Fragomeni
10. LNCS 10910, Virtual, Augmented and Mixed Reality: Applications in Health, Cultural Heritage, and Industry (Part II), edited by Jessie Y. C. Chen and Gino Fragomeni
11. LNCS 10911, Cross-Cultural Design: Methods, Tools, and Users (Part I), edited by Pei-Luen Patrick Rau
12. LNCS 10912, Cross-Cultural Design: Applications in Cultural Heritage, Creativity, and Social Development (Part II), edited by Pei-Luen Patrick Rau
13. LNCS 10913, Social Computing and Social Media: User Experience and Behavior (Part I), edited by Gabriele Meiselwitz
14. LNCS 10914, Social Computing and Social Media: Technologies and Analytics (Part II), edited by Gabriele Meiselwitz
15. LNAI 10915, Augmented Cognition: Intelligent Technologies (Part I), edited by Dylan D. Schmorrow and Cali M. Fidopiastis
16. LNAI 10916, Augmented Cognition: Users and Contexts (Part II), edited by Dylan D. Schmorrow and Cali M. Fidopiastis
17. LNCS 10917, Digital Human Modeling and Applications in Health, Safety, Ergonomics, and Risk Management, edited by Vincent G. Duffy
18. LNCS 10918, Design, User Experience, and Usability: Theory and Practice (Part I), edited by Aaron Marcus and Wentao Wang

19. LNCS 10919, Design, User Experience, and Usability: Designing Interactions (Part II), edited by Aaron Marcus and Wentao Wang
20. LNCS 10920, Design, User Experience, and Usability: Users, Contexts, and Case Studies (Part III), edited by Aaron Marcus and Wentao Wang
21. LNCS 10921, Distributed, Ambient, and Pervasive Interactions: Understanding Humans (Part I), edited by Norbert Streitz and Shin'ichi Konomi
22. LNCS 10922, Distributed, Ambient, and Pervasive Interactions: Technologies and Contexts (Part II), edited by Norbert Streitz and Shin'ichi Konomi
23. LNCS 10923, HCI in Business, Government, and Organizations, edited by Fiona Fui-Hoon Nah and Bo Sophia Xiao
24. LNCS 10924, Learning and Collaboration Technologies: Design, Development and Technological Innovation (Part I), edited by Panayiotis Zaphiris and Andri Ioannou
25. LNCS 10925, Learning and Collaboration Technologies: Learning and Teaching (Part II), edited by Panayiotis Zaphiris and Andri Ioannou
26. LNCS 10926, Human Aspects of IT for the Aged Population: Acceptance, Communication, and Participation (Part I), edited by Jia Zhou and Gavriel Salvendy
27. LNCS 10927, Human Aspects of IT for the Aged Population: Applications in Health, Assistance, and Entertainment (Part II), edited by Jia Zhou and Gavriel Salvendy
28. CCIS 850, HCI International 2018 Posters Extended Abstracts (Part I), edited by Constantine Stephanidis
29. CCIS 851, HCI International 2018 Posters Extended Abstracts (Part II), edited by Constantine Stephanidis
30. CCIS 852, HCI International 2018 Posters Extended Abstracts (Part III), edited by Constantine Stephanidis

http://2018.hci.international/proceedings

10th International Conference on Virtual, Augmented and Mixed Reality

Program Board Chair(s): **Jessie Y. C. Chen
and Gino Fragomeni, *USA***

- Jacob Crandall, USA
- Tami Griffith, USA
- Stephanie J. Lackey, USA
- Fotis Liarokapis, Czech Republic
- Joseph Lyons, USA
- Philip Mangos, USA
- Amar Marathe, USA

- Rafael Radkowski, USA
- Maria Olinda Rodas, USA
- José San Martín, Spain
- Peter A. Smith, USA
- Tom Williams, USA
- Denny Yu, USA

The full list with the Program Board Chairs and the members of the Program Boards of all thematic areas and affiliated conferences is available online at:

http://www.hci.international/board-members-2018.php

HCI International 2019

The 21st International Conference on Human-Computer Interaction, HCI International 2019, will be held jointly with the affiliated conferences in Orlando, FL, USA, at Walt Disney World Swan and Dolphin Resort, July 26–31, 2019. It will cover a broad spectrum of themes related to Human-Computer Interaction, including theoretical issues, methods, tools, processes, and case studies in HCI design, as well as novel interaction techniques, interfaces, and applications. The proceedings will be published by Springer. More information will be available on the conference website: http://2019.hci.international/.

General Chair
Prof. Constantine Stephanidis
University of Crete and ICS-FORTH
Heraklion, Crete, Greece
E-mail: general_chair@hcii2019.org

http://2019.hci.international/

Contents – Part II

Contents – Part I

Education, Training and Simulation

VAMR in Psychotherapy, Exercising and Health

A Case Study: Chronic Pain Patients' Preferences for Virtual Reality Games for Pain Distraction

Xin Tong[1(✉)], Weina Jin[1], Kathryn Cruz[1], Diane Gromala[1],
Bernie Garret[2], and Tarnia Taverner[2]

[1] Pain Studies Lab, Simon Fraser University, Surrey, Canada
{tongxint,weinaj,kathryn_cruz,gromala}@sfu.ca
[2] School of Nursing, University of British Columbia, Vancouver, Canada
{bernie.garret,tarnia.taverner}@nursing.ubc.ca

Abstract. We plan to conduct a longitudinal mixed-methods study to evaluate the impact of home-use Virtual Reality (VR) for chronic pain (CP) management with cancer survivors over a six-week period. The participants will play VR games for a minimum of 30 min per day for at least three days per week. Each week, the participants are required to use randomly assigned VR content from a group of VR titles that ranged from commercially-available VR games to VR meditation designed specifically for people with CP. Well before launching the longitudinal study, we compiled, tested, categorized and eliminated commercial VR titles, and developed a short list that varied by genre and methods of interaction. Therefore, to better understand which are the best VR games to use, how to offer good VR gaming experiences, and validate our choices, we compared CP patients' experiences of some selected games in VR and non-VR conditions in this research. Seven pain patients took part in the focus group study; initial results suggest participants preferred VR conditions compared to PC games according to both of the quantitative ratings and the qualitative interviews. They also liked puzzle-solving game mechanism comparing to exploration games. Participants also mentioned that the platform (VR vs. PC monitor) is more important than the actual content. This result will be helpful for the researchers to select proper VR games to test in the longitudinal study for pain distraction and management purposes since it has been done with patients.

Keywords: Virtual reality games · Pain distraction · Chronic pain
Gaming preferences · Case study

1 Introduction

Video games—especially immersive Virtual Reality (VR) games—are considered to be an effective method of pain distraction in short-term, acute conditions [1]. Among these relatively small but numerous studies [2], however, the efficacy of VR typically ends when the Head-Mounted Display (HMD) is removed or persists for a few minutes after that [3]. For Chronic Pain (CP) conditions, however, only a few studies of the

© Springer International Publishing AG, part of Springer Nature 2018
J. Y. C. Chen and G. Fragomeni (Eds.): VAMR 2018, LNCS 10910, pp. 3–11, 2018.
https://doi.org/10.1007/978-3-319-91584-5_1

effectiveness of VR have been conducted [4]; among these, the long-term impact of VR on CP management and pain perceptions is unknown. Therefore, we proposed and received funding to conduct a longitudinal mixed-methods study to evaluate the impact of home-use VR for chronic pain management. The plan is to recruit 100 participants with CP; each will be randomly assigned to either a VR or control group (50 subjects in each). Each participant is scheduled to undertake either a series of VR interventions or no-VR control sessions using a computer in their own homes over a period of six weeks. The same content is available in both VR and non-VR conditions (i.e., on a non-stereographic computer monitor), and are randomly assigned.

Before the launch of the longitudinal study, it is necessary and important to decide what VR titles (VR "content" such as a game, exploration or training) to use in the study's VR and non-VR conditions.

First, we identified a list of approximately 40 commercially available VR games, each of which is also available as a non-VR option, i.e., as a videogame on a standard PC. We also identified a VR "title" that was designed specifically for chronic pain patients and that also has a non-VR option. Next, the list of titles was categorized regarding game genre, required PC or VR devices, controller schemes, and methods of interactions. Finally, we developed a shortlist of titles that varied by category to assign to our participants. To validate that our choices were usable by and appropriate for CP patients, we conducted a case study described in this paper with CP patients trying out representative games from various game genres. Therefore, the result of this case study could be generalized for choosing games for other patients, and to understand game preferences of CP patients so the conclusions could be used in other VR research for pain management purpose.

Out of the four representative games, which are *Obduction* and *The Witness* for PC games, and *Call for the Starseed* and *Carpe Lucem* (as shown in Fig. 1), we have selected with VR or non-VR versions, and we hypothesize that participants will prefer VR version because its sense of immersion consistently tests greater. Furthermore, comparing all games, we assume that participants would prefer games with less intense gameplay and easier game mechanics and dynamics, rather than complicated or intense game. In this case study, we were trying to assess: (1) Whether these games are suitable for CP patients to play; (2) Whether each game fulfills the intended experience.

2   Related Work

Video games, especially VR games, have been considered to be a good source of distraction for pain management in acute conditions [4–7]. Games can be used in the medical realm as a valuable resource. Games are defined as such by having a goal, rules, feedback, and voluntary participation; all measurable features that can help patients engage in their treatment [8]. Recently, VR games and video games have also been used in chronic pain management [6, 9–11]. In addition to pain management, active video games have been previously examined to improve balance confidence and is additive to normal rehabilitation as a method pain management [5]. *The Virtual*

Meditative Walk (VMW) was one of the VR environments that the Pain Studies Lab has developed. A prior pilot study and publication about VMW validated that this VR environment was able to help patients reduce their pain levels in short-term timeframe [9]. Systems such as the VMW incorporate biofeedback inputs, a rising trend in medical VR, that can provide data integrated and used for feedback to patients and medical personnel [9, 12].

However, very few studies have compared CP patients' preferences of game selections, and to our knowledge, none of the research has compared CP patients' experiences of the same game in VR and non-VR conditions. This study aims to account for a comparison group unlike previously done studies when VR was included [7]. Furthermore, patient preferences have been minimally explored in other respects, such as game controllers used that may enhance or diminish their experience [13]. Therefore, in this study, we invited a few CP patients to experience each game sequentially and then had a focus group discussion to better understand whether the game experiences would help us to investigate further research questions.

3   Research Methodology

3.1   Study Goals

The aim of our study is to find out CP patients' preferences of playing video games in PC and immersive VR conditions. The experiences of CP patients differ regarding game genres, game devices, controller schemes, and whether the experience is on a VR or PC platform.

This study can help the researchers better understand CP patients' gaming choices, knowing what are the potential appropriate games for them to play, and what are the media forms they would prefer to play with. Our hypothesis is that the game content, and the game platform does matter for patients, which will generate effects on their consistency and willingness of using a game for pain management in a long-term run. Further, we hypothesize that participants will prefer games genres which are not mentally demanding since elder CP patients usually could not cope with too complicated game tasks nor can they use the controllers to navigate with physical movement limitations.

For instance, we expect *Carpe Lucem* and *The Witness* to provide a puzzle-solving challenge whereas *Obduction* and *Call for the Starseed* offer exploration. Exploration games are usually less overwhelming and provide more relaxation than a puzzle-solving game. So we hypothesize that our participants would like *Obduction* and *Call for the Starseed* better than *Carpe Lucem* or *The Witness*.

3.2   Participants

Seven chronic pain patients were originally recruited through direct recruitment method (researchers sent emails to potential participants from a list). The participants were all female (Mean = 35.86, SD = 12.64). The average length that they have chronic pain is 7.64 years (SD = 7.16). Five of the participants have experience playing mobile games, and four played it several times per week (P04, P05, P06, P07), one several times per day (P01), while the other two have none experience playing any game (P02, P03). However, P03, P04, and P06 had experienced a VR environment once before (Table 1).

Table 1. Participants' age distribution.

	Amount of people
19–24	2
25–29	1
30–40	2
>40	2

Fig. 1. (Left image) HTC Vive VR device setting. Copyright @ HTC Vive.

3.3 Apparatus

In the VR condition, *HTC Vive* HMD and *Alienware* desktop were used, and in the PC condition participants used another *Alienware* computer and a monitor to play. The VR condition setup was illustrated in Fig. 1, while the player uses a desktop and sit in front of the monitor in the PC condition. Figure 2 shows one of our participants play the game. As for the four games that were chosen, *Call of the Starseed* is a calm and slow First-Person VR adventure game in which players need to a few solve puzzles to progress in the narrative. *The Witness* is a PC title, which is a similar title to *Call of the Starseed* regarding the intended experience: players solve puzzles in an island. The puzzles in *Call of the Starseed* requires bodily movements such as bending, which might not be easy for CP patients. Therefore, we also included the game *Carpe Lucem*, which involves solving physics puzzles in a sitting or standing position. *Obduction* is an exploration game which has both VR and PC versions. The virtual environment in *Obduction* has many sci-fi elements. Figure 3 shows the screenshots of all four games.

Fig. 2. (Right image) A participant interacting with the game in HTC Vive HMD device.

Fig. 3. Screenshots of four games played in this study (from top to bottom) (a) *Call for the Starseed* (VR game); (b) *Obduction* (PC game); (c) *Carpe Lucem* (VR game); (d) *The Witness* (PC game)

3.4 Study Procedures

This is a mixed-method study design with both a quantitative measurement survey and a qualitative interview discussion. Firstly, we gathered their demographic information and assessed their gaming and VR experience in the pretest questionnaire after getting their ethics. Next, the participants were asked to play either two PC or VR games in a random order and then answer their evaluations for this platform. Then they will try out next platform and give ratings regarding the same questions.

We asked them to rate their interest and willingness to play each game in the posttest questionnaire after they play all games. The participants were asked to rate each game on an 11-point Likert scale (0 means dislike the game and 10 means like the game). The post-test interview was audiotaped after getting consent from the participants. One of the researchers led the discussion by asking the major guide questions. The interview guide contains questions like among all games, which VR or PC games do they like best, which platform they'd prefer to use, ease of use of both controllers in VR and in PC platform, as well as the physical effects on them during their play time (such as motion sickness, pain level changes if there is any, etc.). Furthermore, the participants were asked to talk about their own choices of the game for pain distraction purposes if they were the designer.

The study lasts for around 1 to 1.5 h in total with each participant. Two VR games (*Call for the Starseed, Carpe Lucem*) and two PC games (*The Witness, Obduction*) were tested.

4 Results and Discussions

From the demographic information we collected, we conclude that five of them were the casual type of gamers (P01, P04, P05, P06, P07) while the other two were non-gamer at all (P02, P03). They all had no prior experience playing VR games.

4.1 Quantitative Analysis

For the two PC games, participants did not enjoy *Obduction* very much (M = 4.17, SD = 2.40), while they showed moderate interest in playing *The Witness* (M = 5.17, SD = 2.79). For the two VR games, the participants both rated them higher than the PC games, showing a greater interest in *Carpe Lucem* (M = 8.86, SD = 0.90) than *Call for the Starseed* (M = 7.50, SD = 1.38). As for the probability that they will play the game at home, all expressed higher ratings of VR condition (M = 8.43, SD = 1.72) than PC condition (M = 6.17, SD = 2.79).

4.2 Qualitative Analysis

For the game genre, we include a puzzle game and an exploration game both on VR and PC platform. Although our participants gave a higher rating of puzzle games like *Carpe Lucem* overall, each game has its supporters, and participants' taste diverge. Participants' preference on game genre seemed to be dependent on the combination of game design and the platform and did not transfer when game platform changed. For example, P03 enjoyed the puzzle game (*The Witness*) on PC while favored the exploration game (*Call for the Starseed*) on VR. However, the puzzle game is not in favor of all the participants, for example, P04 mentioned "I'm assuming the puzzles... was getting repetitive. That may be the only thing that I would dislike about it. If all the puzzles were kinda the same."

For the gaming platform, 6 out of 7 participants favored VR over PC platform and preferred VR games if they have the freedom to choose any games. "It was more fun to be in it, than staring at it." [P01] "It's virtual reality, it's almost, it feels more tactile." "I think it's more just the spatial awareness." [P03] One participant like the PC game, since she had neck pain and commented that "just because the VR was a little rough on the neck" [P04].

For the physical feelings, most participants felt comfortable and relaxed while playing the VR game. For instance, "Very relaxing playing the VR game... complete body relaxation" [P02]. One participant mentioned the pain level decreased from 6 before the study to 5 during the interview. This effect is after both PC and VR gameplay. "And now it's on 5. ... I found that feeling relieving in a way." [P03] "I feel like the VR, because it's so new to me, because it's so cool, like, it's almost more of a distraction. Afterward, the pain would come back, and it might get worse if I was to play for a long time. But while I'm playing it, I might not notice the pain as much. ... I wasn't really thinking about it (the pain condition)." [P05] "(In VR) I felt more distracted. I was more comfortable in a sense, like, yeah. I didn't feel nauseous. ... Cuz you're doing something, and you're focused and it's, it's very distracting" [P07].

However, due to some participants' pain conditions, playing games on various platforms could cause certain physical discomfort. For the PC platform, some participant report discomfort while sitting and using the mouse and keyboard to control simultaneously. "Like my pain is the worst in my hands and wrists. So it's hard for me to like, use a mouse or a keyboard for extended periods of time." [P05] "The movement (in PC), I felt nauseous for sure, and I don't know if it's because I'm feeling a bit nauseous. When my pain is bad I'm nauseous. But that maybe made it worse. And it's just the walking. So I'm not sure the reason but I did feel really nauseous." [P07] The VR platform also cause certain problems for one participant as she mentioned, "(VR) just increase in neck pain" [P04].

For the navigation and movement in VR, participants have mixed view on the teleporting mechanics used in *Call for the Starseed*. P02 and P03 liked the teleporting experience after figuring out how it works, while P01 didn't like the idea and she said "so I didn't know that I could physically, like me moving, inside the environment for the fine-tuning. I couldn't figure out exactly how I would get myself to exactly where I wanted to be."

For the game control, all participants prefer the VR controller than the joystick controller of the PC games. As P02 mentioned "With the controllers in the PC, you are very static and stationary, whereas with VR, if you had gloves, you would have (a) full range of motion. "It's pretty cool, it's my first time playing with something like that, so it was really interesting. It was cool. I was impressed by how responsive it was. It was like really responsive; it was perfect" [P05].

5 Conclusion

In this case study, to evaluate the CP patients' preferences of playing PC and VR games, we recruited seven CP patients to play four off-the-shelf games. Two are PC and the other two are VR games. Most of the participants prefer VR games over PC games, since they feel more immersed in the virtual space. Most participants did not feel discomfort while playing the two VR games except two patients who had neck pain and arthritis pain.

In conclusion, we need to consider CP patients' individual differences, including pain conditions, player types (casual or hardcore players?) and the attitudes toward VR/PC game interactions. From this study, we understand that the choices of VR content should be validated first, which will be utilized in our longitudinal VR study in the near future. As the VR titles became widely and commercially available, the focus group in this pilot study provided important information about the choices of VR content and revealed important limitations of these games from the perspective of CP patients (such as the ability to sit or stand for certain lengths of time).

Acknowledgement. We thank all of the players who participated in this research and the Natural Sciences and Engineering Research Council of Canada (NSERC) for funding this study.

References

1. Hoffman, H.G., Prothero, J., Wells, M.J., Groen, J.: Virtual chess: meaning enhances users' sense of presence in virtual environments, pp. 251–263, November 2009
2. Mahrer, N.E., Gold, J.I.: The use of virtual reality for pain control: a review. Curr. Pain Headache Rep. **13**(2), 100–109 (2009)
3. Garrett, B., Taverner, T., Masinde, W., Gromala, D., Shaw, C., Negraeff, M.: A rapid evidence assessment of immersive virtual reality as an adjunct therapy in acute pain management in clinical practice. Clin. J. Pain **30**(12), 1089–1098 (2014)
4. Hoffman, H.G., Doctor, J.N., Patterson, D.R., Carrougher, G.J.: Virtual reality as an adjunctive pain control during burn wound care in adolescent patients [burn pain, virtual reality, presence, analgesia, distraction, attention]. IASP **1**(2), 305–309 (2000)
5. Staiano, A.E., Flynn, R.: Therapeutic uses of active videogames: a systematic review. Games Health J. **3**(6), 351–365 (2014)
6. Wiederhold, B.K., Gao, K., Sulea, C., Wiederhold, M.D.: Virtual reality as a distraction technique in chronic pain patients. Cyberpsychol. Behav. Soc. Netw. **17**(6), 346–352 (2014)
7. Jones, T., Moore, T., Rose, H., Choo, J.: The impact of virtual reality on chronic pain. J. Pain **17**(4, Supplement), S102–S103 (2016)
8. Hookham, G., Nesbitt, K., Kay-Lambkin, F.: Comparing usability and engagement between a serious game and a traditional online program. In: Proceedings of the Australasian Computer Science Week Multiconference, New York, NY, USA, pp. 54:1–54:10 (2016)
9. Gromala, D., Tong, X., Choo, A., Karamnejad, M., Shaw, C.D.: The Virtual meditative walk: virtual reality therapy for chronic pain management. In: Proceedings of the 33rd Annual ACM Conference on Human Factors in Computing Systems, New York, NY, USA, pp. 521–524 (2015)

10. Shahrbanian, S., Ma, X., Korner-Bitensky, N., Simmonds, M.J.: Scientific evidence for the effectiveness of virtual reality for pain reduction in adults with acute or chronic pain. Stud. Health Technol. Inf. **144**, 40–43 (2009)
11. Malloy, K.M., Milling, L.S.: The effectiveness of virtual reality distraction for pain reduction: a systematic review. Clin. Psychol. Rev. **30**(8), 1011–1018 (2010)
12. Schonauer, C., Pintaric, T., Kaufmann, H., Jansen-Kosterink, S., Vollenbroek-Hutten, M.: Chronic pain rehabilitation with a serious game using multimodal input. In: 2011 International Conference on Virtual Rehabilitation (ICVR), pp. 1–8 (2011)
13. Mortensen, J., Kristensen, L.Q., Brooks, E.P., Brooks, A.L.: Women with fibromyalgia's experience with three motion-controlled video game consoles and indicators of symptom severity and performance of activities of daily living. Disabil. Rehabil. Assist. Technol. **10**(1), 61–66 (2015)

The Effect of Multimodal Feedback
on Perceived Exertion on a VR Exercise Setting

Jon Ram Bruun-Pedersen[(⊠)], Morten G. Andersen,
Mathias M. Clemmensen, Mads K. Didriksen, Emil J. Wittendorff,
and Stefania Serafin

Aalborg University Copenhagen, A. C. Meyers Vænge 15,
2450 Copenhagen SV, Denmark
{jpe,sts}@create.aau.dk,
{morand14,mclemm14,mdidri14,ewitte14}@student.aau.dk

Abstract. This paper seeks to determine if multimodal feedback, from auditory and haptic stimuli, can affect a user's perceived exertion in a virtual reality setting. A simple virtual environment was created in the style of a desert to minimize the amount of visual distractions; a head mounted display was used to display the environment. Users would in the real world drive a Combi Bike and the velocity generated was translated to a vehicle in the virtual environment, moving it forward on a predetermined path. Each user traversed a total of eight hills, two in each of the four conditions. The perceived exertion was measured several times during each condition using the Borg Scale. The results show that there is no significant difference between the four conditions, which had different combinations of auditory and haptic feedback.

Keywords: Virtual reality · Exertion · Multimodal stimuli · Exercise bike

1 Introduction

It is reasonable, that what we have grown to understand about real life settings, directly influences our perception and interpretation of situations or interactions in virtual reality. The study of perceived exertion from physical activity in this relation is interesting for several reasons. It is not highly documented how individual modalities dominate specific parts of the experience of exertion when physical activities are augmented in virtual reality (VR), and its application might be particularly useful in areas such as exercise or rehabilitation using VR. A manipulation of a user's perceived exertion level, could lead to a change of the sensation of fatigue, or the difference between the experience of accomplishment or failure. For instance, for users not otherwise prone to exercise, regulating their sense of exertion could have an effect on their overall exercise experience. If a sense of accomplishment, e.g. for an elderly practitioner, is in part based on a perception of conquering a vast exercise task (such as lifting a series of objects perceived as heavy), an illusion of high exertion could be constructive. If weakened practitioners (for instance, cancer patients) need to exercise but cannot believe themselves capable, perceiving a lower exertion level with that exercise could make the exercise appear easier, and thus be valuable. VR has

© Springer International Publishing AG, part of Springer Nature 2018
J. Y. C. Chen and G. Fragomeni (Eds.): VAMR 2018, LNCS 10910, pp. 12–30, 2018.
https://doi.org/10.1007/978-3-319-91584-5_2

previously shown its merits as a motivation tool for VR rehabilitation [1–3], and manipulation of users' perception of exertion seems possible [4, 5], while uncharted, especially for VR. This paper seeks to explore how to manipulate a user's perception of exertion in immersive VR. More specifically, the paper presents an experiment where participants are asked to use an immersive VR biking simulation, in which they drive up- or downhill inside the virtual environment, with varying multimodal feedback, and rate the perceived level exertion for each run for each.

2 Related Works

The body of studies on the manipulation of perceived exertion through the use of multimodal feedback are sparse. But while results have not been consistently significant between recent studies on the perceived exertion under certain feedback conditions [4, 5], a shared finding has been that users have indeed perceived a change in perceived exertion, when the activity is augmented with auditory feedback, from variations to pass filters and amplitude.

Looking at studies on behavior related to physical activity based on feedback in VR, Plotnik et al. [6] show how changing the inclination in VR (with walking) altered participants' gait, even when a physical treadmill was level. Meanwhile, Denton [7] investigated how locomotor respiratory coupling was affected by inclined walking in VR but found no significant changes from level walking and inclined walking. However, both studies used projections on canvas and not head mounted displays (HMD), and no additional multisensory feedback. Even so, Plotnik et al. [6] showed participant reactions to the stimuli provided. Looking specifically at studies using non-visual sensory feedback to affect perceived exertion, Bordegoni et al. [4] showed how altering the frequency and amplitude of the sound, produced by friction from a pulley machine, affected the perception of exertion, using the Borg rating of perceived exertion (RPE) scale [8]. By manipulating sound in real-time, generated from the metal wire connecting the pull handle to the weight bricks, the pulling sound was augmented through headphones, as feedback suggesting increased or decreased weight of the pull. After each pull, participants were asked to rate their level of exertion on the RPE scale. Despite the physical weight on the pulley always remained the same for all conditions, results showed significant differences of exertion for frequency content between low-pass filters at 1000 Hz (more exertion), compared to a highpass filter-split at the same frequency (less exertion) [4].

In subsequent study, Bruun-Pedersen et al. [5] investigated the role of similar auditory feedback, to measure the differences in perceived exertion with a VR based biking simulation. The setup used a DeskCycle couch-bike, a 55' LED TV for visuals and speakers for audio [5]. When the user pedaled, the TV would provide visual feedback, of moving through a park VE. The base auditory feedback was the sound of wheels, chain and cabin of recumbent bike. The behavior of the feedback (speed, etc.) corresponded with the speed of a user's pedaling. Similar to Bordegoni et al. [4], this study used 9 conditions; 3 frequency settings and 3 amplitude settings [5]. Participant's rated their perceived exertion level using the RPE scale [8]. RPE results showed no significant differences between conditions, but qualitative measures suggested that the majority of participants perceived gradual changes in exertion between conditions. Changes which many participants described as a difference in mechanical resistance from the bike. Perhaps more interesting, was the fact that no participants had been aware of the differences in auditory feedback, while performing experiment trials. When presented to some participants post-trial, however, participant responses were that the individual feedback conditions were considered very different from each other [5] (Fig. 1).

Fig. 1. The park VE used by Bruun-Pedersen et al. [5]

The different results between the studies by Bordegoni et al. [4] and Bruun-Pedersen et al. [5] came from similar experiment methodologies. Between the studies, the physical demands by the fitness equipment (i.e. the weight load of a pulley machine [4] and resistance from an DeskCycle [5]) remained constant between conditions, and the auditory feedback (despite representing two different mechanical dynamics) had the very similar condition properties. However, the pulley exercise was centered around a visible, mechanical fitness device, placed in a room with no visual distractions other than the exercise and machine itself [4]. In bike study, the DeskCycle was a placeholder for a digital object (recumbent bike) in a digital environment; a park VE with loads of visuals. The park VE was presented on a TV monitor, while the mechanical pulley was a natural extension of the surrounding environment. In essence, there were several differences between the studies in some key areas. And for the experience of a VE, the (multimodal) display used to mediate the VE plays a decisive role for the effect of the experience, and the relation to the activities performed in that environment.

2.1 The Relevance of Immersion and Presence

Studies on the manipulation of perceived exertion through on multimodal feedback are sparse, especially in relation to immersive VR (IVR), which in this paper is to understood through the definitions of immersion (and presence) offered by Slater [9]. In a VR system, increasing the spectrum of sensory stimuli provided by the system to mediate a virtual environment (VE) to a user, corresponds to increasing the immersive properties of that system [9]. Immersive systems can also be characterized by the collective sensorimotor contingencies (SCs) supported by the system, which describes the number of possible 'valid actions' the user is able to perform inside the VE with the system. SCs can be split into two categories; (a) valid sensorimotor actions; actions which changes the current VE perception (in all sensory modalities), and (b) valid effectual actions; which are user actions which affects changes perception of the VE or changes to the VE [9]. The gain from a highly immersive system, is the potential for a sense of presence inside the VE. Slater defines presence as the combination of a place illusion (PS); users' experience of being transported to another place (even despite being certain that are in fact not), and a plausibility illusion (Psi); which is users' belief that behaviors or occurrences inside that (virtual) place are experienced as occurring (even despite being aware that they are not) [9]. But while system immersion is objectively measurable by its stimuli and SCs, presence is not. Two people can experience different sensations of presence, based on how their actions affect their 'journey' in the VE, and how well it feeds their PS and Psi, and thus their experience in the VE [10].

The plausibility illusion is suggested by Rovira et al. [11] to depend on three conditions; (a) user actions must produce correlated reactions in the VE, (b) the VE must respond directly to the user, also in situations where the user is passive, and (c) the VE and the events occurring in it must be credible, based on the life-time, real-world experience of the user. Designing a VR experience for a specific purpose, in a specific context, should therefore appropriately consider what SCs that users are led to experience, how they are mediated by the system and how consistently users are expected to receive and interact with the mediation. Stimuli given from the system needs to meet the expectations of the user, if intended to reflect the behavior and feedback from a real-world environment.

2.2   Issues to Consider for Exertion Manipulation

It can be argued, that the effect of the auditory feedback from pedaling, in the study by Bruun-Pedersen et al. [5], might have been disrupted by the comprehensive audiovisual stimuli from the VE park (visual flora and fauna, soundscape stimuli from running water, birds, wind, etc.). While the ecology of the park VE might have represented such environment faithfully, it was likely unsupportive of participants' focus on- and perception of the feedback. In hindsight, it can also be argued that the study by Bruun-Pedersen [5] failed to afford the focus and attention on the exercise activity, compared to the disturbance-free experience of the purpose-supportive gym environment of the pulley [4]. In addition, the start position of the VR bike changed between participants, meaning that path characteristics and soundscape features in the VE varied slightly between trials, possibly influencing the consistency of the conditions between trials, and thus the results in the study [5]. Another, more general consideration made obvious from the studies, is a likelihood for the Borg scale to be interpreted depending on the physical attributes of the individual participant, potentially resulting in differences between participants' interpretation of the RPE.

Future studies on using feedback stimuli to manipulate perceived exertion, should thus be able to benefit from system with highly immersive properties, based on the potential to (a) escape possible real-world environment distractions of less immersive systems, (b) focus the participants attention on the activity itself by, (c) offering virtual environment-task disturbance-free and purpose-supportive environment, (d) an expanded usage of SCs, providing, (e) a heightened potential for focus on the task from a potentially high sense of presence in terms of both place and plausibility, but (f) upholding the guidelines (for Psi) of how actions must produce correlated reactions in the VE, the VE must respond directly to the user, and how the VE and the events occurring in it must be comparable with real-world experience of the user.

2.3 Haptics as Feedback

Taking reference to the studies from Plotnik et al. [6] and Denton [7], revisiting the idea of users' perception when ascending or descending a virtual hill seems interesting. Only this time with biking, and using audition, visuals and haptics for a multimodal IVR mediation, rather than simply visuals from the previous hill-based studies [6, 7].

The relevance of haptics can be seen in various multimodal uses in VR, such as for instance Nordahl et al. [12], where pressure sensors and actuators were combined with motion capture and implemented into a pair of shoes for use in VR. The shoes served as the controller for a surround sound system, as well as the physically based audio-haptic synthesis engine [12]. This footwear-based interaction simulated the feeling of walking on different surfaces. The goal of the study was two-fold; (a) to test whether multimodal feedback in the form of audio and haptics improved the task of walking on a virtual rope while being blindfolded, and (b) to test the importance of auditory and haptic feedback in a VE [12]. Results indicated that participants who started with the audio-haptic feedback had higher mean presence scores. Besides the effect of the haptic feedback, it also showed that the degree of similarity, of locomotive techniques in VR to real life locomotive movement, had a positive influence on presence [12].

2.4 Biking in IVR

One of the challenges listed by Nordahl et al., was how virtual egocentric motion should try to correspond to the movement in real life, which however often introduces the issue of the physical limitations of room dimensions [12]. Being a stationary exercise tool, an exercise bike such as the manuped is a useful platform to overcome issues of physical room limitations and should support the real-life experience sensation of egocentric motion, even when not physically moving to a degree. A manuped activates (and occupies) both hands and feet, during exercise sessions. This means that the sensation of egocentric motion inside the VE should be connected to the manuped activity, and possibly considered congruent with a real life sensation of driving a biking device.

Contextualizing the manuped inside the VE is necessary for users' association between the real world and VE. As before, this will be based on the combination of pedal activity on the manuped, and a virtual biking-centric device, which a user controls to move forward inside the VE, based on the pedaling [11].

2.5 The Immersive Properties

Increasing visual immersive properties of the biking experience will come from the multiple modalities (including haptics), as well as a significant increase in the visual domain by introducing an Oculus CV1 VR headset, compared to the previously mentioned exertion studies [4, 5]. In addition, the study will introduce a new scenario to the perception of exertion, through the task of riding a path which ascends and descends over a hill, taking inspiration from [6, 7]. According to the real-life experience from biking, going downhill should be considered less exertive than going uphill. Meanwhile, creating the sensation with users of experiencing higher exertion going uphill and lower exertion going downhill in VR is not trivial. The next part of the paper will detail how the VR setup has been designed to mediate the drive across different height levels, and how this should incentivize users to experience a different exertion driving uphill and downhill, concurrent with their real-life experiences.

3 Design

The commercial manuped product 'The Combi Bike' is a state of the art manuped device from Denmark-based company LEMCO, chosen for its quality construction. Besides solving the problem of limited physical space when moving in VR [3], the manuped is also to be considered a very safe biking device for VR, considering that the user is not placed on a saddle, but in a steady chair. To accommodate the requirement of the least disturbing environmental complexity, the VE created for the study was a desert. The desert VE was designed and developed using the Unity3D engine. The design of the desert VE can be seen in Fig. 2.

Fig. 2. Screenshot of the desert VE

The VE was modelled with the aid of GAIA; a plugin that allows for fast and detailed terrain generation, based on only a few guiding parameters. The terrain was generated based on height maps of sand dunes, which resulted in a natural looking landscape, when compared to sand dune reference imagery, but limited to very few visual elements, to not remove focus on the task of pedaling forward along the path.

The choice of angle for the incline of the hills was determined based on the study by Dentorn [7]. As Denton used a 15° incline but was unable to get any conclusive results. Amplifying the incline by doubling the slope to 30°, was initially chosen and later changed to 20°, based on internal and pilot testing on various angles, finding that 20° was considered the spot between a strong sensation of slope, and an angle which a device would realistically be able to climb. To increase consistency and reliability between participant trials, as well as control of the sequencing of hills and valleys for participant to cross, the VE road was made as a straight path. This would remove steering from the VE but retain control of the speed of the buggy. While reducing the level of interactivity and freedom in the VE but maintain control and consistency between participant trials. Two hills were implemented as it makes it possible to get respectively an average RPE exertion rating and standard deviations for up- and downhill driving. This should reduce the uncertainty of participant scores [9], while also making it possible to determine if any fatigue would be created for each run through of the VE. Having several hill types should create a more stable average, but the resource demands on participants, related to a longer and more perceptually demanding session with extended periods in VR, kept the hill count to a single entry.

A virtual vehicle for the participants to occupy while in the VE was implemented (also visible in Fig. 2). The vehicle was a 4-wheel sand dune buggy; fitting the theme of the desert VE and the stability of the manuped Combi Bike.

3.1 Multimodal Feedback

Audio and haptic feedback was based on diegetic stimuli from different VE objects and materials. The auditory and haptic feedback was represented by the surface friction between the wheels of the buggy and the gravel road surface. The auditory and haptic feedback could be presented in two different states; static and dynamic (as part of the condition design). Static feedback had constant pitch, independent from the inclination when driving uphill or downhill. Dynamic auditory and haptic feedback was designed similarly between them. Feedback varied by decreasing the pitch when driving uphill and increasing it when driving downhill, inspired by the findings of Bordegoni et al. [4], where altering the frequency of an auditory feedback was found to affect the perceived level of effort. While the auditory and haptic signals were both based on audio signals, they were different from each other, serving purpose in different parts of the frequency spectrum, with haptics focusing on the lower registers (using a Butt-Kicker motor), as Bordegoni et al. [5] showed that as low frequencies were found to affect perceived effort.

3.2 Auditory Feedback and Soundscape Design

An argument brought up in [5] was how the park VE soundscape might have contained too many different noises, which might have cluttered the implemented sounds of the bike. As such keeping to a more consistent and subtle soundscape for this VE, could potentially produce better results. On a similar note; as participants in [5] did not notice of the auditory feedback, there is a possibility that the auditory feedback was *too* subtle. In this study, was therefore designed to be more pronounced.

Despite needing a subtle representation, the inclusion of soundscapes in mediated environment should not be underestimated, as pointed out by Nordahl [13] who shows how soundscapes are able to increase the sense of presence, as well as promote movement inside a VE. The soundscape for this desert VE consisted of simple and subtle wind sounds, to add contextual stimuli in the auditory domain, while remaining in the background of the multimodal feedback. As previously mentioned, the auditory feedback was the friction sound of the buggy's wheels on the gravel desert road. All sounds were based on recorded samples. The final gravel sound from driving was created by combining several different segments of a gravel friction recording. The combination created variance to avoid an obviously repeating loop of the sample. To control the pitch, the slope of the surface in the VE was remapped, from its minimum negative slope to its maximum slope, for a range of values, which were used as a multiplier for controlling the pitch of the auditory feedback. The pitch varied between a 20% increase and decrease depending on the uphill and downhill slope, which means that when the user is driving up the slope, the pitch would be 80% of its original, and 120% driving downhill. Both static and dynamic conditions saw changes in amplitude to the auditory feedback, controlled from the velocity of the VE vehicle. This meant that when the user was moving fast with high amplitude, low when moving slowly and off when still.

3.3 Haptic Feedback

The haptic feedback was controlled through Pure Data, with a patch created and modified using the guide by Farnell [7]. The patch created random pop sounds, using an audio ramp that jumps to one, creates the pop, and randomly fades out to zero. With three of these patches as sub-patches (all linked to the same output), a sound effect was created which was reminiscent to rain. For the haptic stimuli, the 'Buttkicker Advance', a low frequency transducer, was used to translate the audio signal from Pure data to vibrations. Meanwhile, using the patch without modification created too few vibrations to properly simulate the vibration associated with driving on gravel. To solve this, the minimum delay for creating the pop sound was lowered from 30 to 5 and additional six sub-patches was added. With these modifications the impulses were more densely packed, creating vibrations similar to the gravel sensation intended for the road surface.

The haptic feedback was controlled using a separate audio signal created in Pure Data, as Unity cannot split its auditory output between several audio devices. The dynamic values (slope and velocity) obtained from Unity were sent over the Open Sound Control (OSC) protocol to a Pure Data patch.

3.4 VE Movement Speed

The speed of the buggy inside the desert VE, was controlled by the of the Combi Bike pedal arm revolutions, obtained from a custom-built Arduino based GIRO microcontroller [14] strapped to the pedal arm of the Combi Bike (see Fig. 3). The GIRO is made to tracks rotation activity, which it streams to Unity through a UDP network. A Unity script receives the stream and estimates the driving speed inside the VE, based on the values received from the GIRO, and uses the values to drive the user forward at a corresponding speed, with no noticeable delay. For movement speed, gravitational force was deliberately not included in the VE, as it would require the users to work physically harder driving uphill, and less so driving downhill. This would complicate the results, due to its effects on the Borg scale responses from participants [8].

Fig. 3. The GIRO microcontroller [14] strapped to the pedal arm of the Combi Bike

4 Methods

To determine whether dynamic feedback has an effect on perceived exertion three different hypotheses were created, based on our RQ:

H1: There will be a significant difference in users' perception of exertion between up- and downhill movement by introducing dynamic feedback in a VR exercise setting as opposed to static feedback.

H2: There will be a significant difference in users' perception of exertion when driving uphill by introducing dynamic feedback in a VR exercise setting as opposed to static feedback.

H3: There will be a significant difference in users' perception of exertion when driving downhill by introducing dynamic sensory modalities in a VR exercise setting as opposed to static feedback.

4.1 Pilot Test

A pilot test on the VE interaction design was conducted early, with four participants, to determine if there were any adverse health effects. As previously mentioned, results showed that a 30° incline and decline was too steep, combined with forcing the perspective of the camera to follow the rotation of the vehicle, as it caused several instances of strong cybersickness with users. Another aspect effect on cybersickness from the speed of forward movement inside the VE (relative to the pedal speed). The solution was to separate the Unity camera from the vehicle rotation and lower the speed. Combined with 20° hill-angles, cybersickness was notably reduced, and induced a satisfying indication of driving up- or downhill (as it was steep enough to force the user to physically look upwards and downwards to follow the direction of buggy movement).

4.2   Experiment Design

This study used a within-group design, in order to deduce whether different levels of immersion could affect a user's perceived level of exertion in a virtual reality exercise setting. Using a within-group design means that certain factors have to be considered when designing the experiment. By using the participants more than once creates the risk of carry-over effects, such as fatigue and boredom due to the longer test duration for each participant [9]. Additionally, a factor to be aware of when working in VR, is adverse health effects related to cybersickness [11]. Cybersickness has an immense impact on presence [10], which would most likely affect the results of the experiment. In order to minimize the carry-over effects a counterbalanced list of conditions was used. As the experiment had four conditions this created 24 unique combination of conditions [9]. This means that a minimum of 24 participants or a multiple of 24, i.e. 48, 72, were required. The independent variables of the experiment were auditory and haptic feedback. Both had two levels, static and dynamic. The dependent variable was perceived exertion, measured using the Borg Scale [6]. This created four conditions, see Table 1 for an overview of combinations of auditory and haptic levels.

Table 1. Experimental conditions

Condition A	Condition B	Condition C	Condition D
Static Audio & Static Haptic	Dynamic Audio, Static Haptic	Static Audio, Dynamic Haptic	Dynamic Audio & Dynamic Haptic

The four experimental conditions. Containing the different combinations of audio and haptic feedback.

Demographics on test participants (age, gender and previous VR experiences including experiences with adverse health effects) was collected using a questionnaire. In addition, the SUS-questionnaire [15] was used as a post-questionnaire after each condition, to compare the participants' level of presence for each condition. There exists different versions of the SUS-questionnaire. The one used in this study is the 3-item version [15], where ratings can be given on a Likert scale from 1–7, where 6–7 are indicators of presence. The Borg scale of perceived exertion was applied throughout the test. The scale goes from 6–20, where 6 is resting and 20 is the maximal intensity which can be kept for a very short time [8]. The Borg scale can be seen in Appendix 1. As the final part of the experiment, a short semi-structured interview was executed to determine if participants had noticed any differences between the four conditions and if they had experience any adverse health effects.

4.3   System Setup

The physical setup can be seen in Fig. 4. A Combi Bike with the GIRO strapped to the handles, was connected to a high-end PC, running the Unity build of the desert VE.

Fig. 4. Schematic of the VR setup

The PC's specifications were as follows:

- NVIDIA GeForce GTX 1080
- Intel Core i7-7700K, 4.2 GHz
- 16 GB VRA.

The high-level performance ensured the VE running at a stable 90 fps (frames per second), for the best, and least fatiguing and cybersickness-provoking VR experience [16].

Connected to the PC was an Oculus CV1 headset, and a pair of noise reducing headphones, and a ButtKicker attached to a wooden pallet. Through the pallet, the vibrations could reach the user, from the chair, that was placed on the pallet. A carpet was placed under the pallet to reduce noise generated by the ButtKicker and pallet during instances of strong vibrations. In addition to the PC, demographics data, Borg scale ratings from participants, notes from the trials, debriefings, etc. were typed by an observer on a laptop in the background.

4.4   Procedure

24 participants performed the experiment (6 female). All of the participants were selected through non-probability sampling. Age range was 22–31, average age of 24.75 (SD = 2.56). All of the participants had prior experience with VR systems. 11 participants had never become sick from VR before, whereas the remaining 13 had felt varying degrees of sickness in prior VR experiences. Participants were asked to read and sign a consent form, informing of the risk of cybersickness, and seeking permission to record their performance on video. Afterwards, participant would be introduced to the test itself, and how it would be conducted. They were introduced to the Borg Scale, and tested in their understanding of it, to prevent misinterpretations of the values. The participant would go on to fill the demographic items, whether they had prior experience with VR, and any previous occurrences with motion sickness. The session

procedure was explained to the participant, who was first introduced to a training environment (introducing how to use the RPE scale and introduced to the SUS questionnaire). Participants went through the four different conditions after having completed the training environment. Upon main test start, RPE ratings were requested after each incline/decline, with presence questions asked at the end of each condition. The conditions sequence was controlled using a counterbalancing, to minimize carry-over effects. Each participant drove across 2 hills in each condition, measuring their perceived exertion four times, once at the end of each incline and decline. Therefore, the participant would have given 16 Borg measurements and 4 presence measurements by the end of the experiment. As a participant was asked to say the Borg score out loud, the rating was noted by the experimenter. Presence measurements were filled by the participants, which required them to remove the HMD between conditions. After the test there was a debriefing session, asking the participant if they experienced any adverse health effects and if they noticed any changes between conditions.

The data collected was interval data as the Borg Scale uses a numbered scale similar to the Likert scale, which collects interval data. As the experiment conducted was of a 2^2 factorial design, the rule of sphericity is not valid, as it only applies to studies that have factors with more than two levels. The normality of the data must be determined for each condition, which was done using a Shapiro-Wilk test. To determine the existence of statistical differences in perceived exertion, the data was analyzed using a two-way repeated measures ANOVA.

5 Results

The results were analyzed using SPSS 24 and charts were made using Microsoft Excel 2016. Before analyzing the results, the final requirement for parametric data must be evaluated. In terms of parametric statistics, a Shapiro-Wilk test was performed on the data belonging to each of the four conditions. The result for condition A was $D(24) = 0.93$, $p = 0.09$, for condition B the result was $D(24) = 0.93$, $p = 0.11$, for condition C $D(24) = 0.93$, $p = 0.85$ and finally the result for condition D was $D(24) = 0.968$, $p = 0.62$. This means that all of the data is normally distributed, as none of the results were statistically significant and parametric data analysis can be performed on the experiment data.

5.1 Perceived Exertion for Uphill and Downhill Driving

For uphill driving, results of the two-way repeated measures ANOVA, for the data measured in relation to driving uphill in VR, shows that there is no main effect of audio $F(1, 23) = 0.11$, $p = 0.75$, $r = 0.01$. This is also the case with the haptic feedback as there was no difference between the two levels $F(1, 23) = 0.3$, $p = 0.59$, $r = 0.01$. Average scores from the uphill Borg scores can be seen in Fig. 5. There was not found a significant difference for the interaction between audio and haptic feedback when driving uphill $F(1, 23) = 0.0$, $p = 1.0$, $r < 0.01$.

For downhill driving, results, also analyzed using ANOVA, of driving downhill shows that there is no main effect of audio $F(1, 23) = 0.18$, $p = 0.68$, $r = 0.01$. Again, there was no main effect of haptic feedback $F(1, 23) = 0.278$, $p = 0.6$, $r = 0.01$. The interaction effect between audio and haptic also proved to be non-significant $F(1, 23) = 0.3$, $p = 0.59$, $r = 0.01$. The average scores from the downhill Borg scores can be seen in Fig. 6.

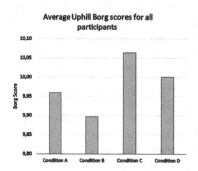

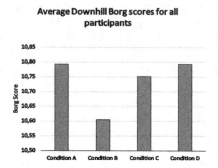

Fig. 5. Averages for each condition, based on participants' RPE ratings for uphill driving (scale ranges from 6–20). Results are very similar between conditions.

Fig. 6. An average for each condition, based on all participants' Borg scores for downhill driving (scale ranges from 6 to 20). Results are very similar between conditions.

5.2 Difference Between Uphill and Downhill Driving

To find the difference between the uphill driving data and the downhill data, each participant had their uphill score subtracted from their downhill score, see Fig. 7 for an average score for all participants.

Using these values, the final hypothesis, which sought to determine if there existed a significant difference in perceived exertion between the up- and downhill driving in VR, was analyzed using ANOVA. Just as there were no significant difference for the other two hypotheses no main effect was found between haptic and dynamic audio $F(1, 23) = 0.004$, $p = 0.95$, $r < 0.01$. The same applied for the haptic feedback $F(1, 23) = 0.4$, $p = 0.838$, $r < 0.01$, this was also the case for the interaction effect $F(1, 23) = 0.624$, $p = 0.438$, $r = 0.03$.

5.3 SUS Questionnaire Presence Scores

From the SUS presence questionnaire items, a score of 6 or 7 indicates a sensation of presence. The overall presence scores from participants were very consistent, between respectively the 3 items per condition per user, and also between conditions. 3 of 24 participant scores suggested a sense of presence while driving the buggy in VR (Table 2).

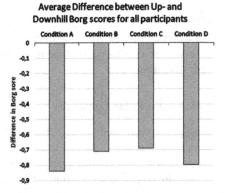

Fig. 7. Average difference between uphill and downhill Borg scores for all participants. Negative scores mean that downhill measurements were higher than uphill measurements.

While only 3 participants felt a strong sense of presence, the score range between participants differs a lot, with most conditions. As such, there are no conditions which induced a higher sense of presence than others, as presence scores for all individual participants scores were very consistent between conditions, and only deviated 0.5 points on average. No one condition was remarkably different from another, in terms of the degree of presence it induced with participants.

Table 2. SUS presence questionnaire results

Condition A	Condition B	Condition C	Condition D
Presence score 4.3	Presence score 4.4	Presence score 4.6	Presence score 4.5
Standard dev. 1.5	Standard dev. 1.4	Standard dev. 2.6	Standard dev. 2.6

6 Discussion

The quantitative results do not illustrate any significant effect of the multimodal stimuli, on participants' perception of exertion. Meanwhile, the somewhat extreme swings in reported presence between participants is curious, despite getting close to *exactly* the same experience, and indicate that there are variables to the IVR biking experiment that cannot be derived simply from the RPE responses. We believe that the large difference in presence scoring can relate to several aspects of the VE design and overall experiment method. As previously stated, the way users relate to VR through their real-life experiences affect their experience in VR, for better or worse. In this case, features from real world physics, as perceived and expected in our VE, did not live up to users' expectations from own experience. Another problem might have been that the experiment asked participants to rate polar opposite mental constructs, in the form of going uphill (more effort) and downhill (less effort), with sounds that have previously suggested a heavier (more effort) and lighter load (less effort). Mixing these in a bag, combining them, and using the combinations to test an illusion (i.e. something that does not exist to begin with) was most likely not a very good proposition. In some senses, the fact that no real differences were felt, might have been due to confusion between certain mixes of less/more effort effects, that users simply became unsusceptible to the perceptual manipulation.

6.1   Participant Expectations and Polar Opposites

In the debriefing, the majority of participants stated that they experienced the VE differently from their expectations to driving up- and downhill. 14 of the participants directly mentioned that driving downhill felt harder than driving straight or uphill. The rationale was that they expected the buggy to keep rolling, when driving downhill, even if they stopped pedaling. Not meeting this expectation, participants felt they had to work harder to get down the hills. Missing indeed from the VE design is gravity, as the buggy behavior on the hills was not affected by a gravitational pull. Leaving out this element could very well be something which affected the gathered data. In Fig. 7, all the mean values are negative, meaning that downhill driving scored higher on the Borg scale, compared to uphill, which supports participants recollections that driving downhill felt harder, compared to uphill driving. Meanwhile, including gravity in the experiment would change the actual exertion needed to drive up- and downhill. Meaning that measuring perceived exertion would no longer make sense, if used in a similar fashion as in this experiment.

In hindsight, this might generally suggest that there are many complexities to exertion perception studies, which need to be takes into consideration for experiment design. However, perhaps two elements or behaviors of a (real or virtual) world, so fundamentally opposite each other (e.g. forces of pull/push, up/down, etc.) should not be measured against each other, when trying to understand illusions and perceptual manipulations. But simply isolated to gradients within their own domain. At least when experimenting with something that could be described as a perceptual and cognitive construct, more than a real thing. And from a design perspective; placing the same manipulation method on two things act opposite to each other, might also be quite dangerous for the success of the effect.

This in part, could be due to the previously mentioned perspective of expectations within certain environmental or physical conditions, which have been confirmed in this study to apply in VR and in relation to perceived exertion, which we will discuss in a moment. But also, from a test design method perspective, it also has to do with changing too many feedback-oriented aspects, when operating in a within-participant design. When testing multimodal feedback to certain conditions, especially a delicate manipulation as the illusion of exertion has shown to be, having two conditions which could be considered polar opposites to each other (going uphill and going downhill) could be a bad choice for the methodology. And as mentioned previously, coupling it with feedback stimuli which also has suggestive properties to opposite exertion effects, the complication might be too high for the delicacy of the desired effect.

6.2 Make It Plausible, Somehow

When suggesting the existence of non-existent physical changes to the real world, the argument needs to be persuasive. In some sense, this might also have to do with what you are implicitly telling the participants to be a plausible part of the scenario. In the previous (bike) study from Bruun-Pedersen et al. [5], the physical attributes of the path (e.g. height) did not change. Meanwhile, a part of the test procedure was a little mind-game, where the researcher turned the bike-resistance knob between each trial, to *suggest* that a perceived change in resistance was a hypothetical possibility, and thereby suggesting that changes in perceived exertion *could* in fact be plausible in the real world. Meanwhile, doing so makes the study manipulate not only the feedback, but prime the user to change his/her perspective and expectations to the world they are entering. This perspective can be both constructive or destructive to the validity of future studies, but is a point that it seems to be hard to neglect.

6.3 Speed of the Virtual Buggy

The velocity of the virtual buggy also mentioned by participants during debriefing. Some participants felt that the speed of the virtual buggy did not correlate well with the force put into the Combi Bike, and felt that the buggy went slower than expected. Meanwhile, high velocity was responsible for some of the cybersickness that pilot testers felt, even if most was related to camera movement. In the final experiment, 7 participants reported affects from cybersickness, meanwhile just slightly (reasons being mixed, for instance whenever a participant were forced to break to give a Borg scale rating, stated to feel unnatural with no force transfer).

6.4 Various Risks from the Within-Group Design

One of the general risks to always consider is the carry-over effect of VR is currently impossible to neglect when working a within-participant design, as it can bias results between conditions. This study used counterbalancing was used to try and counteract or reduce the potential bias created from such an effect. Our participants had to go through several conditions to reach the end of the experiment. Another is the similarity between conditions, as using of the same VE have likely bored some the participants, making them less engaged in the experiment, even if the desert VE environment was selected to avoid other issues. Fatigue played a larger role than anticipated. Since there were two hills for each condition each participant has eight Borg scores for driving up- and downhill. Comparing the difference in Borg score between driving up the first and second hill, in each participant's first condition, shows that the second hill (M = 10.17) scores higher on average compared to the first hill (M = 8.8), see Fig. 8.

Since participants are assigned to conditions using counterbalancing the difference in scores for the two hills indicates that the difference is not created by using dynamic and static feedback. The difference most likely stems from fatigue.

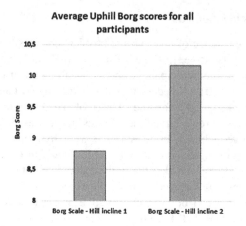

Fig. 8. Average score of the 1 and 2 encountered hill, based on all participants

6.5 Presence

The range of presence scores given to a single item, for a single condition was very different between individual participants, as seen in both Table 3 and Fig. 9.

Table 3. SUS presence questionnaire – score range

Condition A	Condition B	Condition C	Condition D
Lowest average 2.0	Lowest average 1.7	Lowest average 2.0	Lowest average 2.0
Highest average 6.7	Highest average 6.0	Highest average 6.3	Highest average 6.7

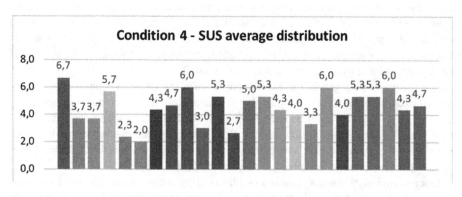

Fig. 9. Averages of the 3 SUS items for each 24 participants, for condition 4. The range is considerable, from almost no sensation - to a powerful sensation of presence.

Over the course of the experiment, we knew there would be several instances where the Oculus headset would have to be removed, resulting in an immersive change, and also risk of this affecting the sensation of presence. For every RPE rating, the participant would be made aware of the test conductor. Between every condition, the participant would also have to remove the Oculus headset to respond to questions. As such, participants were both reminded of the non-virtual world while in VR, and fully switching back and forth. Going forward, all user input should be incorporated into the virtual reality, so that participants would not need interaction with the real world at any point during the experiment (so to speak). Another presence related issue was how in the VE, the buggy had a steering wheel, while in the real world the handles on the Combi Bike were moving hand pedals. As a result, the relationship between VR and real-world interaction was missing, causing a disturbance for the participants, based on the lack of correlation.

6.6 The Individual Interpretation of the Borg Scale

The interpretations of the Borg scale have like varied between participants, which could be a reason for how and why the ratings between participants varied in some circumstances. Meanwhile, the advantage of the within-group design is that it is each participant's own variance that is compared between participants. This eliminates the bias of participants starting with different scores. There is no way to guarantee that the same increase in exertion is scored with the same variance between participants. To give the participants the same interpretation of the scale it would require some method for determining how much more exertion is needed based on an initial score, e.g. this is twice as hard as a score of 5 therefore the new score is 10. Participants would then have a starting point from where they would be able to give more similar changes in score, for similar changes in perceived exertion. The Borg scale does contain definitions for the individual ranges, see appendix 1, but these are rather ambiguous and can be interpreted. Meanwhile, adding some concrete examples could aid to limit the uncertainty.

7 Conclusion

This paper presented an experiment, aiming to investigate the possibility of altering the perceived exertion, using auditory and haptic feedback, during a biking session in VR. The study found no significant difference in any of the presented hypotheses. An interesting discovery was made from the post experiment feedback, as 14 participants mentioned, that the missing effect of gravity made driving downhill feel more difficult compared to driving uphill. This and the almost extremely differentiating presence score, has led to reflections on the experiment methodology, which should lead to improved study designs in the future. This relates to understanding the approach necessary when operating a delicate effect, such as the manipulation of perceived exertion, despite the fact that it is trying to invoke a perceptual construct in the real world, of something that (at best) only exists in the virtual. VR is still very young as a technology, and despite not producing significant differences between conditions, it is important to take notice of how to connect the dots properly to achieve that difference in future studies.

References

1. Bruun-Pedersen, J.R., Serafin, S., Kofoed, L.B.: Motivating elderly to exercise – recreational virtual environment for indoor biking. In: 4th International Conference on Serious Games and Applications for Health, Orlando (2016)
2. Bruun-Pedersen, J.R., Pedersen, K.S., Serafin, S., Kofoed, L.B.: Augmented exercise biking with virtual environments for elderly users - a preliminary study for retirement home physical therapy. In: Proceedings of IEEE VR 2014 - Workshop on Virtual and Augmented Assistive Technology, VAAT, Minneapolis (2014)
3. Bruun-Pedersen, J.R., Serafin, S., Kofoed, L.B.: Restorative virtual environment design for augmenting nursing home rehabilitation. J. Virtual Worlds Res. 9(3), 1–24 (2016)
4. Bordegoni, M., Ferrise, F., Grani, F., Bruun-Pedersen, J.R., Serafin, S.: Auditory feedback affects perception of effort when exercising with a Pulley machine. In: Online Proceedings from the International Conference on Multisensory Motor Behavior: Impact of Sound (2013)
5. Bruun-Pedersen, J.R., Grani, F., Serafin, S.: Investigating the role of auditory feedback in a multimodal biking experience. In: 13th International Symposium on Computer Music Multidisciplinary Research, CMMR (2017)
6. Plotnik, M., Bahat, Y., Akiva, Y.A., Gimmon, Y., Inzelberg, R., Kizony, R.: Can we climb with our eyes? Preliminary report on the effect of conflicting virtual scenery on leveled and inclined gait. In: Virtual Rehabilitation, ICVR (2013)
7. Denton, W.C.: Comparison of uphill walking and visual uphill environments on energy expenditure and locomotor-respiratory coupling. Doctoral dissertation, University of Nebraska at Omaha (2017)
8. Borg, G., Linderholm, H.: Perceived exertion and pulse rate during graded exercise in various age groups. J. Intern. Med. 181(S472), 194–206 (1967)
9. Slater, M.: Place illusion and plausibility can lead to realistic behaviour in immersive virtual environments. Philos. Trans. Roy. Soc. Lond. B: Biol. Sci. 364, 3549–3557 (2009)
10. Nilsson, N.C., Nordahl, R., Serafin, S.: Immersion revisited: a review of existing definitions of immersion and their relation to different theories of presence. Hum. Technol. 12 (2016)
11. Rovira, A., Swapp, D., Spanlang, B., Slater, M.: The use of virtual reality in the study of people's responses to violent incidents. Front. Behav. Neurosci. 3, 59 (2009)
12. Nordahl, R., Serafin, S., Turchet, L., Nilsson, N.C.: A multimodal architecture for simulating natural interactive walking in virtual environments. PsychNol. J. 9(3) (2011)
13. Nordahl, R.: Sonic interaction design to enhance presence and motion in virtual environments. In: Proceedings of CHI 2008 Workshop on Sonic Interaction Design (2008)
14. Grani, F., Bruun-Pedersen, J.R.: Giro: better biking in virtual reality. In: IEEE 3rd Workshop on Everyday Virtual Reality, WEVR (2017)
15. Usoh, M., Catena, E., Arman, S., Slater, M.: Using presence questionnaires in reality. Presence: Teleoper. Virtual Environ. 9(5), 497–503 (2000)
16. Bruun-Pedersen, J.R., Serafin, S., Kofoed, L.: Going outside while staying inside - exercise motivation with immersive vs. non-immersive recreational virtual environment augmentation for older adult nursing home residents. In: IEEE International Conference on Healthcare Informatics, ICHI 2016 (2016)
17. Bruun-Pedersen, J.R., Serafin, S., Kofoed, L.B.: Simulating nature for elderly users - a design approach for recreational virtual environments. In: Proceedings of the 2015 IEEE International Conference on Computer and Information Technology; Ubiquitous Computing and Communications; Dependable, Autonomic and Secure Computing; Pervasive Intelligence and Computing (2015)

xR-Based Systems for Mindfulness Based Training in Clinical Settings

Mark R. Costa[1(✉)], Dessa Bergen-Cico[1], Rocio Hererro[2],
Jessica Navarro[3], Rachel Razza[1], and Qiu Wang[1]

[1] Syracuse University, Syracuse, NY, USA
mrcosta@syr.edu
[2] Universitat Jaume I, Castellón de la Plana, Spain
[3] University de València, Valencia, Spain

Abstract. Chronic and acute stress are persistent and troubling health concerns for many people and military veterans in particular. Clinicians are increasingly turning to mindfulness techniques to provide people with the skills they need to self-manage that stress. However, training and getting people to adhere to the practice is difficult. In this paper, we talk about a virtual reality based system designed specifically to help veterans learn mindfulness-based stress reduction techniques.

Keywords: Mixed reality · Virtual reality · Wellness · Mindfulness
Meditation

1 Introduction

Mindfulness-based techniques (MBT) are useful for managing stress, anxiety, trauma, and pain, as well as for improving concentration and general mood. Practicing mindfulness techniques can help people reduce or eliminate reliance on pharmacological treatment and specialized mental health care treatment providers. Additional potential effects include higher levels of self-efficacy because MBT helps reduce trait anxiety, self-criticism and self-judgment [4, 5] and improves performance through increased ability to focus attention [21]. Practicing mindfulness can also improve interpersonal relationships, which are critical for emotional well-being. The effectiveness of mindfulness-based interventions is well established for physical and mental health. However, effectiveness requires both physical and psychological engagement in mindfulness-based practices.

Given the documented efficacy and breadth of benefits associated with practicing mindfulness, clinicians and researchers are increasingly incorporating mindfulness techniques in clinical settings. The main interest is to test the efficacy of the techniques on specific problems as well as identifying the challenges to implementing effective practices across a wider range of patient populations. Although mindfulness has many positive effects, patient adherence and quality of practice can be challenging. The benefits of mindfulness come through regular practice; that practice can be difficult at first and may even drain attentional resources. Helping patients develop sustainable habits, is a challenge for any person interested in promoting mental and physical wellness.

© Springer International Publishing AG, part of Springer Nature 2018
J. Y. C. Chen and G. Fragomeni (Eds.): VAMR 2018, LNCS 10910, pp. 31–39, 2018.
https://doi.org/10.1007/978-3-319-91584-5_3

This paper discusses our research, which focuses on using cross- or extended-reality (xR) technologies to address some of the challenges related to teaching people mindfulness and developing the necessary habits to make the practice a sustainable part of their daily lives. For this research, we focus on mixed reality and virtual reality xR mindfulness technologies to improve self-regulation and engage the parasympathetic nervous system (PNS).

2   Context and Challenges

Although clinicians apply MBT to a variety of patient populations and treatment problems, our work focuses largely on United States military veterans who use the Department of Veterans Affairs (VA) health care services. The VA patient population presents health care providers with many challenges, including high rates of post-traumatic stress disorder (PTSD) and other mental health problems, traumatic brain injuries (TBI) and musculoskeletal injuries which can present unique barriers to engaging in mindfulness-based practices which we will address in turn. For example, PTSD is characterized by hypervigilance, reductions in working memory, and startle response which can make it difficult to block out environmental distractions. Musculoskeletal injuries can present barriers to extended periods of sitting meditation; although mindfulness-based practice can effectively manage chronic and acute pain. Whereas TBI, PTSD and some mental health conditions reduce working memory and present barriers to engaging in focused attention and metacognitive training of the mind. In addition to the aforementioned potential barriers research has also found that drop out or non-completion rates of mindfulness-based programs may be 30% or higher and those who drop out may be the people who could benefit most (Banarjee, Cavanagh, & Strauss, 2017; Cavanagh, et al., 2014). Disengagement and non-completion of mindfulness programs may be particularly high for people with depression and rumination [3] feeling of being trapped in the long practices [13, 18].

Broadly speaking, the VA is split into primary and specialty clinics. Primary care is analogous to a general practitioner, while specialty clinics (e.g., mental and behavioral health) provide focused support for specific conditions. Understanding this distinction is useful because it highlights the difference in our previous work - much of the research on mindfulness practice focuses on specific chronic conditions and may involve prolonged support from specialized care. The aims of this paper are to examine the use of MBT to help primary care patients manage acute stress without having to visit specialty clinics. One of the driving questions of this research is - *How do we make mindfulness techniques more accessible to VA patients?* Our goal is to provide veterans with the skills needed to manage acute stressors in a limited number of sessions - approximately five over a period of several weeks and have those skills and seedlings of habit continue after the direct intervention.

One of the core problems veterans will face when attempting to learn MBT techniques in a clinical setting is managing external stimuli. In general, it is difficult for any person to tune out external stimuli when it comes to practicing mindfulness meditation. This is why many guided mindfulness meditation exercises start with the suggestion - "Find a quiet, comfortable place with few distractions." The VA's primary care settings are anything but quiet; sound infiltrates individual patient rooms from adjacent offices and hallways. The problem is further exacerbated by the high rates of hypervigilance in the veteran population. Therefore, exposure to external stimuli needs to be controlled to facilitate the mindfulness meditation practice.

Mindfulness-based meditation takes effort and requires ongoing practice. This may make it impractical for clinicians to teach individual patients or directly monitor their practice. Mindfulness based programs are most commonly conducted in a group setting which means that participants need to be available at the designated time and be able to get to the designated central location. This can present scheduling barriers and limitations for people who need child care. The xR mindfulness interface can be self-directed and enable participation for people who may be unable to travel to a central location at the designated time. An additional potential advantage of xR may be the customizability of the xR environment to enhance the cultural relevance and compatibility of the experience thus overcoming cultural barriers identified by researchers (Proulx et al., 2017).

We hypothesize that xR technologies are a solution to the problem of external distractions, stimuli control and access limitations of in-person clinic based training. One of the core capabilities of virtual and mixed reality is that the auditory and visual features of an environment can be precisely controlled. Also, because xR is now a consumer grade information and communication technology (ICT), it can be made readily available to diverse user groups relatively inexpensively.

Other researchers and developers have already identified the potential benefits of using VR for cultivating and training mindfulness [1, 9]. Additionally, virtual reality systems can be coupled with physiological sensors and supported by gamification mechanisms to promote sustained engagement. Popular sensors include heart rate and heart rate variability monitors, EEGs, and breath straps; these sensors are all commonly available in clinics and are increasingly available to consumers. What makes our systems different is that we focus more on designing the system to fit in to the social environment it will be embedded in. That is to say, we are building an xR-based meditation app that should not only work well for users, but also the clinicians supporting those users and the researchers interested in optimizing the experience and impact of the tool.

3   Needs and Design Requirements

In this section, we address the design requirements for our system from three different perspectives: the user's, the clinician's, and the researcher's. Our user population is veterans of the U.S. armed forces, specifically those veterans who use the VA's health care system. Clinicians include licensed clinical health care providers and other trained mental health care providers or team members affiliated with the VA. Researchers may include university and VA research staff who focus on building systems for mental wellness.

3.1 User Needs

Overall, our goal is to develop an xR-based mindfulness application that facilitates practice by providing an idealized, calming environment to meditate in. As authors pointed out, many novice practitioners would benefit from an environment that reduces or eliminates the distracting effects of stimuli present in most office and home environments. The application also needs to include interventions and feedback to maximize the effectiveness of individual sessions, most likely through customized biofeedback [8, 17], and a support system to promote sustained engagement in the practice over time.

We expect most of our initial users to be veterans who are referred to the system to deal with either acute or chronic stress. Access will not be limited to this particular subset of veterans, nor will it be limited to veterans entirely. However, we will be using participatory design techniques [15] to optimize the experience for our target population.

First and foremost, the environment needs to match the expectations and desires of the users of our system. [1, 11] found that users vary in terms of the environments they find naturally calming and conducive to meditation practices, which is why apps like Guided Meditation VR that give users a choice of scenes to meditate in are popular. Overall, we expect to provide a variety of nature inspired themes, based on research findings that have demonstrated the inherent calming effects of nature [19] and the potential of such scenes to support attention restoration therapy [14].

In addition to providing a calm environment, xR environments can be modified or made to be adaptive to the user to either gently direct attention to desired locations, to create optimal challenges to accelerate skill development, and to stimulate curiosity and selectively train specific aspects of mindfulness. We want the xR environments to be conducive to practice but also want the veteran to be able to transfer the skills [6] learned to the real world instead of needing to seek refuge in the virtual environment.

From the perspective that mindfulness is a skill honed through practice, any system intended to support the development of that skill needs to provide an infrastructure to promote sustained engagement and effortful practice. Gamification is a common and effective framework for incentivizing participation and engagement [12]. Popular meditation apps like Headspace use game mechanisms like data driven feedback and badges to encourage and reward practice and to provide feedback and recommendations for future action. Data driven feedback can also be used to guide individual sessions; one of the main advantages of having access to an expert trainer is that trainer can help the practitioner through his or her specific challenges via customized feedback. xR systems can provide customized feedback and guidance if they are coupled with sensors [9]. Users need feedback to enable them to make cognitive and physiological changes that strengthen self-directed mindfulness practices and the targeted neural networks. In terms of whether the sensors should be employed to promote curiosity of internal states or to identify and guide users towards an idealized state is an open question. Finally, we expect to incorporate self-report measures, both to inform our research (see below) and to serve as a limited journal for the users.

The genesis of this system emerged from a clinical need to provide quality care to veterans as well as the desire to provide those same veterans with the tools they need to excel in life. To that end, our system includes the capacity to enable and support clinical supervision of mindfulness practice (see next section). Consequently, our system will need to support patient privacy (HIPAA) rules. However, not all users will be patients and patients should be able to retain the right to use the system anonymously for any given session. Also, we support full user autonomy; therefore, the user should be able to sever the connection with the clinical system.

3.2   Clinical Needs

The main assumption going forward is that a clinician at a VA health care center will conduct a basic patient evaluation procedure and determine whether or not mindfulness-based stress reduction is the most appropriate intervention for that specific patient. If MBSR is the most appropriate choices, the clinician will suggest a 4–5 session MBSR training schedule in the office of the clinician, so s/he can supervise and guide the patient. The xR system will serve to reduce environmental stimuli, which generally makes it difficult for novices to practice.

The clinician will also want to maintain the capacity to override environmental variables in the xR system. There are two reasons for this oversight: first, the user may have little experience in xR environments; consequently, the immediate burden of learning to use the system will detract from the mindfulness experience. Secondly, the clinician may develop a better intuition of which environmental settings will most likely positively impact the users' experience.

Clinicians will also benefit from the data generated to improve user engagement. Common clinical practice is to give patients homework – exercises to strengthen the skill and promote habituation of the practice. But there is no reliable way to monitor patient compliance when practice is not dependent on a system; however, providers discovered that xR systems are very useful for tracking exercise compliance. Not only can the system track whether the patients are practicing, but also the frequency and duration of practices, the impact of the practice on the user's psychophysiological health. For example, sensors can be used to monitor indicators of the parasympathetic nervous system (PNS) with galvanic skin response (GSR) and heart rate during the exercise, track participant GSR and heart rate as an indicator of a state of relaxation and restoration [10, 20]; thus indicating de-escalation of the sympathetic nervous system and the stress response [16], and track attention and engagement of the task positive network (TPN) using as an indication of a state of mindfulness [22].

Ideally, all of the data discussed would be made available to the clinician via the VA's electronic medical record (EMR) system. The EMR system facilitates team care and would make the user's information readily available to other health care providers who may need it to provide the appropriate health care. For the monitoring mental health care provider, data based in the portal would make it easier for him or her to evaluate the patient using multiple data points, including some that are not associated with the xR system. Clinicians may want to take notes or share data with authorized personnel. Finally, clinical providers are responsible for discharging patients; therefore, the clinician also needs to be able to separate the connection to a user's data.

3.3   Researcher Needs

Researchers will need access to many of the same types of usage and environmental statistics that the users and clinicians have. Additionally, researchers will need to be able to explicitly limit the environment and the environmental settings to conduct controlled experiments. We anticipate most of the experimentation to be focused on the dynamic aspects of environments – attempts to instill calmness or focus by manipulating the speed and intensity of lighting, sound and textures, all of which can either serve as focal points or distractors yet are important for increasing the sense of presence we need [2].

In addition to the self-report measures that will serve as a log or diary for the user, researchers will want to collect survey data related to the specific research question. The collection and storage of that data needs to be done in an IRB compliant manner, which may include piping data from the user database to a research database while simultaneously anonymizing the data.

In terms of psychophysiological data, our labs are primarily interested in exploring the effects of mindfulness on the sympathetic and parasympathetic nervous systems, as well as the effects of mindfulness meditation on activation in the task positive network (TPN) versus default mode networks (DMN) [7]. Our core suite of sensors includes: EEG, fNIRS, EDA, HRV monitors, and breath monitors. From the adaptive system perspective, our system needs to be able to ingest streaming data, perform a classification function on the data to determine the user's state, and modify environmental variables based on the difference between the user's current state and idealized state. The classification model should be readily available, easily adjustable, and easily recorded for subsequent analysis.

Mechanisms of Mindfulness

Although it is well known that mindfulness is an effective technique for managing stress, increasing the well-being and improving emotional regulation, there is still room for improvement in how mindfulness is taught and in our knowledge about how the practice works at a deeper level. Specifically, we have gaps in our knowledge about the specific mechanisms of change and how the components of mindfulness work to affect that change. Additionally, it is difficult to get people to adhere to the practice, even when they believe practice will be beneficial.

According to research, beginning with the mindfulness practice can be difficult for novices. One of the main causes is that practice sessions may initially be exhausting, given that need a high demand for the attentional resources. Beginners have to struggle with the distractions in order to learn the attentional regulation skills required in mindfulness and to not be distracted by other stimuli or be able to attend and observe their own emotional states without getting caught up in them, whether the state is positive or negative (Lymeus, Lundgren, Hartig., 2016). This difficulty can cause a lack of adherence to the practice; therefore, there is a need to explore new and simple ways to bring the mindfulness benefits to these people.

In this context, cross- or extended- reality (xR) technologies can be a good tool for people without experience in meditation to begin and be committed to the mindfulness practice. Besides, virtual reality seems to be a perfect lab in order to train a mindfulness state in the mind, given its possibilities to manipulate the environmental stimulus. In this sense, through a VR environment the trainee can develop the skill by doing exercise according to her/his level, as for example a beginner could start the training in a controlled environment without a high number of sensor stimulus (e.g. noises, colors, movements), and progress in his/her training increasing the levels of difficulties. As already mentioned, the auditory and visual features of an environment can be controlled through these technologies and consequently reducing the attentional efforts and improve the skill acquisition. Different studies have already pointed out that the objective of these technologies should be to help beginning meditators to focus on the task of meditation and progressively develop the necessary skills to continue the practice in any noisier context (Kosunen et al. [17]).

In addition to VR being a training tool, it can also be used as an experimental testbed for learning more about and training the specific components of mindfulness, namely, focused attention, sustained attention, emotional regulation, and body scanning. In the previous section we talked about exploring the neural and physiological correlates of mindfulness. However, we do not know the relationship between the practitioner's current state, their ability to engage in the specific components of mindfulness and the effects those states have on their future states. For example, if a user is practicing mindfulness to help manage chronic pain, is it more important to focus on body scanning or attention regulation first? How would we manipulate the environment to emphasize that focus? When is it appropriate to begin transitioning the focus to other components of mindfulness and how do we implement that change?

As we better understand the relationship between the mechanisms of mindfulness practice and the neurophysiological manifestations of a mindful state, we can begin to develop interventions that support nervous system sensitization and to improve the training via a biofeedback system to facilitate the access to Mindfulness state. The general concept is to provide the user with a sense of self-efficacy regarding the practice as well as exposing them to the benefits of mindfulness, which should increase adherence to the training. Over time, we can scale back the utility of the biofeedback to prompt the user to rely more on their own skill to maintain the mindful state. Exactly how that can be done is contingent on developing a better understanding of the relationships between the components of mindfulness and the sustainment of a mindful state.

Transference is another critical concern. Here, we refer to transference as the ability to effectively move from practicing the technique in a structured environment to employing the technique in daily life. Challenges of transference are not limited to mindfulness, it is a common problem in the fields of psychology and education [6]. In contrast to many of the commercially available tools where the ability to transfer is expected or assumed to occur naturally from repeated practice, we are exploring ways to design our system to explicitly facilitate transference. For example, one experimental manipulation might involve progressively adding more stimulus to the training environment to better mimic daily life's distractors.

4 Conclusions and Future Work

Acute and chronic stress continue to be public health concerns, particularly for military veterans. Teaching veterans mindfulness has proven to be an effective approach to manage stress. However, there are still challenges to the process of teaching and practicing mindfulness. In this paper, we discussed some of those environmental and cultural challenges and identified how xR technologies might address those challenges.

Specifically, Virtual and mixed reality (xR) present viable solutions to overcome barriers to engaging in evidence based mindfulness practices. The xR technologies can reduce external distractions, control stimuli and provide flexibility in timing and location of participant practice. Moreover the customizability of xR environments can overcome cultural barriers with culturally relevant contexts and customizable auditory and visual features. The biofeedback interface can provide real time feedback to continue coaching and guiding participants to strengthen participant engagement and improve lifelong outcomes.

In addition to the inherent strengths of xR systems, the fact the xR is a form of ICT affords benefits related to behavioral tracking and feedback. The data gathered from behavioral feedback and tracking can be used by both veterans and their health care providers to encourage sustained engagement in the practice of meditation and monitoring of the efficacy of the intervention to ensure veterans are receiving the care they need. Our paper has outlined the core features xR-based meditation systems shoud have to support user, researcher, and clinician needs. Our next steps involve testing current versions and engaging relevant stakeholders via participatory design methods [15] of system development.

References

1. Andersen, T., Anisimovaite, G., Christiansen, A., Hussein, M., Lund, C., Nielsen, T., Rafferty, E., Nilsson, N.C., Nordahl, R., Serafin, S.: A preliminary study of users' experiences of meditation in virtual reality. In: 2017 IEEE Virtual Reality (VR), pp. 343–344 (2017). https://doi.org/10.1109/VR.2017.7892317
2. Annerstedt, M., Jönsson, P., Wallergård, M., Johansson, G., Karlson, B., Grahn, P., Hansen, Å.M., Währborg, P.: Inducing physiological stress recovery with sounds of nature in a virtual reality forest—Results from a pilot study. Physiol. Behav. **118**, 240–250 (2013). https://doi.org/10.1016/j.physbeh.2013.05.023
3. Atkinson, M.J., Wade, T.D.: Impact of metacognitive acceptance on body dissatisfaction and negative affect: engagement and efficacy. J. Consult. Clin. Psychol. **80**(3), 416 (2012)
4. Bergen-Cico, D., Krishna Kumar, A.: Examining the processes of change associated with mindful-ness-based meditation and reductions in trait anxiety. Sci. Pages Depress Anxiety **1**(1), 1–11 (2017)
5. Bergen-Cico, D., Cheon, S.: The mediating effects of mindfulness and self-compassion on trait anxiety. Mindfulness **5**(5), 505–519 (2014). https://doi.org/10.1007/s12671-013-0205-y
6. Bossard, C., Kermarrec, G., Buche, C., Tisseau, J.: Transfer of learning in virtual environments: a new challenge? Virtual Reality **12**(3), 151–161 (2008). https://doi.org/10.1007/s10055-008-0093-y

7. Buckner, R.L., Andrews-Hanna, J.R., Schacter, D.L.: The brain's default network. Ann. N. Y. Acad. Sci. **1124**(1), 1–38 (2008)
8. Chittaro, L., Sioni, R.: Affective computing vs. affective placebo: study of a biofeedback-controlled game for relaxation training. Int. J. Hum. Comput. Stud. **72**(8), 663–673 (2014). https://doi.org/10.1016/j.ijhcs.2014.01.007
9. Choo, A., May, A.: Virtual mindfulness meditation: virtual reality and electroencephalography for health gamification. In: 2014 IEEE Games Media Entertainment, pp. 1–3 (2014). https://doi.org/10.1109/GEM.2014.7048076
10. Davis, W.B., Thaut, M.H.: The influence of preferred relaxing music on measures of state anxiety, relaxation, and physiological responses. J Music Ther. **26**(4), 168–187 (1989). https://doi.org/10.1093/jmt/26.4.168
11. De Kort, Y.A.W., Meijnders, A.L., Sponselee, A.A.G., IJsselsteijn, W.A.: What's wrong with virtual trees? Restoring from stress in a mediated environment. J. Environ. Psychol. **26** (4), 309–320 (2006)
12. Deterding, S., Dixon, D., Khaled, R., Nacke, L.: From game design elements to gamefulness: defining "gamification". In: Proceedings of the 15th International Academic MindTrek Conference: Envisioning Future Media Environments (MindTrek 2011), pp. 9–15. https://doi.org/10.1145/2181037.2181040
13. Dobkin, P.L., Irving, J.A., Amar, S.: For whom may participation in a mindfulness-based stress reduction program be contraindicated? Mindfulness **3**(1), 44–50 (2012). https://doi.org/10.1007/s12671-011-0079-9
14. Kaplan, S.: The restorative benefits of nature: toward an integrative framework. J. Environ. Psychol. **15**(3), 169–182 (1995). https://doi.org/10.1016/0272-4944(95)90001-2
15. Kensing, F., Blomberg, J.: Participatory design: issues and concerns. Comput. Supp. Cooper. Work (CSCW) **7**(3–4), 167–185 (1998). https://doi.org/10.1023/A:1008689307411
16. Khawaji, A., Zhou, J., Chen, F., Marcus, N.: Using galvanic skin response (GSR) to measure trust and cognitive load in the text-chat environment, pp. 1989–1994. https://doi.org/10.1145/2702613.2732766
17. Kosunen, I., Salminen, M., Järvelä, S., Ruonala, A., Ravaja, N., Jacucci, G.: RelaWorld: neuroadaptive and immersive virtual reality meditation system. In: Proceedings of the 21st International Conference on Intelligent User Interfaces (IUI 2016), pp. 208–217. https://doi.org/10.1145/2856767.2856796
18. Lomas, T., Cartwright, T., Edginton, T., Ridge, D.: A qualitative analysis of experiential challenges associated with meditation practice. Mindfulness **6**(4), 848–860 (2015). https://doi.org/10.1007/s12671-014-0329-8
19. Lymeus, F., Lundgren, T., Hartig, T.: Attentional effort of beginning mindfulness training is offset with practice directed toward images of natural scenery. Environ. Behav. **49**(5), 536–559 (2017). https://doi.org/10.1177/0013916516657390
20. Paul, G.L.: Physiological effects of relaxation training and hypnotic suggestion. J. Abnorm. Psychol. **74**(4), 425 (1969)
21. Zeidan, F., Johnson, S.K., Diamond, B.J., David, Z., Goolkasian, P.: Mindfulness meditation improves cognition: evidence of brief mental training. Conscious. Cogn. **19**(2), 597–605 (2010). https://doi.org/10.1016/j.concog.2010.03.014
22. Zhang, H., Dong, W., Dang, W., Quan, W., Tian, J., Chen, R., Zhan, S., Yu, X.: Near-infrared spectroscopy for examination of prefrontal activation during cognitive tasks in patients with major depressive disorder: a meta-analysis of observational studies. Psychiatry Clin. Neurosci. **69**(1), 22–33 (2015)

A Mixed Reality Based Social Interactions Testbed: A Game Theory Approach

Archi Dasgupta, Nicole Buckingham, Denis Gračanin$^{(\boxtimes)}$, Mohamed Handosa, and Reza Tasooji

Department of Computer Science, Virginia Tech, Blacksburg, VA 24060, USA
gracanin@vt.edu

Abstract. This paper describes a Mixed Reality (MR) based testbed and a framework for studying social interactions using a game theory approach. MR technology enables moving and interacting naturally with the real and virtual world in three dimensions, thereby using affordances for a better sense of presence. That, in turn, provides a unique opportunity to create a realistic but controlled interaction scenario to stimulate the natural response of a subject, making it an efficient platform for studying situated interactions. The users are engaged with digital characters in repetitive social interactions where the behavior of the characters is modeled using game theory. Game theory interaction models stimulate behavioral gestures in subjects that can be studied to explore psychopathological traits or other behavioral aspects of subjects. A proof of concept MR application is presented that provides exposure therapy for treatment of individuals with Social Anxiety Disorder. A case study for exposure therapy treatment using the proposed testbed is also presented. The small pilot study demonstrates the feasibility of the developed approach for studying social situations as well as the influence of the facial expressions displayed by 3D avatars on the user's perception of realism in an MR environment.

Keywords: Mixed reality · Game theory · Social interactions

1 Introduction

Social interactions can take place in a group or individual setting. Studying psychological disorders in a group setting has benefits such as allowing participants to meet people who are struggling with the same issues and having multiple options for role-playing partners. However, the group format also has disadvantages. Conducting a study with a group takes more time and is more expensive. Additionally, the first participant may have to wait before starting the session. This increases the possibility that a participant may drop out. The participant may also become discouraged if another member of the group is advancing more rapidly.

© Springer International Publishing AG, part of Springer Nature 2018
J. Y. C. Chen and G. Fragomeni (Eds.): VAMR 2018, LNCS 10910, pp. 40–56, 2018.
https://doi.org/10.1007/978-3-319-91584-5_4

Mixed reality (MR) can be an enabling technology to address this problem. Artificial experiment settings in MR are realistic enough to stimulate the natural response in a subject making it an efficient platform for studying situated interactions and multi-modal behavior [3]. Virtual Reality Exposure Therapy (VRET) and Computer-assisted Cognitive Behavioral Therapy (CCBT) are already used to incorporate virtual scenarios that resemble real-life interactions. But the advantage of MR over Virtual Reality (VR) is the ability of a user to feel completely present in the exposure therapy environment [10,32]. In MR, the digital or virtual constructs are embedded in the physical world and the user can interact with both the real and virtual objects seamlessly. The user can move naturally in the real-world physical environment making them feel completely present in an MR environment. Consequently, we have developed an MR based social interactions testbed where users are prompted to engage in a social interaction scenario with a digital character.

Another novelty of our approach is the incorporation of game theory techniques for modeling the behavior of the digital characters in a social exchange game for our testbed. Game theory studies and analyzes interaction strategies between the number of interacting agents (players) in mathematically well-defined competitive situations called games [21,34,37]. Fairness games have been used in recent years for studying social exchange [33,35,38]. Our approach offers an interaction scenario using fairness games that in turn stimulates behavioral gestures in subjects that can be used for cognitive studies.

We developed a proof of concept MR application aimed at exposure therapy treatment for Social Anxiety Disorder (SAD) because such treatments use simulated social interaction as a form of therapy. We conducted a small pilot study with five individuals who have SAD. We recorded subject's real-time physiological responses (heart rate, pulse, temperature and electrodermal activity) during the study. We also recorded the numerical investment and return in each round of the economic exchange game. The analysis of results suggests the effectiveness of the proposed approach in classifying psychopathologies and understanding behavioral patterns.

Overall, the novelty of our approach lies in using the MR platform and incorporating the game theory techniques. The MR testbed has the potential to offer a research framework that requires less time, money and effort to arrange than traditional methods. This can be a revolutionary new assistance tool for researchers of behavioral science. Modeling the interactions using game theory techniques enable stimulation of authentic responses in subjects which can be used to study behavioral gestures and identify behavioral patterns. Moreover, the case study application has the potential to be an easily and remotely accessible therapy module for SAD patients who shy away from traditional treatment.

2 Related Work

VR can also be used in applications for simulating social interactions. However, VR requires complete immersion in a virtual world by entirely replacing the physical world using devices such as head-mounted displays etc. As a result, the user can consciously distance themselves from the physical world and feel that the virtual experience is not real [3]. Such simulated situations are not as realistic as a natural social interaction with other people.

Using MR instead of VR can create an experience that is more realistic as it is closer to the real environment in a reality-virtuality continuum. MR allows the user to interact with the real environment as well as the virtual objects and perceive their own body in a natural way against physical surroundings. The 3D avatars are responsive to the user's actions, making the user experience feel like a true social interaction. MR is particularly efficient to investigate situated interaction [3,36].

Anabuki et al. described the design and implementation of an embodied conversational agent into an MR system. They discuss the effects of spatial factors like the distance of the agent from the user, the size of the agent and the location of the agent [1]. Cheok et al. presented a mixed reality game space based on ubiquitous and social computing which utilizes the physical and social aspects of traditional game-play [10]. The importance of incorporating traditional gameplay in virtual interaction for the success of the overall system is evident from their discussion.

The study of social interaction can only be successful if a realistic experience is produced using a high level of immersion. Immersion was shown to increase the transfer or the application of knowledge learned in one situation to another using situated learning techniques [13]. The level of immersion is dependent on the amount of virtual character realism provided. In a study by Volonte et al., the outcomes illustrate that the photo-realistic character was perceived to have more human-like characteristics and conveyed social cues better than the cartoon characters [41]. Bailenson et al. describe the necessary components to consider a VR environment immersive [4].

A study by Borst et al. concludes that when an avatar is created to look enough like a real human, they will be processed in the same manner as a real human [12]. Generating realistic movements for the characters are important based on the study of Geijtenbeek et al. They describe quality measurement techniques to determine physical realism of an animation [15].

Game theory is the science of logical decision making which was used to model the behavior of the digital characters in our testbed. Modern game theory addresses a wide array of behavioral relations [37]. One application of game theory is to model social interactions within a group. A game consists of two or more players, each with a set of strategies, and for each combination of strategies, there is a numerical payoff for each player that reflects the desirability of an outcome to the player. Players are rational and seek to maximize their payoffs. Fairness games have been used as probes for social exchange in recent years [23, 33,35,38]. Koshelev et al. show that this type of economic exchange games can stimulate behavioral gestures in subjects that can be used to classify certain psychopathologies [21].

Our case study application was aimed at providing exposure therapy treatment for people with SAD. SAD is the fear of behaving embarrassingly during social interactions and being negatively evaluated by other people [39]. People with this disorder usually experience a reduced quality of life and suffer greatly in their work and interpersonal relationships [44]. One of the most effective treatments for SAD is exposure therapy, where a patient is gradually exposed to feared stimuli so that over time less anxiety is triggered [17,25]. Exposure therapy needs to be realistic and the patient needs to be actively and willingly participating in the process for the therapy to be successful [5,24,28]. However, in a traditional role play method or an outside situation, if someone interacting with the participant responds negatively, this may reinforce the participant's fear of the situation [16]. As a result, many patients are disinclined to seek exposure-based treatment.

As the traditional methods prove to be unreliable, both MR and VR are gaining interest in the area of exposure therapy because these tools allow implementation of controlled but realistic environments. In recent years, VR technologies were used for VRET to generate a digitally created environment with three-dimensional virtual objects that gives the patient a simulated and controlled exposure to the traumatic stimuli. Such experience causes elevated subjective levels of social anxiety [27,30]. Studies suggest that VRET can provide effective results for the treatment of several anxiety disorders like fear of heights or flying [22,26,27,29,31]. Some studies suggest that VRET can also reduce SAD symptoms [2,19,20].

However, there have been limited randomized controlled trials that specifically tested the effectiveness of VRET in SAD [8,19,42]. Some studies show a positive change in the personal assessment of public speaking anxiety, proving that VRET can reduce this type of anxiety [2,19].

In the majority of previous trials, VRET exercises solely worked with visual stimuli or public-speaking related anxiety and did not address engaging in social interactions. Our proposed approach has the ability to address multiple social fears using dynamic social interaction scenarios.

Augmented virtuality was also proved to be effective in the treatment of stress disorders [11]. MR has not been a focus of exposure therapy research yet as it is a relatively new technology. However, even the limited number of previous studies suggest that the MR treatment has the potential to be more lifelike than VR so that the therapy sessions can generate the typical anxiety reactions that the user encounters due to the disorder [7,14,32]. We explored the potentials of this novel technology for social interaction exposure therapy in our case study.

3   Problem Definition

The study of cognitive and neural systems demands integrative strategies because the human brain and behavior work in complex ways. The artificial experiment settings for the study of social interactions usually take a lot of effort, time and money to arrange and typically lack the contextual complexity of a natural setting. That, in turn fails to stimulate complex natural responses in the user thus limiting the scope of understanding human interchange in action. In the current study, we used the virtual realism facilitated by leveraging immersive environments (e.g., MR) in the experiment settings to offer an interactive social interaction scenario as an alternative approach.

Previous studies used VR predominantly and focused more on visual stimuli. Whereas we proposed an MR based responsive and dynamic situated interaction which enables understanding adaptive processes of the brain during complex social interactions in an authentic way. Our proposed game theory model enables the digital avatar to imitate a real person's behavior in an authentic way. The contributions include:

1. A testbed and a framework for developing MR applications for studying situated social interactions using Game Theory models.
2. Using smart, tangible interface for a dynamic interaction with the MR environment.
3. A proof of concept case study demonstrating the feasibility of the proposed approach for studying social interactions by developing an MR application aimed at exposure therapy treatment for SAD which consists of an interactive social interaction scenario.

We chose to develop the SAD therapy module as a case study because this type of therapy uses exposure to simulated social interaction as a form of treatment. Using our MR based game theory approach provides an opportunity to study the effectiveness of this testbed for understanding the social interaction of people with SAD.

This novel approach has the potential to drastically improve the current VRET and in vivo treatments used for SAD treatment. Overall, in the current study, we have discussed the usability of MR environments as social interaction testbed by exploring its effectiveness as a tool for exposure therapy.

4 Proposed Approach

The testbed provides a social interaction scenario with a collection of avatars. One or more users can interact with the avatars in an environment that is a combination of physical and virtual objects, including electronic devices serving as props with input/output capabilities. The social interactions are structured based on the underlying game theory models and related data sets. Currently, supported game types include sequential games with perfect information. One of the design goals is the ability to study the social exchange component in participating subjects in the game.

The implementation steps for the framework are depicted in the workflow diagram in Fig. 1. The workflow is divided into three phases. Phase 1 comprises of designing the social interaction scenario and generating the virtual characters based on the underlying game model. Phase 2 comprises of implementing social interactions and gestures by animating virtual avatars. Lastly, Phase 3 comprises of programming the behavior of the MR application, programming the behavior of the smart objects for embodied interaction and testing them. The implementation steps are briefly discussed below:

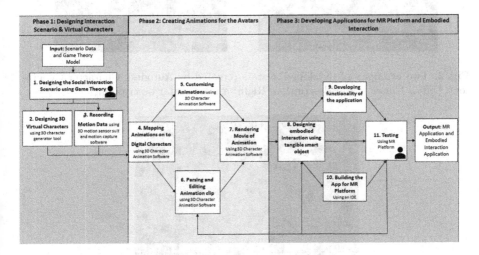

Fig. 1. MR application development workflow based on the proposed approach. Phase 1: requirements gathering and initial scenario design. Phase 2: scenario implementation, including animation. Phase 3: interactions design, including smart objects.

4.1   Phase 1: Designing the Social Scenario and Generating Relevant Avatar and Motion Data

1. **Implementing the social interaction scenario programmatically using Game Theory:** The first step is designing a social situation and creating the interaction scenario based on game theory model according to the requirements specific to the application. The modes and types of interaction between subject and virtual objects need to be decided. A subject matter expert (SME) is particularly important during this step to ensure that the game theory model and the social interaction scenario are well aligned.
2. **Designing 3D avatar:** The next step is designing virtual characters relevant to the social scenario. The characters need to be realistic enough with varying physical and emotional traits to ensure the desired impact on the subject. The appearance of the characters with varying ethnic traits and desired clothing can be generated using 3D character generation tools. Two examples of the avatar's generation characteristics can be seen in Fig. 2.
3. **Recording motion data:** The virtual avatar needs to be animated to make gestures and interact with the subject to facilitate the interaction scenario. This is difficult to accomplish procedurally. Instead, the desired movements can be acted out by a person and captured using a 3D motion sensor suit and motion capture software.

Fig. 2. Two examples of developed avatars (created by Autodesk Character Generator): Left: a female avatar description. Right: a male avatar description.

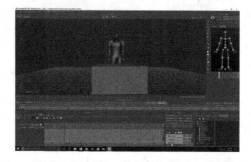

Fig. 3. Animations (movements/gestures) design for an avatar behind a proxy virtual table. The MR application can use an actual, physical table.

4.2 Phase 2: Animating Virtual Avatars for Enabling Interaction with the Users

1. **Mapping Animations onto avatars:** At this phase, the recorded motion data is used to animate the avatars to make the character's movements as realistic as possible. 3D Character Animation Software (e.g., Autodesk Motion-Builder) can be used to map the animation onto the avatars. First, the base avatar in the originally recorded motion needs to be set to T-pose. Then the newly generated target avatar needs to be merged into the same frame. After plotting the original animation onto the new character, the base avatar can be removed from the scene leaving the new avatar with the correct animation. These steps need to be repeated for each avatar. Figure 3 shows an avatar being manipulated in Motion Builder.

2. **Customizing Animations for each avatar:** If the physical measurements of the base avatar and the target avatar vary widely, noise can appear in the newly generated animation. Each of the animations needs to be carefully customized by manipulating individual joints of the avatar's anatomy to make the movements smooth. Sudden changes in the animation can be corrected by adjusting the movements of a joint in X, Y or Z direction at the given point in time. The manipulation needs to be synced properly with the existing animation.

Another challenge is aligning the avatar accurately within the physical space. 3D models of physical objects (e.g., a table) can be used as a proxy in the animation customization phase to ensure alignment (Fig. 3). These alignments can be generated using 3D modeling software tools (e.g., Autodesk Maya). These proxy models need to be removed before building the application.

3. **Creating Animation Movie:** Each newly generated animation needs to be rendered as a video clip. Viewing the video clip helps to decide if the animation needs any more manipulation before begin used in the application, i.e., if it is realistic and smooth enough.

4.3   Phase 3: Building Applications for MR Platform and Embodied Interaction

1. **Designing embodied interactions using a tangible smart object and developing game theory module:** For the user to interact with the virtual world, a tangible interaction is needed. A smart, tangible object can be used for interaction. The interface needs to be small and customizable. It can be any smart tangible object like a smartphone, a tablet or any configurable physical object. An application needs to be developed for the smart object's interface defining the functionality of the interactions. Similarly, a game theory module determines the type and the intensity of interactions (e.g., the amount of monetary exchange).
2. **Developing the functionality of the MR application:** Once the animations and the mode of interaction are finalized, the application can be developed using a game engine (e.g., Unity). The application interface needs to have comprehensible instructions (e.g. visual/audio) for the user to start using the application. Scripts need to be written to enable the functionalities of the program. To assemble all the components, first, the animated avatars need to be imported into a game engine as a component. Next, animator controllers are added for each component. Then, the scripts are added to define the functionality of the program based on user's prompts.
3. **Deploying the developed MR application:** After the completion of assembly, the application is built and deployed onto the selected MR platform.
4. **Testing using MR platform:** Finally, the application needs to be tested extensively with each avatar on the selected MR platform. In case of problems, the editing and customization phases need to be repeated until all of the sessions are deemed fit to be used in the application. This is another step where the participation of SMEs is crucial for completing the development process.

5   Case Study

We used the developed testbed in a pilot study with five subjects for studying social interaction within the context of exposure therapy for individuals with

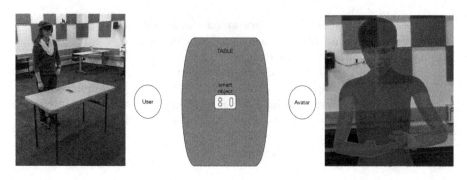

Fig. 4. Left: a user wearing a Microsoft HoloLens device and an Empatica wristband device with a tangible interactions prop (a smartphone) placed on the table. Middle: the graphical outline of the user study setup. Right: the 3D avatar, seen through the Microsoft HoloLens device on the other side of the table.

SAD. Several SMEs were consulted to demonstrate and evaluate the potentials of using MR in behavioral therapy. The social scenario was modeled as a two-party exchange game, called the Trust game [21], in which a subject diagnosed with SAD plays with a virtual avatar. This game has been previously used as a form of treatment for SAD as a web game [40]. The time span and structure of the sessions ensure that the exposure is controlled and does not create an adverse impact contrary to a real-life therapy session where things can go out of hand easily.

Each subject attends six sessions with six different avatars that have neutral facial expressions. There are ten rounds in each session and it takes around 10 min to complete each session. The Microsoft HoloLens device was chosen as the MR platform to test the application. The experiment is conducted in a room that had a $153 \times 91 \times 73.66$ cm table in the middle. The layout of the experiment can be seen in Fig. 4. A user is positioned in front of the table wearing the HoloLens device. A smart object (a smartphone) is used for tangible, embodied interaction to represent a monetary bill. The smart object is placed on the table and is used by the user and the avatar to set the amount of money to be sent. An example of the user handling the phone is shown in Fig. 5. Once the application starts, an avatar appears on the other side of the table.

The subject starts the game with 20 monetary units and chooses to send some fraction of that money to the virtual avatar. The amount invested by the subject is tripled before sending to the avatar. Then the avatar decides which fraction of that tripled money to return to the investor based on the corresponding game theory model in each round. A mathematical model was created for programming the avatar's behavior based on a previous study using an web-based game with live subjects.

The avatar appears to takes some time to 'decide' on the amount to return and then brings a hand to the phone. The phone then displays the returned monetary amount. The avatar's decision is determined by the game theory model.

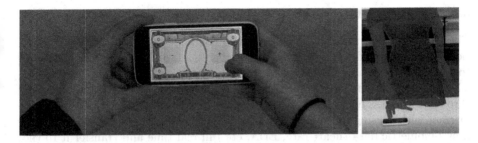

Fig. 5. Left: a view of the smart object displaying the money amount. The user can set the amount between 0 and 20 monetary units using the '-' and '+' icons. Right: the avatar reaching towards the smart object to indicate setting the return value.

The user presses the next button which appears on the phone screen to start a new turn. The user needs to be willing to give back portions of the returned money to the avatar after each round to end up with the most money at the end of the game. We have recorded the initial investment submitted by the subject and the investment returned by the avatar. We also recorded subject's real-time physiological responses (heart rate, pulse, temperature and electrodermal activity) using the Empatica E4 wristband. The game allows the investor (the subject) to build mental models of what to expect from the other player (the avatar) [6,9,43]. The users are asked to complete an assessment pre- and post-treatment to evaluate if the sessions were an effective form of exposure therapy.

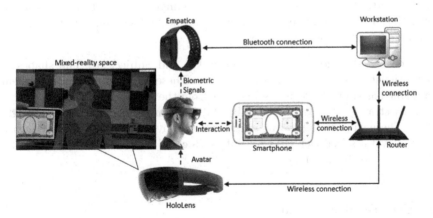

Fig. 6. System architecture for the developed MR application. Empatica E4, HoloLens and smartphone devices are connected to a workstation that controls the experiment and collects the data. The game theory model then uses the data to provide responses and control the avatar's gestures and social interactions.

5.1 System Architecture

The system architecture relies on four main components (Fig. 6). The workstation is responsible for running the server that manages the whole application, collects data and runs the game theory model to produce avatars' responses. The workstation, the smartphone, and the HoloLens device are interconnected through a wireless network. The user sees the avatar through HoloLens and can interact with it using the smartphone. The Empatica E4 device is used to collect user's biometric data (heart rate, EDA, etc.) in real time and transfer it to the workstation using Bluetooth. We aim to analyze the collected biometric data to explore possible effects of social interactions on the user's emotional state.

6 Results

We developed a case study MR application that involved users engaging in a monetary exchange game with virtual avatars. A small pilot study with five users enabled us to analyze users' monetary exchange data to understand their behavioral pattern. The results indicate that the proposed approach can be used to understand how people behave in certain social scenarios.

6.1 Behavioral Analysis Based on Monetary Exchange Data

The play pattern can be used to identify psychological traits of a person. Our observations indicate clear patterns in users' behavior. We present our findings by showing cumulative graphs of investments by the subject (red) and returns by the avatars (blue). These graphs show a distinguishable pattern of behavior among the subjects. Six subjects enrolled but one subject (Subject 4) dropped-out. There are two groups of behaviors:

1. Tic-for-Tac strategy (Subject 2, Subject 5 and Subject 6): The shapes of investment and return graphs are similar. These subjects decide investment amount based on the avatar's feedback from the previous round (Fig. 7).
2. Steady strategy (Subject 1 and Subject 3): The investment graph is a straight line. These subjects follow a specific trend in investment without any regard to the avatar's feedback (Fig. 8). Subject 3 could also be considered a combination of two behaviors.

6.2 User Feedback Form

We collected user feedback at the end of the study. Each user filled out a feedback form with the following questions: a rating on how helpful the social exchange was for the user's personality disorder, a description of what the user learned, lists of any particular aspects that the user found helpful and unhelpful, and any recommendations for improvement.

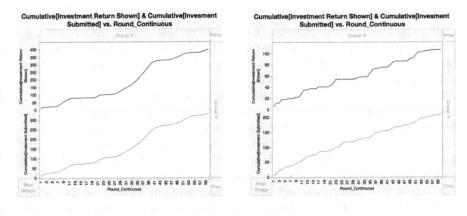

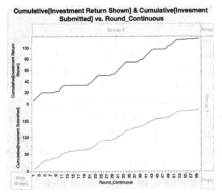

Fig. 7. Cumulative graph of investment and return (Tic-for-Tac strategy): subjects 2, 5 and 6. (Color figure online)

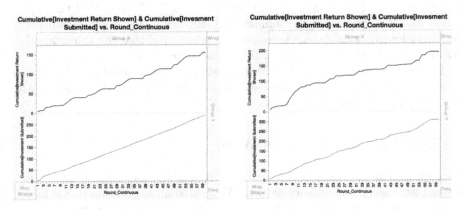

Fig. 8. Cumulative graph of investment and return (steady strategy): subjects 1 and 3. (Color figure online)

The mean rating for the helpfulness of the interaction was 4.4 out of 10, with 10 being the most helpful. However, four out of the five participants specifically stated that they gained knowledge regarding building trust and recognizing emotions. The feedback about building trust also shows that the users treated the situations as real life-like interactions.

The additional statement that this study helped users recognize emotions is interesting because the avatars were given one standard facial expression. This feedback leads us to conclude that the users felt that the avatars were human enough to contain emotions, which led them to focus on the avatar's face during interactions, and to interact with them as if they were normal humans. However, people with SAD display biases in recognizing emotional facial expressions [18], so we aim to look into this aspect as an extension of our study. One user added that they felt that the setting was an interesting way of introducing a stranger to be interacted with. Additionally, they added that this study served as a good easing mechanism into treatment.

On the other hand, one user reported that the level of anxiety provoked from the avatar was not as high as it would have been by a human. This statement, along with the feedback that showed a high interest in facial expressions, led us to a conclusion that the use of avatars with varying facial expressions should be explored.

Some users reported that some type of feedback regarding how they were doing in the game would be helpful. There are many possibilities for adding real-time user progress, including adding a visual, audio or physical feedback. These possibilities may be researched in future work. Altogether, the feedback was mostly positive and provided us with useful ideas for improvement.

It is important to note the complexities and technological challenges encompassed in this approach. Recording motion data and making the avatars' movements realistic, is arguably the most time consuming and problem-ridden step. The movements of the avatar play a vital role in the life-likeness that the application has. It is important to eliminate any glitches in the original animation data in order to obtain a clean movement. It is also vital that the animations be customized to fit the body shape of the avatar being used.

Finally, designing embodied interaction using a tangible smart object requires time and creativity. The object used and the functionality needed can vary vastly depending on the research at hand.

7   Conclusion and Future Work

We presented an approach to developing a mixed reality based social interaction testbed leveraging game theory models. We created an application to conduct a proof of concept pilot study for the proposed approach. The pilot study demonstrates the effectiveness of the approach as we were able to study subjects' behavioral pattern in a social interaction scenario. Analyzing the monetary exchange data between the subject and the avatar, we were able to identify specific behavioral patterns among subjects. This proves the potential of the proposed testbed for studying behavioral gestures and identifying psychopathological patterns. Moreover, the case study application has the potential to be an easily accessible therapy module for SAD patients who shy away from traditional treatment. This type of MR based exposure therapy can serve as a good easing mechanism into treatment. The feedback from the participants suggests that they found the approach to be novel and effective.

As the logical next step, we aim to compare the effectiveness of existing exposure therapy treatments with our proposed framework. For improving the framework, we intend to focus more on streamlining the operations, faster development of scenario, support for non-technical users and better adjustment of motion to create characters of different sizes. Another topic for further research is integrating and testing a variety of game theory models that are complemented by diverse facial and emotional expressions of the avatars.

The influence of the quality of the facial expressions displayed by 3D avatars on the user's perception of the realism of the MR environment is another important topic. Additional technical aspects like the distance of the digital character from the user, the size of the character and the location of the character would also be interesting to study. One approach is to monitor user's physiological signals and biometric data to quantify the effects on the users for comparing the effectiveness of an MR-based framework against a web-based therapy as a part of the future work. We hope our study will be helpful in the ongoing research on this topic.

References

1. Anabuki, M., Kakuta, H., Yamamoto, H., Tamura, H.: Welbo: an embodied conversational agent living in mixed reality space. In: Proceedings of the CHI 2000 Extended Abstracts on Human Factors in Computing Systems, pp. 10–11. ACM, New York (2000)
2. Anderson, P.L., Zimand, E., Hodges, L.F., Rothbaum, B.O.: Cognitive behavioral therapy for public-speaking anxiety using virtual reality for exposure. Depress. Anxiety **22**(3), 156–158 (2005)
3. Avramova, V., Yang, F., Li, C., Peters, C., Skantze, G.: A virtual poster presenter using mixed reality. Intelligent Virtual Agents. LNCS (LNAI), vol. 10498, pp. 25–28. Springer, Cham (2017). https://doi.org/10.1007/978-3-319-67401-8_3
4. Bailenson, J.N., Yee, N., Blascovich, J., Beall, A.C., Lundblad, N., Jin, M.: The use of immersive virtual reality in the learning sciences: digital transformations of teachers, students, and social context. J. Learn. Sci. **17**(1), 102–141 (2008)
5. Beck, J.S.: Cognitive Behavior Therapy: Basics and Beyond, 2nd edn. The Guilford Press, New York (2011)
6. Berg, J., Dickhaut, J., McCabe, K.: Trust, reciprocity, and social history. Games Econ. Behav. **10**(1), 122–142 (1995)
7. Botella, C., Juan, M., Baños, R., Alcañiz, M., Guillén, V., Rey, B.: Mixing realities? An application of augmented reality for the treatment of cockroach phobia. Cyberpsychology Behav. **8**(2), 162–171 (2005)

8. Bouchard, S., Dumoulin, S., Robillard, G., Guitard, T., Klinger, É., Forget, H., Loranger, C., Roucaut, F.X.: Virtual reality compared with in vivo exposure in the treatment of social anxiety disorder: a three-arm randomised controlled trial. Br. J. Psychiatry **210**(4), 276–283 (2017)
9. Camerer, C., Weigelt, K.: Experimental tests of a sequential equilibrium reputation model. Econometrica **56**(1), 1–36 (1988)
10. Cheok, A.D., Yang, X., Ying, Z.Z., Billinghurs, M., Kato, H.: Touch-space: mixed reality game space based on ubiquitous, tangible, and social computing. Pers. Ubiquit. Comput. **6**(5), 430–442 (2002)
11. Cipresso, P., Gaggioli, A., Serino, S., Raspelli, S., Vigna, C., Pallavicini, F., Riva, G.: Inter-reality in the evaluation and treatment of psychological stress disorders: the INTERSTRESS project. Stud. Health Technol. Inform. **181**, 8–11 (2012)
12. de Borst, A.W., de Gelder, B.: Is it the real deal? Perception of virtual characters versus humans: an affective cognitive neuroscience perspective. Front. Psychol. **6**, 576 (2015)
13. Dede, C.: Immersive interfaces for engagement and learning. Science **323**(5910), 66–69 (2009)
14. Dünser, A., Grasset, R., Seichter, H., Billinghurst, M.: Applying HCI principles in AR systems design. In: Proceedings of the 2nd International Workshop on Mixed Reality User Interfaces: Specification, Authoring, Adaptation (MRUI 2007) (2007)
15. Geijtenbeek, T., van den Bogert, A.J., van Basten, B.J.H., Egges, A.: Evaluating the physical realism of character animations using musculoskeletal models. In: Boulic, R., Chrysanthou, Y., Komura, T. (eds.) MIG 2010. LNCS, vol. 6459, pp. 11–22. Springer, Heidelberg (2010). https://doi.org/10.1007/978-3-642-16958-8_2
16. Heimberg, R.G., Magee, L.: Social anxiety disorder. In: Barlow, D.H. (ed.) Clinical Handbook of Psychological Disorders: A Step-by-Step Treatment Manual, 5th edn. The Guilford Press, New York (2014)
17. Hofmann, S.G., Smits, J.A.J.: Cognitive-behavioral therapy for adult anxiety disorders: a meta-analysis of randomized placebo-controlled trials. J. Clin. Psychiatry **69**(4), 621–632 (2008)
18. Joormann, J., Gotlib, I.H.: Is this happiness I see? Biases in the identification of emotional facial expressions in depression and social phobia. J. Abnorm. Psychol. **115**(4), 705–714 (2006)
19. Kampmann, I.L., Emmelkamp, P.M.G., Hartanto, D., Brinkman, W.P., Zijlstra, B.J.H., Morina, N.: Exposure to virtual social interactions in the treatment of social anxiety disorder: a randomized controlled trial. Behav. Res. Ther. **77**, 147–156 (2016)
20. Klinger, E., Bouchard, S., Légeron, P., Roy, S., Lauer, F., Chemin, I., Nugues, P.: Virtual reality therapy versus cognitive behavior therapy for social phobia: a preliminary controlled study. CyberPsychology Behav. **8**(1), 76–88 (2005)
21. Koshelev, M., Lohrenz, T., Vannucci, M., Montague, P.R.: Biosensor approach to psychopathology classification. PLoS Comput. Biol. **6**(10), 1–12 (2010)
22. Krijn, M., Emmelkamp, P.M.G., Olafsson, R.P., Biemond, R.: Virtual reality exposure therapy of anxiety disorders: a review. Clin. Psychol. Rev. **24**(3), 259–281 (2004)
23. Lazem, S., Gračanin, D.: An experimental analysis of social traps: a second life analog. In: Proceedings of the 2010 IEEE Virtual Reality Conference (IEEE VR 2010), pp. 283–284, 22–24 March 2010
24. Lilienfeld, S.O.: Psychological treatments that cause harm. Perspect. Psychol. Sci. **2**(1), 53–70 (2007)

25. Mayo-Wilson, E., Dias, S., Mavranezouli, I., Kew, K., Clark, D.M., Ades, A.E., Pilling, S.: Psychological and pharmacological interventions for social anxiety disorder in adults: a systematic review and network meta-analysis. Lancet Psychiatry **1**(5), 368–376 (2014)

26. Meyerbröker, K., Emmelkamp, P.M.G.: Virtual reality exposure therapy in anxiety disorders: a systematic review of process-and-outcome studies. Depress. Anxiety **27**(10), 933–944 (2010)

27. Morina, N., Brinkman, W.P., Hartanto, D., Kampmann, I.L., Emmelkamp, P.M.G.: Social interactions in virtual reality exposure therapy: a proof-of-concept pilot study. Technol. Health Care **23**(5), 581–589 (2015)

28. Parikh, S.V., Zaretsky, A., Beaulieu, S., Yatham, L.N., Young, L.T., Patelis-Siotis, I., MacQueen, G.M., Levitt, A., Arenovich, T., Cervantes, P., Velyvis, V., Kennedy, S.H., Streiner, D.L.: A randomized controlled trial of psychoeducation or cognitive-behavioral therapy in bipolar disorder: a Canadian network for mood and anxiety treatments (CANMAT) study [CME]. J. Clin. Psychiatry **73**(6), 803–810 (2012)

29. Parsons, T.D., Rizzo, A.A.: Affective outcomes of virtual reality exposure therapy for anxiety and specific phobias: a meta-analysis. J. Behav. Ther. Exp. Psychiatry **39**(3), 250–261 (2008)

30. Powers, M.B., Briceno, N.F., Gresham, R., Jouriles, E.N., Emmelkamp, P.M.G., Smits, J.A.J.: Do conversations with virtual avatars increase feelings of social anxiety? J. Anxiety Disord. **27**(4), 398–403 (2013)

31. Powers, M.B., Emmelkamp, P.M.G.: Virtual reality exposure therapy for anxiety disorders: a meta-analysis. J. Anxiety Disord. **22**(3), 561–569 (2008)

32. Regenbrecht, H., Wickeroth, D., Dixon, B., Mueller, S.: Collaborative mixed reality exposure therapy. In: Proceedings of the 2006 International Conference on Cyberworlds, pp. 25–32, November 2006

33. Rilling, J.K., Gutman, D.A., Zeh, T.R., Pagnoni, G., Berns, G.S., Kilts, C.D.: A neural basis for social cooperation. Neuron **35**(2), 395–405 (2002)

34. Rubinstein, A.: Comments on the interpretation of game theory. Econometrica **59**(4), 909–924 (1991)

35. Sanfey, A.G., Rilling, J.K., Aronson, J.A., Nystrom, L.E., Cohen, J.D.: The neural basis of economic decision-making in the ultimatum game. Science **300**(5626), 1755–1758 (2003)

36. Suchman, L.A.: Human-Machine Reconfigurations: Plans and Situated Actions, 2nd edn. Cambridge University Press, Cambridge (2007)

37. Swedberg, R.: Sociology and game theory: contemporary and historical perspectives. Theory Soc. **30**, 301–335 (2001)

38. Trivers, R.L.: The evolution of reciprocal altruism. Q. Rev. Biol. **46**(1), 35–57 (1971)

39. VandenBos, G.R. (ed.): Publication Manual of the American Psychological Association, 6th edn. American Psychological Association, Washington, D.C. (2010)

40. Virginia Tech Carilion Institute: Web ganmes index. https://ckc.vtc.vt.edu/webgames/ (2018). Accessed 28 Feb 2018

41. Volonte, M., Babu, S.V., Chaturvedi, H., Newsome, N., Ebrahimi, E., Roy, T., Daily, S.B., Fasolino, T.: Effects of virtual human appearance fidelity on emotion contagion in affective inter-personal simulations. IEEE Trans. Vis. Comput. Graph. **22**(4), 1326–1335 (2016)

42. Wallach, H.S., Safir, M.P., Bar-Zvi, M.: Virtual reality cognitive behavior therapy for public speaking anxiety: a randomized clinical trial. Behav. Modif. **33**(3), 314–338 (2009)

43. Weigelt, K., Camerer, C.: Reputation and corporate strategy: a review of recent theory and applications. Strateg. Manag. J. **9**(5), 443–454 (1988)
44. Wittchen, H.U., Fuetsch, M., Sonntag, H., Müller, N., Liebowitz, M.: Disability and quality of life in pure and comorbid social phobia – findings from a controlled study. Eur. Psychiatry **14**(3), 118–131 (1999)

Escape from the Dark Jungle: A 3D Audio Game for Emotion Regulation

Jiangtao Gong[1(✉)], Yin Shi[2(✉)], Jue Wang[3(✉)], Danqing Shi[1(✉)], and Yingqing Xu[1(✉)]

[1] Department of Information Art and Design, Tsinghua University, Beijing 100084, China
gjt15@mails.tsinghua.edu.cn,
{shidanqing,yqxu}@tsinghua.edu.cn
[2] Department of Psychology, Tsinghua University, Beijing 100084, China
shiy16@mails.tsinghua.edu.cn
[3] Megvii Inc., Seattle, WA 98052, USA
wangjue@megvii.com

Abstract. In this paper, we introduce a new 3D-sound-based VR game named Escape from Dark Jungle, with the design goal of regulating players' emotion. Our game design is based on the "Stimulus - Response" theory of behavioral method, implemented using Low-cost, real-time 3D audio technologies. We conducted an extensive user study to evaluate the game's effectiveness on emotion regulation. The results show that this game achieves this goal by effectively making players more positive or negative, excite or calm.

Keywords: Emotion regulation · Game design · Emotion measurement
Stimulus response theory · 3D sound · Virtual reality

1 Introduction

Emotion is an important psychological indicator that can affect human cognition and decision-making. Emotional disability as a serious mental disorders is concerned by psychiatrists widely.

As we all know, games can regulate emotion, making players stressed, excited or happy. With the recent development of computer technologies, new VR games can bring the players a more realistic experience that is useful in the field of psychological therapy for the treatment of anxiety disorders, phobia, etc. For instance, Rothbaum et al. have successfully used VR technologies typical imaginal exposure treatment for Vietnam combat veterans with posttraumatic stress disorder (PTSD) [1].

In this paper, we study whether audio-based VR games can be effectively used for emotion regulation. To this end we designed and implemented the first 3D-audio-based VR game that aims at emotion regulation, called "Escape from the Dark Jungle". We recorded the player's emotion before and after playing game, and use it to evaluate the game's effectiveness. Our main contributions include:

1. A novel 3D-sound-based VR game designed for emotion regulation;
2. An extensive user study that evaluates the effectiveness of the game.

© Springer International Publishing AG, part of Springer Nature 2018
J. Y. C. Chen and G. Fragomeni (Eds.): VAMR 2018, LNCS 10910, pp. 57–76, 2018.
https://doi.org/10.1007/978-3-319-91584-5_5

2 Related Work

2.1 Emotion and Emotion Regulation

Following the "ecological rationality" theory proposed by Gigerenzer and Todd [2], extensive research has been conducted on emotions and decision making [3, 4]. Research show that emotion can influence our decision-making behavior to a great extent. In a study related to emotion and economic decision-making [5, 6], Harle and Sanfey asked subjects to participate UG tasks after induced positive, negative and neutral emotions. The results showed that subjects in the sad level had lower acceptance rates of unfair offers than others. On the other hand, when the subjects were induced to the four kinds of emotions are amusement (positive, approach), serenity (positive, withdrawal), anger (negative, approach), disgust (negative, withdrawal), emotional impact on the decision-making has more significant effect.

In the field of emotion regulation, Panney Baker's paradigm [7] on emotional storytelling is a method of regulating strong negative emotions. It requires the subjects to make self-disclosure of emotional volatility using writing. This emotional storytelling has a quite strong long-term positive effect. Besides, in contrast to less hostile people, a highly hostile person (an individual who is difficult to manage emotions) exhibits a more aggressive immune response, and people with high levels of alexithymia (difficult to recognize and understand emotions) experience more benefits than those with low levels of alexithymia [8]. Those who cannot handle emotional events in their lives will benefit most from Panney Baker's paradigm.

2.2 Games for Emotional Regulation

There exist a few games for emotional regulation. These games mainly target on people with special needs, such as regulating emotion of adolescents with emotional disorders like depression or anxiety disorder [9, 10]; regulating the eating mood of people with anorexia or bulimia eating disorder or treatment of other neuropsychiatric disorder [11, 12]. Other games are used to train players' emotional self-regulation through biofeedback, in order to achieve better job performance [13–15].

Despite all these efforts, there are not many emotion regulation games that target on regular users. To the best of knowledge, there is no emotion regulation games that use "Stimulus - Response" theory of behavioral method as we do in this work.

2.3 Psychoacoustics and Immersive Audio Technology

Psychoacoustics studies have measured the human perception of sound using psychophysical method, including loudness level, tone, direction hearing, hearing sensitivity, etc. [16] The most typical characteristics of sound perception include the binaural effect and the auricle effect. The binaural effect refers to the ability of localizing the sound source position with two ears. The auricle effect refers to the ability to determine the sound source position assisted by the shape characteristics of the auricle. Immersive audio technology is an application of psychological acoustics research, which uses head-related transfer function to render real-time 3D surround sound [17, 18].

Nowadays, there are many low-cost real-time 3D rendering technologies that allow users to enjoy immersive 3D audio though regular headsets.

3   Game Design

Our goal is to design an audio-only game that has no visual elements. Compared with a regular VR game that contains both visual and audial components, we believe a sound-only game could have the following unique advantages on emotion regulation:

1. The amount of visual information in a regular VR game could be overwhelming. In contrast, a sound-only game leaves a much greater degree of freedom to players' imagination. It can even wake the players' subconscious like hypnosis, bringing greater emotional impact on them.
2. Creating realistic VR game is expensive and time-consuming. In contrast, low-cost real-time 3D audio rendering technology based on psychoacoustics has been available for years.
3. Rich visual information may introduce too many uncontrollable factors in our user study. It is instead easier to control and evaluate only sound information for emotion regulation.

3.1   Scenario Design

Considering the above reasons, we designed a game scenario in which the player plays the game only by listening in the dark. In this game, the player falls into a dark jungle due to a plane crash, with temporary blindness caused by injury. The player needs to explore the jungle and find a way to escape from it. The start interface of this game is shown in Fig. 1. The player can hear different sounds based on his/her location in the jungle, and make real-time navigation decisions based on the sound he/she is hearing.

Fig. 1. Start Interface of "Escape from the dark jungle"

Fig. 2. Players play with a headset and game paddle

3.2   Core Play Rule

To play the game, the player sits alone in the dark, wearing a headset and uses a game paddle, as shown in Fig. 2. The player uses the joystick on the game paddle to move north/south/east/west on the virtual map. When the player moves to a specific location on the map, some sound sources that are nearby will be triggered to play through the headset, such as intensive explosion, beast roaring, wind and rain, farm dog barking, etc. The player needs to move away from the dangerous sounds, move towards safe sounds to find a safe path to escape from the jungle. In the process of the game, the player relies mainly on his/her own exploration to make progress, and the system will

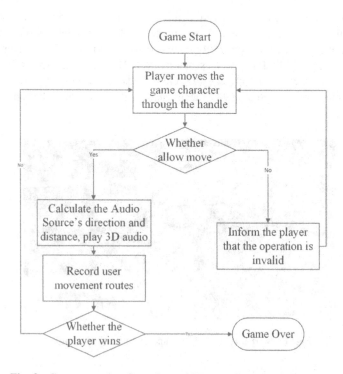

Fig. 3. Game operation flow chart of "Escape from the dark jungle"

give them a little voice guidance when necessary (e.g. stuck at the same location for too long). During the game, the system will automatically record the players' trajectory and all the sound sources that are triggered. The game operation flow is shown as Fig. 3.

3.3   Audio Material Selection

This Game requires a lot of sound sources with positive and negative attributes, which need to be carefully selected and prepared.

Firstly, we selected 88 original sounds from an audio material website [sc.chinaz. com], which are suitable for our game scenario, like explosion, fire, jungle, farm, etc.

Next, we invited seven subjects to evaluate these sound pieces from two aspects: recognizability and positivity. The subjects gave a score from 1 to 7 for each aspect. Based on the evaluation results, we deleted sounds that could not be recognized by more than half of the subjects. 44 sounds are removed in this step. For the remaining ones, we mark those sounds whose average positivity score is more than 5 as positive sound, less than 3 as negative sound and between 3 and 5 as neutral sound. The results of audio material selection experiment are shown in Table 1.

Table 1. Results of audio material selection

No.	Score		No.	Score	
	M	SD		M	SD
1	4.22	0.88	23	1.72	0.69
2	4.22	0.73	24	1.06	0.73
3	4.0	0.59	25	3.32	0.50
4	1.89	0.96	26	1.16	0.13
5	1.77	0.35	27	2.27	0.35
6	2.35	0.27	28	6.27	0.45
7	5.58	0.42	29	1.69	0.44
8	4.83	0.51	30	5.83	0.42
9	6.60	0.25	31	5.79	0.39
10	4.17	0.46	32	1.69	0.76
11	6.52	0.74	33	4.78	0.43
12	5.78	0.32	34	3.36	0.28
13	1.72	0.70	35	6.15	0.72
14	1.83	0.38	36	1.44	0.54
15	5.13	0.25	37	1.06	0.59
16	6.68	0.89	38	6.59	0.18
17	4.52	0.75	39	5.24	0.35
18	3.90	0.29	40	4.5	0.69
19	5.52	0.45	41	2.24	0.21
20	3.21	0.72	42	3.45	0.44
21	4.06	0.64	43	2.56	0.24
22	4.44	0.9	44	4.72	0.73

3.4   Map Design

We designed three types of audio maps: Positive, Negative and Neutral. The Map design principle is based on the behavioral method of the "Stimulus - Response" theory.

Behaviorists believe that human behavior and emotion heavily depends on the feedback form the environment. People feel good when the results match with their expectations, and feel bad otherwise. In our game, the positive sounds represent positive feedback, encouraging players to continue with their current movement, while the negative sounds are negative feedback that urges the players to change their current moving pattern.

For the design of the Positive Map, we follow the "Stimulus-Response" pattern of behavior: when the player triggers a positive sound, he/she will receive positive feedback, meaning that the player will encounter more positive sounds. When the player triggers a negative sound and dodge, he will avoid more negative sounds. In this way, the player can gradually build up confidence during the game and their emotion will hopefully become more positive. On the other hand, the Negative Map is completely opposite to the "Stimulus-Response" behavior mode. If the player triggers a positive sound and decides to continue to move forward, a negative sound will be triggered. If the player triggers a negative sound and dodges, he/she will trigger more negative sounds. This will force the player to make unnatural decisions constantly and their emotion may be negatively affected. Besides, the Neutral Map is designed with random sound distribution.

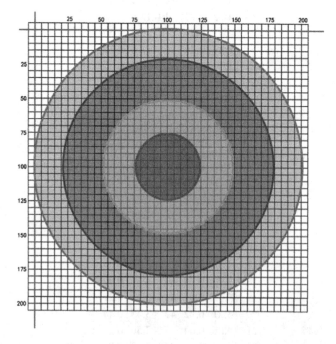

Fig. 4. Audio Map of "Escape from the dark Jungle" (Color figure online)

The size of the audio map is 200 × 200, the center of the map is the player's starting position. The audio map, as shown in Fig. 4, is divided into four areas: the Explosion Zone (red), the Vacuum Zone (yellow), the Battle Zone (green) and the Safe Zone (blue). The number of three types of sound sources in the map is shown in Table 2. The Explosion Zone is where the crash happens, and the second layer is a vacuum region due to radiation of the explosion. The third layer is the battle area full of beasts from the vacuum area, and the most outer layer is the safe zone with some villages and farms. The player wins the game by stepping into the Safe Zone and triggering the first positive sound source.

Table 2. Number of three sound sources in the map

Map area	Positive sound source	Negative sound source	Neutral sound source
Explosion zone	0	4	1
Vacuum zone	4	4	3
Battle zone	4	7	6
Safe zone	4	2	5

The Neutral Map in Fig. 5, the Positive Map in Fig. 6, the Negative Map in Fig. 7, are all designed based on "Stimulus - Response" behavioral theory and design.

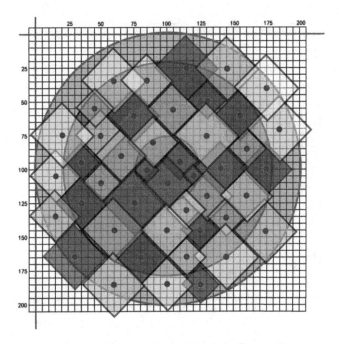

Fig. 5. Audio source distribution of the Neutral Map

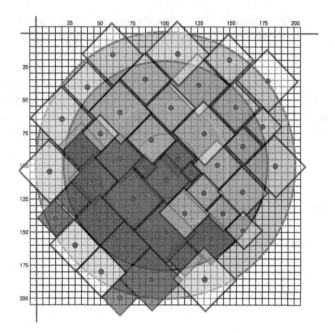

Fig. 6. Audio source distribution of the Positive Map

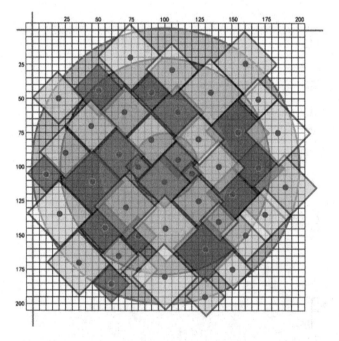

Fig. 7. Audio source distribution of the Negative Map

4 Evaluation

We conducted a user study to find out whether or not our VR Game can effectively regulate players' emotion. We set up our system at a five-day university art exhibition, and invited people who were attending the exhibition to play our game. We recorded their emotions both before and after playing game for analysis.

As shown in Table 3, we arrange a 2.5 m * 1.5 m dark space enclosed by black cloth. A computer with a 28-in. display is placed in the dark room. A regular Philip headset and a Sony PlayStation4 game paddle are used for the game play.

Table 3. List of equipment and materials

Equipment/material	Details
Dark space	a 2.5 m * 1.5 m dark space enclosed by black cloth
Display device	Crown micro E2817, 28-in. MVA wide viewing angle slim LCD monitor, the best resolution of 1920 * 1080, viewing angle of 178/178° Video Interface: D-Sub (VGA), DVI-D
Handle	Sony PlayStation4 handle, model CUH-ZCT1NA, wireless connection, size of about $162 \times 52 \times 98$ mm, weighs about 210 g, ergonomic
Emotion scale	Using the concise map of core emotions revised by Barrett and Russell [20]. The player can mark his/her emotions on the map
Audio material	Through the sound material website to obtain, the specific screening method see the audio material selection section. Adobe Audition CS6 software processing, wav format, mono, sampling frequency of 44100 Hz, 32-bit. Moderate volume, no head and tail, the length of less than 5 s
Guidance audio	The game guidance audio sources are recorded. The recording sound files are made by Adobe Audition CS6 software processing, wav format, mono, sampling frequency of 44100 Hz, 32-bit. Moderate volume, no gap at first and last
Opening animation	The opening animation taken from the game "Survivors: Mission"
Game map	Sound source distribution map, with the size of 200×200

When a subject enters the dark space, the display shows simple instructions on how to play the game, and reminds the player to keep the headset on all the time when playing the game. After that, we conduct an emotion test on the player before starting the game. Next, the player watches the opening CG and starts the game adventure using the game paddle. After the player finishes the game, we conduct another emotion test on this player, and save all the playing history and emotion test results. The experiment flow chat is shown in Fig. 8 and the instruction audio source list is shown in Table 4. In the emotion test, we use the core emotions concise measure map revised by Barrett and Russell [20]. Our emotion test interface is shown in Fig. 9. Every subject takes about 10 to 15 min to complete our user study.

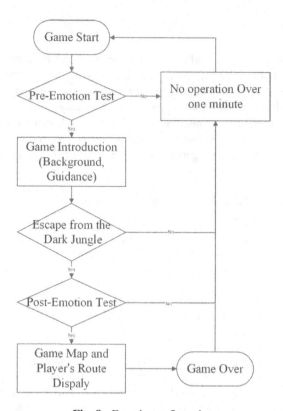

Fig. 8. Experiment flow chat

We recruited 150 participants from the visitors to the art exhibition. Among them, 14 subjects did not complete the game, therefore their data are excluded. In the remaining 134 game sessions, 29 used the positive sound map, 56 used the negative sound map and 49 used the neutral map. We did not record their gender nor their age. Table 5 shows the mean and standard deviation of the 134 pre and post emotion test.

As shown in Figs. 10 and 11, we compared the emotional status of the participants before and after playing the game. According to a 2D emotion model [19], the emotional status can be divided into two dimensions of valence and arousal. We found that in games using negative and neutral sound map, the emotional status of the participants significantly changed after the game play. The scores of our participants' emotional status in both dimensions were significantly lower after the playing negative map game (Valence: $M_{before} = 529.55$, $SD_{before} = 30.43$, $M_{after} = 434.82$, $SD_{after} = 33.67$, $t(55) = 2.089$, $p = 0.041$; Arousal: $M_{before} = 1367.29$, $SD_{before} = 38.57$, $M_{after} = 1265.32$, $SD_{after} = 36.45$, $t(55) = 2.002$, $p = 0.05$). This result indicates that participants were less pleasant and calmer after playing the game. When playing the neutral map game, the emotional arousal scores were significantly lower after the game ($M_{before} = 1445.20$, $SD_{before} = 49.60$, $M_{after} = 1228.67$, $SD_{after} = 41.05$, $t(48) = 4.294$, $p < 0.001$), and there is no significant difference before and after the game in emotional

Table 4. Instruction sound source list

Instruction sound	Detail	Note
Pre-emotion test instruction	Hello, welcome to experience "Escape from the dark jungle." Before the game begins, we want you to mark your emotional state in the appropriate area of the Emotional Axis. You can operate the handle up, down, left and right keys to control the cursor position, and press "O" key to confirm	Start after the player enter the game and looping until the player is finished
Background introduction	You are a photographer from the National Geographic and take pictures of the Amazon jungle. However, you are riding a single-jet jets meeting the inexplicable impact of the air flow, which leads to a plane crash. Although you escaped unharmed, but the brain was still hit hardly and there were some blood clots your nerve which leads to temporary blindness	After press the Enter button to start the game; play once
Play rule instruction	Dangerous! It's full of explosions. Try to manipulate the left rocker or press the up, down, left and right keys to move. You can judge the position by the change of sound around you. Here are different sounds representing different levels of danger, and your job is to escape from the forest to reach the village and find the safe place there. Come on, go find the village!	After the game background Introduction played
Game victory	Congratulations! You successfully escaped from the dark jungle!	After trigger the first positive source in the safe zone
Game over	Game Over	After stay in the negative sound source area for more than 1 min
Post-emotion test instruction	Please mark your emotions in the appropriate area of the emotional axis again. You can operate the handle up, down, left and right keys to control the cursor position, and press "O" key to confirm	After the success of escaped

valence ($M_{before} = 452.76$, $SD_{before} = 32.44$, $M_{after} = 379.29$, $SD_{after} = 34.16$, $t(48) = 1.631$, $p = 0.109$). No significant difference is observed in both dimensions of valence and arousal after playing the positive map game (Valence: $M_{before} = 443.97$, $SD_{before} = 48.68$, $M_{after} = 455.69$, $SD_{after} = 46.13$, $t(28) = -0.180$, $p = 0.858$; Arousal: $M_{before} = 1337.41$, $SD_{before} = 38.47$, $M_{after} = 1361.90$, $SD_{after} = 55.78$, $t(28) = -0.401$, $p = 0.692$).

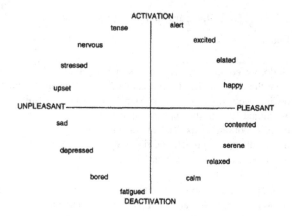

Fig. 9. Emotion test interface.

Table 5. Emotion test results

		Positive (n = 29)		Negative (n = 56)		Neutral (n = 49)	
		M	SD	M	SD	M	SD
Valance	Pre	443.97	48.68	529.55	30.43	452.76	32.44
	Post	455.69	46.13	434.82	33.67	379.29	34.16
Arousal	Pre	1337.41	38.47	1367.29	38.57	1445.2	49.6
	Post	1361.9	55.78	1265.32	36.45	1228.67	41.05

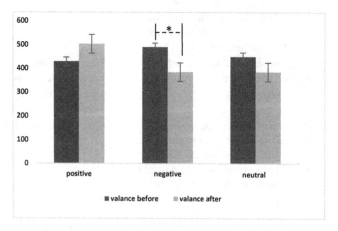

Fig. 10. Emotional valance change. (* represents $p < 0.05$ in the paired sample t-test)

We conducted an ANOVA using the score of emotional arousal as the dependent variable, and game and map type as independent variables, as shown Fig. 12. We found a very significant effect on emotional arousal before and after game

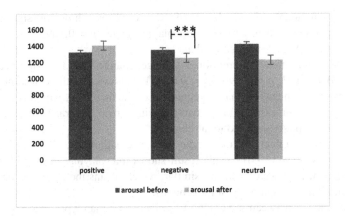

Fig. 11. Emotional arousal change (* represents $p < 0.05$ in the paired sample t-test, *** represents $p < 0.001$ in the paired sample t-test)

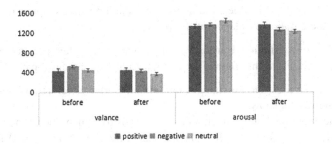

Fig. 12. Map comparison

($F(1, 131) = 9.155$, $p = 0.003$, $\eta^2 = 0.065$). The participants were calmer after playing game in all types of maps. We did not find the main effect of the map type ($F(2, 131) = 0.230$, $p = 0.795$, $\eta^2 = 0.003$). The connection between emotional arousal and the map type was significant ($F(2, 131) = 4.155$, $p = 0.018$, $\eta^2 = 0.06$). The effect of the negative and neutral map types was very significant ($F_{negative}(1, 131) = 4.486$, $p = 0.036$, $\eta^2 = 0.033$; $F_{neutral}(1, 131) = 17.701$, $p < 0.001$, $\eta^2 = 0.119$). No significant difference was observed for the positive map type ($F_{positive}(1, 131) = 0.134$, $p = 0.715$, $\eta^2 = 0.001$).

Figure 10 shows emotional valance change before and after playing game with different map type. From this figure, we can get following conclusions:

(a) Paired-sample t-test on the changes in emotional valance before and after playing game, the results shows:

    i. The emotional valance change of positive map shows no significant difference before and after playing game, $t(24) = -1.140$, $p = 0.266$.

    ii. The emotional valance change of negative maps shows significant difference before and after playing game, $t(42) = 2.287$, $p = 0.027$. Which means, after playing game with negative map, the player's mood was significantly worsen.

iii. The emotional valance change of the neutral map shows no significant difference between before and after playing game, $p = 0.109$.

(b) Two-way ANOVA results show that,

i. The main effect of emotional valance change was not significant, $F(1, 113) = 1.132$, $p = 0.290$, $\eta^2 = 0.01$. This shows that there was no positive change nor negative change regardless of the map type, which is basically in line with our expectation because positive map, neutral map and negative map can offset the emotional change.

ii. The main effect of map type was not significant $F(2, 113) = 0.701$, $p = 0.498$, $\eta^2 = 0.012$. This result shows that playing game with the three types of map were basically similar, which means the influence on players' emotion was relatively homogeneous.

iii. Interaction between the emotional valance and map types was Significant, $F(2, 113) = 2.703$, $p = 0.071$, $\eta^2 = 0.046$. However, when analyzing each simple effect, we found that playing with negative maps could significantly decrease the valance scores of players, which made the players' emotion more negative. Besides, the neutral maps and positive maps had little effect on the emotional valance of the players.

Figure 11 shows emotional arousal change before and after playing game with different map type. From this figure, we can get following conclusions:

(a) Paired-sample t-test on the changes in emotional arousal before and after playing game, the results shows:

i The emotional arousal change of the positive map shows no significant difference before and after playing game, $t(24) = -1.437$, $p = 0.164$.

ii The emotional arousal change of the negative map shows no significant difference before and after playing game, $t(42) = 1.661$, $p = 0.104$.

iii The emotional arousal change of the neutral map shows the extremely significant difference between before and after playing game, $t(47) = 4.307$, $p < 0.001$.

(b) Two-way ANOVA results show that,

i The main effect of emotional arousal change was significant $F(1, 113) = 4.393$, $p = 0.038$, $\eta^2 = 0.037$. The emotional arousal score of players was significantly decreased after playing the game. This result shows that the emotion of players became calmer after playing the game regardless of map type.

ii The main effect of the map type was not significant $F(2, 113) = 0.617$, $p = 0.542$, $\eta^2 = 0.011$. This shows that the emotional arousal level change after playing game with three different map type was basically similar, which means the influence on players' emotion was relatively homogeneous.

iii The interaction between map types and emotional arousal was extremely significant $F(2, 113) = 5.496$, $p = 0.005$, $\eta^2 = 0.089$. This shows that the impact of different maps on the player's emotional arousal was different. when analyzing each simple effect, we find that there was no change on the players' emotional arousal before and after playing game with the positive map and the negative map, that is, the player always maintained a high emotional arousal (continuous excitement), while the neutral map significantly decreased the player's emotional arousal. The players became calmer after playing game with neutral map.

We conducted another ANOVA using the score of emotional valence as dependent variable and game and map type as independent variables. No significant difference was observed in the main effect of emotional valence before-and-after game ($F(1, 131) = 3.033$, $p = 0.084$, $\eta^2 = 0.023$) and with the map type ($F(2, 131) = 1.886$, $p = 0.156$, $\eta^2 = 0.028$). There is no significant difference in the interaction between the two independent variables ($F(2, 131) = 1.007$, $p = 0.368$, $\eta^2 = 0.015$).

In order to exclude the impact of the game itself (such as game is boring, too difficult and so on) on the players' emotion, we use the neutral map (random distribution of sound source) as a reference. We compare the positive map and the negative map with the neutral map respectively, to observe the impact of the positive map and negative map on the players' emotion.

Figure 13 shows emotional valance change before and after playing game with the positive map and the neutral map;

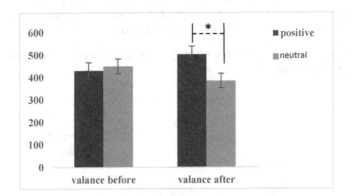

Fig. 13. Valance comparison between positive map and neutral map (* represents $p < 0.05$ in the paired sample t-test)

In this figure, an independent sample t-test was conducted on the positive map and the neutral map, which illustrates the following conclusions:

(1) Before playing game, there was no significant difference in emotional valance between the positive map and neutral map, $t(71) = -0.348$, $p = 0.729$.
(2) After playing game, Emotional valance of the positive map and the neutral map was significantly different, $t(71) = 2.025$, $p = 0.047$.

Figure 14 shows emotional arousal change before and after playing game with the positive map and the neutral map;

In this figure, an independent sample t-test was conducted on the positive map and the neutral map, which illustrates the following conclusions:

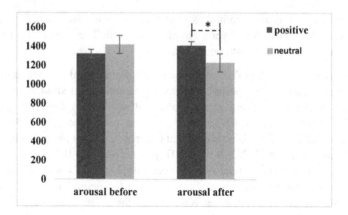

Fig. 14. Arousal comparison between positive map and neutral map (* represents $p < 0.05$ in the paired sample t-test)

(1) Before playing game, there was no significant difference in emotional arousal between the positive map and neutral map, $t(71) = -1.418$, $p = 0.161$.

(2) After playing game, Emotional arousal of the positive map and the neutral map was significantly different, $t(71) = 2.611$, $p = 0.011$.

Figure 15 shows emotional valance change before and after playing game with the negative map and the neutral map;

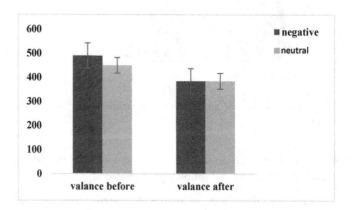

Fig. 15. Valance comparison between negative map and neutral map

In this figure, an independent sample t-test was conducted on the negative map and the neutral map, which illustrates the following conclusions:

(1) Before playing game, there was no significant difference in emotional valance between the negative map and neutral map, $t(89) = 0.833$, $p = 0.407$.

(2) After playing game, here was no significant difference in emotional valance between the negative map and neutral map, $t(89) = -0.005$, $p = 0.996$.

Figure 16 shows emotional arousal change before and after playing game with the negative map and the neutral map;

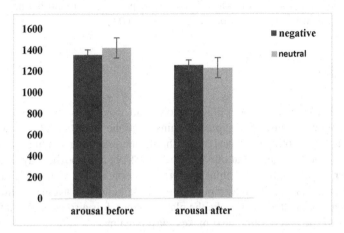

Fig. 16. Arousal comparison between negative map and neutral map

In this figure, an independent sample t-test was conducted on the negative map and the neutral map, which illustrates the following conclusions:

(1) Before playing game, there was no significant difference in emotional arousal between the negative map and neutral map, $t(89) = -1.040$, $p = 0.301$.
(2) After playing game, here was no significant difference in emotional arousal between the negative map and neutral map, $t(89) = 0.431$, $p = 0.667$.

Figure 17 shows emotional valance change before and after playing game with the positive map and the negative map;

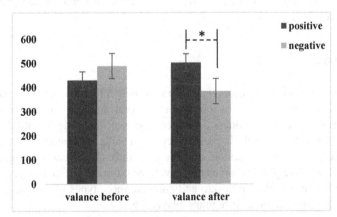

Fig. 17. Valance comparison between negative map and positive map (* represents $p < 0.05$ in the independent sample t-test)

In this figure, an independent sample t-test was conducted on the positive map and the negative map, which illustrates the following conclusions:

(1) Before playing game, there was no significant difference in emotional valance between the positive map and negative map, $t(66) = -1.016$, $p = 0.314$.
(2) After playing game, Emotional valance of the positive map and the negative map was significantly different, $t(66) = 2.188$, $p = 0.032$.

5 Discussion

Finding 1: This VR Game makes players more calm, especially using the neutral map.

As our common sense, we typically think that the game would make players exciting, thus the emotional arousal score should increase after playing game. However, our user study suggests that our VR game works in an opposite way: it calms the players down significantly. We think the main reason is that our VR game is not competitive and there is no failure punishment. We believe that other games with a similar design would effectively make the player calmer. It is also possible that the dark environment of the audio game also makes players calmer.

We also find that using the positive map, the players' emotional arousal score does not decrease. This suggests that the Positive map is effective to keep players' excitement level during the game.

Finding 2: The negative map makes players feel obviously worse, while the Positive Map makes people feel slightly better.

Our user study results show that the negative map can significantly reduce the players' emotional valence score. In contrast, the positive map makes people's emotional valence somewhat better, though not significantly. This finding is largely in line with our experimental hypothesis. The reason why the effect of the positive map is insignificant is inconclusive. One possible explanation is that the game is not challenging enough to play using the positive map, so it does not have a strong impact on the players' mood.

6 Conclusion

In this paper, we introduce a novel 3D-sound-based VR game that is designed to regulate players' emotion, based on the behavioral method of the "Stimulus - Response" theory. We also evaluate the effectiveness of this design method through a user study. Although our study is preliminary, the results suggest that we can potentially influence the plays' emotion purposefully through specially-designed audio games, so that negative players can be changed to positive and excited players can calm down. In the future, we plan to design and compare more types of games, and to find more effective design method to regulate players' emotion.

Acknowledgments. We thank all the 150 subjects taking part in our experiment. This work is supported by National Key research and development Program (2016YFB1001402).

References

1. Rothbaum, B.O., Hodges, L.F., Ready, D., et al.: Virtual reality exposure therapy for Vietnam veterans with posttraumatic stress disorder. J. Clin. Psychiatry **62**(8), 617–622 (2001)
2. Gigerenzer, G., Todd, P.M.: Simple Heuristics that Make us Smart. Oxford University Press, New York (1999)
3. Loewenstein, G.F., Weber, E.U., Hsee, C.K., et al.: Risk as feelings. Psychol. Bull. **127**(2), 267 (2001)
4. Loewenstein, G., Lerner, J.S.: The role of affect in decision making. Handb. Affect. Sci. **619** (642), 3 (2003)
5. Harlé, K.M., Allen, J.J.B., Sanfey, A.G.: The impact of depression on social economic decision making. J. Abnorm. Psychol. **119**(2), 440 (2010)
6. Harlé, K.M., Sanfey, A.G.: Effects of approach and withdrawal motivation on interactive economic decisions. Cogn. Emot. **24**(8), 1456–1465 (2010)
7. Christensen, P.R., Anderson, D.L., Chase, S.C., et al.: Results from the Mars global surveyor thermal emission spectrometer. Science **279**(5357), 1692–1698 (1998)
8. Páez, D., Velasco, C., González, J.L.: Expressive writing and the role of alexythimia as a dispositional deficit in self-disclosure and psychological health. J. Pers. Soc. Psychol. **77**(3), 630 (1999)
9. Rodriguez, A., Rey, B., Vara, M.D., et al.: A VR-based serious game for studying emotional regulation in adolescents. IEEE Comput. Graph. Appl. **35**(1), 65–73 (2015)
10. Vara, M.D., Baños, R.M., Rasal, P., et al.: A game for emotional regulation in adolescents: the (body) interface device matters. Comput. Hum. Behav. **57**, 267–273 (2016)
11. Claes, L., Jiménez-Murcia, S., Santamaría, J.J., et al.: The facial and subjective emotional reaction in response to a video game designed to train emotional regulation (Playmancer). Eur. Eat. Disord. Rev. **20**(6), 484–489 (2012)
12. Fagundo, A.B., Santamaría, J.J., Forcano, L., et al.: Video game therapy for emotional regulation and impulsivity control in a series of treated cases with bulimia nervosa. Eur. Eat. Disord. Rev. **21**(6), 493–499 (2013)
13. Ducharme, P., Wharff, E., Hutchinson, E., et al.: Videogame assisted emotional regulation training: an ACT with RAGE-control case illustration. Clin. Soc. Work J. **40**(1), 75–84 (2012)
14. Cederholm, H., Hilborn, O., Lindley, C., et al.: The aiming game: using a game with biofeedback for training in emotion regulation. In: Proceeding of DiGRA 2011 Conference: Think Design Play (2011)
15. Jercic, P., Astor, P.J., Adam, M.T.P., et al.: A serious game using physiological interfaces for emotion regulation training in the context of financial decision-making. In: ECIS 2012, vol. 207 (2012)
16. Howard, D.M., Angus, J.: Acoustics and Psychoacoustics. Taylor & Francis, Routledge (2009)
17. Burgess, D.A.: Techniques for low cost spatial audio. In: Proceedings of the 5th Annual ACM Symposium on User Interface Software and Technology, pp. 53–59. ACM (1992)

18. Cheng, C.I., Wakefield, G.H.: Introduction to head-related transfer functions (HRTFs): representations of HRTFs in time, frequency, and space. In: Audio Engineering Society Convention 107. Audio Engineering Society (1999)

19. Lang, P.J.: The emotion probe. studies of motivation and attention. Am. Psychol. **50**(5), 372–385 (1995)

20. Russell, J.A., Barrett, L.F.: Core affect, prototypical emotional episodes, and other things called emotion: dissecting the elephant. J. Pers. Soc. Psychol. **76**(5), 805 (1999)

Virtual-Reality Videos to Relieve Depression

Syed Ali Hussain[1(✉)], Taiwoo Park[2], Irem Yildirim[2], Zihan Xiang[2], and Farha Abbasi[3]

[1] School of Journalism, College of Communication Arts and Sciences, Michigan State University, Room 305, 404 Wilson Road, East Lansing, MI 48824, USA
hussai52@msu.edu
[2] Department of Media and Information, College of Communication Arts and Sciences, Michigan State University, East Lansing, USA
[3] Psychiatry Department, Michigan State University, East Lansing, USA

Abstract. Depression is a serious public health concern. The problem is further exacerbated due to social stigma and stereotypical attitudes. Thus, many people with depression keep the suffering to themselves and avoid seeking professional psychological help. Virtual reality applications offer a way to provide a virtual counseling experience without being stigmatized. In this study, we produced 360-degree virtual reality videos in which a person is shown sharing stories about his experience of living with depression. The participants (n = 12), with mild and moderate levels of depression, were invited in the lab and watched the 360-degree videos using Oculus Rift. After each video, participants were asked to say-out-loud their personal experiences about living with depression. We hypothesize that such private and confidential experience of talking about one's illness will help the users to express their feelings without the fear of being stigmatized. Results show that participants expressed more positive emotions, compared with negative emotions, after watching the 360-degree videos. Participants also expressed high positive attitude toward help seeking behavior. However, the study did not find an above average behavioral intention to seek help. Qualitative data gathered from the thought-listing exercise provides further insights about the effectiveness of virtual reality videos to promote help seeking behavior among depressed individuals. The study offers implications for improving mental health help-seeking, specifically on college campuses.

Keywords: Virtual reality · 360-degree videos · Self-disclosure
Depression · Mental health · Campus health

1 Introduction

1.1 Depression: A Serious Problem

Worldwide, depression is among the leading causes of death [1]. Roughly 20% of people experience depression at some point in their lives [2]. Prevalence of depression is particularly high among college students [3, 4], who often do not seek professional

© Springer International Publishing AG, part of Springer Nature 2018
J. Y. C. Chen and G. Fragomeni (Eds.): VAMR 2018, LNCS 10910, pp. 77–85, 2018.
https://doi.org/10.1007/978-3-319-91584-5_6

psychological help [5], and leave the symptoms untreated [6]. The problem of not seeking help during depression is evident from the fact that almost 50% of young people who complete suicide had a diagnosable mood disorder, including depression [7].

1.2 Social Stigma and Help-Seeking for Depression

Social stigma is a significant barrier in help-seeking for people living with depression [10]. Giving such people an opportunity to tell their stories of illness helps them actively participate in improving their wellness [8] and empowering both story-tellers and listeners to seek and offer help [9]. Hearing others' stories helps them cope with their own illness by realizing that they are not alone. Individuals with stigmatized health conditions, specifically individuals with depression are more inclined to suppress thoughts and keep the sufferings in themselves [11, 12]. Due to such discriminatory attitudes, even if an individual develops behavioral intention to seek help; stigma interferes to weaken caregiving relationship [13].

Help-seeking, through therapy and counseling, is a significant determinant for ones with stigma to recover from depression at an early stage. To facilitate these process, research on depression-related narratives has employed a method called 'expressive writing' [14]; a form of storytelling that involves journaling and diary writing. Expressive writing of one's thoughts has shown to positively affect mental and physical health [15]. We envision that expressive storytelling can be effective to address depression. In this study, we enhance the benefits of expressive writing by introducing it in an immersive Virtual Reality (VR) environment. We propose that VR videos will result in a more interactive and engaged experience of expressing one's depression-related thoughts and would in turn facilitate positivity and help-seeking behavior.

2   360-Degree Virtual Reality Videos

VR is defined as "an application allowing a user to navigate and interact in real time with a computer-generated three-dimensional environment" [16; p. 17]. Several studies have explored the benefits of VR-based interventions for social issues. For example, VR videos have been employed for educational setting [17], immersive story telling [18], virtual tourism [19], and learning a new language [20]. VR based interventions have shown positive results such as increased enjoyment [21], higher motivation [22], message retention [23], and positive mood induction [24]. The feasibility of VR interventions has surged due to the emergence of low cost headsets.

This study introduces two innovations. First, we produced VR videos, using 360-degree video camera, to provide a user with an immersive experience of listening to narratives of depression. Second, the VR video is made interactive by inviting participants to 'speak-out' and share their personal narratives of living with depression. This confidential and private nature of evoking depression-related narrative is hypothesized to result in positive emotions, reduced sadness, and positive attitude toward seeking professional psychological help (Fig. 1).

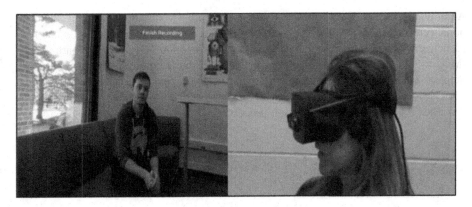

Fig. 1. Virtual reality 360-degree video showing a male individual sharing his story of living with depression while the participant listens and then shares her story. The people shown in this video are not real participants.

Hypothesis and Research Question

As such, the study proposes the following hypotheses and a research question.

Hypothesis 1: Participants exposed to the interactive VR video will express more positive, and less negative emotions.
Hypothesis 2a: Participants exposed to the interactive VR video will express a positive attitude toward seeking a professional psychological help.
Hypothesis 2b: Participants exposed to the interactive VR video will express high behavioral intention to contact counseling center.

As discussed above, an important objective of the proposed approach is to provide participants with an opportunity to express their thoughts and feelings. Thus, in addition to the quantitative results, we will also administer a thought-listing exercise after watching the VR videos. Our research question is:
Research Question: What are the prominent themes emerging from the thought-listing exercise, expressed by the participants after watching the interactive VR video.

The research group comprise of an interdisciplinary team of professionals from computer science, psychiatry, interactive game design, health communication and information and media program at Michigan State University.

3   Method

3.1   Participants

Recruitment criteria and measurements for the study were developed and administered in collaboration with a clinical psychiatrist. The study was approved by institutional review board. Participants were recruited from a student subject pool. The recruitment criteria included scoring mild or moderate level of depression as per PHQ-9 scale.

Additionally, respondents who are currently attending counseling or taking medications were excluded. Seven participants screened as a mild level of depression and five participants screened as moderate levels of depression. Overall, 12 participants (Male = 3, Female = 9) eventually participated in the main study. Most of the participants were single (n = 9), English as first language (n = 10), and in ages ranging from 18 to 26 years. The recruitment process started in October 2017. Figure 2 describes the inclusion and exclusion process.

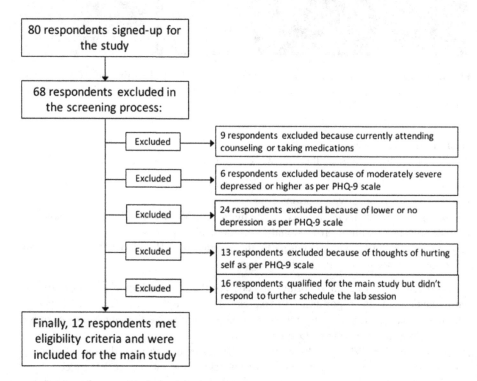

Fig. 2. Process of including/excluding participants based on the recruitment criteria.

3.2 Measurement

Positive and Negative Emotions. The study measured ten positive and negative emotions selected from a battery of emotions provided in a study about hierarchical emotions in consumer behavior [25]. Participants were asked to rate their response on a seven-point scale. Positive emotions: Warm, Peaceful, Hopeful, Joyful, Relaxed, Purposeful, Secure, I can do it, Determined, and Helpful. Negative emotions: Sadness, Overwhelmed, Anxious, Hopelessness, Tense, Guilty, Tired, Helplessness, Unwanted, and Misunderstood. Higher score indicates more emotions evoked.

Attitude Toward Help Seeking. Attitude toward help seeking was measured on a seven-point Attitude Toward Seeking Professional Psychological Help Scale (ATSPPHS) [26]. This is a shorter 10-item version of the original 29-item scale developed by Fischer and Turner [27]. Sample items include "If I believed I was having a mental breakdown, my first inclination would be to get professional attention." The revised scale strongly correlated with the longer version (.87) suggesting the measurement of the same construct [26].

Behavioral Intentions to Seek Help. The scale to measure behavioral intention to seek help is adopted from Park and Smith [28]. The scale employs a 7-point response format (1 = strongly disagree, 7 = strongly agree). Example item: "I intend to contact the counseling center when experiencing a personal or emotional problem in the future." Higher score indicates more behavioral intention. Descriptive and correlation matrix of all scales is presented in Table 1.

Table 1. Correlation matrix and descriptive statistics for positive emotion, negative emotion, attitude toward help seeking, behavioral intention to contact counseling center

	Positive emotions	Negative emotions	Attitude counseling	Behavioral intention	Mean	SD	Alpha
Positive emotions	1				4.89	.81	.82
Negative emotions	.169	1			2.34	.66	.72
Attitude counseling	.573	.434	1		4.34	.96	.79
Behavioral intention	.494	.018	.629*	1	2.86	1.6	.91

Note: Significant at * $p < .05$, ** $p < .01$

3.3   Procedure

For the screening phase, participants first completed an online survey using Qualtrics survey platform. Based on the recruitment criteria adopted for this study, the respondents were screened and then invited to participate in an hour-long study. Participant was first provided a consent form. After providing consent, the participant wore the Oculus Rift VR headset and watched the interactive VR video produced specifically for this study. The video first showed a 360-degree video with a calm and soothing lake scene to familiarize the participants with the 3D environment. The participant could interact with the contents using a gaze pointer which was placed as a red dot at the center of the screen. Using the pointer, the participant moved to the next scene that introduced the study purpose while showing another scene of campus life. Next, the participant proceeded to an indoor scene where they see a person sitting in front of them. A voiceover explains (Appendix) the next steps of the video that includes clicking on a button through the gaze pointer to listen to his experience of living with depression, and then click on the record button to share participants' own experience.

Overall, five different main scenes were designed to engage participants. At the end of each scene, participants were invited to express their personal experience which was recorded through an audio recorder and later transcribed.

After completing all main scenes, the participant took off the VR headset and completed an online survey using Qualtrics platform. Finally, the participant completed demographic scales and concluded the study. At the end of study, the participant received a debriefing form to provide information about the study purpose as well as the contact information of campus counseling center and other helpful sources to seek help during depression. The participant then received a course credit and left the lab.

4 Results

After going through the VR session, participants expressed more positive emotions ($M = 4.89$, $SD = .81$), compared with negative emotions ($M = 2.34$, $SD = .66$), thus supporting hypothesis 1. Additionally, participants expressed a considerably high positive attitude toward help seeking behavior ($M = 4.34$, $SD = .96$), supporting hypothesis 2a. However, participants reported below average behavioral intentions to seek help ($M = 2.86$, $SD = 1.59$), i.e., not supporting hypothesis 2b. A linear regression analysis entering positive emotions as predictor variable and attitude toward help seeking as criterion variable showed that positive emotions predicted a positive attitude toward help seeking behavior with marginal significance ($R = .57$, $SE = .82$, $F(1,10) = 4.89$, $p = .052$). This effect was absent in predicting behavioral intentions to seek help.

The research question stated: what are the prominent themes emerging from the thought-listing exercise, expressed by the participants after watching the VR video. To answer this question, we present here quotes from the thought-listing exercise written by participants after watching the VR videos. Our objective here is to understand the usefulness of the interactive VR videos and identify any signs of distress caused by the sharing experience. One participant expressed this as:

"I love the idea to express my story in a virtual context rather than a real counselor center, as I think psychological counselors are listening to me and taking good care of me because they are professional, but what I want more is to express what I am going through in a more natural context. This might be my biased view rather than a fact."

Another participant talked about how the videos may help in improving help seeking intentions in the future:

"I think these videos were very helpful in making me feel like I am not alone in this work dealing with depression and there are ways to make things easier. The visuals and audio were great and really made me feel like I was in a room talking with someone also dealing with these issues."

Another participant stated the same as:

"I think this study has encouraged me to talk to someone else about my depression."

Specifically, talking about the use of VR for this purpose, one participant said:

"VR is the coolest new technology that many people can use. That entire experience was so cool. Being in a different place talking to someone that isn't real. I know this sort of tech can be used for more serious things like mental health."

Another participant, elaborating on the 360-degree aspect of the videos said:

"I thought the videos were cool through the headset because it was more than just a video. You knew about a real person who had similar issues and outlooks."

Another participant elaborated the need for such interventions to improve counseling or help-seeking behavior and said:

"I thought talking about what depression is and looks like was an interesting idea and something more people could consider. I think it is easy to glance over depression, anxiety or panic that you might have but talking through it or acknowledging it in some way is helpful and can be a therapeutic experience."

However, the study is not without its limitations as expressed by one participant who felt the whole experience weird, thus pointing towards further modifications and testing of the study.

"It was kind of uncomfortable to talk out loud about depression. I think having the other person share experiences first helped, but overall it felt weird."

5   Discussion

To the best of our knowledge, this is a new study to experimentally test the effectiveness of VR videos to encourage self-disclosure and expression from individuals living with mild and moderate levels of depression. This study, by no means, claims to replace the counseling session, instead, it proposes VR as a medium to motivate individuals who avoid seeking help and promote help-seeking attitudes and behaviors. In other words, the VR may serve as a foot-in-the-door technique to increase help-seeking intentions while respecting users' privacy and self-esteem. In terms of ecological validity, the VR approach is viable because of the easy access and availability of smartphones and cost-effective VR headsets now available off-the-shelf. In addition, the users can experience the VR sessions in the comfort of their homes without having to visit a counseling center. Based on this initial experience, they may feel more efficacious to seek professional help from a real counselor or seek social support from friends and family. Finally, the proposed approach is expected to result in a more immersive experience with better retention of messages and higher engagement.

Appendix: Script of 360-Degree Videos

Campus Scene

What you see around is a typical day on a college campus. Even though college is one of the best days in life, it could also be one of the most difficult ones when feeling depressed or stressed out which is a serious health concern among younger population.

Prevalence of depression is particularly high among college students, who often do not seek professional psychological help, and leave the symptoms untreated. According to research, most students report feeling overwhelmed at least once during past academic year and depressed to such an extent that it became difficult to function.

Indoor Scene

Today, you are being asked to participate in a research study about videos on mental health.

In this session, you will go through a series of videos in which you will watch a person briefly talking about his experiences of living with depression. At the end of each video, you will be invited to share your thoughts and opinion. Please speak-out loud when sharing your thoughts.

If you feel uncomfortable, you can withdraw from the study anytime without any consequences. The information you provide will not be linked to you and your privacy will be strictly maintained throughout the project.

References

1. World Health Organization. Suicide prevention [Fact sheet]. World Health Organization (2007). http://www.who.int/mental_health/prevention/suicide/suicideprevent/en/. Accessed 1 May 2008
2. Gotlib, H., Hammen, L.: Handbook of Depression. The Guilford Press, New York (2008)
3. Chang, H.: Depressive symptom manifestation and help-seeking among Chinese college students in Taiwan. Int. J. Psychol. **42**, 200–206 (2007). https://doi.org/10.1080/002075 90600878665
4. Lucas, S., Berke, A.: Counseling needs of students who seek help at a university counseling center: a closer look at gender and multicultural issues. J. Coll. Stud. Dev. **46**, 251–266 (2005). https://doi.org/10.1353/csd.2005.0029
5. Vogel, L., Gentile, A., Kaplan, A.: The influence of television on willingness to seek therapy. J. Clin. Psychol. **64**, 276–295 (2008). https://doi.org/10.1002/jclp.20446
6. Schomerus, G., Matschinger, H., Angermeyer, C.: The stigma of psychiatric treatment and help-seeking intentions for depression. Eur. Arch. Psychiatry Clin. Neurosci. **259**, 298–306 (2009). https://doi.org/10.1007/s00406-009-0870-y
7. Cheung, H., Dewa, S.: Mental health service use among adolescents and young adults with major depressive disorder and suicidality. Can. J. Psychiatry **52**(4), 228–232 (2007)
8. Herek, G., Glunt, K.: An epidemic of stigma: public reactions to AIDS. Am. Psychol. **43**, 886–891 (1988)
9. Reavey, P., Johnson, K.: Visual approaches: using and interpreting images. In: The SAGE Handbook of Qualitative Research in Psychology, pp. 296–314 (2008)
10. Frank, A.W.: The Wounded Storyteller: Body, Illness, and Ethics. University of Chicago Press (2013)
11. Wenzlaff, M.: The mental control of depression: psychological obstacles to emotional well-being. In: Wegner, D.M., Pennebaker, J.W. (eds.) (1993)
12. Rude, S., Wenzlaff, M., Gibbs, B., Vane, J., Whitney, T.: Negative processing biases predict subsequent depressive symptoms. Cogn. Emot. **16**, 423–440 (2002)
13. Gulliver, A., Griffiths, K.M., Christensen, H.: Perceived barriers and facilitators to mental health help-seeking in young people: a systematic review. BMC Psychiatry **10**(1), 113 (2010)

14. Pennebaker, W.: Writing about emotional experiences as a therapeutic process. Psychol. Sci. **8**(3), 162–166 (1997)
15. Sloan, M., Marx, P.: A closer examination of the structured written disclosure procedure. J. Consult. Clin. Psychol. **72**(2), 165 (2004)
16. Pratt, R., Zyda, M., Kelleher, K.: Virtual reality: in the mind of the beholder. IEEE Comput. **28**(7), 17–19 (1995)
17. Kavanagh, S., Luxton-Reilly, A., Wüensche, B., Plimmer, B.: Creating 360 educational video: a case study. In: Proceedings of the 28th Australian Conference on Computer-Human Interaction, pp. 34–39. ACM (2016)
18. Assilmia, F., Pai, S., Okawa, K., Kunze, K.: In360: a 360-degree-video platform to change students preconceived notions on their career. In: 2017 ACM SIGCHI Conference on Human Factors in Computing Systems, CHI EA 2017. Association for Computing Machinery (2017)
19. BBC: British Museum offers virtual reality tour of Bronze Age, BBC News (2015). http://www.bbc.com/news/technology-33772694
20. Cheng, A., Yang, L., Andersen, E.: Teaching language and culture with a virtual reality game. In: Proceedings of the 2017 CHI Conference on Human Factors in Computing Systems, pp. 541–549. ACM (2017)
21. Apostolellis, P., Bowman, A.: Evaluating the effects of orchestrated, game-based learning in virtual environments for informal education. In: Proceedings of the 11th Conference on Advances in Computer Entertainment Technology - ACE 2014, pp. 1–10. ACM Press, New York (2014). https://doi.org/10.1145/2663806.2663821
22. Sharma, S., Agada, R., Ruffin, J.: Virtual reality classroom as a constructivist approach. In: 2013 Proceedings of IEEE Southeastcon, pp. 1–5. IEEE (2013). https://doi.org/10.1109/secon.2013.6567441
23. Huang, M., Rauch, U., Liaw, S.: Investigating learners' attitudes toward virtual reality learning environments: based on a constructivist approach. Comput. Educ. **55**(3), 1171–1182 (2010). https://doi.org/10.1016/j.compedu.2010.05.014
24. Riva, G., Mantovani, F., Capideville, M., Preziosa, A., Morganti, F., Villani, D., Gaggioli, A., Botella, C., Alcaniz, M.: Affective interactions using virtual reality: the link between presence and emotions. CyberPsychol. Behav. **10**(1), 45–56 (2007)
25. Laros, F.J., Steenkamp, J.-B.E.M.: Emotions in consumer behavior: a hierarchical approach. J. Bus. Res. **58**(10), 1437–1445 (2005). https://doi.org/10.1016/j.jbusres.2003.09.013
26. Fischer, H., Farina, A.: Attitudes toward seeking professional psychological help: a shortened form and considerations for research. J. Coll. Stud. Dev. **36**, 368–373 (1995)
27. Fischer, H., Turner, I.: Orientations to seeking professional help: development and research utility of an attitude scale. J. Consult. Clin. Psychol. **35**(1p1), 79 (1970)
28. Park, S., Smith, W.: Distinctiveness and influence of subjective norms, personal descriptive and injunctive norms, and societal descriptive and injunctive norms on behavioral intent: a case of two behaviors critical to organ donation. Hum. Commun. Res. **33**(2), 194–218 (2007)

The Message Effect of Augmented Health Messages on Body

Soyoung Jung[(✉)]

MIND Lab, S.I. Newhouse School of Public Communication,
Syracuse University, Syracuse, NY, USA
sjung01@syr.edu

Abstract. This study investigates the health message effect of Spatial Augmented Reality (SAR) with projection mapping technology while comparing a two-dimensional flat screen and three-dimensional image of a participant's body. This current study offers insight that the dualprocess model occurs when people experiencing spatial presence, also known as feeling of "being there," are particularly experiencing affective feeling, not cognitive feeling. In turn, the affective feeling as spatial presence enhances negative attitudes on cigarette smoking and online viral behavior intentions while demonstrating heuristic-systematic process model (HSM).

Keywords: Augmented Reality (AR) · Spatially Augmented Reality (SAR)
Spatial presence · Affective attitude · Heuristic-Systematic process Model (HSM)
Persuasion · Cigarette cessation campaign

1 Introduction

1.1 Backgrounds

Many medical Augmented Reality (AR) applications attempt to help surgical processes; for example, projecting guidance with medical imaging to help develop physician's intuitive abilities [1]. Also, medical AR have been applied for rehabilitation of various areas such as post-stroke rehabilitation and physical therapy [2, 3]. In addition, medical AR include psychological disorder treatments; while the AR technology allows patients to experience a phobic simulation, e.g., cockroach phobia, the patient may experience a reduction in the mental disorder because they can expose themselves to virtual cockroaches through the AR technology [4].

Exposing people to impossible experiences with augmented reality technology may have great benfit for attitude change but that effect has been relatively disregarded. Recently, communication technology scholars have attempted to demonstrate AR's persuasive effects [2, 4–9].

This study is particularly focused on the effects of an anti-smoking message by turning the 3D objects in the message into embodied parts of the participants' bodies. The purpose of this study is to gain better understanding of the persuasive effects of the projected health message through the SAR form by comparing the threedimensional human body and two-dimensional flat screen of an identical antismoking message.

© Springer International Publishing AG, part of Springer Nature 2018
J. Y. C. Chen and G. Fragomeni (Eds.): VAMR 2018, LNCS 10910, pp. 86–93, 2018.
https://doi.org/10.1007/978-3-319-91584-5_7

Definition of Augmented Reality (AR) and Spatial Augmented Reality (SAR).
Based on the real, physical world, projecting and overlaying virtual images is the
definition of augmented reality (AR) [10]. The projection mapping is known as a
variation of spatial augmented reality (SAR), or a projection-based AR, that augments
images based on the physical 3D objects or spaces in the real world [11]. Utilizing the
real environment doesn't require having the higher resolution of a hologram, which is
solely depending on the lumens of projector. Instead, SAR uses the depth of threed-
iemnsional effect and stereognostic perception to help perceivers' simulation process
[6]. Therefore, its strong affordnace based on three-dimensional depth has occured
sense of immersion and presence [12].

1.2 SAR and Spatial Presence

The feeling of presence, "being there," also known as spatial presence, has been
discussed for the whole of a virtual environment; however, it could be extended to the
virtual objected and mixed reality, which is rendered by augmented reality systems [6,
12]. When the virtual objects evoke the unconscious spatial cognition processes and
check for the possibility of interaction with the AR, it enhances the affordances of the
virtual objects. In the moment, the spatial presence is feedback of the potential interactivity from AR [12].

The feeling of "being-there" presence is developed by tele-communication scholarship to explain the experience of transcendence [13] that is beyond the physical place
and being, existing in another place mediated by a medium, e.g., book, TV, movie,
phone, or VR. The extended experiences, emergent through the new medium, have
developed along with technological advancement.

The novel experience—an impossible visual representation in the physical world—
created by SAR provides the feeling of spatial presence, which is a transcendent feeling
of immersion; while the SAR projects anatomical images of lung and fetus onto the
perceiver's body.

The role of the feeling of spatial presence in the model here was how the perceivers
were involved in the environment and how the participants were immersed in the
projected AR.

The feeling of presence generally demonstrates that it results in better evaluation on
content and system [6], and also shows attitude change [13]. However, the scholarship
of theory of presence has attempted to explain the hidden meaning and relationship
between presence and the dual model process in perception [12, 14]. According to
Schubert [12], the presence is demonstrated as affective feeling associated with
experiences. The presence occurs by experiencing a mediated situation; the involvement in the experience can then be applied to when a perceiver judges the information
that is provided from the mediated situation. The feelings have also been considered as
affective influence on information processing during persuasion process [15, 16].

Before making an affirmation on persuasion's effect on the feeling of presence, we
must retrace the information processing model for persuasion to systematically expli-
cate how the heuristic-systematic model of information processing occurred when
presence emerged.

1.3   Heuristic-Systematic Model (HSM) of Information Processing

In social psychology scholarship, it is understood that affective influence results better on persuasion than cognition [17–19]. This phenomenon can be explained with a unique peripheral persuasion process, which is known as the theory of persuasion heuristic-systematic model (HSM) [18, 20–23]. Chaiken attempts to explain that while people process persuasive information in one of two ways—a heuristic or systematic process—they tend to minimize their cognitive process so that they utilize their memory and experience to determine whether the information is valid. Thus, the processing of messages can be affected by pre-existing memory and experience in terms of "principle of least effort" (p. 269, Kluckhohn [31]).

Also, when forming an attitude, people carefully consider any available information to determine whether the information is accurate or valid. However, this systematic process requires more time and is a cognitively effortful process. According to the heuristic-systematic model, when people developed and changed their attitude by utilizing their knowledge based on memory and experiences, this demonstrated that people used a simplified form of attitude judgment—e.g., heuristic processing—and it is likely to be less stable and less resistant information [24]. Hence, the source of information is cue for the judgement, e.g., when a doctor or specialist endorses the information, people use the credibility of the source to judge whether the information is credible or not.

In addition, feeling is an important influential factor on information processing [16, 25]. Consistent with logic of feeling as information theory, Krishna and Schwarz [25] argued that bodily experience is a source of information and is used for judgement [26].

Therefore, three-dimensionally mapped out onto body images can give a novel experience to see one's organs—which is impossible to see in the physical world—and demonstrate significant effect on anti-smoking. This novel experience provides affective feeling while perceivers experience feeling of presence, and it results in a better persuasive effect [27], e.g., information sharing intention or intention to engage the campaign with PSA video rather than cognitive feelings.

In sum, what is the persuasion effect of SAR on anti-smoking messages which is projecting anatomical images directly onto perceiver's body by examining how the perceiver's overall impressions of and the negative attitudes toward cigarette smoking have changed and how the affective feeling is and with this persuasion process.

The role of spatial presence, and its affective feeling, enhanced negative attitude toward cigarette smoking, and lead to better motivation to engage the cigarette cessation campaign.

2   Methodology

In this study, the two conditions were compared: projecting health information onto a two-dimensional flat screen versus projecting health information onto the three-dimensional body of the participant. The embodied augmented message has greater persuasive effect on health messages than a two-dimensional flat screen. The imbedded video is edited with the existing cigarette cessation campaign Public Service

Announcement (PSA) video, which contains anatomical moving images of a polluted lung and fetus by cigarette smoking.

2.1 Procedure

For this study, we hired college students (n = 58) from one of the Northern East college. The recruited students were rewarded with class extra credit. When they entered the experiment room, they were told about the experiment and were randomly assigned to either the flat screen or body mapping condition. Before they were exposed to the stimulus video, they were asked to start the survey questionnaire to measure their backgrounds, i.e., age, gender, education, pre-existing attitude toward cigarette smoking, and technology usage. The two-minute long identical video was played for them two times for each condition in the dark room. Both conditions were prepared as an identical situation—the same size of images and the same distance between projector and image of 6 feet. The body condition was shown to the participants through a mirror.

2.2 Participants

All 58 participants (men = 37, women = 21) were recruited at a university in the Northeastern U.S. The mean age was 19.17 (SD = 2.93). Most of them were Caucasians (74.1%), the next dominant group was Asian/Pacific Islanders (10%), 6.9% were Hispanic/Latino, 5.2% were African and 3.4% were other racial/ethnic groups.

3 Measures

Spatial Presence and Immersion. Spatial presence and immersion were measured by the ITC-SOPI multidimensional scale [26], which was developed for measuring virtual reality. The original scale consists of four subfactors—spatial presence, immersion, ecological validity, and negative effects. We adopted the two primary factors of spatial presence and immersion to measure the variables of interest. Hence, in the present study, the questionnaire was comprised of 33 items on a 7-point scale (1 = never, 7 = very much). First, to measure spatial presence, 20 items were employed (e.g., "I felt like the content was live," "I had a sense of being in the scenes displayed," "I had the sensation that parts of the displayed environment [e.g. characters or objects] were responding to me"), M = 3.09, SD = 1.20, Cronbach's α = .95. Next, to measure immersion, 13 items were employed (e.g., "I felt involved [in the displayed environment]," "I paid more attention to the displayed environment than I did to my thoughts," "I lost track of time"), M = 3.79, SD = 1.06, Cronbach's α = .89. The items were averaged to create each of the scales.

Change in Negative Emotions Toward Smoking. Negative emotions toward smoking were measured by 6 items adopted [26]. These items include, "I am afraid of the effects of smoking on health," "I am frightened by the effects of smoking on health," "I feel tense when I think about the effects of smoking on health," "I am worried about the

effects of smoking on health." All items were rated on a 7-point scale (1 = strongly disagree, 7 = strongly agree). Negative emotions were measured two times in the pre- and post-test (pre-test: M = 5.54, SD = 1.12, Cronbach's α = .87; post-test: M = 5.55, SD = 1.34, Cronbach's α = .89. Change in negative emotions was calculated by subtracting pre-test ratings from post-test ratings, M = .003, SD = 1.05.
Cognitive and affective attitudes toward the message.

Attitudes toward the smoking cessation message were assessed in the two dimensions—cognitive and affective attitudes—based on previous research by Yoo and MacInnis [28]. First, cognitive attitude toward the message was measured using a 7-point semantic differential scale with 3 pairs of adjectives (unpersuasive/persuasive, uninformative/informative, unbelievable/believable), M = 5.59, SD = .85, Cronbach's α = .71. Similarly, affective attitude toward the message was measured using a 7-point semantic differential scale with 3 pairs of adjectives (negative/positive, bad/good, unfavorable/favorable), M = 4.31, SD = 1.19, Cronbach's α = .81. The items were averaged to create each of the attitude scales.

Intentions to Engage in Smoking Cessation Campaign. Intentions to engage in a smoking cessation campaign were measured using a 7point scale (1 = strongly disagree, 7 = strongly agree) modified from Alhabash, McAlister, Lou, and Hagerstrom [29]. The wordings of the items were modified specifically to smoking cessation campaigns. Items for online behavioral intentions (8 items) include, "Smoking cessation campaigns are worth sharing with others through online media," "I would recommend smoking cessation campaigns to others through online media," and "I would "SHARE" online smoking cessation campaigns on my social media pages (e.g., Facebook, Twitter, Instagram, etc.)." Items for offline behavioral intentions (5 items) include, "Smoking cessation campaigns make me want to volunteer for an organization that manages smoking problems, "Smoking cessation campaign makes me want to attend a community or neighborhood meeting dealing with the issue of smoking," and "Smoking cessation campaign makes me want to sign a petition for governments to design more campaigns to decrease smoking rates." All items were averaged to create a single scale of behavioral intentions, M = 3.82, SD = 1.23, Cronbach's α = .93.

4   Results

Therefore, this finding gives interesting insights into AR and health related message delivery; first, the mapping out the body gives novel and personalized experience. Second, it raises higher spatial presence and higher affective attitude than flat and normal images. Third, only the spatial presence and affective attitude results in persuasive effects, e.g., enhancing negative attitude toward cigarette smoking and willingness to engage the cigarette cessation campaign (Fig. 1).

The path model was performed with WarpPLS [30]; its model fit, average path coefficient (APC) = 0.21, p = 0.008, average R-squared (ARS) = 0.136, p = 0.044 and average adjusted R-squared (AARS) = .119, p = 0.061 support significant results. The average block VIF (AVIF) <= 5 is acceptable; if AVIF <3.3 is ideally acceptable but the path model's AVIF = 1.237, it shows ideal acceptable AVIF value (Fig. 2).

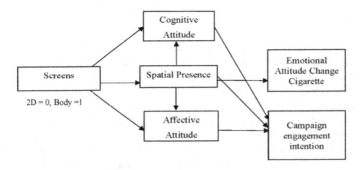

Fig. 1. Proposed model

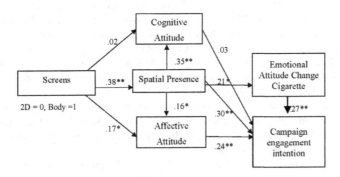

Fig. 2. Model analysis

5 Discussion

The judgement process of humans has been considered a logical and objective process; however, social psychology scholarship has introduced that how information judgement process is how affective process when people make judgement. In other words, when people perceive the certain information, they use their heuristic experience from their memory [24]. The current research has implications for the impact of an SAR experience on change, enhancement, or persistence in opinion. In fact, that an SAR experience exerted no direct effect on opinion change. However, the cognitive and affective feeling analysis, which argues that greater spatial presence heightens the participants' negative attitude on cigarette smoking and heighten their behavior intention to engage the cessation campaign. The feeling of spatial presence resulted when the message was projected on to the recipient's body directly. This result can be explained with feeling as information theory [25] that emphasizes the embodiment is important input sensory system for judgment on information processing. The embodied message on cigarette cessation has shown significant effect. Therefore, the results of this study suggest that applying a health message with SAR technology to a patient's body directly would have a positive persuasive effect on enhancing attitude and engagement of health-related information, such as sharing the health campaign information.

References

1. Bichlmeier, C., Wimmer, F., Heining, S.M., Navab, N.: Contextual anatomic mimesis hybrid in-situ visualization method for improving multisensory depth perception in medical augmented reality. In: 2007 6th IEEE and ACM International Symposium on Mixed and Augmented Reality, pp. 1–10 (2007)
2. Hondori, H.M., Khademi, M., Dodakian, L., Cramer, S.C., Lopes, C.V.: A spatial augmented reality rehab system for post-stroke hand rehabilitation. Stud. Health Technol. Inform. **184**, 279–285 (2013)
3. Mousavi Hondori, H., Khademi, M.: A review on technical and clinical impact of Microsoft Kinect on physical therapy and rehabilitation. J. Med. Eng. **2014**, 846514 (2014)
4. Juan, M.C., et al.: An augmented reality system for treating psychological disorders: application to phobia to cockroaches. In: ISMAR 2004: Proceedings of the Third IEEE and ACM International Symposium on Mixed and Augmented Reality, pp. 256–257 (2004)
5. Chang, H.-Y., Hsu, Y.-S., Wu, H.-K.: A comparison study of augmented reality versus interactive simulation technology to support student learning of a socio-scientific issue. Interact. Learn. Environ. **24**(6), 1148–1161 (2016)
6. Jung, S., Lee, D., Biocca, F.: Psychological effects on 3 dimensions projection mapping versus 2 dimensions: exploratory study. In: Proceedings of the International Society for Presence Research, pp. 213–222 (2014)
7. Javornik, A.: Augmented reality: research agenda for studying the impact of its media characteristics on consumer behaviour. J. Retail. Consum. Serv. **30**, 252–261 (2016)
8. Taylor, C.A., Lord, C.G., Bond, C.F.: Embodiment, agency, and attitude change. J. Pers. Soc. Psychol. **97**(6), 946–962 (2009)
9. Yee, N., Bailenson, J.: The proteus effect: the effect of transformed self-representation on behavior. Hum. Commun. Res. **33**(3), 271–290 (2007)
10. Bajura, M., Fuchs, H., Ohbuchi, R., Bajura, M., Fuchs, H., Ohbuchi, R.: Merging virtual objects with the real world. ACM SIGGRAPH Comput. Graph. **26**(2), 203–210 (1992)
11. Bimber, O., Raskar, R.: Spatial Augmented Reality: Merging Real and Virtual Worlds. Books24x7.com, Boston (2005)
12. Schubert, T.W.: A new conception of spatial presence: once again, with feeling. Commun. Theory **19**(2), 161–187 (2009)
13. Lee, K.M.: Presence, explicated. Commun. Theory **14**(1), 27–50 (2004)
14. Greifeneder, R., Bless, H., Pham, M.T.: When do people rely on affective and cognitive feelings in judgment? A review. Pers. Soc. Psychol. Rev. **15**(2), 107–141 (2011)
15. Schwarz, N.: Feelings as information: implications for affective influences on information processing (1999)
16. Mayer, N.D., Tormala, Z.L.: 'Think' versus 'feel' framing effects in persuasion. Pers. Soc. Psychol. Bull. **36**(4), 443–454 (2010)
17. Petty, R.E., Wegener, D.T.: Attitude change: multiple roles for persuasion variables. Annu. Rev. Psychol **48**, 609–647 (1997)
18. Rhodes, N.: Fear-appeal messages: message processing and affective attitudes. Commun. Res. **44**(7), 952–975 (2017)
19. Smith, E.R., et al.: Dual-process models in social and cognitive psychology: conceptual integration and links to underlying memory systems for helpful comments on earlier drafts. requests for reprints should be sent to. Pers. Soc. Psychol. Rev. **4**(2), 108–131 (2000)
20. Chaiken, S., Trope, Y.: Dual-Process Theories in Social Psychology. Guilford Press, New York (1999)

21. Chen, S., Chaiken, S.: The heuristic-systematic model in its broader context. Dual-process Theor. Soc. Psychol. **15**, 73–96 (1999)
22. Press, A.: The Navaho. Library (Lond) **52**(2), 268–270 (1950)
23. Chaiken, S., Fee Iii, J.W., John, K.: Heuristic versus systematic information processing and the use of source versus message cues in persuasion. J. Pers. Soc. Psychol. **39**(5), 752–766 (1980)
24. Schwarz, N., Van Lange, P., Kruglanski, A., Higgins, E.T.: Feelings-as Information Theory (2010)
25. Krishna, A., Schwarz, N.: Sensory marketing, embodiment, and grounded cognition: a review and introduction. J. Consum. Psychol. **24**, 159–168 (2013)
26. Lessiter, J., Freeman, J., Keogh, E., Davidoff, J.: A cross-media presence questionnaire: the ITC-Sense of presence inventory. Presence **10**(3), 282–297 (2001)
27. Dillard, J., Peck, E.: Affect and persuasion: emotional responses to public service announcements. Commun. Res. **27**(4), 461–495 (2000)
28. Yoo, C., MacInnis, D.: The brand attitude formation process of emotional and informational ads. J. Bus. Res. **58**(10), 1397–1406 (2005)
29. Alhabash, S., McAlister, A.R., Lou, C., Hagerstrom, A.: From clicks to behaviors: the mediating effect of intentions to like, share, and comment on the relationship between message evaluations and offline behavioral intentions. J. Interact. Advert. **15**(2), 82–96 (2015)
30. Henseler, J., Hubona, G., Ray, P.A.: Using PLS path modeling in new technology research: updated guidelines. Ind. Manag. Data Syst. **116**(1), 2–20 (2016)
31. Kluckhohn, C.: Human behavior and the principle of least effort. Am. Anthropol. **52**(2), 268–270 (1950)

Immersion in Virtual Reality Can Increase Exercise Motivation and Physical Performance

Gyoung Kim and Frank Biocca[✉]

Media, Interface, and Network Design Lab,
S.I. Newhouse School of Public Communications,
Syracuse University, Syracuse, NY, USA
{gmkim, fbiocca}@syr.edu

Abstract. We present an experimental study evaluating the effectiveness of immersive virtual reality games (combined with stationary cycling) on health-related physical activity in comparison to stationary cycling with the same game in a non-immersive (2D) setting. In the experiment, participants were asked to play a cycling video game with a stationary bike either in the immersive virtual reality (3D VR) environment or in a traditional 2D (Non-VR) display setting. Based on several theories, we anticipate that users of immersive virtual reality will feel more present in the game be induced to physically performed better than when they played the same game with a traditional 2D screen. In addition, we also expect to see people who are eager to accept and use a new technology will show better cycling performance in an immersive virtual environment than people who think accepting the newest technology in a timely manner is not very important for their lives.

Keywords: Health · Exercise · Virtual reality · Biking · VR workout
VR bike

1 Introduction

Tech Used for Health

Today, computer games have been considered as a tool for health promotions [1, 2] and for actual physical activity and exercise [3, 4]. In other words, computer games can be attractive because game mechanics engage users inactivity. Video games, so players spontaneously accept them during gameplay [5]. In addition, because of characteristics of games, players have unlimited chances to repetition of messages [6] and those can be individualized based on their game performance [5].

So, games are seen as tools for both promoting healthy behavior by modeling it, and more recently by engaging in the user in actual physical behavior via more embodied physical games. A key question explored in this study is whether the technological platform of a game dramatically influences user behavior and performance. A fundamental assumption of the technology is that playing a game in a more immersive or embodied platform will make the game appear more real and lead to more physical activity. Or to put it another way as the game simulation becomes more embodied the simulated game comes closer to the actual "real" activity.

© Springer International Publishing AG, part of Springer Nature 2018
J. Y. C. Chen and G. Fragomeni (Eds.): VAMR 2018, LNCS 10910, pp. 94–102, 2018.
https://doi.org/10.1007/978-3-319-91584-5_8

1.1   Activity and Interactivity in Simulated Gaming

Beyond just having fun during gameplay, video games for health (exergames) engage users in physical activity by motion-based interfaces mentioned above. One of key benefits of consuming interactive media at the user's level is that game platforms engage user's physical activity or involvement more so than non-interactive media consumption such as television viewing or reading printed articles, very sedentary behavior [7, 8]. In particular, body movements or a certain part of user's body can work as an input device during interaction with media [9]. For instance, most of major video game consoles today such as Nintendo Wii, Microsoft Xbox one, and Sony PlayStation 4 have their own motion recognition sensors to capture user's body movements and use them as controls in the game. With this benefit, users not only play video games but also expect more physical activity during gameplay.

Most games simulations do not fully reproduce the physical movement associated with the real-world equivalent of the simulated games such a biking, golfing, tennis, football, etc. Some simulation or restriction of the environment or movement is involved. Depending on the platform, for example, golf might be "played" by timing the push of a button or by swinging a stick with a sensor. To put it more broadly consoles and platforms vary in the degree to which the user is immersed or embodied in the virtual environment. How much does this matter and how much does it affect performance? We turn to this variable.

2   Immersion and Embodiment: Factors that Differentiate Virtual Reality

Game consoles vary technologically in the degree to which the user is immersed and embodied. Embodiment can be broadly defined as the degree to which the body of the user is captured, represented, and inside the virtual environment. More specifically we define the level of embodiment as the degree to which: (1) the senses are immersed in the virtual environment, (2) the user's body or motor activity is sensed by the technology, and (3) there is sensorimotor integration of sensory information with bodily activity [9]. Sensory immersion is defined as the degree to which the range of sensory channel is engaged by the virtual simulation. For example, immersion of a user's vision (visual channel) is influenced by field-of-view of the image and the resolution of the imagery among other variables. For instance, for any two media platforms say from Imax, PC, to virtual reality, we can distinguish them from a purely experiential viewpoint by the level of sensory immersion and embodiment. So that when the same "content" is shown across these platforms it is level of immersion and embodiment that varies.

In this study, we will explore whether higher levels of immersion and embodiment affect the users level of presence, arousal, and physical performance. We examine to two levels of immersion and embodiment that are encapsulated in two platforms: a virtual reality system and a standard fixed screen PC system extended with additional sensors and input devices (a bike a simulator).

Previous studies have looked the effects of level of embodiment and immersion on user motivation and exercise performance. Kim et al. [10] found that increased levels of embodiment operationalized as different forms of physical input and representations of body motion increased levels of presence in the game, motivation, and some aspect of physical exercise (performance).

Avatar

Several studies have kept the platform fixed and focused on the aspect of embodiment the effect of the representation of the user's body, the avatar, in the game. The avatar is the agent inside the virtual environment, the virtual body the user controls. In the game, the avatar represents a user; if you move left, your avatar also moves left in the game. Therefore, self-representation was a key role in exergames [11]. For this reason, the effect of the avatar in the game was widely explored in the past [12, 13]. Some studies focused on the identification of avatar [14] and how much does a player get immersed into that. Even though we have created a realistic avatar that resembles you, there is an always lag of reflecting yourself because it is not you. In other words, the avatar is communicating with virtual objects for you; you are not directly interacting with them.

3 Effects of Embodiment in More Immersive Virtual Environments: What If You Feel as If You Are There Exercising?

The goal of more immersive media like virtual reality and more realistic and body responsive input devices is to make the user feel as if they are "really there" So when it comes to virtual exercise, what if the user feels as if they are actually there? If the user feels as if they are there in the virtual environment without a third-person avatar, then can they focus more on the exercise?

3.1   The Users Sense of Presence in the Virtual Environment

Presence, or the users sense of presence, is the term coined to capture the degree to which a user has a sense of 'being there' in the virtual environment, or to put it another way the user's sense that their body is located not in the physical environment but in the virtual environment [15]. Numerous studies show that the level of embodiment and immersion affects users sense of presence, or more simply that virtual reality systems, which have higher levels of body motion sensing (head movement) and increased sensory immersion (field of view) and higher levels of sensorimotor integration (head movements linked to visual flow) increase levels of presence.

We hypothesize that:

H1. An exercise game platform with a higher level of embodiment and immersion will increase the user's sense of presence in the exercise environment.

3.2 Feeling More Aroused While Exercising in the Virtual Environment

While manipulating a user's sense of "being there" or presence is often a goal of virtual reality systems, it is often assumed that higher levels of presence are related to other desirable psychological outcomes such as increased performance, enjoyment, memory, persuasion, and other effects. For example, with the content of gaming Calvert and Tan found that a greater immersion and realism in a video game would influence players' emotional state [16]. Similarly, it is assumed that a more embodied media platform such as virtual reality may influence players' level of psychological or physiological states directly or mediated by the degree to which they feel present in the environment. One component that can contribute to presence is interactivity [17, 18]. Heeter [19] suggests responsiveness is one dimension of interactivity and that a highly responsive virtual environment could induce a higher sense of presence than less responsive environments.

Arousal. Arousal is a psychological and physiological state marked by the individual's level of alertness, attention, and readiness for physical response [20]. Both exercise and virtual environments affect user arousal. Scholars suggest that technological advancement in video game realism (including graphics, sounds, and controllers) could increase not only players' presence but also their arousal [21]. Arousal can be measured in different ways: broadly by assessing physiological arousal and/or psychological arousal. Physiological arousal has been measured by body sensors that assess blood flow and muscle activation such as skin conductance, muscle movement, or heart rate. Arousal and presence are sometimes correlated [17]. Therefore, we hypothesize that:

H2. An exercise game platform with a higher level of embodiment and immersion will increase the user's arousal in the exercise environment.

H3. A user's level of presence will affect the users level of arousal in an exercise environment.

3.3 Increasing "Real" Exercise Performance in the Virtual Environment

At some point, we can suggest or theorize that increasing levels of realism and presence make the virtual exercise indistinguishable from "real" exercise or activity. Of course, no medium or game platform comes close to mapping all the sensory cues and motor activity of the simulated sport or activity in the physical world. But we can theorize that with increasing levels of embodiment that actual exercise performance should increase. Of course, it is that case that pressing a button to play golf will involve less physical performance that swinging a stick sensor. But holding the physical sensor or activity constant do other levels of embodiment affect actual physical exercise performance?

We hypothesize that:

H4. Higher levels of sensory immersion (embodiment) will lead to higher levels of physical exertion and performance in the virtual exercise environment (Fig. 1).

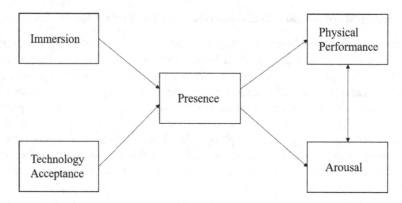

Fig. 1. Research model of the study

4 Method

We conducted an experiment to explore whether a platform with increased levels of embodiment, operationalized as virtual reality system, affected user cognition and performance. A within-subjects experiment was conducted with one independent variable, level of immersion, with two levels high immersion (virtual reality) and low immersion (a standard PC screen platform). We explored the effect on several dependent variables: user sense of presence, psychological arousal, and exercise performance. We also explored a control variable, user's individual differences in technology acceptance, as this might affect a user's comfort and interest in using a new technology.

4.1 Apparatus

Media Platforms. The independent variable was operationalized using two media platforms, an immersive virtual reality system, was used to manipulate high levels of immersion, and a standard PC platform with a fixed screen was used for low levels of immersion. On the level embodiment, the systems vary in the degree of visual immersion (VR = closed visual field and large field of view; PC open visual field and smaller field of view) and sensorimotor immersion.

(VR = head motion slaved visual feedback, PC = input sensor visual feedback only).

We controlled for input device so that the sports input device would be the same. Since current head-mounted display system for VR for a consumer market (e.g. HTC Vive or Oculus Rift) only recognizes user's movement within 10 ft. from the sensor, we used an exercise that does not need huge play area but requires enough workout intensity for a cardiovascular exercise. Therefore, we use cycling system and an input device for the experiment. The exercise bike (developed by VirZOOM) can interact with VR headsets and can be used with a simulated cyber cycling trail. In addition, the bike has a speedometer sensor sending bike's current speed into the immersive environment (See Fig. 2). We used Le Tour simulation race as the stimulus in both conditions (See Fig. 3).

High Immersion: Virtual Reality Cycling Platform	Low Immersion: External Monitor Cycling Platform

Fig. 2. Experimental conditions of the study

Fig. 3. Gameplay of bike simulation, Le Tour (First-person point of view)

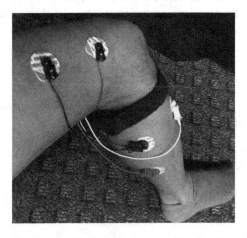

Fig. 4. Wireless EMG measurement setup for the study

Electromyography (EMG). Participants were instrumented with electromyography (EMG) to measure their physical muscle activity (Fig. 4).

4.2   Measures

Presence. Presence was measured using the ITC-SOPI questionnaire [22]. The scale includes three factors "Sense of Physical Space," "Engagement," and "Ecological Validity." Participants rated their levels of agreement using a ten-point scale, anchored by 1 (strongly disagree) to 10 (strongly agree) and a total of 12 items was used. Example items include: "I had a sense of being in the scenes displayed," "I felt that the characters and/or objects could almost touch me," and "I felt I was visiting the places in the displayed environment."

Psychological Arousal. Psychological arousal was measured using the Perceived Arousal Scale [23] which contains 24 items. Participants rated their levels of agreement using a ten-point scale, anchored by 1 (strongly disagree) to 10 (strongly agree). Example items included: "Active," "Energetic," "Exhausted," and "Inactive."

Physical Exercise Performance (by EMG). To measure participants' exercise performance, their muscle power was measured by electromyography, a physiological measurement. It was measured from two main muscles (vastus lateralis and gastrocnemius) of the leg used for cycling. Then in each condition, we found the peak and mean values of the EMG signal that is a valid EMG measurement for biking [24, 25].

4.3   Procedure

Participants were instrumented with the EMG sensors. Since each participant's muscle strength is different, we measured their baseline of muscle strength by averaging their 90 s of natural pedaling of the bike. After testing, instrumentation, and baseline measurement, they were asked to ride a bike for 10 min in each condition. The order of conditions was randomized for each participant. A rest period of 5 min was used between conditions. EMG data were collected throughout. After each condition (ride), participants completed a questionnaire assessing their level of presence and arousal.

5   Conclusion

Based on theories and concepts we discussed above, it's highly anticipated that the interactive immersive environment affects user's level of immersion and this could finally induce or dissuade his or her work performance.

Acknowledgments. We would like to thank research assistants Tony Yao and Jessica Navarro who worked on the pilot study. This project is funded by M.I.N.D. Lab at Syracuse University.

References

1. Gerling, K.M., Schild, J., Masuch, M.: Exergame design for elderly users: the case study of SilverBalance. In: Proceedings of the 7th International Conference on Advances in Computer Entertainment Technology, pp. 66–69. ACM (2010)
2. Staiano, A.E., Abraham, A.A., Calvert, S.L.: Adolescent exergame play for weight loss and psychosocial improvement: a controlled physical activity intervention. Obesity. 21, 598–601 (2013). https://doi.org/10.1002/oby.20282
3. Russell, W.D., Newton, M.: Short-term psychological effects of interactive video game technology exercise on mood and attention. Educ. Technol. Soc. 11, 294–308 (2008). citeulike-article-id:7693606
4. Warburton, D.E.R., Bredin, S.S.D., Horita, L.T.L., Zbogar, D., Scott, J.M., Esch, B.T., Rhodes, R.E.: The health benefits of interactive video game exercise. Appl. Physiol. Nutr. Metab. 32, 655–663 (2007). https://doi.org/10.1139/h07-038
5. Lieberman, D.A.: Interactive video games for health promotion: effects on knowledge, self-efficacy, social support, and health. In: Health Promotion and Interactive Technology Theoretical Applications and Future Directions, pp. 103–120 (1997)
6. Sy, S., Zichermann, G., Cunningham, C.: Gamification by Design: Implementing Game Mechanics in Web and Mobile Apps. O'Reilly Media Inc., Newton (2011)
7. Dunstan, D.W., Salmon, J., Owen, N., Armstrong, T., Zimmet, P.Z., Welborn, T.A., Cameron, A.J., Dwyer, T., Jolley, D., Shaw, J.E.: Associations of TV viewing and physical activity with the metabolic syndrome in Australian adults. Diabetologia 48, 2254–2261 (2005). https://doi.org/10.1007/s00125-005-1963-4
8. Dunstan, D.W., Barr, E.L.M., Healy, G.N., Salmon, J., Shaw, J.E., Balkau, B., Magliano, D. J., Cameron, A.J., Zimmet, P.Z., Owen, N.: Television viewing time and mortality: The australian diabetes, obesity and lifestyle study (AusDiab). Circulation 121, 384–391 (2010). https://doi.org/10.1161/CIRCULATIONAHA.109.894824
9. Biocca, F.: The cyborg's dilemma: progressive embodiment in virtual environments minding the body, the primordial communication medium. JCMC 3, 1–29 (1997). https://doi.org/10. 1111/j.1083-6101.1997.tb00070.x
10. Kim, S.Y., Prestopnik, N., Biocca, F.A.: Body in the interactive game: how interface embodiment affects physical activity and health behavior change. Comput. Hum. Behav. 36, 376–384 (2014). https://doi.org/10.1016/j.chb.2014.03.067
11. Fox, J., Bailenson, J.N.: Virtual self-modeling: the effects of vicarious reinforcement and identification on exercise behaviors. Media Psychol. 12, 1–25 (2009). https://doi.org/10. 1080/15213260802669474
12. Jin, S.-A.A.: Does imposing a goal always improve exercise intentions in avatar-based exergames? The moderating role of interdependent self-construal on exercise intentions and self-presence. Cyberpsychol. Behav. Soc. Netw. 13, 335–339 (2010). https://doi.org/10. 1089/cyber.2009.0186
13. Peña, J., Kim, E.: Increasing exergame physical activity through self and opponent avatar appearance. Comput. Hum. Behav. 41, 262–267 (2014). https://doi.org/10.1016/j.chb.2014. 09.038
14. Jin, S.-A.A.: Avatars mirroring the actual self versus projecting the ideal self: the effects of self-priming on interactivity and immersion in an exergame, Wii Fit. CyberPsychol. Behav. 12, 761–765 (2009). https://doi.org/10.1089/cpb.2009.0130
15. Sallnäs, E.-L., Rassmus-Gröhn, K., Sjöström, C.: Supporting presence in collaborative environments by haptic force feedback. ACM Trans. Comput. Interact. 7, 461–476 (2000). https://doi.org/10.1145/365058.365086

16. Calvert, S.L., Tan, S.L.: Impact of virtual reality on young adults' physiological arousal and aggressive thoughts: interaction versus observation. J. Appl. Dev. Psychol. **15**, 125–139 (1994). https://doi.org/10.1016/0193-3973(94)90009-4

17. Lombard, M., Ditton, T.: At the heart of it all: the concept of presence. J. Comput. Commun. **3**, 0 (2006). https://doi.org/10.1111/j.1083-6101.1997.tb00072.x

18. Steuer, J.: Defining virtual reality: dimensions determining telepresence. J. Commun. **42**, 73–93 (1992). https://doi.org/10.1111/j.1460-2466.1992.tb00812.x

19. Heeter, C.: Being there: the subjective experience of presence. Presence **1**, 262–271 (1992). https://doi.org/10.1109/VRAIS.1995.512482

20. Barlett, C.P., Rodeheffer, C.: Effects of realism on extended violent and nonviolent video game play on aggressive thoughts, feelings, and physiological arousal. Aggress. Behav. **35**, 213–224 (2009). https://doi.org/10.1002/ab.20279

21. Ivory, J.D., Kalyanaraman, S.: The effects of technological advancement and violent content in video games on players' feelings of presence, involvement, physiological arousal, and aggression. J. Commun. **57**, 532–555 (2007). https://doi.org/10.1111/j.1460-2466.2007.00356.x

22. Lessiter, J., Freeman, J., Keogh, E., Davidoff, J.: A cross-media presence questionnaire: the ITC-sense of presence inventory. Presence Teleoper. Virtual Environ. **10**, 282–297 (2001). https://doi.org/10.1162/105474601300343612

23. Anderson, C., Deuser, W.E., DeNeve, K.M.: Hot temperatures, hostile affect, hostile cognition, and arousal: Tests of a general model of affective aggression. Pers. Soc. Psychol. Bull. **21**, 434–448 (1995). Perceived Arousal Scale

24. Hunter, A.M., Gibson, A.S.C., Lambert, M., Noakes, T.D.: Electromyographic (EMG) normalization method for cycle fatigue protocols. Med. Sci. Sports Exerc. **34**, 857–861 (2002). https://doi.org/10.1097/00005768-200205000-00020

25. Pringle, J.S.M., Jones, A.M.: Maximal lactate steady state, critical power and EMG during cycling. Eur. J. Appl. Physiol. **88**, 214–226 (2002). https://doi.org/10.1007/s00421-002-0703-4

Design of Virtual Reality Scenes with Variable Levels of Fear Evocation

Dan Liao[1,2], Yanping Huang[1,3], Zhizhen Tan[2], Jiong Yang[4],
and Xiangmin Xu[1(✉)]

[1] School of Electronic and Information Engineering,
South China University of Technology, Guangzhou, Guangdong, China
{danl,xmxu}@scut.edu.cn
[2] School of Design, South China University of Technology,
Guangzhou, Guangdong, China
[3] School of Physics and Optoelectronic Engineering, Foshan University,
Foshan, Guangdong, China
[4] Goku Design Studio, Guangzhou, China

Abstract. Fear is one of the basic emotions of human which are comprehensive representations of human psychology and consciousness. The evocation of emotion has been applied to many fields, such as mental diseases diagnosis, mental health assessment, study of cognitive science and game design. The present methods for affective stimuli mainly include texts, pictures, sounds, odors and computer games. However, they have some limitations in terms of inefficient emotion elicitation and high susceptibility to ambient interferences. Virtual reality technology is a potential technology to solve some of these problems by providing immersive and realistic experience in terms of emotion elicitation. Therefore, in this study we set up a systematic approach for the design of emotion evocative VR scenes, using fear as an example. Firstly, we extracted fear evocative elements from the International Affective Picture System (IAPS), the Chinese Affective Digital Sound System (CADS), the Chinese Affective Video System (CAVS), horror films and video clips. Secondly, we developed three virtual reality fear scenes using the classified evocative elements. At last, we used the Self-Assessment Manikin (SAM) scale to test the effectiveness of fear evocation using these VR scenes. In conclusion we have built up a series of fear evocative VR scenes, which can induce different levels of fear with high effectiveness of fear elicitation in the VR environment.

Keywords: Virtual reality · Scenes design · Fear evocation

1 Introduction

Emotions are the psychological and physiological states associated with cognitive and epistemological processes and play a very important role in human communication. Fear is considered as one of the basic emotions of human.

In term of fear, there are various definitions made by many scholars. King et al. [1] considered that fear is a normal reaction to real or imaginary threats in psychology, which is considered as an integral part of development and adaptability. In physiology,

© Springer International Publishing AG, part of Springer Nature 2018
J. Y. C. Chen and G. Fragomeni (Eds.): VAMR 2018, LNCS 10910, pp. 103–115, 2018.
https://doi.org/10.1007/978-3-319-91584-5_9

Johansen et al. [2] believe that fear is a motivational state that has a strong biological drive, driving organisms to choose external stimuli in their environment, especially those with dangerous signals. In 1991 Izard [3] put forward that relative to other basic emotions, fear has huge potential. That is why the fear becomes one of the most widely studied emotions. Since Hall started to study fear [4], researches on fear have attracted great attention. Especially after 1980s, the study of fear has become a field which is concerned and interested in various disciplines.

The evocation of emotion has been applied to the diagnosis of mental illness, mental health assessment [5], cognitive science research [6], game design [7] and many other areas. Emotional evocation can also be used as a tool to enhance user experience in design process [8]. As emotion have a significant impact on many cognitive activities, such as perception, attention, memory and decision making, an important way to study emotions is to induce desirable emotion, so as to observe and measure physiological, psychological and behavioral changes of subjects under the corresponding emotional state.

At present there are several ways to evocate different emotions in the laboratory:

Visual stimuli - Visual stimuli induce emotions by pictures of various contents. Related databases include the International Affective Picture System (IAPS) [9] established by the National Institute of Mental Health (NIMH) and the Chinese Affective Picture System (CAPS) launched by Bai et al. [10].

Auditory stimuli - Auditory stimuli induce emotions by nature's voice recordings, nonverbal syllables and music material. Related databases include the International Affective Digital Sounds (IADS) [11] and the Chinese Affective Digital Sounds (CADS) [12].

Video stimuli - Video stimuli are combinations of visual and auditory stimuli. The main materials are movie clips based on the study of Gross and Levenson [13] and Chinese Emotional Visual Stimulus (CEVS) established by Xu et al. [14].

Olfactory stimuli - Olfactory stimuli induce emotions by having the subjects smell sniffing either intentionally or unconsciously. A large database called the Consumer Fragrance Thesaurus is such a kind of system [15].

Imagination stimuli - In imagination stimuli, subjects are guided to imagine or recall a certain situation to induce emotions. Related materials are the Affective Norms for English Words (ANEW) [16] and the Affective Norms for English Text (ANET) launched by Bradley and Lang [17].

Expression stimuli - Subjects are instructed to control their own facial muscles, making their facial expressions consistent with the reference facial expressions reflecting the target emotions, thereby inducing the target emotions [18].

Situational stimuli - Situational stimuli induce emotions by placing the subjects in a simulated or real life situation, such as public speaking, mock exams, parachuting, and surgery [19].

In above methods, visual and auditory stimuli are single channel stimuli with low ecological effect. Situational stimuli create virtual environments for the subjects, but the effects will be greatly affected once the subjects know the purpose of the experiment. Expression stimuli have greater limitations because they demand the subjects have some performance skills, and it is not easy to take the sample. Imagination stimuli are greatly influenced by individual's imagination ability. Video stimuli combine the image and music to induce the mood of the subject, which could be effective. But the number of related material is small and the generated fear level is not clear.

Therefore, in this study we analyzed the design elements from existing materials which can evocate fear, and then built up a series of fear evocative VR scenes, which can evocate different levels of fear with improved efficiency of elicitation.

About the research of emotion measurement, Ekman [20] believes that nine characteristics can distinguish one emotion from another. However, his method can hardly provide a quantitative definition for an emotion, including fear. Many scientists have tried to develop a quantitative reference range for fear and other emotions. Kim and André [21] establishes the two-dimensional emotion model of valence and arousal, according to which an emotion with high arousal and negative valence may be fear. The Self-Assessment Manikin (SAM) [22] is a non-verbal pictorial assessment technique that directly measures the valence, arousal, and dominance associated with a person's affective reaction to a wide variety of stimuli. The SAM scale is a 1–9 scale. Two critical dimensions used to measure emotions are valence and arousal. Valence is the degree of pleasure; for instance, pleasure has high valence and disgust has low valence. Arousal is the degree of activation, for instance, surprise has high arousal and sadness has low arousal.

In this paper, we defined fear as the emotion with valence of no more than 4 and arousal greater than 4. And the level of arousal could be further classified as 4 classes: slight fear (4–5), mild fear (5–6), moderate fear (6–7) and severe fear (>7).

This study consists of three parts: the first part is the extraction of features of fear evocative elements, the second part is design of VR fear scenes, and the last part is the assessment of the effectiveness of VR fear scenes using the SAM scale.

2 Feature Extraction of Critical Element for Fear-Evocation

VR technology is a combination of visual media and audio media. Therefore, we extracted fear evocative elements from emotional evoked material libraries which can provide visual stimuli, auditory stimuli and video stimuli. Fear evocative elements are extracted from the International Affective Picture System (IAPS), the Chinese Affective Digital Sound System (CADS), the Chinese Affective Video System (CAVS) and other horror films and video clips.

2.1 Fear Feature Analysis of International Affective Picture System (IAPS)

International Affective Picture System (IAPS) is made by National Institute of Mental Health (NIMH). It is a standardized picture system of stimulating the target mood. IAPS is widely used in the study of all kinds of emotional problems abroad such as the physiological mechanism of emotion, emotion regulation, and relationship on the memory of emotion and other cognitive activities. The way of using it is to identify mental state of subjects by showing them the emotional picture materials.

With the classification above, we analyzed the features of the elements in each class of evocation from three aspects: attributes, semantic features and expressive features. Specific contents are shown in Table 1.

Attribute is the nature of the element; for instance, a decaying corpse and a skull share the same attribute of human body. Semanteme refers to the meaning of the element; for instance, a decaying corpse means a horrible death and a sharp knife means hurt. Expression means the morphological character of the elements; for instance, a decaying corpse is designed to be twisted and incompleteness.

Table 1. Features of the elements in IAPS.

Level of arousal	Attributes	Semanteme	Expression
Severe fear (>7)	Severely bloody, deformed human body	Horrible death, Extremely Severe hurt	Blood red, incompleteness, deformity
Moderate fear (6-7)	Bloody or deformed human body, aggressive animal, lethal weapon or tool, severe catastrophe	Severe hurt, Death threat	Sharp, medium saturation colors, strong light and shade contrast, incompleteness
Mild fear (5-6)	Wounded human body, mummification, wounding weapon or tool, catastrophe	Hurt, pain	Abnormality
Slight fear (4-5)	Skull, graveyard, disgusting animal	Death, plague, dinginess	Low saturation color, chaos

2.2 Fear Feature Analysis of the Chinese Affective Digital Sound System (CADS)

In the establishment of CADS, Liu et al. [12] sums up the sound materials into 6 categories: surprise, neutrality, activation, pleasure, disgust and fear. We analyzed the sound materials of the type of fear. According to the sources of the sounds, we divided these voices into the sound of role and the sound of environment.

The Sound of Role. The sound is mainly made by the narrative subjects itself with clear meanings. It contains the sounds of the process of violence, such as the sound of shrill cry and the unusual sound, such as strange noises and grinning sound. The specific classification information is shown in Table 2:

Table 2. Features of the sound of role in CADS.

Level of arousal	Attributes	Semanteme	Expression
Severe fear (>7)	Heartrending scream and moan, sound of hitting human body	Torture, pain, hurt	Sudden and intermittent voice, sharp yell
Moderate fear (6–7)	Moan and wail, weird sound made by human	Sorrow and unluckiness, unknown and abnormal situation	Trembling faint voice, fierce cry and wail

The Sound of Environment. The environmental sound could be helped to set the mood and narrate. It can be divided into natural sound, artificial sound and background music. The specific classification information is shown in the Table 3:

Table 3. Features of the environmental sound in CADS.

Level of arousal	Attributes	Semanteme	Expression
Severe fear (>7)	Alarm, sound of accident	Severe disaster	Sudden and intermittent voice
Moderate fear (6–7)	Alarm, sound of dangerous object	Danger, disaster	Sharp and hasty sound
Mild fear (5–6)	Sound of dangerous object	Danger	Sudden sharp sound

2.3 Fear Feature Analysis of the Chinese Affective Video System (CEVS) and Other Horror Films and Video Clips

The Chinese Affective Video System (CEVS) [14] contains 30 film clips, which can induce six emotions including anger, fear, sadness, happiness, disgust and neutrality. There are five film clips which could induce fear. We also analyzed a number of horror films and television works. We analyzed the feature elements in the following aspects: role design, scene design, rhythm design and plot design, as shown in Table 4:

Table 4. Fear features of the elements in CAVS, horror films and video clips.

Level of arousal	Attributes	Semanteme	Expression
Character Design	The symbol of abnormal death, such as deformed body	Abnormal death, undead retaliation,	Bloody body, pale body, twisted and incomplete body
Scene design	Sealed space, endless space, dusky space	Loneliness , helplessness, confinement, unknown	Colors of cold hue and low saturation; cold and hard material
Rhythm design	Fast, slow, alternating rhythm,	Nervous, Perturbed, calm, complicated	Rhythm alternating, the horror scenes are usually set after a person feels safe.
Plot design	Escape, mystery, numinous phenomena	Unknown, precarious, creepy	Escape, suspense, confrontation, break taboos

2.4   Summary of Fear Feature Analysis

Based on abovementioned analysis, we found that the fear features of different levels can be clearly distinguished. This regularity can be used as a rationale for further design of VR fear provoked scenarios that can evoke different levels of fear.

3   Development of Virtual Reality Fear Scenes

3.1   Fear Scenes Development Process

The development of virtual reality fear scene was divided into three steps. At first, we selected appropriate music fragments, such as character settings, theme colors, scenes settings. Then we consequently finished the scripting, role design, interactive interface design and scene design. At last, we integrated models in Unreal Engine 4 and created special effects for the scenes. Main components of the development process are shown in Fig. 1.

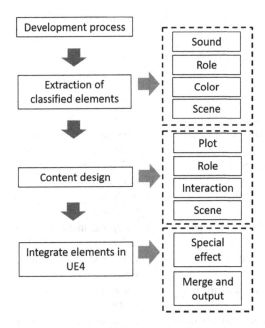

Fig. 1. Schematics of VR scene development process

3.2   Fear VR Scenes Design

According to our research, we designed three fear VR scenes. The contents of the scenes are shown in Table 5. Snapshots of the designed scenes are shown in Figs. 2, 3 and 4.

Dilapidated Basement. The Snapshot of the scene as shown in Fig. 2.

0–81 s: The scene begins in a narrow dingy corridor on the first floor of a two-story building. The height of camera is low and in a creeping perspective. The camera advances at a slow pace and the slow background music creates a mysterious and horrible atmosphere. Sudden lightning (5 s) illuminates a twisted body monster standing by the window. The corridor is covered with mosaics and other construction waste shedding from the broken wall (Fig. 2a). A male corpse in a suit with a heavy makeup mouth and a grin lies on the ground. The camera moves forward slowly, the lightning suddenly flashes again (36 s) and the monster standing by the window roars backwards and falls in front of the camera (Fig. 2b). The camera bypasses the fallen monster slowly, approaching the window. A blood soaked woman flashes through the window (55 s), accompanied by a shrill scream. The camera accelerates slightly towards the door of a red room in the front and a horned head zombie in a prison uniform suddenly falls from the broken ceiling onto the ground in front of the camera (75 s).

81–97 s: The camera moves slowly towards the door, and cries of a girl and singing of a soprano appear, which echo in the room (81 s). The camera goes through the door into the red and confined staircase. A strong ghost walks toward the camera, chasing the camera (Fig. 2c) and at the same time the background music switches to fast-paced music (88 s). The camera accelerates again, begins to escape and races up the shabby stairs.

Table 5. Description of three fear scenes.

	1	2	3
Name	Dilapidated Basement	Horrible Underground Palace	Abandoned Factory
Scene	Basement	Palace	Factory
Element	Zombies, Residual limbs, a broken stair, construction rubbishes	Zombies, skulls, a bat, torches, snakes	Centipedes, mosquitoes, black bugs, construction rubbishes
Color	Black, red, green	Brown, grey, red, blue	Green, grey
Lighting effect	Low brightness	Medium brightness	High brightness
Dynamic effect	Crawl forward, capture	Creep and attack	Creep and attack
Plot	Chase and escape	Guide and observe	Guide and observe
Rhythm	An alternating rhythm	An alternating rhythm	A smooth rhythm
Sound	Cries of a girl, Soprano singing, roars of monsters	Sound of water, sound of zombies	Sound of insects
Sound effect	Asymptotically increasing	Surrounding sound	Asymptotically increasing
Camera perspective	Low height	Normal height	Low height

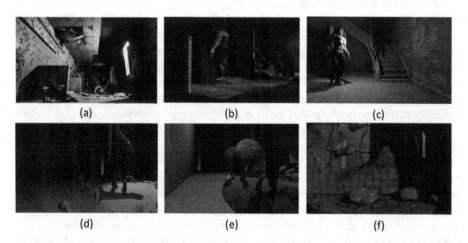

(a)   (b)   (c)

(d)   (e)   (f)

Fig. 2. Snapshot of fear Scene 1: Dilapidated Basement. (See text for the detailed description of different sub-figures) (Color figure online)

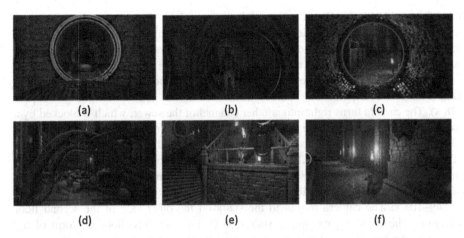

Fig. 3. Snapshot of fear Scene 2: Horrible Underground Palace. (See text for the detailed description of different sub-figures) (Color figure online)

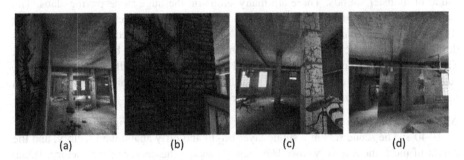

Fig. 4. Snapshot of fear Scene 3: Abandoned Factory. (See text for the detailed description of different sub-figures)

97–115 s: The camera enters the second floor, which is a dark and confined cement space. Some areas are illuminated with red and green lights and some are dark areas with no light. Three huge brick balls are hung on the ceiling and many moving hands and feet are out from the concrete floor and ceiling (Fig. 2d). Suddenly a woman screams (110 s), and the shadow of a dancing ghost appears on the wall (Fig. 2e). Looking down the direction of the light, a ghost has come to the camera, ready to throw the camera down. A dancing shadow of a ghost appears on the wall, moving forward. Looking down the direction of the light source, the ghost has come to the camera, trying to catch the camera. (Figure 2f).

Horrible Underground Palace. The Snapshot of the scene as shown in Fig. 3.

0–21 s: The scene sets in a darkened three-story confined castle and the scene begins under the steps of a palace. The underground palace is dimly lit by candle-light in the distance and the height of the camera is normal. The camera slowly moves to the stairs, suddenly neon lights come on and a fierce snake comes out behind the guardrail

(Fig. 3a), making a sound and tearing at the camera (5 s). The camera moves upstairs, and water sound becomes louder and louder. The camera enters the second floor, where there are sewer exits on the wall, flowing water, and forming waterfalls. The camera turns left into one of the sewer exits.

21–49 s: The camera enters the brick sewer and the sewer has shallow water (Fig. 3b). The camera moves forward in the sewer, and cries of a little girl appear (28 s). The camera turns right into another channel of the sewer, which is blocked by a steel bar gate. Cries continue and the camera turns away in the opposite direction (35 s). Footsteps sound (38 s), and a green-eyed zombie walks past the camera (Fig. 3c). The camera turns left to leave the sewer in the original way. The little girl's cry gradually disappears, the sound of water getting stronger. The camera leaves the sewer and enters the second floor platform of the palace (49 s).

49–103 s: The camera moves to the stairs on the other side of the second floor platform. The camera goes up the stairs (65 s), into the third floor platform of the palace. In the torchlight, a huge group of worm-like monsters creep toward the camera (70 s) (Fig. 3d). The camera turns right (76 s) and goes through a narrow, dark aisle into the magnificent main hall of the palace. The sound of water disappears and the sound of monster sounds. There are many skulls on the huge stone paving slabs. The camera continues to advance and there are many snakes dancing under the vault (Fig. 3e). The red candlesticks shine the stone columns to red. The camera goes through mouths of the snakes, with fangs and eyes of the snakes being clearly visible. The camera moves forward to a dry well (104 s) in the middle of the main hall, suddenly accelerates, climbs over the guardrail, turns over the railing and then jumps into the dry well, hitting a bat-like monster (Fig. 3f).

Abandoned Factory. The Snapshot of the scene as shown in Fig. 4.

0–40 s: The scene sets in a single layer bright and dirty abandoned factory, and the height of the camera is very low. The scene begins at the corner of the factory. When the camera moves out of the corner, the picture becomes brighter and shrill mosquitoes vibrate its wings (4 s) (Fig. 4a). A lot of trashes, a couple of wood boards and a broken table are on the floor. A group of mosquitoes are hovering above the table. After the camera goes through the table (10 s), a large, white spider can be seen, crawling back and forth on the ground and rubbing against the ground (Fig. 4b). The camera passes through the spider and a huge centipede are creeping on the front wall. The camera gradually approaches the door of a room filled with centipedes.

40–56 s: The camera enters the room where hundreds of centipedes are creeping on the floor, wall and ceiling, making a loud noise. The camera moves forward into the middle of the room, above a dense group of centipedes (Fig. 4c), turns around and returns in the same way.

56–86 s: The camera leaves the room and the sound of centipede gradually disappears. There are a few dancing centipedes on the ground, and a few huge worms wriggling in the ground not far away, making loud noise. Several white spiders are crawling back and forth on a distant pillar. The camera passes by the giant worms and the sound of the worms gradually disappears. Suddenly the sound of the mosquito wings sounds (77 s) and a huge mosquito hovers over the left front of the camera (Fig. 4d).

4 Evaluation of Designed Fear VR Scenes by Self-Assessment Manikin (SAM)

4.1 Experiment

We used the Self-Assessment Manikin (SAM) scale to test effectiveness of the designed VR scene. 30 subjects with no history of mental disorders (15 males and 15 females, age: 21–37 years) were recruited for tests.

At first, we introduced the SAM scale test process to the subjects, and illustrated its usage with some examples. Then we asked the subjects wore the experimental equipment on the subjects, including VR glasses and multi-channel physiological recorder. The subjects were requested to rest, including thirty seconds with eyes closed and ten seconds with eyes open for rest. Three VR scene videos were played to subjects in random order, and the subjects completed the corresponding SAM scale after each VR scene video was played. The experimental procedure is shown in Fig. 5.

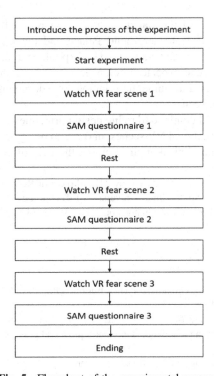

Fig. 5. Flowchart of the experimental process.

4.2 Results

Table 6 shows the mean score of valence, arousal and dominance. The arousal scores are 7.4, 7.0 and 6.4. According to the predefined levels of fear, the main factors that affect evocation of emotion are valence and arousal. When valence <4, arousal >7, the

Table 6. The mean score of valence, arousal and dominance.

No.	Scene	Valence	Arousal	Dominance
1	Dilapidated Basement	2.6	7.4	4.2
2	Horrible Underground Palace	2.7	7.0	5.0
3	Abandoned Factory	3.1	6.4	5.0

evocation of emotion is severe fear. When valence <4, arousal between 6–7 is moderate fear. The reason why Scene 1 got the highest arousal and Scene 3 got the lowest arousal mainly lay in the color and lighting effect of the scenes. Higher contrast of the color in environment could induce higher arousal. Another important reason for the difference in arousal among three scenes is the sound with the narrative rhythm. Scene 1 has the sound of weeping of people with escape. Scenes 2 and 3 have more natural sounds and noises.

5   Conclusion

According to the result, the Dilapidated Basement has reached the level of inducing severe fear, and the Horrible Underground Palace and the Abandoned Factory has reached the level of inducing moderate fear. The experimental results above show that designed fear VR scenes can evocate different levels of fear. Our design approach is effective, which can be used as guideline principles for designing more fear scenes or other types of emotional scenes.

In future work, we will continue to refine design principles and design more scenes to enrich the library of emotional VR scenes, in order to bring a new and more effective tool for both research and clinical applications in the field of emotion study.

Acknowledgement. This work is supported by "The Project of Research and Reform based on Undergraduate Education in South China University of Technology in 2017" (Y1171080) and "Science and Technology Program of Guangzhou" (201704020043).

References

1. King, N.J., Hamilton, D.I., Ollendick, T.H.: Children's Phobias: A Behavioural Perspective. Wiley, Hoboken (1988)
2. Johansen, J.P., Tarpley, J.W., Ledoux, J.E., et al.: Neural substrates for expectation-modulated fear learning in the amygdala and periaqueductal gray. Nat. Neurosci. **13**(8), 979–986 (2010)
3. Izard, C.E.: The Psychology of Emotions. Springer, Berlin (1991). vol. 6, no. 61, pp. 198–209
4. Hall, G.S.: Thanatophobia and immortality. Am. J. Psychol. **26**(4), 550–613 (1915)
5. Young, M.E., Bemak, F.: The role of emotional arousal and expression in mental health counseling. J. Ment. Health Couns. **18**, 316–332 (1996)
6. Salterspedneault, K., Gentes, E., Roemer, L.: The role of fear of emotion in distress, arousal, and cognitive interference following an emotional stimulus. Cogn. Behav. Ther. **36**(1), 12–22 (2007)

7. Ravaja, N., Salminen, M., Holopainen, J., et al.: Emotional response patterns and sense of presence during video games: potential criterion variables for game design. In: Nordic Conference on Human-Computer Interaction, pp. 339–347 (2004)

8. Piqueras-Fiszman, B., Jaeger, S.R.: The impact of the means of context evocation on consumers' emotion associations towards eating occasions. Food Qual. Prefer. 37(37), 61–70 (2014)

9. Center for the Study of Emotion and Attention (CSEA-NIMH).: The International Affective Picture System: Digitized Photographs. Center for Research in Psychophysiology, University of Florida (1995)

10. Bai, L., Ma, H., Huang, Y.X., Luo, Y.J.: The development of native Chinese affective picture system–a pretest in 46 college students. Chin. Ment. Health J. 19(11), 719–722 (2005). (in Chinese)

11. Bradley, M.M., Lang, P.J.: The International Affective Digitized Sounds Affective Ratings of Sounds and Instruction Manual. University of Florida (2007)

12. Liu, T.S., Luo, Y.J., Ma, H., et al.: The compilation and evaluation of localized emotional sound library. Psychosoc. Sci. 29(2), 406–408 (2006). (in Chinese)

13. Gross, J.J., Levenson, R.W.: Emotion elicitation using films. Cogn. Emot. 9(1), 87–108 (1995)

14. Xu, P.F., Huang, Y.X., Luo, Y.J.: Preliminary compilation and evaluation of Chinese emotional image materials library. Chin. J. Ment. Health 24(7), 551–554 (2010). (in Chinese)

15. Warrenburg, S.: Measurement of emotion in olfactory research. In: ACS Symposium, vol. 825, pp. 243–260 (2002)

16. Bradley, M.M., Lang, P.J.: Affective norms for English words (ANEW): instruction manual and affective ratings. J. Roy. Microsc. Soc. 88(1), 630–634 (1999)

17. Bradley, M.M., Lang, P.J.: Affective norms for English text (ANET): affective ratings of text and instruction manual, pp. 1–25. Technical report D1. University of Florida (2007)

18. Xin, W., Jingna, J., Li, S., et al.: Study on the early metaphase component difference of ERP induced by scene situation and facial expression picture. Chin. J. Biomed. Eng. 34(3), 257–263 (2015). (in Chinese)

19. Siemer, M., Mauss, I., Gross, J.: Same situation–different emotions: how appraisals shape our emotions. Emotion 7(3), 592 (2007)

20. Ekman, P.: An argument for basic emotions. Cogn. Emot. 6(3–4), 169–200 (1992)

21. Kim, J., André, E.: Emotion recognition based on physiological changes in music listening. IEEE Trans. Pattern Anal. Mach. Intell. 30(12), 2067–2083 (2008)

22. Bradley, M.M., Lang, P.J.: Measuring emotion: the self-assessment manikin and the semantic differential. J. Behav. Ther. Exp. Psychiatry 25(1), 49 (1994)

Scenes Design in Virtual Reality for Depression Assessment

Dan Liao[1,2], Lin Shu[1], Yanping Huang[1,3], Jiong Yang[4],
and Xiangmin Xu[1(✉)]

[1] School of Electronic and Information Engineering,
South China University of Technology, Guangzhou, Guangdong, China
{danl,xmxu}@scut.edu.cn
[2] School of Design, South China University of Technology,
Guangzhou, Guangdong, China
[3] School of Physics and Optoelectronic Engineering, Foshan University,
Foshan, Guangdong, China
[4] Goku Design Studio, Guangzhou, China

Abstract. Depression has caused serious problems and attracted extensive attention in our society nowadays. Traditional depression diagnosis methods mainly include scale examination, blood test and medical imaging. But they did not obtain promising performance because of patient's stigma, arbitrariness and distraction. The virtual reality technology can solve some of those problems by providing immersive experience and rich interaction in terms of detecting patient's emotions. In this paper, we propose utilizing VR in the field of depression assessment. Specifically, we have designed a personalized VR depression diagnosis scene and interactive models for depression assessment. To validate the effectiveness of our approach, preliminary experiments were carried out and good results were obtained from survey of user experience. The average score of each ten questions is over 3.2 points with a total score of 5 points. The visibility of doctor's position obtains the highest score. The lowest is naturalness of the scene, the main factor being the coordination between the human doctor image and the virtual scene. In future work, we are going to further improve the user experience and the efficiency of assessment.

Keywords: Virtual reality · Scenes design · Depression assessment

1 Introduction

Recently, depression has caused serious problems and attracted extensive attention in our society. According to WHO statistics, the number of suicide deaths per year is estimated 1 million due to depression. By 2020, depression might become the second largest disease after heart disease.

Traditional depression diagnosis methods are based on the scale examination [1], blood biochemical examination [2] and imaging examination [3]. In addition, many experts developed the software of the Beating the Blues (BTB) for diagnosis and treatment of depression. Although the used methods have been helpful, they have some fundamental problems, such as stigma, arbitrariness and distraction. Whereas the VR

© Springer International Publishing AG, part of Springer Nature 2018
J. Y. C. Chen and G. Fragomeni (Eds.): VAMR 2018, LNCS 10910, pp. 116–125, 2018.
https://doi.org/10.1007/978-3-319-91584-5_10

technology could provide patients an immersed experience and improve the accuracy of interrogation.

In the aspect of psychological disease treatment, psychologists use VR scenes to trigger the emotion of the patients, such as claustrophobia [4], acrophobia [5], flying phobia [6], spatial neglect disease [7], eating disorders [8], post-traumatic stress disorder [9], male sexual dysfunction [10], relieve pain [11], schizophrenia [12]. In cross research area, "computational psychiatry" had grown up, which could use some new technologies like artificial intelligence, virtual reality and deep learning techniques to treat mental disease [13]. However, the current research mainly focuses on the process of mental treatment, and explores the physiological and psychological mechanisms of disease. However, the VR depression diagnosis has not yet been carried out, as well as the mechanism research.

In conclusion, according to the related research at home and abroad, the research of depression diagnosis based on virtual reality technology is less concerned. In this study, we design the personalized VR depression scene and interactive diagnosis models which can early identify the patients' disease and improve the efficiency of diagnosis.

2 VR Scene Design Element Analysis

The elements of VR scene design, which are both conventional and personalized, are critical for the success of this study. They are symbols of emotions and meanings. So a reasonable design of content and form is of particularly importance, which directly influences the level of user experience and affect whether user can answer questions objectively and easily. Therefore, in the design of VR scene, we should follow the design principle of user experiences and balance the relationship between aesthetics and function in order to achieve good diagnosis results. In terms of design of VR scene for depression diagnosis, this paper first conducted a literature research, then analyzed on space design, role design and interactive technique.

2.1 Space Design

Space Decoration. Pressly and Heesacker [14] suggested that it was important to make environment more appealing and comfortable by decoration. The appealing environment can allude to counselors' personality and character, and can increase feelings of ownership for patients. Designers should consider surrounding the counselors with accessories that are visually pleasing to patients (e.g. family pictures, artwork and objects that are meaningful and attractive). Research also indicated that plant could have a positive effect on some patients who were sick or old, because it symbolizes vitality, growth and regeneration.

Gass et al. [15] found that the first impression of counselors' attire and seating was highly related to the willingness of the patients. The scene of consultants with casual clothes in the room without any desk would be attractive to patients. In contrast, consultants sitting behind the desk with formal clothes always be perceived as experts. But females would give a lower score to consultants sitting behind desk.

Space Color. In psychological counseling space, consultants were advised to choose different design rooms for subjects based on age and gender [16]. The research shows that bright colors are accompanied by positive emotional expression for children and young people, while dark colors are accompanied by negative emotional expression. Therefore, it is recommended to use pink wall colors instead of dark ones, and the colorful walls and highly bright ceilings are more suitable for children. Blue is one of the most popular colors for young people and elderly. Next is green and red in turn.

Space Light. Comparing with bright light, dim light is easier to make the counselees relaxed in the psychological counseling room, and more favorable to expose themselves. The research on psychophysics and environmental psychology have evaluated the relationship between light intensity and task productivity, revealing the personal perception of light and their views on the environment. For instance, the researchers have found that participants held more positive perceptions for a task and reported decreased boredom in a room with windows than that without windows.

2.2   Role Design

Gender Setting. The role of psychological consultant needs to be more genial with subjects. The famous feminism psychologist Gilligan suggested that females have often been a caregiver that put the relationship and the care of others on the significant position. Compared to male, female is more suitable to be a psychological consultant. A research about the attitude of college freshmen towards psychological consultation indicated that the female is more favored than the male by the respondents [17].

Suits Setting. Heitmeyer and Goldsmith [18] found that the requirement for consultants clothing style was between formal and casual. Hubble and Gelso [19] noticed that counselees prefer the consultants with formal clothes. Kerr and Dell [20] suggested that professional attire would help the consultants make a professional judgment; if not, it would take an attraction judgment on it. The research indicated that the professional comment on counselors were not only influenced by clothing but also by role. Bailey-Hamptom [21] investigated more precisely the influence of clothing. He noticed that the subject's evaluation of the consultant in education, knowledge, experience and compassion presented of the following order: "traditional attire > informal attire > casual wear".

2.3   Interactive Technology

Besides visual interaction, we mainly apply voice interaction. Voice interaction is the core of the depression diagnosis system. The diagnosis questions can be transformed into voice information and delivered to counselees. The elements of voices include volume, tone, speed and timbre.

Sausure, the father of modern language, in his book: Cours de linguistique générale, recorded the psychological attributes of voice, and pointed out the concept of "sound image", that is the psychological feeling of voice. The psychological attributes of voice mainly are reflected in the two basic psychological processes of voices delivery and voices perception. The measurement of speed is the number of syllables per second. Different consulting speed would result in different time pressure, lead to a diverse counseling effect. Bass music reduces θ wave activity and increases α wave activity, which is good for relaxation and concentration. High volume helps activate arousal levels, but may lead to distraction. Low speed is more conducive to network consultancy than high speed [22]. According to [23], the network interrogation had a better effect on reducing the subjects' anxiety by using 60 dB and low speed 160 words/minute than using high speed and high volume.

3 Development of Virtual Reality Diagnosis Scene

3.1 Scene Development Process

The development of virtual diagnosis scene is divided into three parts: material design, interaction design and the output, as shown in Fig. 1. Main components of the development process are detailed as follows:

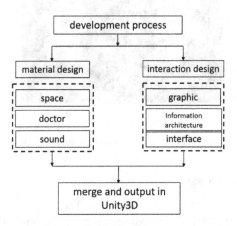

Fig. 1. Schematics of VR scene development process.

3.2 Doctor Material Design

There are mainly two methods of doctor material design. The first method is role model after investigation of a doctor's countenance and behavior at the hospital. The advantage is that the character's style can be freely defined by designers. But the character design requires a good aesthetics basic, which takes a long time to complete the sketches, map design, texture, character dubbing and mouth shape design etc. The second method is shooting the human characters, then importing it into the VR engine.

The role of the character is similar to real diagnosis environment with a higher shooting efficiency. But the role image, language and gesture are defined, which requires coordination with the virtual scene. In this paper, we adopted the role shooting method and specific requirements are shown in Table 1 and Fig. 2.

Table 1. Role requirements.

Gender	Female
Age	25
Clothing	White nurse uniform
Posture	Body 3/4 side sitting
Action	Head up to ask questions, down to write
Expression	Natural, amiable, nod and wink
Position	Placed at the golden section on the left side of the screen where questions are arranged on the right

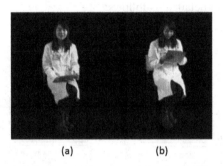

(a)   (b)

Fig. 2. Postures of questioning (a) and recording (b) of the doctor.

3.3 Diagnosis Space Design

Space design can be divided into two methods. The first method is simulating the virtual scene according to the design requirements of the actual diagnosis room. The advantage is that the size, light and ornaments of the diagnosis room can be designed freely. But the design needs good aesthetic skill during the sketch design, effect diagram design, mapping, baking design and other design steps. The second method is utilizing existing 360° spatial material provided by the engine store of Unity 3D (Unity is the ultimate game development platform developed by Unity Technologies). In this paper, we use 360° spatial material complemented by 3D plants to adjust the spatial extent of the brightness so as to fit our requirements for the diagnosis environment. Specific requirements are shown in Table 2 and Fig. 3.

Table 2. Space design requirements.

Content	Requirement	Design
Decoration	Vitality	Plant
Ground	Affinity	Carpet, wood floor
Wall	Professional and friendly	Shelves, books
Light	Breathable, relaxed	Window, Chandelier
Hue	Lively	Cool hue
Soft outfit	Comfortable	Sofa

Fig. 3. Snapshot of the designed scene.

3.4 Audio Material Design

Audio material includes the following aspects: starting sound, sound in resting state, sound in diagnosis, special sound for encouragement, and ending sound. Specific contents are shown in Table 3.

Table 3. Audio material.

Category	Aim	Audio source
Starting sound	A sense of science and technology	Childhood's memory
Resting state sound	Help the subjects calm down and relax	The sound of silence
Diagnosis sound	Clear, kind	Real recording
Special sound for encouragement	Encourage the subject to answer question, with coupled screens	Bird
Ending sound	Relaxed and appreciation	Fire

3.5 Interface Design

Before we began interface design, we established the flow chart of the diagnosis system as shown in Fig. 4. Then we have established a VR system based on the DPVR (give company name related to this device) device and Unity engine for the purpose of

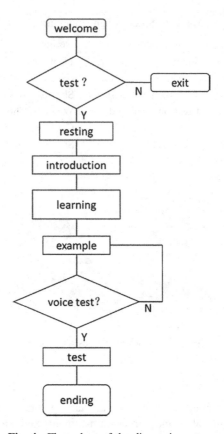

Fig. 4. Flow chart of the diagnosis system.

depression assessment, which is described as follows. In the Welcome scene (Fig. 5a), a cursor is indicated which will rotate with the head's rotation in order to enhance user interaction. Then it will go to the Resting scene (Fig. 5b) where a green grove shows up. At the same time, low volume music Sound Of Silence will be played to lead users to a relaxation state before real test. After that, it goes to a Test Reminding scene (Fig. 5c) and fades away into a Q&A Demo scene (Fig. 5d), where a demonstration is shown to the tested subject on how to answer questions. The place is a quiet and comfortable room with a large sofa placed in a half rectangle and bookshelf full of colorful books and bright windows in the background. After the Demo section is finished, the real testing session (Fig. 5e) starts where a female doctor of 25 years old appears at a position on the golden section of the left side. On the right side it is the text part including questions and answers. After a question is played, the subject need to answer in his/her own voice. This answer is automatically recognized by natural language processing embedded in the VR device. Then the chosen answer is partially flashed to attract the attention of the subject. After all the questions are answered, the scene goes to the End stage (Fig. 5f) with a title of thanks shown to the subject for his/her participation in the study.

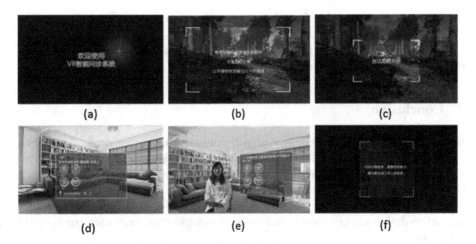

Fig. 5. The designed VR interface showing different stages in the assessment of depression (see text for the detailed description of different sub-figures)

4   Experiment and Results

4.1   Experiment

We designed a survey to test user experience of the designed VR scene. 10 subjects (5 males and 5 females, age: 21–37 years) were recruited for a questionnaire test.

We set up a user experience questionnaire containing 8 topics, including the effectiveness, efficiency, attractiveness, ease of learning and human-computer interaction of VR scene design. A No from 1 to 5 is given to indicate the user's satisfaction to each item with 3 meaning general, 1 meaning dissatisfaction and 5 meaning satisfaction. The subject was asked to fill the user experience questionnaire after a test was conducted using the design VR depression diagnosis system.

4.2   The Result

Table 4 illustrates the content of the questionnaire and score obtained from each tested subjects.

Table 4.   The content of the questionnaire and score.

Title	1	2	3	4	5	6	7	8	9	10	Mean (SD)
Easy to learn	3	3	3	4	4	4	3	3	3	3	3.3
Interest	3	3	3	3	3	5	4	4	4	5	3.7
Complexity	4	3	5	4	4	4	3	3	3	4	3.7
Attractiveness	4	3	5	4	4	5	4	1	3	5	3.8
Naturalness	1	4	3	2	4	4	3	4	3	4	3.2
Definition	4	4	3	4	4	4	4	4	4	3	3.8
Visibility	4	5	5	4	4	5	5	3	4	5	4.1
Vertigo	4	3	3	4	5	5	4	4	4	5	3.7

The experimental results show that the user experience was generally quite good. The score of satisfaction is over 3 points. The visibility of doctor's position obtains the highest score. The lowest is naturalness of the scene, mainly affected by the coordination between the human doctor and the virtual scene.

5 Conclusion

In this study, we have successfully designed interactive scenes for depression assessment in VR environment, following a specific route of design element analysis. Preliminary normal user assessment confirmed good user experience. In future work, a clinical trial will be conducted to verify the effectiveness of the system with targeted subject population, and long term research is needed to investigate the emotional interaction design and graphical visualization in order to improve its user experience in patient test.

Acknowledgement. This work is supported by "The Project of Research and Reform based on Undergraduate Education in South China University of Technology in 2017" (Y1171080) and "Science and Technology Program of Guangzhou" (201704020043).

References

1. Waraich, P., Goldner, E.M., Somers, J.M., et al.: Prevalence and incidence studies of mood disorders; a systematic review of the literature. Can. J. Psychiatry 49(2), 124 (2004)
2. Van Reedt Dortland, A.K., Giltay, E.J., van Veen, T., et al.: Longitudinal relationship of depressive and anxiety symptoms with dyslipidemia and abdominal obesity. Psychosom. Med. 75(1), 83–90 (2013)
3. Fernandez, A., Maestu, F., Amo, C., et al.: Focal temporoparietal slow activity in Alzheimer's disease revealed by magnetoen cephalography. Biol. Psychiatry 62, 764–770 (2012)
4. Botella, C., Baños, R.M., Perpiñá, C., Villa, H., Alcañiz, M., Rey, A.: Virtual reality treatment of claustrophobia: a case report. Behav. Res. Ther. 36, 239–246 (1998)
5. Jang, D.P., Ku, J.H., Shin, M.B., Choi, Y.H., Kim, S.I.: Objective validation of the effectiveness of virtual reality psychotherapy. Cyberpsychology Behav. 3, 369–374 (2000)
6. Rothbaum, B.O., Hodges, L., Anderson, P.L., Price, L., Smith, S.: Twelve month follow-up of virtual reality and standard exposure therapies for the fear of flying. J. Consult. Clin. Psychol. 70, 428–432 (2002)
7. Yoshizawa, M., Yishida, Y., Baheux, K., et al.: Development of virtual reality systems for tests and rehabilitation of patients with hemispatial neglect. In: Complex Medical Engineering, pp. 1313–1316. Beijing Institute of Technology (2007)
8. Mclay, R.N., Graap, K., Spira, J., et al.: Development and testing of virtual reality exposure therapy for post-traumatic stress disorder in active duty service members who served in Iraq and Afghanistan. Mil. Med. 177(6), 635–642 (2012)
9. Rica, G., Bacchetta, M., Baruffi, M., et al.: Vitual reality environments for body image modification: a multidimension therapy for the treatment of body image in obesity and related pathologies. Cyberosychology Behav. 3(3), 421–431 (2000)

10. Rica, G., Bacchetta, M., Baruffi, M., et al.: Vitual reality based multidimensional theapy for the treatment of body image disturbances in obesity: a controlled study. Cyberosychology Behav. 4(4), 356–368 (2001)
11. Hoffman, H.G., Garcia-Palacios, A., Patterson, D.R., et al.: The effectiveness of virtual reality for dental pain control: a case study. CyberPsychology Behav. 4(4), 527–535 (2001)
12. Horan, W.P., Kern, R.S., Tripp, C., et al.: Efficacy and specificity of socialcognitive skills training for outpatients with psychotic disorders. J. Psychiatr. Res. 45(8), 1113–1122 (2011)
13. http://www.techdog.cn/news/32592.htm
14. Pressly, P.K., Heesacker, M.: The physical environment and counseling: a review of theory and research. J. Couns. Dev. 79(2), 148–160 (2001)
15. Gass, C.S.: Therapeutic influence as a function of therapist attire and the seating arrangement in an initial interview. J. Clin. Psychol. 40(1), 52–57 (1984)
16. Miwa, Y., Hanyu, K.: The effects of interior design on communication and impressions of a counselor in a counseling room. Environ. Behav. 38(4), 484–502 (2006)
17. Jiang, Z., Li, M., Meng, S.: The attitude of psychological counselling of college freshman. China J. Health Psychol., 527–519 (2006). (in Chinese)
18. Heitmeyer, J.R., Goldsmith, E.B.: Attire, an influence on perceptions of counselors' characteristics. Percept. Mot. Skills 70(1), 923–929 (1990)
19. Hubble, M.A., Gelso, C.J.: Effect of counselor attire in an initial interview. J. Couns. Psychol. 25(6), 581–584 (1978)
20. Kerr, D.: Perceived interviewer expertness and attractiveness: effects of interviewer behavior and attire and interview setting. J. Couns. Psychol. 23(6), 553–556 (1976)
21. Bailey-Hamptom, B.S.: Effects of counselor attire on subject perceptions of counselor expertness, empathy, and counselor preference. Unpublished doctoral dissertation, Texas Tech University (1982)
22. Wang, L.: The Effect of Teacher's Speed and Students' Working Memory on Classroom Learning. Henan University (2008, in Chinese)
23. Chen, G.: An empirical study of the effect of language speed and volume on relaxation therapy in Internet counseling. Wuhan Institute of Sport (2015, in Chinese)

The Use of Virtual and Augmented Reality to Prevent the Physical Effects Caused by Diabetes Melitus Type 2: An Integrative Review

Leticia Neira-Tovar[1(✉)] and Ivan Castilla Rodriguez[2]

[1] Universidad Autónoma de Nuevo León, San Nicolás de los Garza, Mexico
leticia.neira@gmail.com
[2] Universidad de la Laguna, San Cristóbal de La Laguna, Tenerife, Spain

Abstract. Virtual Reality, (VR), and Augmented Reality, (AR), have been used for business, social life, culture, education and health. As a part of information technology, VR is a tool with the potential to improve the quality of life of people. Currently, it is possible to use tools in combination with IT, such as for situations related to entertainment and education activities, as well as in health treatments. This work is focus on health area mainly on how to prevent the Diabetes effects using applications based on a Virtual Reality.

An analysis of the state of the art in relation to the articles and authors who have worked on the subject of this study is presented, with such analysis we can summarize the actual situation and position this study within the framework of knowledge found.

An integrative review of the areas of knowledge is presented in relation to the objective, which are Virtual Reality in health, Diabetes Studies, in turn this is subdivided into Virtual Reality applied in chronic degenerative diseases treatments and works related to physical and emotional rehabilitation. Regarding the area of studies on diabetes, it is subdivided into the literature focused on the prevention of this condition and in the literature dedicated to the population of young people and adults at México and Spain.

Keywords: Virtual Reality · Diabetes effects · Serious game · Gamification
User experience · Games for health

1 Introduction

Information technology, IT, is a tool with the potential to improve the quality of life of people, currently, it is possible to use tools in combination with IT, such as Virtual Reality, (RV), and Augmented Reality, (RA), combined and using different bio-sensors to know the user experience and to improve the results. The objective of this review is to show the actual state of related works that intended to address some of the physical rehabilitation treatments using at DM2 diseases, and that are supported using Virtual and Augmented reality tools.

There are a number of successful examples on the use of virtual reality technology [1], to prevent and empower people on the consequences of this terrible disease. These examples include prototypes to teach healthy food habits [3, 4] to perform physical

© Springer International Publishing AG, part of Springer Nature 2018
J. Y. C. Chen and G. Fragomeni (Eds.): VAMR 2018, LNCS 10910, pp. 126–133, 2018.
https://doi.org/10.1007/978-3-319-91584-5_11

activity [5] and some special cases using exergames [2], mainly in diabetic patients of a single community. Although the causes of this effect are not yet completely determined, it is usually associated with poor disease control, adverse health outcomes and quality of life impairment [3, 4]. This gives rise to the search of the most relevant literature that will serve as a basis for proposed model of use of VR in prevention of the damages caused by DM2.

2 Method

A literature research criteria process is designed, it relies on five steps, Fig. 1, which one includes elements that integrate the research involved areas:

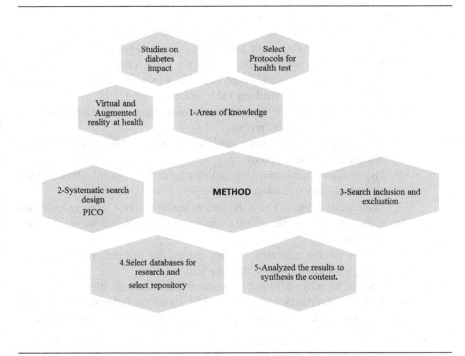

Fig. 1. Model based on related areas

Step 1   First, the areas of knowledge related to the research objective are identified, which are: Virtual Reality for health, Studies on Diabetes using information technology that includes VR and AR, also involving videogames, Studies about protocols and instruments used in health tests for medical research.

This in turn is subdivided into virtual reality applied in chronic degenerative disease treatments and works dedicated to physical and emotional rehabilitation related with

Diabetes cases. Regarding the area of diabetes studies, it is subdivided into literature focused on the prevalence of this condition, separating the literature of youth population from the adult ones.

Step 2   A systematic search criteria is designed, based on the PICO protocol, [6], for being this focused on health research, which consists of the combination of controlled terminology and texts that express the concepts of games, exercise, physical effects of diabetes DM2 and prevalence. A separate search criteria is applied for health test area, this is based on terminology that includes mobility, self-care, usual activities, pain, discomfort, depression and anxiety.

This criteria represents each of the parties in relation to the patient, the intervention and the comparison.

Step 3   Inclusion and exclusion search criteria is designed based on relevant studies of the last 10 years according the next parameters:
a-   The study population must be less than 60 years old.
b-   The exposed studies must have previous and subsequent results.
c-   Virtual Reality studies should contain some of the following tests: physical activities, weight care and cases of stress and depression. Also studies that use eye tracking tools, are considered.
d-   English and Spanish literature are considering, excluding articles in review and re-sums in process.
e-   The VR and AR tools used must include Kinect. Wii, Oculus rift, leap motion and gloves, mainly.
f-   The computer hardware used includes lightweight mobile devices, such as smartphones or tablets.
f-   Studies that relate to know the patient health before a tests, and after test must present examples results, excluding those applied for no chronical diseases.
g-   Studies on the economic impact caused by diabetes in México and Spain, excluding those with more than 6 years.
Step 4   The criteria to select a search instrument includes only electronical databases. These databases are used to find abstracts, full-text articles from journals, magazines, and newspapers and government documents related.

The search is carried out at the selected electronic media: SCOPUS and WOS are used to find scientific journals related with virtual and augmented reality as multidisciplinary topics. WebSpirs-medline, OVID and PUBMED for medical topics.

Search of public journals of the year in which this research begins, only published in Mexico and Spain are also included at this step.

The Mendeley, appointment repository, is used as a reference manager, to organize the search findings and to discover the latest related research.

Step 5   A selection of results is done, emphasizing the title name first, to proceed with an analysis of their content and the presented results. Here, what is relevant to the locations of Spain and Mexico is highlighted. Findings from international organizations are used to compare the selected population with the worldwide situation. After the readings is done, the literature that don't represent enough relation, is discriminated.

After completing the stages, it is suggested to carry out the searches again, in case of not finding enough literature from any of the study areas.

3 Research Analysis

After the search were done, the selected articles were analyzing, by area, to obtain the information relevant to be presented at the below Table 1.

That will be used to support the Model proposal in a VR game research, to prevent some physical effects on joints caused by DM2.

Table 1. Analysis report table

Selected work	Main
Breton, M.-C., Guénette, L., Amiche, M. A., Kayibanda, J.-F., Grégoire, J.-P., & Moisan, J. (2013). Burden of Diabetes on the Ability to Work: A systematic review. Diabetes Care, 36(3), 740–749. https://doi.org/10.2337/dc12-0354	The economic burden represented by Diabetes, projected on the population worldwide, current and a projection to the future is observed
Burgos LÁ, Hurtado LC, Cuentas en diabetes mellitus, enfermedades cardiovasculares y obesidad: México 2006. editors. Secretaría de Salud. 2009 [cited 2016 Jul 10]. Available: http://www.insp.mx/images/stories/Produccion/pdf/101203_cdiabetes.pdf	This work provides a comprehensive review of the epidemiological, clinical considerations and management strategies that affect depression in patients with diabetes mellitus
Cristina Mamédio da Costa Santos, Cibele Andrucioli de Mattos Pimenta, Moacyr Roberto Cuce ESTRATEGIA PICO PARA LA CONSTRUCCIÓN DE LA PREGUNTA DE INVESTIGACIÓN Y LA BÚSQUEDA DE EVIDENCIAS, Rev Latino-am Enfermagem 2007 maio-junho; 15(3) www.eerp.usp.br/rlae	It describes the need to know what to select, from a large amount of information and how to do it. Orientation for the construction of the research question and the search of bibliography
Cuentame Población, INEGI, http://cuentame.inegi.org.mx/poblacion/habitantes.aspx?tema=P	Display data about the population in Mexico and the amount that has access to information and communication technologies
El uso de las nuevas tecnología en España, https://www.tecnohotelnews.com/2016/04/espana-a-la-cabeza-europea-en-el-uso-de-las-nuevas-tecnologias/	In the exposed article, we talk about the increase in the use of information technology in Spain, mainly smartphones
Este es el costo por tener diabetes en México, 2016, http://www.excelsior.com.mx/nacional/2016/11/14/1128184	We talk about the cost of having diabetes in Mexico, and it also provides some information about the disease
Federación Internacional de la Diabetes, http://www.sld.cu/noticia/2016/11/14/atlas-de-la-diabetes-de-la-federacion-internacional-de-diabetes-6ta-edicion,14 Noviembre 2016	In this work the number of patients with diabetes today is exposed, a projection to 2035, in addition to exposing that people with lower social class are more vulnerable to contracting the disease

(*continued*)

Table 1. (*continued*)

Selected work	Main
Global Alliance for Chronic Diseases, http://www.gacd.org/	This web page provides us with general data on the main chronic diseases in the world, as well as data resulting from advances in research in the countries with the greatest suffering with chronic diseases
Informe mundial sobre la diabetes, Organización Mundial de la Salud, Ginebra, 2016	It presents figures on the situation and increase of Diabetes as well as its social and economic effects
OCDE, Estadísticas sanitarias de la OCDE 2015. Disponible en: http://www.oecd.org/els/health-systems/health-data.htm	Statistics of the health situation worldwide are shown
Perestelo-Pérez L, Rivero-Santana A, García-Lorenzo B, Vallejo-Torres L, De la Rosa-Merino H, Castellano-Fuentes CL, Guerra Marrero C, Castilla-Rodríguez I, García-Pérez L, Cuéllar-Pompa L, Toledo-Chavarri A, Serrano-Aguilar P., Efectividad, seguridad y coste-efectividad de los sistemas de monitorización continua de glucosa intersticial en tiempo real (SMCG-TR) para la Diabetes Mellitus tipo 1 y 2	The objective of this paper is to review the effectiveness, safety, cost-effectiveness and cost-utility of SMCG-TR (from the Spanish NHS perspective), compared to traditional self-monitoring, in patients with DM1 and DM2
Ramallo-Fariña Y, García-Pérez L, Castilla-Rodríguez I, Perestelo-Pérez L, Wägner AM, De Pablos-Velasco P, et al. Effectiveness and cost-effectiveness of knowledge transfer and behavior modification interventions in type 2 diabetes mellitus patients—the INDICA study: a cluster randomized controlled trial. Implement Sci. 2015;10	Information about a study for the scientific community is obtained by presenting a modem for the formulation of pre-questions. Case studies of the Spanish population of the Canary Islands
Sagarra R, Costa B, Cabré JJ, Solà-Morales O, Barrio F, el Grupo de Investigación DE-PLAN-CAT/PREDICE. Coste-efectividad de la intervención sobre el estilo de vida para prevenir la diabetes tipo 2. Rev Clin Esp. 2014;214:59–68	It shows results and values of the cost-effectiveness ratio of the preventive interventions of the T2D, Diabetes in Europe-Prevention using Lifestyle, Physical Activity and Nutritional intervention (DE-PLAN)
Secretaría de Salud. Boletín de información estadística. Volumen IV. Recursos financieros. Número 31, Año 2011. 2016 [cited 2016 Jul 10]. Available: http://www.dgis.salud.gob.mx/contenidos/publicaciones/p_bie.html	Presents report on the financial recourses that Mexico allocates to the health sector
Stephen Bouchard, A. Aime, Johana Monthuy-Blanc, Using Virtual Reality to Study, Assess and Treat Obesity, Illustrations of The Use of an Emerging Tool. Canadian Journal of Diabetes. 2013 37	It shows how to tackle childhood obesity with emerging technologies
The living text book for diabetes, https://www.diapedia.org/	It is a dedicated page to know most of the aspects of Diabetes Mellitus disease
Villalobos Hernández A, Ham Chande R. 2014 [cited 2016 Jul 10]. Gasto por diabetes en el sistema público de salud en México, 2010–2030. Available: http://colmex.alma.exlibrisgroup.com/view/delivery/52COLMEX_INST/1264973160002716	Report dedicated to the projections of expenses, applied surveys, epidemiology and other aspects of diabetes in Mexico

(*continued*)

Table 1. (*continued*)

Selected work	Main
González-Ortega, D., Díaz-Pernas, F. J., Martínez-Zarzuela, M., & Antón-Rodríguez, M. (2014). A Kinect-based system for cognitive rehabilitation exercises monitoring. Computer Methods and Programs in Biomedicine, 113(2), 620–631. https://doi.org/10.1016/j.cmpb.2013.10.014	This work present the use of a 3D application using Kinect to support a psychomotor exercises, It achieves left and right-hand tracking, and face and facial feature detection. The system is easily implemented with a consumer-grade computer
Pedraza-Hueso, M., Martin-Calzon, S., Javier Diaz-Pernas, F., & Martinez-Zarzuela, M. (2015). Rehabilitation using Kinect-based Games and Virtual Reality. In GonzalezMendivil, E and Flores, PGR and Gutierrez, JM and Ginters, E (Ed.), 2015 INTERNATIONAL CONFERENCE VIRTUAL AND AUGMENTED REALITY IN EDUCATION (Vol. 75, pp. 161–168). https://doi.org/10.1016/j.procs.2015.12.233	It research present a serious games, where some exergames are used. It is a type of serious game to stimulate body mobility through an immersive experience
Soler-Dominguez, J. L., Camba, J. D., Contero, M., & Alcañiz, M. (2017). A proposal for the selection of eye-tracking metrics for the implementation of adaptive gameplay in virtual reality based games. In Lecture Notes in Computer Science (including subseries Lecture Notes in Artificial Intelligence and Lecture Notes in Bioinformatics) (Vol. 10280, pp. 369–380). Springer Verlag. https://doi.org/10.1007/978-3-319-57987-0_30	This work shows the effectiveness of the use of eye tracking as a test of evaluation of the user experience in virtual reality games
Brooksby, A. (2008). Exploring the Representation of Health in Videogames: A Content Analysis. CyberPsychology & Behavior, 11(6), 771–773. https://doi.org/10.1089/cpb.2007.0007	At this work the author explores the different ways in which health concepts are represented in videogames. The content of the games analyzed in this study, such as mobility, capacity and psychology, are key aspects for the design of tests in new proposed games
Howard, M. C. (2017). A meta-analysis and systematic literature review of virtual reality rehabilitation programs. Computers in Human Behavior, 70. https://doi.org/10.1016/j.chb.2017.01.013	In this document, a systematic review of the effectiveness of virtual reality rehabilitation programs, VRR, is carried out. positive results of the use of VRR on traditional rehabilitation programs are shown. Three mechanisms are proposed to improve the results
Cordella, F., Di Corato, F., Zollo, L., Siciliano, B., & Van Der Smagt, P. (2012). Patient performance evaluation using Kinect and Monte Carlo-based finger tracking. In Proceedings of the IEEE RAS and EMBS International Conference on Biomedical Robotics and Biomechatronics (pp. 1967–1972). https://doi.org/10.1109/BioRob.2012.6290794	This article shows the use of movement through the Kinect as a method of evaluation of the rehabilitation activities of the patient
Chao, Y. Y., Scherer, Y. K., Wu, Y. W., Lucke, K. T., & Montgomery, C. A. (2013). The feasibility of an intervention combining self-efficacy theory and Wii Fit exergames in assisted living residents: A pilot study. Geriatric Nursing, 34(5), 377–382. https://doi.org/10.1016/j.gerinurse.2013.05.006	The author examines the intervention in rehabilitation exercises using the Wii, although the population is above the criterion established in this analysis, it is considered as an exception when having simple physical mobility

(*continued*)

Table 1. (*continued*)

Selected work	Main
Pirovano, M., Surer, E., Mainetti, R., Lanzi, P. L., & Alberto Borghese, N. (2016). Exergaming and rehabilitation: A methodology for the design of effective and safe therapeutic exergames. Entertainment Computing, 14, 55–65. https://doi. org/10.1016/j.entcom.2015.10.002	In this article, we expose a methodology to create safe exercise games for therapeutic purposes. The games are transformed into a virtual environment
Song, H., Kim, J., & Lee, K. M. (2014). Virtual vs. real body in exergames: Reducing social physique anxiety in exercise experiences. Computers in Human Behavior, 36, 282–285. https://doi.org/10.1016/j.chb.2014.03.059	In this study, videogames of exercises with the use of avatars are tested. the results show positive experiences and reduction of anxiety in the game
Koivisto, A., Merilampi, S., & Kiili, K. (2011). Mobile exergames for preventing diseases related to childhood obesity. In Proceedings of the 4th International Symposium on Applied Sciences in Biomedical and Communication Technologies - ISABEL'11 (pp. 1–5). New York, New York, USA: ACM Press. https://doi.org/10.1145/2093698. 2093727	This study shows how the exergames motivate the exercise in the players, also highlights the importance of group participation. Mobile phones are used for game interaction

4   Results

From the analysis of information related to the used technologies, it can be assumed that what has been found provides a basis for the justification of the uses of VR and AR tools, to prevent some physical impacts of diabetes. Despite a high prevalence of the use of games in rehabilitation, it can be inferred from the selected readings the lack of activities to prevent the physical effects caused by DM2 on the joints.

It is observed that the topic video games is being used to address health situations and social effects.

The use of videogames controllers applied to physical activities, appears more frequently in recent works. Immersive games for health rehabilitation are funded just in last two years.

The use of mobile devices is present as a game controller.

Regarding medical test for health, two instruments already validated were found. It is decided to select the one that it can be applied in México and Spain.

The results found about national spending due to DM2, reflect the increase in recent years, however, they do not show evidence of the use of technology in prevention programs.

5   Conclusion and Next Works

The advancement in this research allows us to evaluate the acceptability of the game interactions proposal and to continue to design the usability test and the patient health instrument to be applied before using the game.

The implications of the results permit the possibility of new ways to support the rehabilitation using mixed reality concept. Also, the benefit of using validated instruments for health tests is reflected on the time to complete this research.

This results leads to the formulation of the next activities to build the proposal model.

References

1. Gillies, C.L., Abrams, K.R., Lambert, P.C., Cooper, N.J., Sutton, A.J., Hsu, R.T., et al.: Pharmacological and lifestyle interventions to preventor delay type 2 DM in people with IGT: systematic review and meta-analysis. BMJ **334**(229–37), 2 (2007)
2. Skjaeret, N., Nawaz, A., Morat, T.: Exercise and rehabilitation delivered through exergames in older adults: an integrative review of technologies, safety and efficacy. Int. J. Med. Inf. **85** (1), 1–16 (2016)
3. Bouchard, S., Aime, S., Monthuy-Blanc, J.: Using virtual reality to study, assess and treat obesity, illustrations of the use of an emerging tool. Can. J. Diab. **37**, S249 (2013)
4. Breton, M.-C., Guénette, L., Amiche, M.A., Kayibanda, J.-F., Grégoire, J.-P., Moisan, J.: Burden of diabetes on the ability to work: a systematic review. Diab. Care 36(3), 740–749 (2013). https://doi.org/10.2337/dc12-0354
5. Finco, M., Maass, R.: The history of exergames: promotion of exercise and active living through body. In: SeGAH 2014 IEEE 3er International Conference on Serious Games and Applications for Health, books of proceedings (2014)
6. da Costa Santos, C.M., de Mattos, C.A.: ESTRATEGIA PICO PARA LA CONSTRUCCIÓN DE LA PREGUNTA DE INVESTIGACIÓN Y LA BÚSQUEDA DE EVIDENCIAS. Rev Latino-am Enfermagem 2007; maio-junho **15**(3) (2007). www.eerp.usp.br/rlae

Reducing Fear or Anxiety by Simulating Breathing Movements as Physical Contact with an Unrelated Person

Shunsuke Yanaka[1(✉)], Motofumi Hattori[2], and Takayuki Kosaka[2]

[1] Graduate School of Engineering, Kanagawa Institute of Technology,
Atsugi, Japan
s1495001@cce.kanagawa-it.ac.jp
[2] Kanagawa Institute of Technology, Atsugi, Japan
{hattori,kosaka}@ic.kanagawa-it.ac.jp

Abstract. In this paper, we verify the effect of the chair system which we developed as "Breath Chair." If a person sits in the "Breath Chair," the subject can be contacted with the movement which was simulated as human's breathing motion. We verified that the chair system's breathing movement reduced fear or anxiety of the person who sit in the chair system. Furthermore, the person's fear or anxiety was reduced even if the chair system's breathing movement was generated by a human who was not familiar with that person.

Keywords: Substitute robot · Simulating breathing · Fear · Anxiety

1 Introduction

The processes of how human emotions arise and functions of emotions have been studied since ancient times. Recently, in the field of information engineering, there have been many studies to measure and control emotions. Among the basic human emotions as classified by Ekman, we focus on fear or anxiety [1, 2].

Fear or anxiety are closely associated with anxiety disorder. Approximately 40% of cases of depression is preceded by anxiety disorder, and anxiety disorder is closely associated with increasing societal cost of mental disorders [3]. The Ministry of Health, Labour and Welfare [4] in the 2014 patient survey estimated the number of patients with depression to be 112,000, and the number of patients with neurotic disorder to be more than 59,000. These numbers have been increasing since 1996. Cabinet Office, Government of Japan [5] has reported that based on the Japanese citizen poll conducted in June 2014, approximately 67% of Japanese people have worry or anxiety in their daily lives.

When human is contact with a person physically, his/her fear or anxiety will be reduced as Gergen et al. [6] shows. In this research [6], people were divided into several groups. Each group contained approximately eight persons. Some groups were left in the bright room and other groups were left in dark room. In the dark room, the people lost spatial sense of direction and visual communication with others became impossible. Although the subjects did not know each other, approximately 90% of

J. Y. C. Chen and G. Fragomeni (Eds.): VAMR 2018, LNCS 10910, pp. 134–149, 2018.
https://doi.org/10.1007/978-3-319-91584-5_12

them intentionally sought physical contact with others in the dark room. Furthermore, approximately 50% of the subjects hugged each other. In the bright room, there was no physical contact or hug. In response to this experimental result, Yamaguchi [7] suggested that the physical contact can reduce humans' anxiety. Further-more, the experimental results that showed the human's fear or anxiety will be reduced when he/she is contacted with other person physically. The person is not need to be a specific people, such as close friends, a romantic partner, or family. Even physical contact with an unrelated person can reduce fear or anxiety.

Although physical contact with an unrelated person is successful in reducing fear or anxiety in a dark environment, that person is usually someone in close relationship such as friends, romantic partners, and family. Hall [8] categorized interpersonal distance into four categories—close, personal, social, and public distances—and describes how physical distance between people communicating with each other is proportional to psychological distance. This suggests that physical contact with an unrelated person is hard to establish and in usual cases the physical contact is established with the specific person such as friends, romantic partners, and family. Since unmarried people are increasing [9] and single-person households are increasing [10] in Japan recently, it is becoming difficult to realize physical contact in daily life.

In associated with the above problem, there are attempts to support communication between specific people in some fields including tele-existence [11]. However there are few attempts to support communication between unrelated people and to validate its effect, although fear or anxiety will be reduced by communication with unrelated person.

Therefore, we attempt to reduce fear or anxiety by supporting physical contact with unrelated person instead of physical contact with specific person. We developed "Breath Chair," a chair system that aims to reduce fear or anxiety [12] (Fig. 1).

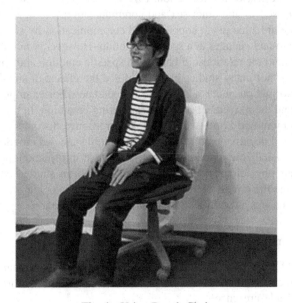

Fig. 1. Using Breath Chair

It simulates the movement of a person's thorax when he/she is breathing. When the user sit in this chair system, the user feels the sense as if the user is physically contact with him/her. In this paper, we refer to the movement of the thorax during breathing simply as "breath." The objective of this paper is to perform an experiment using Breath Chair and show that fear or anxiety are reduced by physical contact via simulated breath. In addition, we aimed to show that fear or anxiety are reduced by physical contact with one, even if one is an unrelated person to the subject.

2   Related Work

In this Section, we will discuss related works on transmission of physiological information and to affect emotions, followed by tele-existence and communication.

2.1   Transmission of Physiological Information and Effect on Emotions

The relationship between changes in emotion and physiological responses has been discussed for a long time [13]. For change in emotions and physiological responses, Nishimura et al. [14] aimed to artificially manipulate fondness for people by externally reinforcing or suppressing changes in physiological responses of liking people and developed a device that provides tactile presentation of one's own heartbeat.

"Lovable Couch" developed by Iwamoto et al. [15] visualizes heartbeat as an information to judge the level of romantic interest between a male and a female who met for the first time. By visualizing the heartbeat of the communication partner, it provides a factor for judging the level of interest expressed by the communication partner. In this manner, it experimentally derives a positive correlation between the actual affection and heartbeat information. Based on this result, it supports judgement of affection expressed by the other sex and communication.

As such, there are attempts to support good communication by visualizing physiological information and changes at a specific emotion. However, while there have been studies to understand the relationship between a specific emotion and changes in physiological response, not many studies have examined the effects of simulating constant physiological information under normal and rested states. For example, the vibration from heart beat and the movement of the thorax during breathing. In the estimation and evaluation of emotions and associated physiological response, not only are happiness and fear, or positive and negative emotions, but also neutral state and emotion are assumed [16, 17]. Yet, in visualizing emotions and physiological information, neutral state and emotion and their physiological information have not been studied much. Thus, we attempt to examine the effects of simulating constant physiological information under normal and rested states as well as under neutral state and emotions.

2.2   Tele-Existence in Communication

Tanaka et al. [11] added remote contact using a robot hand for handshaking to a conventional video conference system with audiovisual information in order to strengthen social tele-presence.

Sakamoto et al. [18] performed an experiment in which the experimenter and subjects have a conversation. This experiment evaluated the impression of the sense of presence under three different conditions: with a remotely operated robot modeled after and closely resembling a real person, with a video conference system, or with a speaker like a telephone.

Yamaoka et al. [19] used an autonomous robot and created two conditions: one where subjects were told that robot movements were based on a program and another where subjects were told that robot movements are controlled by an operator. In this manner, they examined differences in impression of the robot. The result showed that regardless of the condition, 2/3 of subjects felt that they were interacting with the robot itself.

As shown by these studies, the sense of presence with video conference system and robots are being examined. When a communication is made through a remotely operated robot, does the user recognize the communication as interaction with the robot or with the operator? However, in many cases, most subjects assume that they are communicating with a specific person under a specified situation. When using a video conference system, visual information clearly defines the communication partner. Even when using a robot, most subjects feel that they are interacting with the robot itself, regardless of the condition; thus, it is assumed that the robot in front of the subject is the communication partner.

Although fear or anxiety can be reduced via physical contact with an unrelated person, there have been few efforts and studies to support and validate the value of communication with an unrelated person. Thus, in this study, the proposed system will not provide physical characteristics or information that will allow subjects to identify an actual person and will define such object without identity as an unrelated person. We will then examine if fear or anxiety can be reduced by having simulated physical contact with such unrelated person.

3 Breathing Movement Simulation System

We developed a chair system (called "Breath Chair") which simulates the movement of a person's thorax when he/she is breathing. When the user sit in this chair system, the user feels the sense as if the user is physically contact with him/her [12]. In this study, we assume simulated physical contact with an unrelated person. If we prepare the robot-type medium with only torso (without head or limbs), the subjects do not identify specified communication partner and are not influenced by the shape of the robot-type medium [20]. Also considering the lifestyle of Japanese people [21], we designed our system as chair-style system which has only chest and which does not have head, limb, and so on.

The schematics of this system is shown in Fig. 2. This system has sealed polyurethane sponge in the back of the chair. This polyurethane sponge is compressed and expanded with a vacuum pump, and these volume changes simulate breathing, providing a sense of physical contact to reduce fear or anxiety.

The objective of this paper was to show that fear or anxiety are reduced by physical contact through simulated breathing, even if the physical contact is made with a person

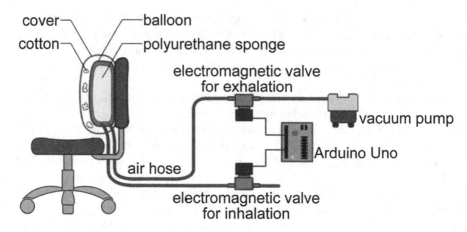

Fig. 2. System configuration

unrelated to the subject. Breathing in this system was visualized through controlled volume change of polyurethane sponge using compression and expansion based on average adult respiratory rate to avoid presenting characteristics such as sex and age of a person by basing on the breathing of an actual person.

Based on the reports that chest expansion, or the difference in chest circumference between maximal inhalation and exhalation, is approximately 3.3 cm [22], volume change of polyurethane sponge between compression and decompression was controlled to approximately 3.3 cm in perimeter while the seat was vacant. Therefore, changes in perimeter occur when a user is seated in the present system due to changes in pressure on the back of the chair depending on the user's weight and the way the user sits. Since, the rate of breathing in this system and ratio of rhythm associated with inhalation and exhalation were designed based on the average adult's respiratory rate [23], the rhythm polyurethane sponge's movement was regulated 12 times in a minute. Since the ratio of inspiration and expiration in adults is 1:3, we set the rhythm of inhalation and discharge of air in this system at 1:3.

4 Experiment: Effect on User's Fear and Anxiety

We conducted experiments using our system "Breath Chair" which aims to reduce fear or anxiety. The objective of these experiments was to show that physical contact using simulated breathing can reduce fear or anxiety. We also aimed to show that fear or anxiety are reduced even if simulated physical contact is caused as breathing movement of an unrelated person. When conducting such experiments, the recognition for the system's movement by the subject must be distinguished. We must distinguish whether the subject recognizes the system's movement as the movement of the thorax during human breathing or the subject recognizes it as a simple physical movement. Thus, we conducted the following two identical experiments. Between two experiments, our system Breath Chair gave same movements to subjects, but information provided to the subjects differed as follows. In Experiment 1, we informed each subject that Breath Chair's movements were only physical movement and consequent external stimulation. In Experiment 2, we informed each subject that Breath Chair's movements were breathing movements which were simulated by measuring someone's breath who was located at a distance through real-time remote sensing. Although the true objective of our experiments was to reduce fear or anxiety using our system "Breath Chair," in order to remove bias in the subjectivity and recognition of every subject, we informed each subject that "The aim of these experiments is to examine the effects of our system Breath Chair regardless whether the effect is positive or negative" at the beginning of experiments. After these experiments were completed, we explained the true objective of our study to each subject.

In this chapter, we first noted the common contents between Experiment 1 and Experiment 2. Then, we discuss Experiment 1 in Sect. 4.6 and Experiment 2 in Sect. 4.7.

4.1   The Subjects and the Experimental Environment

In our experiments, we used a questionnaire, State-Trait Anxiety Inventory (STAI), that evaluates anxiety by dividing anxiety into state and trait anxieties. Since, Spielberger et al. [24], who developed the STAI conducted his experiment on university students, we also selected university students and graduate students as subjects of our experiment. We informed the objective and methods of our experiments to these subjects. Also each subject was informed that there is no disadvantage if they reject our experiments, that they are free to discontinue our experiments at any moment, that obtained data are statistically processed, that there is no identification of individuals in analysis, and that privacy is protected, by our verbal explanation and a written format. In this manner, informed consent was obtained. This study was approved by the Ethical Review Board for the use of human subjects of Kanagawa Institute of Technology.

The experiment used an air-conditioned room into which other people did not enter or leave. Based on the experiment conducted by Honda et al. [25], the lighting in the room was set to approximately 30 lx. To eliminate factors affecting the sympathetic nervous system as much as possible, each subject was instructed to refrain from alcohol the day before, exercise on the day in question, and was not given any food except for water 2 h before the start of the experiment. A visual stimulation was presented by placing a 23-inch display approximately 1 m in front of the test subject. During the experiment in the test room, the examiner was absent, and the test subject was left alone.

4.2   Evaluation Indicators

In these experiments, we used both psychological indicator and physiological indicator. The psychological indicator STAI (state anxiety scale) was used as an anxiety indicator. The STAI includes scales for both the state anxieties and the trait anxieties. As STAI expresses anxiety, the higher the value, the greater the anxiety. The distribution of STAI value occurs within the range of 20 and 80 points. State anxiety is a transient state reaction to the phenomenon invoking the anxiety and it measures "what I am actually feeling now." On the contrary, trait anxiety measures long-term result and indicates "how do I feel normally in general." Based on the STAI created by Spielberger et al. [24], Hidano et al. [26] developed new items to consider Japanese culture and checked its reliability. We used Hidano's STAI in these experiments.

As a physiological indicator, the fingertip surface skin temperature was used to indicate fear or anxiety. The fingertip surface skin temperature was calculated as the average value for every 30 s, using a thermistor thermometer (NXFT15XH103FA2B) attached to the fingertip ventral section of the index finger of the left hand. When the sympathetic nervous system is excited, that excitation constricts the peripheral blood vessels and reduces blood flow, then it decreases the skin surface temperature in the peripheral area. Such decrease in the skin surface temperature was also reported by Kumamoto et al. [27] in their study, where the perception level for pain, etc., and psychological anxiety increased.

4.3 Stimulus Invoking Emotion Such as Fear or Anxiety

In order to invoke emotion such as fear or anxiety to each subject, we gave load stimulus to the subject. Although visual stimulus is not invasive to subject, it invokes comparatively strong emotion to the subject in the test room. Many researchers [28, 29] studied visual stimuli which invoke specific emotions to subject. Furthermore, Honda et al. [HMY02] reported that if the subject is given visual stimulus, the fingertip skin surface temperature of the subject changes significantly. Based on these findings, we gave visual stimulus to each subject in order to invoke fear or anxiety to each subject in our experiments.

As visual stimuli in our experiment, we used the same images which Alexandre et al. [30] used in their experiment, in order to invoke emotion such as fear or anxiety to each subject. We used the same videos which were exactly the same movies used by Alexandre et al. with the same start point and stop point, but we used the Japanese versions of the movies. In their experiment, the researchers used movies of virtually the same length, 210 s, which none of the test subjects in the experiment had seen up to that point. The two movies used were "Misery" (copyright; Castle Rock Entertainment, 1990) and "Scream 2" (copyright; Miramax Film Corp., 1997).

4.4 Experimental Protocol

Figure 3 shows the procedures of Experiment 1 and Experiment 2. In these experiments, each subject sat in our chair system Breath Chair under the experimental environment and relaxed for 3 min with his (her) eyes closed. Then, we measured the subject's emotion by the questionnaires of STAI state anxiety scale and STAI trait anxiety scale. Next, as intervention 1, each subject viewed a video. Subsequently, we measured the subject's emotion by the questionnaires of STAI state anxiety scale. Then the subject relaxed for a total of 6 min. Intervention 2 involved the same operations as intervention 1. After these experiments were completed, we asked each subject about impressions and opinions to the experiment. In these experiments, if our system Breath Chair worked during intervention 1, it did not work during intervention 2. If our system Breath Chair worked during intervention 2, it did not work during intervention 1.

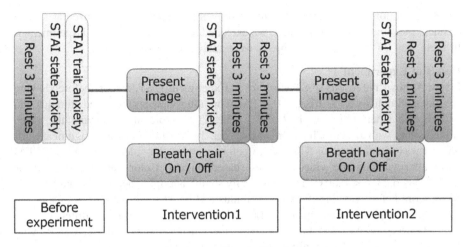

Fig. 3. Experimental protocol

We assigned these combinations of Breath Chair On and Breath Chair Off randomly, in order to counterbalance the order effect and interaction. Also we assigned the combinations of two kinds of video randomly, in order to counterbalance the order effect and interaction.

4.5   Analytical Methods

To analyze the result of the questionnaires of STAI state anxiety scale, we performed one factor analysis of variance. For the fingertip surface skin temperature, we calculated the mean for each 30-s interval based on the experiment by Honda et al. [25]. We calculated each baseline as the mean of values which were measured when each subject relaxed before viewing each video in interventions 1 and 2. Then we calculated the amount of change by subtracting the baseline from value which was measured when the subject viewed each video in interventions 1 and 2. For multiple comparison of each variance analysis, we used Tukey's method. A p value of < 0.05 was considered as significant.

4.6   Experiment 1: The Chair System's Movement as Physical Motion

In Experiment 1, we informed to each subject that chair system's movement was simple physical movement. We in-formed each subject that the objective of this experiment was to evaluate the effects of the simple physical movement to the subject's emotion. Experiment 1 was conducted with 26 subjects (22 men and 4 women, aged 20.5 ± 1.7 years, mean ± S.D.). There were 7 subjects whose STAI scores after viewing the video stimulus were smaller than STAI score before viewing the video stimulus. We judged that the video stimulus did not invoke anxiety to these 7 subjects and excluded these 7 subjects from Experiment 1. There was one subject who reported that the subject thought that the chair system's movement was generated by human's breathing motion. Since the chair system's movement should be recognized as simple physical movement in Experiment 1, we excluded this one subject from Experiment 1. In these way 26 − 7 − 1 = 18 subjects were analyzed in Experiment 1.

Result of Experiment 1

Figure 4 shows the results of STAI scores in Experiment 1. STAI score before viewing the video stimulus was 37.67 ± 7.0. STAI score after viewing the video stimulus and with Breath Chair Off was 49.7 ± 9.3. The STAI score after viewing the video stimulus and with Breath Chair On was 47.2 ± 11.7. The statistically significant difference was found between STAI score before viewing the video stimulus and STAI score after viewing the video stimulus based on one factor variance of analysis ($F(2, 12) = 6.23$, $p < 0.001$). The statistically significant difference was found between STAI score before viewing the video stimulus and STAI score with Breath Chair Off based on multiple comparison ($p < 0.001$). The statistically significant difference was found between STAI score before viewing the video stimulus and STAI score with Breath Chair On based on multiple comparison ($p < 0.001$).

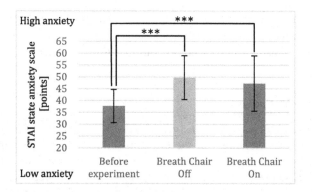

Fig. 4. Results of STAI score in experiment 1 (n = 18, ***p < 0.001)

The results for fingertip surface skin temperature are shown in Fig. 5 (210 s during the video) and in Fig. 6 (210 s immediately after the video). Two factor variance of analysis showed that video results had no significant difference. Results from immediately after the video showed main effect from presence or absence of Breath Chair On ($F(1, 244) = 9.26$, $p < 0.05$).

4.7   Experiment 2: The Chair System's Movement as Breathing Motion

In Experiment 2, we informed to each subject that the chair system's movement was simulated by measuring human's breathing motion. We informed each subject that the objective of this experiment was to evaluate the effects of the human's breathing motion to the subject's emotion. To let the subjects believe that the chair system's movement was generated by measuring human's breathing motion, we gave subjects wrong information that "there is another person in an adjacent room, who is comfortably

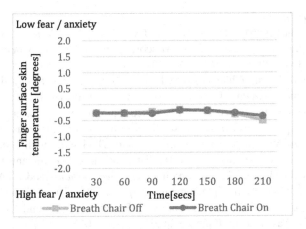

Fig. 5. Results of fingertip surface skin temperature during video in experiment 1 (n = 18)

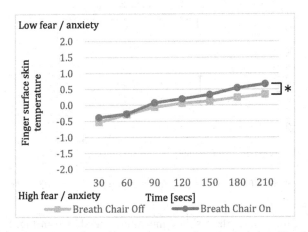

Fig. 6. Results of fingertip surface skin temperature after viewing the video in experiment 1 (n = 18, *p < 0.05)

resting, and this person's breathing motion is remote sensed in real time and this measured motion generates the chair system's movement" before Experiment 2.

Experiment 2 was conducted with 30 subjects (23 men and 7 women, aged 21.5 ± 1.6 years) who did not conduct Experiment 1. There were 6 subjects whose STAI scores after viewing the video stimulus were smaller than STAI score before viewing the video stimulus. We judged that the video stimulus did not invoke anxiety to these 6 subjects and excluded these 6 subjects from Experiment 1. There were 3 subjects who reported that the subjects thought that the chair system's movement was not caused by human's breathing motion. Since the chair system's movement should be recognized as human's breathing motion in Experiment 2, we excluded this one subject from Experiment 1. In these way 30 – 6 – 3 = 21 subjects were analyzed in Experiment 2.

Result of Experiment 2

Figure 7 shows the results of STAI scores in Experiment 2. STAI score before viewing the video stimulus was 36.2 ± 6.5. STAI score after viewing the video stimulus and with Breath Chair Off was 49.6 ± 9.7. The STAI score after viewing the video stimulus and with Breath Chair On was 44.7 ± 10.9. The statistically significant difference was found between STAI score before viewing the video stimulus and STAI score after viewing the video stimulus based on one factor variance of analysis ($F(2, 40) = 25.3, p < 0.001$). The statistically significant difference was found between STAI score before viewing the video stimulus and STAI score with Breath Chair Off based on multiple comparison ($p < 0.001$). The statistically significant difference was found between STAI score before viewing the video stimulus and STAI score with Breath Chair On based on multiple comparison ($p < 0.001$). The statistically significant difference was found between STAI score with Breath Chair On and STAI score with Breath Chair On based on multiple comparison ($p < 0.05$).

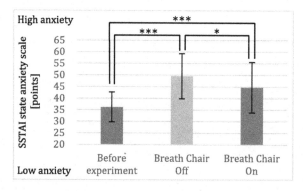

Fig. 7. Results of STAI score in experiment 2 (n = 21, *p < 0.05, ***p < 0.001)

The results of fingertip surface skin temperature are shown in Fig. 8 (210 s when each subject was seeing the video stimulus) and in Fig. 9 (210 s immediately after each subject had shown the video stimulus). Based on two factor variance of analysis, there was no statistically significant difference during the video. After viewing the video, there was statistically significant difference between Breath Chair On and Breath Chair Off ($F(1, 286) = 5.57, p < 0.05$).

Among 21 subjects in total, only 2 subjects reported that the chair system's movement disturbed the subjects to focus on the video at the discussion after each experiment, At the discussion after each experiment, we asked the question "Did you imagine the human's persona whose breathing motion generates the chair system's movement while you were in contact with the chair system's movement?" to each subject. Among 21 subjects in total. 18 subjects answered that they did not imagine the human's persona who generates the chair system's movement. Other 3 subject thought that the experimenter's breathing motion generated the chair system's movement.

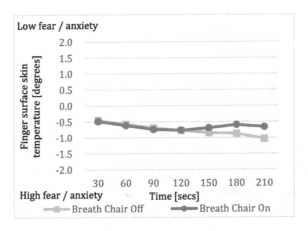

Fig. 8. Results of fingertip surface skin temperature during video in experiment 2 (n = 21)

5   Discussion

Let us discuss the results of STAI state anxiety scale. In these experiments, we analyzed subjects whose fear or anxiety were invoked by the video stimulus (STAI scores of these subjects became higher by viewing the video stimulus under the condition with Breath Chair Off, in other words, the same condition as sitting in a regular chair). In Experiment 1, each subject recognized the chair system's movements as simple physical movements, and in Experiment 2, each subject recognized the chair system's movements as human's breathing motions. There was statistically significant difference between the STAI score before viewing the video stimulus and the STAI score after viewing the video stimulus with Breath Chair Off. Thus video stimulus did invoke fear or anxiety to most subjects' emotion. Although the STAI score with Breath Chair On was smaller than the STAI score with Breath Chair Off, there is a possibility that the fear or anxiety of the subjects did not reduced by the human's breathing motion. There is a possibility that the subject's attention to the video stimulus was distracted due to the chair system's movement. However, in Experiment 1, the STAI score with Breath Chair On is bigger significantly than the STAI score before viewing the video stimulus and there was no significant difference between the STAI score with Breath Chair On and the STAI score with Breath Chair Off. Therefore, Breath Chair's movement did not distract each subject's attention to the video stimulus, and the video stimulus did invoke anxiety to each subject's emotion. Furthermore, although in Experiment 1 (each subject recognized the chair system's movements as simple physical movements), there was no significant difference between the STAI score with Breath Chair On and the STAI score with Breath Chair off, in Experiment 2 (each subject recognized the chair system's movements as human's breathing movements) the STAI score with Breath Chair On was significantly smaller than the STAI score with Breath Chair off. Therefore, simple physical movement cannot reduce the subject's fear or anxiety, but human's breathing motion can reduce the subject's fear or anxiety. We want to conclude that since the subject thought the chair system's movements as human's

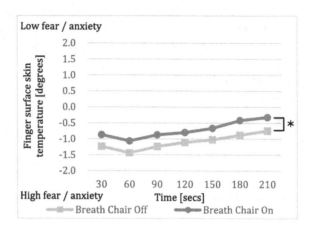

Fig. 9. Results of fingertip surface skin temperature after viewing the video in experiment 2 (n = 21, *p < 0.05)

breathing movements, the movements reduced the subject's fear or anxiety. Nevertheless, there is a possibility that since the subjects was aware of the human whose breath generated the chair system's movement in the adjacent room, this awareness distracted the subject's attention to the video stimulus. However, at the discussion after the experiments, only 2 subjects reported that they were aware of the human in the adjacent room, and other 19 subjects were not aware of the human. These facts deny the above capability and we can conclude that since the subject recognized the chair system's movement as human breath movement, it reduced the subject's fear or anxiety.

Due to the stimulus which causes fear or anxiety, the autonomic nervous system shrinks peripheral blood vessels and the fingertip surface skin temperature decreases [31, 32]. The experiment of Kistler et al. [33] reported that fear or anxiety caused by video stimulus shrinks peripheral blood vessels and the fingertip surface skin temperature decreases. In our experiment also, we observed that the video stimulus caused fear or anxiety in the test subjects and decreased their fingertip surface skin temperature.

To analyze the fingertip surface skin temperature, the amount of change of it from the baseline is calculated, as we noticed in Sect. 4.5. This value becomes negative i.e. it is smaller than 0.

The amount of change of the fingertip surface skin temperature with Breath Chair On is larger than one with Breath Chair Off significantly in Experiment 2. The chair system's movement might reduce fear and anxiety of each subject. There is another possibility that each subject's fear and anxiety were reduced by the security feeling which was caused by the information that "there is another person in an adjacent room." But the latter possibility is denied by the Experiment 1. The amount of change of the fingertip surface skin temperature with Breath Chair On is larger than one with Breath Chair Off significantly also in Experiment 1 in which the chair system's movement was simple physical movement and there are no another person who gave security feeling from an adjacent room. Thus we claim that the chair system's movement reduced the subject's fear and anxiety. There was no statistically significant difference between the amount of change of the fingertip surface skin temperature with Breath Chair On and one with Breath Chair Off during viewing the video stimulus in Experiment 1 and 2. While each subject was viewing the video stimulus, it was invoking fear or anxiety to the subject and the effect of the chair system's movement did not appear. After viewing the video stimulus, it stopped to invoke fear or anxiety to the subject and the effect of the chair system's movement appeared.

By analyzing the results of STAI state anxiety scale, fingertip surface skin temperature, and the subjects' reports after experiment, we claim that physical contact using simulated breath in our system Breath Chair reduced fear or anxiety.

Furthermore, when the subject was contact with Breath Chair's movement as human's breathing motion, the subject did not even imagine specific person whose breath generated the Breath Chair's movement. This fact indicates that the simulated breath movement does not have to be caused by a related person who is familiar with the subject, and the simulated breath movement caused by an unrelated person may reduce the subject's fear or anxiety.

6 Conclusion

We conducted experiments using a chair system "Breath Chair" which was developed by us [12]. We verified that the subject's fear or anxiety could be reduced when the subject contact physically with the simulated breath which are caused by a per-son who is unrelated to the subject.

Starting with the field of tele-existence, there are attempts to support communication with specific people. However, there is little effort and study to support communication with unrelated person although the communication with unrelated person can reduce fear or anxiety. As a future outlook, we plan to develop and study systems about the positive effects caused by the coexistence of people who are not limited to those in close relationships such as friends, romantic partners, and family.

References

1. Ekman, P.: Basic Emotions. In: Dalgleish, T., Power, M. (eds.) Handbook of Cognition and Emotion, pp. 45–60. New York, Wiley (1999)
2. May, R.: The Meaning of Anxiety. Ronald Press Co, New York (1950)
3. Kaiya, H., Tsuchida, H., Suyama, H., Kaneko, Y.: Recent advances in the studies of anxiety disorders—an overview. Anxiety Disord. Res. 4(1), 20–36 (2013)
4. Ministry of Health: Labour and Welfare, Summary of 2014 Patient Surveys. http://www.mhlw.go.jp/toukei/saikin/hw/kanja/14/index.html. Accessed 10 Feb 2016 (in Japanese)
5. Cabinet Office: National Opinion on People's Life. http://survey.gov-online.go.jp/h26/h26-life/index.html. Accessed 14 July 2016 (in Japanese)
6. Gergen, K.J., Gergen, M.M., Barton, W.H.: Deviance in the dark. Psychol. Today 7(5), 129–130 (1973)

7. Yamaguchi, H.: Aibu hito no kokoro ni fureru chikara. NHK Publishing Inc., Tokyo (2003). (in Japanese)
8. Hall, E.T.: The Hidden Dimension. Doubleday & Company, New York (1966)
9. Iwai, N.: The current picture and overall trends of the Japanese family based on JGSS cumulative data from 2000–2010. Jpn. Soc. Fam. Sociol. **23**(1), 20–42 (2011)
10. Ministry of Health: Labour and Welfare, Summary of 2016 Comprehensive Survey of Living Conditions. http://www.mhlw.go.jp/toukei/saikin/hw/k-tyosa/k-tyosa16/index.html. Accessed 4 July 2017 (in Japanese)
11. Tanaka, K., Wada, Y., Nakanishi, H.: Remote handshaking: integration of a haptic device and videoconferencing to enhance social telepresence. IPSJ J. **56**(4), 1228–1236 (2015)
12. Yanaka, S., Kosaka, T.: Breath Chair: reduce fear and anxiety by simulating breathing movements. In: Lackey, S., Chen, J. (eds.) VAMR 2017. LNCS, vol. 10280, pp. 478–492. Springer, Cham (2017). https://doi.org/10.1007/978-3-319-57987-0_39
13. Okada, A., Abe, J.: Emotion research in psychology: past and current trends. J. Jpn. Soc. Fuzzy Theory Syst. **12**(6), 730–740 (2000)
14. Nishimura, N., Ishii, A., Sato, M., Fukushima, S., Kajimoto, H.: Study of tactile device for presenting heartbeat of one-self. In: Interaction 2012, pp.849–854 (2012)
15. Iwamoto, T., Masuko, S.: Lovable couch: supporting dispelling distrust feelings using heartbeat variability at the meeting place. In: Interaction 2015, pp. 866–871 (2015)
16. Masai, K., Sugiura, Y., Ogata, M., Kunze, K., Inami, M., Sugimoto, M.: Affective wear: recognizing wearer's facial expression by embedded optical sensors on smart eye-wear. Trans. Virtual Real. Soc. Jpn. **21**(2), 385–394 (2016)
17. Mizuko, M., Terasaki, M., Kanemitsu, Y.: Effects of positive and negative affectivity on interpersonal interaction: mediating roles of outcome and efficacy expectations. Jpn. J. Pers. **10**(2), 98–107 (2002)
18. Sakamoto, D., Kanda, T., Ono, T., Ishiguro, H., Hagita, N.: Android as a telecommunication medium with a human-like presence. Inf. Process. Soc. Jpn. J. **48**(12), 3729–3738 (2007)
19. Yamaoka, F., Kanda, T., Ishiguro, H., Hagita, N.: Interacting with a human or a humanoid robot? Inf. Process. Soc. Jpn. J. **48**(11), 3577–3587 (2007)
20. Minato, T., Ishiguro, H.: Elfoid: a robotic communication media with a minimalistic human design. J. Robot. Soc. Jpn. **32**(8), 704–708 (2014)
21. Bauman, A., Ainsworth, B.E., Sallis, J.F., et al.: The descriptive epidemiology of sitting. a 20-country comparison using the International Physical Activity Questionnaire (IPAQ). Am. J. Prev. Med. **41**(2), 228–235 (2011)
22. Shôbo, A., Kakizaki, F.: Relationship between chest expansion and the change in chest volume. J. Exerc. Physiol. **29**(6), 881–884 (2014)
23. Onodera, A., Jindai, Y.: Seijin naika 1, Chûôhôkishuppan (2011)
24. Spielberger, C.D., Reheiser, E.C.: Assessment of emotions: anxiety, anger, depression, and curiosity. Appl. Psychol. Health Well-Being **1**(3), 271–302 (2009)
25. Honda, A., Masaki, H., Yamazaki, K.: Influence of emotion-inducing film stimuli on autonomic response specificity. Jpn. J. Physiol. Psychol. Psychophysiol. **20**(1), 9–17 (2002)
26. Hidano, N., Fukuhara, M., Iwawaki, M., Soga, S., Charles, D.S.: State-Trait Anxiety Inventory-Form JYZ. Jitsumukyoiku-shuppan, Tokyo (2000)
27. Kumamoto, M., Yanagida, M., Hotomi, S., et al.: Study on evaluation method of stress and recovery: nasal skin temperature and perception levels and psychological states. Jpn. J. Pediatr. Dent. **46**(5), 578–584 (2008)
28. Gross, J.J., Levenson, R.W.: Emotion elicitation using films. Cogn. Emot. **9**, 87–108 (1995)
29. Noguchi, M., Sato, W., Yoshikawa, S.: Films as emotion-eliciting stimuli: the ratings by Japanese subjects, Technical report of IEICE. HCS, vol. 104, no. 745, pp. 1–6 (2005)

30. Schaefera, A., Nilsb, F., Sanchezc, X., Philippotb, P.: Assessing the effectiveness of a large database of emotion-eliciting films: a new tool for emotion researchers. Cogn. Emot. **24**(7), 1153–1172 (2010)
31. Collet, C., Vernet-Maury, E., Delhomme, G., et al.: Autonomic nervous system response patterns specificity to basic emotions. J. Auton. Nerv. Syst. **62**, 45–57 (1997)
32. Levenson, R.W., Ekman, P., Friesen, W.V.: Voluntary facial action generates emotion-specific autonomic nervous system activity. Psychophysiology **27**(4), 363–384 (1990)
33. Kistler, A., Mariauzouls, C., von Berlepsch, K.: Fingertip temperature as an indicator for sympathetic responses. Int. J. Psychophysiol. **29**(1), 35–41 (1998)

Virtual Reality for Cultural Heritage, Entertainment and Games

The Impact of Augmented Reality on Art Engagement: Liking, Impression of Learning, and Distraction

Tanja Aitamurto[1(✉)], Jean-Baptiste Boin[1], Kaiping Chen[1], Ahmed Cherif[2], and Skanda Shridhar[1]

[1] Stanford University, Stanford, CA 93405, USA
tanjaa@stanford.edu
[2] UC Berkeley, Berkeley, CA 94720, USA

Abstract. This paper examines the impact of an augmented reality (AR) tour guide on users' art engagement. In a between-subjects experiment in an art museum, users' art engagement with a novel video see-through augmented reality guide was examined against user behavior with a book guide. The AR users' liking of art increased more than the book users', whereas the book users learned more. The AR users enjoyed using the application, and it helped them engage with art; however, they felt physical fatigue from holding the tablet and preferred interacting with a still image over the live augmentations. The users were concerned about the screen time the AR guide required; it distracted them from looking at the art with the naked eye, creating more of an impression of learning rather than actual learning. The findings call for more impactful AR applications with art as the focal point.

Keywords: Augmented reality · Art · Human-computer interaction
Learning · Museum · Mobile

1 Augmented Reality as an Interpretive Technology

1.1 Immediate Apprehendability Supporting Art Engagement

In an ideal art engagement experience, the artwork provokes the visitors' interest, raises their emotions, and leads to learning and further interest in the artwork. Tour guides, whether virtual or human, are intended to support visitors' interpretation of art. Art interpretation refers to visitors' engagement with and understanding of art [29]. Tour guides can mitigate the cognitive overload that results when visitors are exposed to overwhelming stimuli and distracted from the art [1, 15]. Enabling immediate apprehendability during tours can help reduce visitors' cognitive overload [2, 22]. Immediate apprehendability refers to providing a focused stimulus for users that allows them to quickly understand an object's properties without excessive effort, even when they experience it for the first time [1]. Immediate apprehendability provides users with quick access points into the artwork, enabling them to engage with the art by focusing on only some of its properties. Immediate apprehendability is mediated through affordances like labels or digital features on tour guides, which support users' learning and their interaction with art [1, 14, 38].

© Springer International Publishing AG, part of Springer Nature 2018
J. Y. C. Chen and G. Fragomeni (Eds.): VAMR 2018, LNCS 10910, pp. 153–171, 2018.
https://doi.org/10.1007/978-3-319-91584-5_13

Ideally, an art tour guide provides users with guidance, supporting a flow-style experience in which they feel a deep sense of engagement with the art. That flow is possible when the activity matches users' previous skills and knowledge and they feel comfortable and well-oriented [1]. For such a flow to be achieved, the user must be in control of the experience, with the artwork as the primary focal point and the tour guide as the secondary focal point, allowing the user to experience both emotional and intellectual engagement with the art. Emotional engagement refers to feelings that the artwork provokes, while intellectual engagement refers to interest and learning that the artwork provokes [1, 2].

1.2   Augmented Reality as an Interpretive Technology in Museums

Interpretive technologies, including AR, are increasingly central in guiding visitors' experiences in art museums. AR experiences are mediated by stationary multimedia kiosks [30, 31], wearable displays such as Google Glass [19, 28], reflective mirrors [27], projections on objects [5, 18, 37, 38], and handheld devices [10, 21, 26].

AR tour guides have been shown to enhance users' learning in museum contexts. A user study of a vision-based mobile AR tour guide at the Taipei Fine Arts Museum showed that, compared to visitors using audio guides or no guides, visitors using an AR guide learned more and a had better flow experience. The AR guide also increased the amount of time visitors spent focusing on the paintings as opposed to other stimuli [8]. Studies also report increased engagement times during AR device use in science learning [17]. Previous work on AR as an interpretive technology indicates that designing a simple and effective user interface for AR tour guide applications is a persistent challenge. An interface must provide enough support for the user to navigate the system and receive the needed information while not distracting the user from the art [8].

AR has a number of definitions, ranging from showing related content based on mobile location [11, 20] to video see-through AR [3, 25]. This study focuses on video see-through AR, in which images are captured by a camera and displayed on a screen with augmented data overlaid on the objects. Video see-through AR applications recognize the object and track its position to correctly position the augmentations. In vision-based mobile AR, users point the camera of their mobile device at an exhibited object, and automatic image recognition provides more information about the object. One advantage of vision-based AR is that it is situated in the same visual field as the artwork; when using an AR tour guide, users do not need to shift their field of vision from the artwork to the tour guide or to a wall label next to the artwork [8, 10]. By pointing a mobile device camera at the artwork, the user can see overlaid information on the device's screen while examining the artwork.

Despite increasing AR use in museums, there is a lack of knowledge about the impact of mobile video see-through AR tour guides on users' engagement and interaction with art. Most of the work on video see-through has been focused on reporting technical advances in AR [26]. Controlled, between-subjects studies examining the impact of AR on the user experience are scarce, and though one such experiment shows that AR can enhance learning about art [8], other aspects of engagement with art mediated by AR remain largely unstudied. Art engagement includes not only one's learning about art but also one's emotional connection to art, enjoyment of art, and interest in art [1, 14]. There is also a lack of knowledge about the users' interaction with mobile see-through AR applications for art. More knowledge is needed on how to design mobile AR tour guide systems that support immediate apprehendability in art engagement and offer a high level of usability. The usability of the tour guide can affect art engagement by either supporting or obstructing the user's interaction with art.

To address these questions, we developed a novel AR tour guide system, Art++, with the Cantor Arts Center at Stanford University. Using the AR guide, we conducted an on-site user testing study in a between-subjects experiment to address the following questions: (1) How does a mobile-based video see-through AR tour guide application affect a user's engagement with art, namely their learning of, interest in, emotional connection to and liking of art? (2) How does an AR tour guide affect a user's interaction and experience in the art gallery in relation to the artwork, the tour guide, and the broader gallery context? (3) How usable is the mobile video see-through AR tour guide application in an art museum? (4) How should the user interface be designed to maximize usability and support immediate apprehendability in an art museum? By addressing these questions, this paper focuses on three aspects to examine the value and role of AR in art engagement: the user's intellectual and emotional engagement with art, the interaction patterns between the user and the AR guide, and usability of the AR guide.

2 System Description, Methods and Data

2.1 Art++, an AR Application for Art Tours

The AR tour guide developed for this study, Art++, is a video see-through AR guide based on image recognition for tablet devices. When a user points a tablet device at a painting, the application provides information about that painting by highlighting elements, augmenting perspective lines, and supplying textual content on the painting's features. Art++ has three modes: resting, scanning, and reading. The resting mode displays the camera view, as shown in Fig. 1a. Paintings are recognized at runtime using an image retrieval algorithm. After a query frame is captured, visual features (SURF) [4] are extracted and aggregated into a compact low-dimensional signature (REVV) [9] that retains most of the visual information of the image. The geometric consistency of the matches is ensured via a robust RANSAC procedure [13], which is a very common step in image matching [7].

When the painting is recognized by the system, the scanning mode is activated and the application provides information with video see-through overlays. The two AR tour guide designs tested in this study differ in the parent layer. The design in condition A, shown in Fig. 1b, uses button icons to switch to a child layer. These buttons are static on the screen and give the title of the layer. Condition B, shown in Fig. 1c, uses red dots that appear directly on the view of the painting, requiring the user to touch the dot to enter a child layer. These markers give the location of the element about which information is provided, but they do not give the title of the layer.

There are two types of child layers in the application. The point-of-interest layer, shown in Fig. 1d, draws the user's attention to a specific part of the painting by

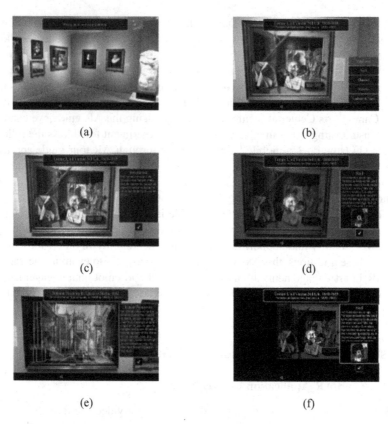

(a)

(b)

(c)

(d)

(e)

(f)

Fig. 1. Screenshots of the six views in Art++: (a) camera view, (b) parent layer in mode A, (c) parent layer in mode B, (d) point of interest child layer, (e) overlay child layer, (f) reading mode. (Color figure online)

desaturating and darkening the background, while the overlay layer, shown in Fig. 1e, superimposes an image onto the painting itself. The visual information is updated in real time to align with the real-world content and is complemented by a text paragraph shown in a layer on the side. The user can switch from scanning mode to reading mode by positioning the tablet as if reading a book (Fig. 1f), and the screen will show a reference image of the recognized artwork instead of the live images from the camera. The other interface elements remain the same; the user can switch between layers as in scanning mode, using buttons (A) or touch markers (B) to go from the parent layer to any child layer and using the "back" or "check" buttons to return from a child layer to a parent layer. The switch between reading and scanning modes is based on the orientation of the device, which is accessed by the program via data from the Android's accelerometer sensors.

The application was developed for and with Cantor Arts Center at Stanford University with the goal of finding a meaningful way to provide visitors with information about the museum's art. The development and testing of an AR application was part of the museum's strategy to identify ways of meaningfully integrating technologies into its visitor experience. Audio features were not developed at this stage, as the goal of this research was to develop a simple-to-use AR tour guide and examine the impact of AR on art engagement.

2.2   Experiment Design

The between-subjects experiment was conducted at the Cantor Arts Center in 2015. Forty-six participants were randomly assigned to use (A) one version of the AR application (Art++) in the art tour (Fig. 1b), (B) another version of Art++ (Fig. 1c), or (C) a book tour guide with the same information as the AR application. Condition A had 16 participants, and B and C each had 15. The participants were recruited on-site at the art museum, through museum member email lists, and through social media, and they each received a $20 gift card for their participation. The experiment was carried out on second-generation Android Nexus 7 tablets with 7-inch displays.

To examine the impact of the AR guide on user behavior, a book guide was used as a control to represent a traditional, analog tour guide, the booklet, which is widely used in museums. The book guide had the same information as the AR guide. Two versions of the AR application were tested to compare two designs for providing information to the user. The goal was to find the best design to support immediate apprehendability in art engagement to inform future designs of AR mediated art tour guides. The study was approved by the Institutional Review Board (IRB) at the museum's parent university.

The experiment had three parts: pre-evaluation, the activity phase, and post-evaluation. The experiment began on-site at the museum as the subjects filled out a consent form and a pre-evaluation survey that inquired about their relationship to art and technology. The survey showed pictures of paintings that subjects would later see on the tour of the Dutch collection in the museum. Offering a 7-point Likert scale for responses, the following questions were posed in pre- and post-surveys to examine the users' interest in, knowledge of, enjoyment of, and emotional connection to the paintings: "How interested are you in this painting?" "How much do you know about this painting?" "How much do you like this painting?" "How emotionally connected you are with this painting?"

In the activity phase, the users received an AR tour guide for the Dutch collection at the museum's visitor service desk. The researcher gave them a prompt to find the collection and interact with the paintings in the collection as naturally as possible. The tour guide offered a full set of information on six of the 13 paintings in the gallery, while it listed only the name of the painting and the artist for the rest. The tour guide provided instructions on navigating to find the collection in the gallery, and the application included a tutorial that every user watched before starting the application. The activity phase was recorded on video, and users' interactions with the application were screen-captured and recorded in activity logs built into the application. Each interaction (e.g., button pressed, painting scanned) was logged with a timestamp, thus recording analytics such as the duration of the tour and the paintings and layers viewed. On average, a tour lasted 15 min and 20 s in condition A, 14 min and 2 s in B, and 14 min and 10 s minutes in C.

Users were asked to narrate their thoughts, feelings, and motivations for behavioral decisions during the tour, following the think-aloud method used in design evaluation [35]. Two researchers observed the users' behavior during the tour; one took notes as the other recorded the tours on video. In two occasions, there were three researchers on-site for researchers' training purposes. The users were instructed to interact with the paintings as they normally would. The users were interviewed after their tours, and they filled out post-evaluation surveys at the research site that inquired about their interest in, knowledge of, enjoyment of, and emotional connection to the paintings they had seen in the gallery, and their experience with the tour guide. The post-survey also inquired about the usability of the tour guides. The usability measures were adapted from Brooke's set of measures [6], following the example of Wein's [33] study about the usability of visual recognition-based mobile museum applications.

2.3 Sample Profile

Of the 46 participants, 36 (78.3%) were women and 10 (21.7%) men. The largest group of users, one third (30.4%), were 55–64 years old. The second-largest group, almost one third (28.3%), were 18–25 years old. About one fifth (19.6%) were 35–54 years old, and another one fifth (17.4%) were 65 or older. Most of the users were working full-time (44%), a quarter (26%) were students, and one fifth (17%) were retired. The users' professions varied, including information technology-, science-, and education-related positions. All users had a good proficiency in English, and 90% spoke English as their first language.

The majority of the participants were occasional museumgoers: over half (54%) reported visiting art museums and galleries only once or twice a year. A large portion of the users were very active museumgoers: 37% visited once a month or more often. Most users (85%) had previously visited at least once the museum where the experiment was conducted. The majority of users could be described as art lovers, as 89% stated that they "loved art" and 80% "enjoyed seeing art very much." However, the users did not consider themselves very knowledgeable about art, even if they visited art museums often: almost half (48%) said their knowledge about art was moderate at best. They considered themselves to have even weaker knowledge about European art than art in general, as 69% said their knowledge in that field was moderate at best. The users were relatively technologically savvy. Slightly more than a majority (55%) used tablet devices frequently, whereas about a quarter (24%) used them rarely or never. Almost all (93%) used mobile touchscreen phones frequently. Most users liked using new technologies (75%) and found technologies easy to learn (65%).

3 Findings

3.1 Interest, Liking, Learning and Emotional Connection to Art

To examine changes in interest in, enjoyment of, knowledge of, and emotional connection to art, we analyzed the survey results by one-way ANOVA with Tukey's HSD test as the post hoc method. When referring to "change," we mean the change in the dependent variables between pre- and post-surveys. The results show a statistically significant difference between the three conditions in the change in liking of the paintings, as Table 1 shows; it reports the ANOVA results of the impact of the three conditions on the key dependent variables, considering all the paintings together. The differences in liking of the paintings were significant at the 0.01 level (p = 0.008). This indicates that the AR users' liking of the paintings increased more during the tour than did the book users'. We did not find a statistically significant association between the dependent variables and independent variables such as age, relationship to technology, or relationship to art.

Table 1. The change between the pre- and post-surveys in the users' liking of, interest in, and emotional connection to the paintings and the perceived and objective knowledge gain.

Factor	Condition A mean (sd)	Condition B mean (sd)	Condition C mean (sd)	Df	F	p
Change in liking	0.34 (1.01)	0.06 (1.03)	−0.03 (0.99)	2	4.892	0.008*
Change in interest	0.325 (1.47)	0.02 (1.34)	0.17 (1.75)	2	1.266	0.283
Change in emotional connection	0.48 (1.44)	0.51 (1.52)	0.24 (1.37)	2	1.465	0.232
Change in perceived knowledge	1.28 (1.70)	1.29 (1.89)	1.13 (1.57)	2	0.587	0.533
Change in objective knowledge	2.10 (1.99)	1.88 (1.77)	2.51 (1.96)	2	4.115	0.017**

*p < 0.01, **p < 0.05

3.2   Objective and Subjective Knowledge Gain

We examined users' learning with two sets of measures: one set for objective knowledge gain (actual learning) and another for subjective knowledge gain (the users' self-perceived learning). Objective knowledge gain was measured by analyzing answers to the following question about each painting in both pre- and post-surveys: "What do you know about this painting? List everything you know." This question measured the baseline of the users' actual knowledge about the paintings before the tour, and the same question was asked after the tour. We counted each new piece of information the users learned during the tour. For example, when a user said in the post-survey, "The crab is a symbol of vanity in life," but did not note that in the pre-survey, the user would receive a point. The users learned the most information with the book, with an average of 2.5 points per painting, whereas with the AR application version A users earned 2.1 points and version B 1.9 points. The differences are significant at the 0.05 level (p = 0.017), as reported in Table 1.

To examine the reasons for the difference between learning with the AR guide and with the book, we also analyzed objective learning with each painting in each condition, as shown in Fig. 2. The users learned the least about the two paintings for which the guides did not supply further information. The difference in objective learning between the AR and book users was significant with those paintings, which is explained by the fact that the book users relied more on wall labels than the AR users did; the book users read the wall labels when they were curious to learn more about a painting, whereas the AR users largely ignored the wall labels, which we will elaborate on later in the Findings section.

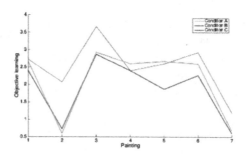

Fig. 2. Objective knowledge gain per painting in each condition.

Self-perceived learning was measured on a 7-point Likert scale with the question: "How much do you know about this painting?" There were no statistically significant differences in self-perceived learning between the conditions. When we examined self-perceived learning in greater depth, we found a trend: the less the users knew, the more they thought they learned in all conditions. The users' previous knowledge affected the amount of self-perceived learning in all conditions, as shown in Fig. 3. For each user and each painting, we recorded the integer-valued knowledge in the pre-evaluation survey and the change in knowledge, which are represented by differences between the pre-survey and post-survey. The plots in Fig. 3 show the values as blue tokens; the shade of blue is darker for the values that contain more occurrences. The red line is the result of a linear regression between the two quantities.

However, when analyzing the impact of the users' previous level of objective knowledge as measured in the pre-survey on their objective knowledge gain, their previous level of objective knowledge did not affect their actual learning, as Fig. 4 shows. The AR conditions did not show any association, while the book condition showed only a very weak association. One potential explanation for the difference between the impact of previous level of knowledge on self-perceived and objective learning lies in user perception. For those who did not have much knowledge at the outset of the experiment, learning even one thing about the paintings may have felt like learning a lot, and they thus these users viewed their experience as a significant gain over their previous knowledge, increasing their self-perceived learning scores. However, when those who already knew a bit about art learned one thing, they perceived it as a lesser knowledge gain. In reality, those with lesser knowledge and more knowledge learned fairly equal amounts, as the objective knowledge values show.

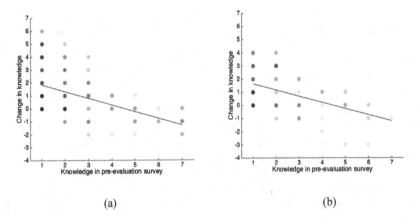

(a)   (b)

Fig. 3. Impact of users' previous self-perceived knowledge on learning for (a) conditions A and B (Art++) and (b) condition C (book). The red line is the result of a linear regression between the two quantities. (Color figure online)

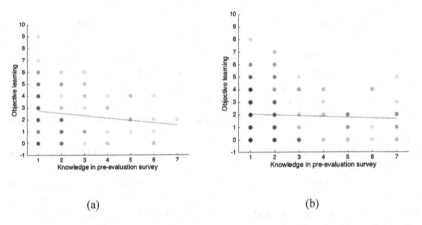

(a)   (b)

Fig. 4. The impact of users' previous objective knowledge on learning for (a) conditions A and B (Art++) and (b) condition C. The red line is the result of a linear regression between the two quantities. (Color figure online)

3.3   User Experience with the AR Tour Guide

In this section we compare user interactions with the AR application and the book guide using data from the on-site observations, videos, interviews, activity logs, and surveys. The findings are organized around three elements: interaction with art, the tour guide, and wall labels. The users are referred to by alphanumeric combinations, such as 28C, with the number referring to the anonymized number of the user and the letter to the condition to which they were assigned.

Interaction with Art. *Discovering hidden aspects.* The AR users felt they interacted directly with the art and that the tour guide application heightened their interest in the paintings: "It got me to look closer at the actual work, not just at the screen. It made me want to learn more" (1A). The augmentations, such as the highlighting of elements in paintings and perspective lines, helped the AR users understand the artwork, and directed their attention to aspects that might otherwise have remained hidden, leading to excitement and even joy: "It helped me to focus on subtleties in the art that I may have missed. Some surprising and fun details! It added to my understanding of each painting" (6A). The users perceived that the visual overlays helped them focus on and learn about certain aspects of the paintings: "I liked how I could learn how the art works in a visual way, rather than being limited to an auditory lecture" (26B). The augmentations helped the users better comprehend the paintings, sparking discovery and focus in particular. Some users also liked the feeling of achievement and gameplay in their art exploration: "[I enjoyed] the immediacy of learning facts and the game-like quality of hide-and-seek within the images" (30A). These feelings of excitement, joy, and achievement were not found among the book users.

Too Much Screen Time. There was a clear difference in the AR users' and book users' interaction with the art: The AR users typically started with only a quick glance at the painting before focusing on the tablet. The book users, by contrast, typically first went closer to the painting, looked at it for some time, and then flipped open the relevant page in the book. A number of book users also began to interpret the painting vocally before even looking at the tour guide; this never occurred with the AR guide. Thus, for the book users the painting was the primary object of engagement, and the book guide was secondary. Whereas for the AR users, the tour guide application was the primary object of engagement, and the artwork was secondary.

The users' interaction patterns can also be found in the time distributions between the conditions. The AR users spent more time than the book users in engaging with each painting, when we combine time spent looking at the painting and the application, only at the painting, and only at the wall label. The AR users spent less time looking at the art with the naked eye (without mediation of the tablet screen) than those who used the book as a guide. The AR users spent almost 70% of their time looking at the art in the application and at the painting through the tablet's screen. Looking at the painting with the naked eye occupied a small part of the time for AR users (about 25%), whereas for book users it occupied more than half of the time (54%). Figures 5 and 6 show with 90% confidence intervals that this quantity was consistently higher for condition C (disjoint confidence intervals), while conditions A and B are indistinguishable using this metric (overlapping confidence intervals). We found that for the naked eye mode, the difference between the AR conditions (condition A and condition B in Fig. 6) and the book was significant at the 0.01 level ($p = 9.506^{e-05}$ comparing condition A and condition C; $p = 0.0008$ comparing condition B and condition C). For other modes, there were not statistically significant differences between the AR conditions and the book.

The AR users did not like having so much screen time during their art experience. They felt that the tour guide application interfered with their engagement with the art: "I felt a bit disconnected from the artwork during the time I was looking at the screen. I didn't like spending too much time looking at the screen" (41A). The users felt the experience became "too technological" (40A), and were worried they did not spend

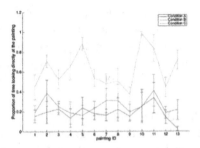

Fig. 5. Average ratio of the time spent looking directly at the painting over the total time spent interacting with it.

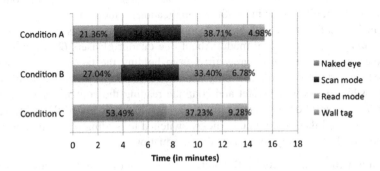

Fig. 6. The time distributions between modes of engagement and conditions.

enough time simply looking at the art. Even though the book guide also required the users' attention, the book users were not as concerned about the time they spent reading the book. This difference suggests that users experienced the properties of the technologically mediated tour guide as more distracting than a book. The AR application thus distracted the users from their art experience; it became the object of their attention even more than the art. At the same time, it supplied the users with information that they found useful. This tension between the utility provided by the application and the concern about excess screen time resulted in a continual balancing act: the users tried to negotiate between focusing on the application and the customary behavior of paying more attention to the paintings.

Somewhat surprisingly, considering the AR users' complaints about being distracted from the artwork, when combining the time looking at the painting through the screen and with the naked eye, the AR users looked at the paintings longer than book users (Fig. 6). However, looking at the paintings *through the screen* and with the naked eye are two different experiences; some of the paintings' features become much more apparent when seen with the naked eye than through the screen. The screen limits the user's visual field, the mediating tablet screen always moves in the user's hands, and the user's eyes get tired of watching the painting through a moving screen. But to see the live augmentations, the user had to point the tablet at the screen and look at the painting through the screen.

Text played a crucial role both in the AR application and the book guide by directing the users' attention from the guide to the painting. When the text encouraged the user to have a closer look at the painting, for instance by saying, "Look closely at the reflection painted into this silver jug, and you can dimly make out an image of the artist at his canvas," most users with all tour guides went closer to the painting to find the reflection.

User Experience with the AR Tour Guide. The users were generally comfortable using all tour guides. The level of comfort using the guides was rated on a scale of 1 to 3, with 3 being very comfortable, 2 comfortable, and 1 not comfortable. The ratings were tabulated by two researchers based on the videos filmed on-site during the experiment. Most users, 43 out of 46, were rated as comfortable or very comfortable using the guides. All book users were at least comfortable. A minority, three out of 31 AR users, had trouble interacting with the application or the tablet.

The main usability issue with both versions of the AR guide was learning to switch from scanning mode to reading mode. About one quarter of users (23%) complained during the tour that their arms grew tired from holding the tablet up. The physical fatigue began early in the tour, after only one or two paintings. When the users noticed it was possible to lower the tablet and continue reading the content, most users (24, which is 77%) started doing so once the application had recognized the painting. The users then scanned the painting and quickly switched to reading mode, finding that to be a more comfortable way to explore the information.

Interaction with Wall Labels. Beyond the tour guides, the only other available information about the paintings could be found in the gallery wall labels. The book users paid more attention to the wall labels than the AR users did. The former looked at about five wall labels on average and spent about 80 s per a label—about 9% of their total time—reading them. The AR users looked at three wall labels on average and spent 52 s per a label—about 6% of their time—reading them. The role of wall labels in art engagement thus varied: for the AR users, the labels were clearly a secondary source of information. For the book users, the labels had more significance as information providers. But several sources of information created confusion: "I am sometimes a little unsure of where to direct my attention between the piece, the screen, and the info card [wall label]" (21B). The users had trouble deciding which field of vision to use and which source of information to focus on. This confusion about the information sources mitigates the potential advantage of AR in helping the user achieve immediate apprehendability in art engagement by providing ease of focus.

Usability and Suitability of the Tour Guides. Based on usability measures in the survey, the participants liked the AR guide and perceived it as suitable for use as a tour guide in art museums. The differences between AR and the book guide were modest. The AR users enjoyed their guide slightly more than the book users enjoyed theirs, as Fig. 7 shows. The difference in enjoyment of use between the AR version A users (menu version) and the book users (condition C) was significant at a 0.05 level ($p = 0.04994$). Regarding comfort of use, users felt nearly equally comfortable using the AR and book guides. The users, however, found only the AR condition B, the dot version, easier to use than the book. The users felt they had the most control over the

AR dot version (condition B), the least control over the AR menu version (condition A), and the most control over the book. The lower usability scores for the menu version are explained by its navigational difficulties, which were not present in the dot version (condition B). The difficulty in the menu version was caused by a lack of visual cues when navigating from parent to child layers, resulting in users feeling a loss of control. The dot version of AR provided clearer support to the users with the red blinking dots. As Fig. 7 shows, visitors were more likely to use both versions of AR in their future visits to art museums than the book guide. The difference between the AR menu version (condition A) and the book (condition C) was significant at the 0.01 level ($p = 0.007036$). We did not find a statistically significant association between the usability measures and independent variables such as age, relationship to technology, or relationship to art.

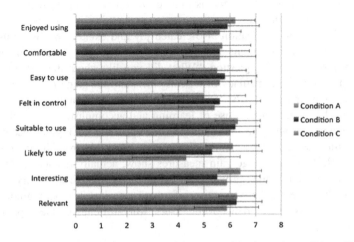

Fig. 7. Enjoyment, usability, and suitability of the tour guides in each condition. (Color figure online)

4 Discussion and Limitations

4.1 Augmented Reality: Compromised Impact on Art Engagement

The findings show that the mobile video see-through AR tour guide application supports users' engagement with art. The augmented information helped users understand and interpret the paintings and engage with them. The AR users began to like the art more than the book users did during their tour. The less knowledgeable the users perceived themselves to be, the more they felt they learned. This suggests that AR provides immediate apprehendability to users and may help decrease visitors' cognitive overload in museums. However, when compared to the book guide, there was very little or no statistical significance in the differences between the conditions. Only one of the examined aspects in art engagement, liking the paintings, performed better in the AR guide than the book with a statistically significant difference.

According to measures of changes in objective knowledge gain, the book users learned more about the paintings than the AR users. One potential explanation for the difference is the book users' greater reliance on wall labels. The AR users, however, tended to continue clicking on the application and thus were trying to find more information in it and were largely ignoring the wall labels. Another explanation is that the book users focused more on the actual content of the tour guide, and thus learned more, whereas the AR users were more occupied by clicking around in the application than reading the content. However, based on the mean values of perceived learning, the AR users *thought* they learned more than the book users, even though they didn't. The AR guide thus created more of *an impression of learning* than actual learning.

The differences between actual learning and perceived learning between users of AR and the book may be explained by the interactivity of the application: the AR user can click around in the application and skim through the information. This action itself can create a sense of accomplishment, as some of the users noted: "It made me feel like I was accomplishing something by going to each painting in the app" (15B). The experience of using the application also created joy and excitement. Some users also liked the feeling of achievement and game play in their art exploration, as a user explained in response to the question, "What did you like about the AR guide in the survey?": "(I liked) The immediacy of learning facts and the game-like quality of hide and seek within the images" (30A). The active role of the user can thus create a false or at least somewhat exaggerated sense of learning and accomplishment simply through the act of clicking through the information in the app. The book guide users focused more on reading the actual information without any distraction from digital affordances and, as the objective knowledge gain measures show, actually learned more than the AR users. The AR guide thus provided an experience of active discovery and entertainment, in which the users are an active information-seeker. The book guide, instead, provided a more passive experience to the users, who still enjoyed the experience and learned more.

4.2   The Value of Augmented Reality

The users' behavioral patterns show they didn't take advantage of viewing art in the same visual field as the augmentations, which is considered a benefit of AR tour guides. Instead, they preferred to review the live augmentations quickly by pointing the tablet at the paintings to activate the parent information layer and then switching to reading mode. They users became quickly tired of holding the tablet up. Furthermore, the users were uncomfortable with switching between several fields of vision: the screen, the painting, and the wall labels. One reason for the lack of interest in live augmentations could be that their content was not compelling enough to merit the effort of holding the device up. Future research should experiment with content that leverages the possibilities of AR more richly and should test a tour guide with different types of augmentations that may yield different results. However, the physical fatigue of holding the tablet up remains a serious concern, regardless of the type of augmentation: If experiencing an augmentation requires holding a tablet up for long periods of time, the users will undoubtedly become fatigued. They might not hold the tablet up for more than a few paintings, as the users' behavior in this study demonstrated.

Apart from liking the paintings, in which the AR guide performed better than the book, and objective learning, in which the book performed better than the AR guide, both the AR application and the book served as a tour guide. Therefore, it is worth investigating the actual value of AR in art engagement. One benefit of AR shown in this study was users learning about the art through application, and AR *was* part of that experience. For instance, seeing the augmented perspective lines on a large painting was a powerful learning experience for several users, as user 26B made clear: "I've never understood what a perspective really is before seeing this." The scaffolding of information with visual overlays, mixing the real (the painting) and the virtual (augmented perspective lines) helped the user understand a key concept in visual art that had not previously been accessible to him. The augmentations also helped users notice details that otherwise would likely have been missed. Learning can even lead to a sense of excitement and joy in exploring hidden aspects in the paintings, as happened with some users in the study. The excitement has also been noted in other AR studies in museum contexts [16, 19]. It can lead to longer engagement times with the artworks, as has been detected by other scholars [17, 32, 36, 38], but that was not the case in this study. However, excitement and joy may translate into liking the paintings, and this could be one explanation for the difference between the stronger enjoyment of the paintings with the AR condition over the book condition.

4.3   Design Implications: Increasing Naked Eye Time

The AR guide's distracting nature was its downside, drawing users' attention away from the artwork toward the screen. The users felt disconnected from the art and were concerned about the excess screen time. This concern is borne out by the data: The AR users looked at the art for less time with the naked eye than did the book users. The distracting property of the AR guide is similar to other technologically mediated tour guides [16, 19, 34]. Contrary to the findings of our study, previous user studies on AR in art engagement haven't shown the distractive nature of the AR systems [8]. The findings of this present study show that when using AR, the users slipped further away from the art. The user was pulled into the influence sphere of the tour guide and became subsumed by the technological experience. The artwork became the secondary focus of attention. When the content of the application instructed the user to look more closely at the painting, most users did. The application's content thus played an important role in negotiating the balance between engaging with the tablet screen and the art object.

The AR users felt conflicted; they wanted to read the information on the AR app, but at the same time felt they should look at the paintings with the naked eye instead. Such anxiety was not found among the book users. To resolve this conflict, measures to mitigate this concern must be developed. Decreasing the screen time is the most obviously promising avenue. Another avenue is adding an audio feature to the application that allows users to obtain the same information by listening, likely increasing the naked eye time with art. However, not all users like using audio guides, as the users' testimonies show, so not all users would benefit from the audio feature. A third possible avenue is content. The content already plays a crucial role in pulling the user back to the actual painting, as when the text prompts the user to find details in the painting. Adding more of these elements would remind the user to focus on the art itself.

Navigation difficulties in the AR menu version (condition A) led to a feeling of lack of control of the application, and disturbed the users' interactions with the art. The blinking red dots in condition B clearly provided more support for focus and discovery, thus supporting immediate apprehendability of art and creating a sense of control. This finding offers a design implication for preferring instant, clear access points in a mobile see-through AR app for art engagement.

4.4   Limitations

The main limitation of this study was its observational nature. The users' interactions with the paintings were observed by two researchers, which could have affected the users' behavior. The users were encouraged to interact with the paintings as naturally as possible, but they most likely paid more attention to the paintings than they would have otherwise, in accordance with the Hawthorne effect [23], which occurs when users try to please researchers [12]. However, on-site, in-person observation is a validated field-research method commonly used in design ethnography in human–computer interaction. This method was crucial for our study, because the observers on the ground provided the users' perspective, which is important in user studies [24]. On-site observations could not be replaced by other methods without compromising the data quality. We did not notice the users having issues with our presence, nor did we notice the users trying to please us; they listed both positive and negative aspects of their experiences, and didn't hesitate to express their concerns. The users completed anonymous pre- and post-surveys on a laptop-based digital survey interface at the research site without the researchers' interference, so it is unlikely they would have altered their survey scores and answers to please the researchers. Finally, the conditions were the same for each user in each condition, so the Hawthorne effect would have affected them equally and should not have skewed the results.

5   Conclusion

This study examined the impact of a mobile video see-through AR tour guide on users' engagement with art. The findings show that AR enhances users' liking of the paintings more than an analog guide, which functioned as a control condition. When measuring actual learning (objective knowledge gain), the book users learned more than the AR guide users did, contradicting previous findings of AR as a medium for increasing learning. The AR guide enhanced the users' art engagement by strengthening both their emotional and intellectual connections to the art, and it supported immediate appre-hendability by providing clear focus points and sequenced information about the art-work, revealing hidden aspects about the paintings. The users enjoyed using the AR application, found it easy to operate, and the system brought joy to their experience in the art museum. The AR guide, however, was not superior to the book guide; the AR application provided equally good support for art engagement as a book guide, and it was equally easy to use, even for the less technologically savvy users.

AR also presented serious downsides, which mitigate the value of AR in art engagement. The users felt distracted by the AR guide and were worried about excessive screen time. They felt physical fatigue holding the tablet up when reviewing the live augmentations. The users had difficulty switching between the three fields of vision: the art, the screen, and the wall labels. The difficulty is paradoxical; mobile see-through video AR is argued to ease art engagement because it is located in the same field of vision as the art object.

These complications partly compromised the AR users' art experience and could be a reason for their weaker learning performance. Ideally, there should be no compromises when using new technologies, only benefits. That might not, however, be possible to achieve in this case. Video see-through, AR-mediated experiences on mobile devices require a certain amount of screen time; to benefit from using these systems, users may have to compromise their instinct to avoid screen time. Moreover, it may be the case that users employ AR applications in museums only occasionally, so screen time might not be a major issue in the long run. AR technologies situated in the same field of vision as the user, such as HoloLense, could be a more fitting platform to art engagement, yet they provide new challenges in user interactions. The findings demonstrate that to add value by deploying AR in art engagement, we must explore further ways of implementing AR applications in art museums with designs that keep the art objects as the main focus of art engagement.

References

1. Allen, S.: Designs for learning: studying science museum exhibits that do more than entertain. Sci. Educ. **88**(1), 17–33 (2004)
2. Allen, S.: Exhibit design in science museums: dealing with a constructivist dilemma. In: Falk, J., Dierking, L., Foutz, S. (eds.) Principle, in practice: museums as learning institutions, pp. 43–56. Altamira Press, Lanham (2007)
3. Azuma, R.: A survey of augmented reality. Presence: Teleoperators Virtual Environ. **6**(4), 355–385 (1997)
4. Bay, H., Tuytelaars, T., Van Gool, L.: SURF: speeded up robust features. In: Leonardis, A., Bischof, H., Pinz, A. (eds.) ECCV 2006. LNCS, vol. 3951, pp. 404–417. Springer, Heidelberg (2006). https://doi.org/10.1007/11744023_32
5. Bimber, O., Coriand, F., Kleppe, A., Bruns, E., Zollmann, S., Langlotz, T.: Superimposing pictorial artwork with projected imagery. In: ACM SIGGRAPH 2006 Courses, p. 10. ACM Press, New York (2006)
6. Brooke, J.: SUS—a quick and dirty usability scale. Usability Eval. Ind. **189**(194), 4–7 (1996)
7. Brown, M., Lowe, D.: Recognising panoramas. In: ICCV, vol. 3, p. 1218 (2003). http://faculty.cse.tamu.edu/jchai/CPSC641/iccv2003.pdf
8. Chang, K., Chang, T., Hou, H., Sung, Y., Chao, H., Lee, C.: Development and behavioral pattern analysis of a mobile guide system with augmented reality for painting application instruction in an art museum. Comput. Educ. **71**, 185–197 (2014)
9. Chen, D., Tsai, S., Chandrasekhar, V., Takacs, G., Vedantham, R., Grzeszczuk, R., Girod, B.: Residual enhanced visual vector as a compact signature for mobile visual search. Sig. Process. **93**(8), 2316–2327 (2013)
10. Damala, A., Cubaud, P., Bationo, A., Houlier, P., Marchal, I.: Bridging the gap between the digital and the physical: design and evaluation of a mobile augmented reality guide for the museum visit. In: 3rd ACM International Conference on Digital and Interactive Media in Entertainment and Arts, pp. 120–128. ACM Press, New York (2008)

11. Dunleavy, M., Dede, C.: Augmented reality teaching and learning. In: Spector, J., Merrill, M., Elen, J., Bishop, M. (eds.) Handbook of Research on Educational Communications and Technology, pp. 735–745. Springer, New York (2014). https://doi.org/10.1007/978-1-4614-3185-5_59

12. Egelman, S., Bernheim A., Brush, A., Inkpen, K.: Family accounts: a new paradigm for user accounts within the home environment. In: Proceedings of the 2008 ACM Conference on Computer-Supported Cooperative Work, pp. 669–678 ACM Press, New York (2008)

13. Fischler, M., Bolles, R.: Random sample consensus: a paradigm for model fitting with applications to image analysis and automated cartography. Commun. ACM **24**(6), 381–395 (1981)

14. Hooper-Greenhill, E.: Museum learners as active postmodernists: contextualizing construc-tivism. In: The Educational Role of the Museum. Routledge, London (1994)

15. Hedge, A.: Human-factor considerations in the design of museums to optimize their impact on learning. In: Falk, J., Dierking, L. (eds.) Public Institutions for Personal Learning: Establishing a Research Agenda, pp. 105–117. American Association of Museums, Washington, DC (1995)

16. Hsi, S.: The electronic guidebook: study of user experiences using mobile web content in a museum setting. In: International Workshop on Wireless and Mobile Technologies in Education, Växjö, Sweden, pp. 48–54 (2002)

17. Huang, T., Chou, Y., Shu, Y., Yeh, T.: Activating natural science learning by augmented reality and indoor positioning technology. In: Huang, Y., Chao, H., Deng, D., Park, J. (eds.) Advanced Technologies, Embedded and Multimedia for Human-centric Computing, pp. 229–238. Springer, Dordrecht (2004). https://doi.org/10.1007/978-94-007-7262-5_27

18. Karnik, A., Mayol-Cuevas, W., Subramanian, S.: MUSTARD: a multi-user see-through AR display. In: Konstan, J., Chi, E., Hook, K. (eds.) Proceedings of the SIGCHI Conference on Human Factors in Computing Systems, pp. 2541–2550. ACM Press, New York (2012)

19. Leue, C., Jung, T., Dieck, D.: Google Glass augmented reality: generic learning outcomes for art galleries. In: Tussyadiah, I., Inversini, A. (eds.) Information and Communication Technologies in Tourism 2015, pp. 463–476. Springer, New York (2015). https://doi.org/10.1007/978-3-319-14343-9_34

20. Liao, T.: Is it "augmented reality"? Contesting boundary work over the definitions and organizing visions for an emerging technology across field-configuring events. Inf. Organ. **26**(3), 45–62 (2016)

21. Lu, W., Nguyen, L., Chuah, T., Do, E.: Effects of mobile AR-enabled interactions on retention and transfer for learning in art museum contexts. In: Mixed and Augmented Reality-Media, Art, Social Science, Humanities and Design (ISMAR-MASH'D), pp. 3–11. IEEE (2014)

22. Mayer, R., Moreno, R.: Nine ways to reduce cognitive load in multimedia learning. Educ. Psychol. **38**(1), 43–52 (2003)

23. McCarney, R., Warner, J., Iliffe, S., Haselen, R., Griffin, M., Fisher, P.: The Hawthorne effect: a randomised, controlled trial. BMC Med. Res. Methodol. **7**(1), 1–8 (2007)

24. Millen, D.: Rapid ethnography: time-deepening strategies for HCI field research. In: Proceedings of the 3rd Conference on Designing Interactive Systems: Processes, Practices, Methods, and Techniques, pp. 280–286. ACM Press, New York (2000)

25. Mohring, M., Lessig, C., Bimber, O.: Video see-through AR on consumer cell-phones. In: Proceedings of the 3rd IEEE/ACM International Symposium on Mixed and Augmented Reality. IEEE Computer Society (2004)

26. Pierdicca, R., Frontoni, E., Zingaretti, P., Sturari, M., Clini, P., Quattrini, R.: Advanced interaction with paintings by augmented reality and high-resolution visualization: a real-case exhibition. In: Paolis, L., Mongelli, A. (eds.) Augmented and Virtual Reality, pp. 38–50. Springer, New York (2015). https://doi.org/10.1007/978-3-319-22888-4_4

27. Plasencia, D., Berthaut, F., Karnik, A., Subramanian, S.: Through the combining glass. In: Proceedings of the 27th Annual ACM Symposium on User Interface Software and Technology (UIST 2014), pp. 341–350. ACM Press, New York (2014)

28. Rhodes, T., Allen, S.: Through the looking glass: how Google Glass will change the performing arts. Arts Management and Technology Laboratory, pp. 1–12. Carnegie-Mellon University (2014)

29. Stecker, R.: Art interpretation. J. Aesthetics Art Criticism **52**(2), 193–206 (1994)

30. Sylaiou, S., Mania, S., Karoulis, A., White, M.: Exploring the relationship between presence and enjoyment in a virtual museum. Int. J. Hum Comput Stud. **68**(5), 243–253 (2010)

31. Sylaiou, S., Economou, M., Karoulis, A., White, M.: Evaluation of ARCO: a lesson in curatorial competence and intuition with new technology. Comput. Entertainment **6**(2), 23 (2008)

32. Szymanski, M., Aoki, P., Grinter, R., Hurst, A., Thornton, J., Woodruff, A.: Sotto Voce: facilitating social learning in a historic house. Comput.-Support. Coop. Work (CSCW) **17** (1), 5–34 (2008)

33. Wein, L.: Visual recognition in museum guide applications: do visitors want it? In: Proceedings of the SIGCHI Conference on Human Factors in Computing Systems (CHI 2014), pp. 635–638. ACM Press, New York (2014)

34. Woodruff, A., Aoki, P., Hurst, A., Szymanski, M.: Electronic guidebooks and visitor attention. In: Trant, J., Bearman, D. (eds.) International Cultural Heritage Informatics Meeting, Milan, Italy, pp. 437–454 (2001)

35. Wright, P., Monk, A.: The use of think-aloud evaluation methods in design. ACM SIGCHI Bull. **23**(1), 55–57 (1991)

36. Wu, H., Lee, S., Chang, H., Liang, J.: Current status, opportunities and challenges of augmented reality in education. Comput. Educ. **62**, 41–49 (2013)

37. Yoon, S., Elinich, K., Wang, J., Steinmeier, S., Tucker, S.: Using augmented reality and knowledge-building scaffolds to improve learning in a science museum. Int. J. Comput.-Support. Collaborative Learn. **7**(4), 519–541 (2012)

38. Yoon, S., Wang, J.: Making the invisible visible in science museums through augmented reality devices. TechTrends **58**(1), 49–55 (2014)

Following the White Rabbit: The Virtual Reality for Games

Paulo Carvalho(✉)

SIDIA (Samsung R&D Institute Brazil), Manaus, Brazil
p.alexandre@samsung.com

Abstract. In recent years, virtual reality has seen a growth in its investments by the technology industry, despite all the experts' predictions about the duration of the hype around this technology and also with some problems still unresolved, such as motion sickness. One of the segments that receive most of these investments is the Games Area for VR, supported by technology enthusiasts, wishful for technological innovation. This essay analyzes some studies about the VR gaming industry for the understanding of all its actors: from manufacturers to their consumers, including developers, artists and researchers.

Keywords: Games · Virtual reality · Head-mounted display · Smartphones
Industry

1 Introduction

Virtual reality (VR) is a computer system that simulates an immersive environment through three-dimensional (3D) objects and scenarios. This technology can have its prolonged immersion effect with the combination of tactile sounds and devices for interaction with the objects and scenarios designed by the system [1]. In recent years, we have witnessed a rush by various technology companies toward popularizing their VR devices, and in recent years have released new versions with updates and new devices. At the same time that several segments such as education, health, simulations and military training have used this technology. However, it is the entertainment industry that concentrates most of the investments related to VR, especially to video games [2]. What is the reason for VR gaming industry to attract more investment than other segments? The present essay aims to analyze some of the key factors that make technology companies make heavy investments in VR for games, as well as provide an overview of the industry.

1.1 Digital Games: The Beginning

The first games were designed to be played by two people with the support of two controls or using digital interfaces such as a light weapon, which would make the gameplay experience more engaging. Designed at first for a single game, the home game consoles were being rapidly improved to support multiple games thanks to the arrival of companies to the game market like Nintendo and SEGA. These companies are among the first to propose that their own consoles have exclusive games, a practice

© Springer International Publishing AG, part of Springer Nature 2018
J. Y. C. Chen and G. Fragomeni (Eds.): VAMR 2018, LNCS 10910, pp. 172–183, 2018.
https://doi.org/10.1007/978-3-319-91584-5_14

quite common today. But the great innovation of the time was the launch of Atari in 1977 with its Atari 2600 that replaced the simple sound signal by a real sound based on two mono channels [3].

1.2 Virtual Reality: The Next Step

Virtual reality, like the digital game, adds a set of scientific areas, such as computer graphics, electronics, cognitive science, etc. A virtual reality system aims to immerse its user in an artificial environment where it is possible to feel and interact with objects and scenarios in real time thanks to sensorimotor interfaces [11]. Experience in a virtual environment must be believable enough that the user's senses are stimulated to generate their self-image within that virtual environment. According to Bouvier et al. [3], the sense of presence can be acquired by combining five pillars: immersion, interaction, real time, emotions, and cognitive science.

- Immersion is the introduction of the user into the virtual environment through the senses of vision and hearing that stimulates his perception and understanding in this environment;
- The interaction enables communication between the user and the environment in which he is inserted;
- The real-time system is in its set of tasks and actions to be executed at the expected moment and its perception occur simultaneously to its execution;
- The emotions originated from the virtual experience stimulate the user to make the experience believable with the aid of the interaction devices, which draws his attention from the real world;
- The last pillar is cognitive science that relates, among other things, human behavior with the capacity for interaction and understanding of the environment in which it is inserted, which contributes to the improvement of immersion and interaction in virtual systems [3].

The definition of the term Virtual Reality was created after the second world war, through the simulators of flight of the United States Air Force. In the 1950s, Morton Heiling developed Sensorama, a machine that allowed users to immerse themselves in an experience that consisted of a motorcycle ride in Manhattan. This multi-sensory experience was accompanied by a three-dimensional and colorful film, supported by sounds and smells that simulated the sensation of movement, as well as the wind in the spectator's face [4] (Fig. 1).

In 1966, Ivan Sutherland released The Sword of Damocles [5], an installation that merges head tracking and the Head Mounted Display (HMD) making a virtual environment connected to the user's point of view. As early as 1975, Myron Krueger devises an installation called Videoplace, in which the user uses his avatar to interact within a simple virtual environment through a camera. However, the popularization of the concept occurred only from the 1980s with Jaron Lanier, in order to differentiate traditional simulations from those involving multiple users. Lanier founded VPL, one of the first companies to market exclusive equipment to virtual reality, such as data gloves and HMDs [6].

Fig. 1. Sensorama [4]

VR glasses, as well as Head Mounted Displays (HMDs), are commonly accompanied by headphones for enhancing the feeling of immersion in the virtual environment. It is a fact that complete immersion in the virtual world occurs as a result of the involvement of the five senses. However, most VR environments cannot make use of all of them, usually using two senses: vision and hearing [4].

2   The First VR Games

The first releases of games using virtual reality focused on immersing the user's sense of the virtual world. The users performed their interactions in the virtual environment with limitations in their movements - the equipment in which the simulations ran did not allow physical walks or races because it was not portable [7].

The first models of videogames that used the RV were launched in the 1990s, such as Dactyl Nightmare [8] and Grid Busters [9]. In the same period the Japanese company Nintendo made its investment in virtual reality games through Virtual Boy, which proved to be a major failure [10]. Released in July 1995, Virtual Boy wasted tremendous potential for success by the time it was released, being referred to as one of Nintendo's biggest failures after being released from the market less than a year after its release and for not meeting expectations of sales, although it was an original system. The company failed to launch a very expensive product, with many technical problems, among them: the lack of head movement tracking, which could rotate the virtual environment relative to the user's head. Another technical factor relates to the absence of the input device that was commonly associated with the VR: the glove. A curious fact is that its display only displays the red color, due to the cost limitations, which made it even more uninteresting for the public, in addition to the many physical discomforts to the players [10].

Currently, the biggest technology companies are present in the market with their virtual reality devices: Facebook Oculus Rift, Google Cardboard, Daydream, HTC Live, Playstation VR and Samsung Gear VR. All have games released or under development for their respective VR systems.

3 The Gaming Industry

The gaming industry is relatively new, as the popularization of the games occurred only between the 1970s and 1980s. The gaming industry is constantly shaped by technology and technological development, while the industry feels pressure to meet its demand not to lose market share to other competitors in the industry [17].

The gaming industry is at the top of the entertainment industry, and continues to grow rapidly. Computer science techniques are primarily responsible for the basis of game industry, and new challenges for computer scientists are represented by new developments in video games. Across the globe, there are massive investments in study programs to expand the workforce in game industry, as the number of computer science academics committed to solving problems and developing algorithms for video games. This set of issues often requires mastery and knowledge of various lines of research, such as psychology and arts, leading to a relevant interdisciplinary field of research, which characterizes the creative games industry [15].

Higgs and Cunningham [18] characterizes the creative industries as those that assure individual creativity, skill and talent as agents for enhancing wealth and job creation by exploiting these intellectual properties. The creative industries have subdivisions spanning ancient arts and literature to contemporary industries based on technological developments such as graphic design, software development and video games [17].

The attributes of the creative industries presented by the gaming industry are essential to understand how they differ from industries in other sectors [17]. Caves [19] defines well the creative industry resources that make up these attributes:

3.1 Uncertainty of Demand

There is considerable uncertainty about demand in the creative industries because reactions to a finished product are unpredictable and subject to certain variables such as individual taste, joint consumption, and others. Therefore, uncertainty of demand may hinder budget projections [19].

3.2 The Respect of the Actors of the Industry for the Originality, Technical Prowess, Harmony

Jobseekers in the creative industries are subject to several sources of motivation to carry out their functions more than, for example, in the manufacturing industries, whose employees have external motivation, generally linked to financial stability [19]. Creative industry workers are usually intrinsically motivated as they see their line of work as an artistic ensemble where originality, technical prowess and harmony are the ultimate results of that association. Due to the nature of creative work, its employees demonstrate characteristics that are more similar to entrepreneurs than to employees in other industries, a factor that draws attention to companies. These employees have a greater tolerance for risk and uncertainty in relation to a creative company in the industry [19]. It is also emphasized that its employees have intrinsic motivation rather than external motivation to carry out their functions, which makes them oblivious to the traditional control systems adopted by other industries where the motivation usually comes from the financial rewards and financial stability offered by your company [19].

3.3   Diversified Inputs

Because it is too broad, production in the creative industries may require a variety of skills. These skills may include design, writing code, conceptual design, marketing, and finance. This effectiveness in attracting talented employees enough to accomplish their tasks opens up possibilities for new challenges [19].

3.4   Products Discerned by Quality and Uniqueness

The products of the creative industries have their market value tied to their technical quality, which characterizes the industry with a solid foundation in knowledge, making it unique in comparison to other industries. Since uniqueness is so valued, traditional controls from other industries will not have the same effectiveness for standardization in product manufacturing or work philosophy, since different work styles will lead to unique results [19].

3.5   Vertically Differentiated Skills

Abundance of talent can be estimated to a certain extent, since a subtle variation in talent can be a factor of great relevance in success [19].

3.6   Time Is of the Essence

The development and creation of products and services by the creative industries are appropriate processes at the moment of their idealization and, once it is initiated, it is fundamental that all its stages are concluded by seeking their relevance within the market at the moment of their launch [19]. And this is a guiding principle for video games: a new game based on an emerging trend will only be interesting at its launch if its features are contemporaneous with those trends. Monitoring the current scenario and the speed of understanding the reaction to trends and changes are fundamental for gaming companies, which creates an interesting challenge in trying to reconcile the search for success and budget balance together with the previously defined deadline [19].

3.7   Aspects of Durability that Require Copyright Protection

Because they are products originating from the creative industries, with unique characteristics, there is a certain facility in duplicating them and copying them, thus, it is necessary that copyright protections be made [19].

The gaming industry has many characteristics, a singular one where a small number of companies make huge profits compared to other companies in the industry, although most are really interested in creating a great demand for their products [17]. One thing that reinforces this standard of modus operandi is the fact that only 5% of the companies with more talents among their employees amplifies in the differences of gains, especially when approaching the reference company of the area [17].

In relation to customers, they tend to wait, and in some situations to request, continuous improvements in the products/services they acquire [17]. A technology client usually takes into account an upgrade or improvement in a replacement, even if this set of services has a high cost. The gaming industry has a similar attitude, with its consumers awaiting continuous improvement [17], as interaction and market share in technology are the main sources of information about the next set of product/service requirements [17].

Gaming companies keep up with market trends, so investment decisions are made based on existing companies' gains and technology requirements in the industry [20].

In the gaming industry, startups seek to ensure stable cash flow into the future, while larger companies deal with the uncertainties the industry brings while seeking to maximize shareholder profits [20]. And as industry relies on new investments due to the short life cycle of the games, the capital reserve plays an important role in growth opportunities. Technology has enabled the emergence of new investment opportunities due to the growth of the mobile game industry, and thus other interactive entertainment alternatives such as virtual reality [20].

4   The Psychological Strategies of VR in Users

Most VR games and environments show the strategies of intrinsic motivation, emphasizing the internal motivation of its users to perform a task, which comes from their own participation in the virtual environment [21, 22]. A research conducted with a focus on intrinsic motivation turned out to be successful from the time students engaged in tasks that required creativity or presented themselves with a certain degree of complexity [23]. However, we cannot say that extrinsic motivation has a negligible role in the game, since intrinsic and extrinsic goals are often mixed. A VR environment can present a very impacting experience, which will cause in its user a pleasurable sensation, as well as disturbing or frightening sensations [24]. The immersion in the virtual environment is a state of consciousness of the physical self that simultaneously diminishes the sensation of physical presence of the world around, intensifying the experience [25]. Being immersed in a virtual environment demands a very specific series of resources internal and external to the environment itself [14].

The public's fervent adoption of new technologies has made it possible to evolve from a resounding need for informal education institutions to the projection of increasingly elaborate exposures that integrate immersive VR, game-based technologies, augmented reality, visualizations, and other emerging media. Advances in simulations for pilot and astronaut training; ubiquitous robots and nanotechnology; satellite image; and the emerging and sophisticated visual data were responsible for creating new opportunities to engage the public in modern science [24]. Data collected from a study of a virtual reality science exhibition [24] revealed that some learners were alarmed by some samples of unrealistic virtual environments and were positively affected by realistic images. The unrealistic images reduced the immersion sensations while some visual images moved or were alternated to try to induce any sensation of immersion [14].

5   The Current VR Scenario for Games

In the past there were certain barriers to the propagation of technology or the use of HMDs. There was the fact that these technological devices were not widely diffused and were generally very expensive. If on the one hand the devices were not widely diffused, in addition to being very expensive, on the other hand their aspects were peculiar to the point of causing aversion to their potential users, generally due to the mismatch between the movements of the head and the corresponding change in the scene [4].

Currently there is a diversity of options of VR devices offering a good virtual simulation at affordable prices, making possible the use of the systems in other areas, such as education and training. In addition, the technology has improved its systems by providing accurate tracking of movements and low latency, making its usability more user-friendly and thus enhancing the feeling of immersion [4]. All this ends up facilitating the way for the development of games for the VR platform.

In current scene, games find a very wide audience due to the young people's taste for entertainment. This broad public encouraged the creation of portable and more accessible virtual reality systems, developed in laboratories around the world. With this, a global community with property was created to validate a growing ecosystem, using its different concepts and interfaces chosen for a VR application [1].

The market has released many haptic devices because of the immersive interactivity between the user and the virtual environment being increasingly demanded by virtual reality systems. In this way several tools are designed for digital games, adding elements of vibration or feedback [1].

6   The VR Games User's Profile in Brazil

In Brazil, according to a survey conducted in 2014 by BNDES (Banco Nacional do Desenvolvimento Econômico e Social) [26] about digital games, video game is the fourth activity most practiced by young people. According to their data, 35% of children and adolescents aged 9 to 16 years play daily, 45% play at least once a week and 19% at least once a month [16].

In a survey conducted with consumers of digital games at some of the major malls in the city of Manaus and São Paulo, Brazil, tests were done with two games, the Finding Monsters [28] (Fig. 2) and Rock & Rails [29] (Fig. 3), produced by Black River Studio for Samsung Gear VR.

From this approach we can gather data that clarify the preference of these consumers, according to the Tables 1 and 2 below:

Fig. 2. Finding monsters [28]

Fig. 3. Rock & Rails [29]

Another research was conducted by Wilson Silva (UX Researcher) and Mamoru Miyagawa (Game Producer) at the VR Gamer game store in São Paulo, Brazil, about the Highlander game for Gear VR, with purpose of validating some elements of the game, such as narrative, mechanics and emotional aspects. Important data were collected on the profile of the consumers of games for the VR [27]:

Table 1. Survey about digital games and VR.

Gender	Age	How often do you play?	Which platform?	Have you ever had contact with VR?	Rate the game Finding Monsters VR with grades (1–5)	Rate the game Rock & Rails VR with grades (1–5)
Male	26 to 34 years	2–6 day	Mobile, PC	Yes	5	Not available
Male	19 to 25 years	Rarely	Mobile	Yes	5	3
Male	>45 years	Rarely	Mobile	Yes	5	5
Male	<16 years	2–6 day	Console	Yes	5	4
Male	26 to 34 years	Rarely	PC	Yes	5	3

Table 2. Survey about VR.

Gender	Age	What content do you expect to find in VR?	Evaluate your VR experience	Would you buy VR?	Would you recommend the Samsung Gear VR?
Male	26 to 34 years	Entertainment, games, sports	5	No	Yes
Male	19 to 25 years	Entertainment, games	4	Yes	Yes
Male	>45 years	Entertainment, education	5	Yes	Yes
Male	<16 years	Entertainment	5	Yes	Yes
Male	26 to 34 years	Entertainment, sports	5	No	Yes

- Total number of participants: 23;
- Average gameplay time: 15 min, with a maximum of 21 min and a minimum of 07 min;
- Target audience: all player profiles, non-gamers, casual, mid-core and hard-core profiles were addressed.

Non-gamers had difficulty with tutorials, while casual and mid-core gamers liked the mechanics but criticized the detail poverty in the story. Hard-core gamers have criticized technical aspects of the game, especially in relation to graphics, character design and movement, as well as the poverty of details in the story as well. When asked, most would like to play the game again in order to better explore the scenario and environment. In relation to the narrative most liked, but they would like to know more about the world and have more details about the mission, the reason why they failed to create any emotional bond with protagonist of the game, precisely because of lack of information about this character [27].

However, for gamers there is a general perception that the Samsung Gear VR is the weakest VR game platform (especially comparing with Rift and Playstation VR), also that mobile game is not as good and well made as other video games. Thus, the survey revealed that the game has more potential of success with casual and average players [27].

7 The VR Obstacles for Video Games

Possibly, in terms of sales, one of the big competitors of commercial video games and VR games are mobile games, due to its ease in being marketed, for its practicality of use. The development of smartphones applications and games becomes practical, as well as their academic study, since it uses small teams of academics and students who are able to work with reduced budgets. Using the specifications of a smartphones as an example, we have a reduced graphics screen with limited hardware, common to mobile devices, which will lead to the production of games with simple graphics with often only 2 or 2.5 dimensions of resolution, which need for large teams of highly skilled artists and 3D modelers. Not to mention the wide variety of inputs that mobile devices offer (touch, images, sound, acceleration, orientation, personal data, etc.) and more output options (images, video, animation), sound, vibration, wireless, bluetooth, infrared) that is usually made available on a desktop or laptop computer. It also adds to the popularity of mobile devices that naturally attracts a large number of casual users, thereby providing a virtually large data source [15].

One of the factors that still hinders the popularization of games for VR is Cyber-sickness, even with content-producing companies and manufacturers investing in surveys that seek solutions to such problems. Most VR device manufacturers as well as game producers have invested a lot of time and money into research to find alternatives that reduce the discomfort caused by prolonged use of devices. In some cases, circumstances are becoming clearer, for example the Oculus Rift, where the design of some games could have favored the induction of some diseases due to a large volume of rather complex interactions over prolonged periods [12]. In other cases, improving interfaces in flight simulation games at their 360° related locomotion interfaces can make them promising. They are fundamental elements in games, as well as spatial orientation or navigation tasks. Many developers devise alternatives in an attempt to minimize the effects of cybersickness, such as the design of hands-free locomotion interfaces with full rotation and tilt-based translation [13].

8 Conclusion

The research made it possible to have a deeper understanding of the gears of the ga-ming industry focused on VR, essentially because virtual reality is a gathering of multiple scientific domains rather than a single one. These various areas of research are enhanced by the needs of VR applications. Some of these improvements generally move to the mass market since the cost of development is reasonable. One of the main goals in virtual reality applications is to provide means to immerse the user's senses in an artificial virtual environment (VE) through an interactive experience. A key factor on how this interactive immersive experience is successful refers to the sense of presence. Another factor is the ability to simulate environments that exist in our physical world, makes the virtual reality system for games to be chosen among players, to the point where game producers develop highly realistic graphics, such as first person shooter games (FPS).

Although VR is over 50 years old, there have been many failed attempts in the period, until in recent years, from the last decade there has been an intensification in device-related research, often thanks to the creativity of game producers in creating thinking platforms the maximum immersion provided to the user. And the gaming industry has expanded the immersion barrier, especially with VR. Due to being naturally followed by ardent fans of technology, the gaming industry determines the trends of the times to come, specifying the requirements of each technology feature implemented in the systems so that they can be constantly improved as the capacity of their hardware components increases, whether they aimed at the platform or VR games.

Acknowledgments. This essay was the result of the combined efforts of the SIDIA Solution Team, the Black River Studios game team and the UX & Design team. It is also important to highlight the company's performance in supporting and promoting the research and development of systems that are present in the main technology products in the domestic market. We thank Samsung Eletronics da Amazonia Ltda., as part of the results presented in this study were obtained from Project VR/AR Apps, financed by the company under the Law 8387 (art.2)/91. For all the people involved in this project, our sincere thanks.

References

1. Desai, P.R., Desai, P.N., Ajmera, K.D., Mehta, K.: A review paper on oculus rift-A virtual reality headset. Int. J. Eng. Trends Technol. V **13**(4), 175–179 (2014). https://doi.org/10.14445/22315381/ijett-v13p237. ISSN 2231-5381
2. Sachs, G.: Virtual and augmented reality: understanding the race for the next computing platform (2016). http://www.goldmansachs.com/our-thinking/pages/technology-driving-innovation-folder/virtual-and-augmented-reality/report.pdf
3. Bouvier, P., Sorbier, F., Chaudeyrac, P., Biri, V.: Cross benefits between virtual reality and games (2008). https://www.researchgate.net/publication/236260040_Cross_Benefits_Between_Virtual_Reality_And_Games. https://doi.org/10.5176/978-981-08-8227-3_cgat08-26
4. Freina, F., Ott, M.: A Literature Review on Immersive VR in Education (2015). https://www.researchgate.net/publication/280566372_A_Literature_Review_on_Immersive_Virtual_Reality_in_Education_State_Of_The_Art_and_Perspectives
5. LaValle, S.M.: Virtual Reality. Cambridge University Press, Cambridge (2017). http://vr.cs.uiuc.edu/vrbooka4.pdf. University of Illinois
6. Kirner, C., Kirner, T.G.: Evolução e tendências da realidade virtual e da realidade aumentada. Symp. Virtual Augmented Reality **13**, 10–25 (2011)
7. Silva, A.R., Clua, E., Valente, L., Feijó, B.: First steps towards live-action virtual reality games (2016). http://seer.ufrgs.br/index.php/jis/article/view/63117
8. Gaming history: Dactyl Nightmare 1991 (2014). https://www.arcade-history.com/?n=dactylnightmare&page=detail&id=12493

9. Gaming history: Grid busters 1991 (2013).https://www.arcade-history.com/?n=grid-busters&page=detail&id=12498
10. Zachara, M., Zagal, J.P.: Challenges for Success in Stereo Gaming: A Virtual Boy Case Study (2009). https://www.researchgate.net/publication/220982585_Challenges_for_success_in_stereo_gaming_a_Virtual_Boy_case_studyDOI10.1145/1690388.1690406
11. King, G., Krzywinska, T.: Tomb Raiders and Space Invaders: Videogame Forms and Contexts. London; New York: New York: I.B. Tauris Publisher: I.B. Tauris; Distributed in the U.S. by Palgrave Macmillan ISBN: 1845111087
12. Tan, C.T., Leong, T.W., Shen, S., Dubravs, C., Si, C.: Exploring Gameplay Experiences on the Oculus Rift (2015). https://www.researchgate.net/profile/Chen_Si14/publication/299441373_Exploring_Gameplay_Experiences_on_the_Oculus_Rift/links/56f761d408ae95e8b6d2bfc3.pdf. https://doi.org/10.1145/2793107.2793117
13. Hashemian, A.M., Riecke, B.E.: Leaning-Based 360° Interfaces: Investigating Virtual Reality Navigation Interfaces with Leaning-Based-Translation and Full Rotation (2017). https://www.researchgate.net/publication/317008262_Leaning-Based_360_Interfaces_Investigating_Virtual_Reality_Navigation_Interfaces_with_Leaning-Based-_Translation_and_Full-Rotation. https://doi.org/10.1007/978-3-319-57987-0_2
14. Psotka, J.: Educational games and virtual reality as disruptive technologies. Edu. Technol. Soc. 16(2), 69–80 (2013)
15. Lucas, S., Mateas, M., Preuss, M., Spronck, P., Togelius, J.: Artif. Comput. Intell. Games (2012). https://doi.org/10.1109/TCIAIG.2014.2339221
16. Frade, B., Alexandre, B., Sousa, P.: Desenvolvimento de um jogo Sério com uso de Realidade Virtual Aplicado ao Ensino de Matemática (2015)
17. Lustig, J., Toiviainen, A., Nikku, I.: Management Control Systems in Game Industry (2016)
18. Higgs, P., Cunningham, S.: Creative industries mapping: where have we come from and where are we going? Creative Ind. J. http://portal2.ntua.edu.tw/~dc/files/F04_3.pdf. https://doi.org/10.1386/cij.1.1.7_1
19. Caves, R.: Creative Industries: Contracts Between Art and Commerce. Harvard University Press, Cambridge (2001). https://doi.org/10.2307/3094879
20. Annual Report 2015 Activision Blizzard Inc. http://investor.activision.com/common/download/download.cfm?companyid=ACTI&fileid=887600&filekey=BE853918-329D-4E90-ABDC-E669E9D097B9&filename=Activision_Blizzard_2015_Annual_Report.pdf
21. Malone, T.W.: Towards a theory of intrinsically motivating instruction. Cogn. Sci. 4, 333–369 (1981). https://doi.org/10.1207/s15516709cog0504_2
22. Malone, T.W., Lepper, M.R.: Making learning fun: taxonomy of intrinsic motivations for learning. In: Snow, R.E., Farr, M.J. (eds.) Aptitude, Learning and Instruction: Cognitive and Affective Process Analysis, vol. 3, pp. 223–252. Erlbaum, Hillsdale (1987)
23. Utman, C.H.: Performance effects of motivational states: a meta-analysis. Pers. Soc. Psychol. Rev. 1, 170–182 (1997). https://doi.org/10.1207/s15327957pspr0102_4
24. deStrulle, A.: Effects of virtual reality on learning at a science exhibit. In: Tettegah, S., Calongne, C. (eds.) Identity, Learning and Support in Virtual Environments, pp. 87–118. Sense Publishers, Rotterdam (2009)
25. Psotka, J.: Immersive training systems: virtual reality and education and training. Instr. Sci. 23(5), 405–431 (1995). https://doi.org/10.1007/BF00896880
26. BNDES (2015). Mapeamento da indústria brasileira e global de jogos digitais
27. Prata, W., Miyagawa, M.: Highlander Report (2017)
28. Finding Monsters VR App on Oculus Store. https://www.oculus.com/experiences/gear-vr/1011054248914698/
29. Rock and Rails VR App on Oculus Store. https://www.oculus.com/experiences/gear-vr/1239388509475291/

Cinematic Narration in VR – Rethinking Film Conventions for 360 Degrees

Michael Gödde[1](✉), Frank Gabler[1], Dirk Siegmund[2](✉),
and Andreas Braun[2]

[1] Hochschule Darmstadt, University of Applied Sciences, Darmstadt, Germany
m.goedde@videoreality.de
[2] Fraunhofer Institute for Computer Graphics Research IGD,
Darmstadt, Germany
frank.gabler@h-da.de,
{dirk.siegmund,andreas.braun}@igd.fraunhofer.de

Abstract. The rapid development of VR technology in the past three years allowed artists, filmmakers and other media producers to create great experiences in this new medium. But filmmakers are, however, facing big challenges, when it comes to cinematic narration in VR. The old, established rules of filmmaking do not apply for VR films and important techniques of cinematography and editing must be completely rethought. Possibly, a new filmic language will be found. But even though filmmakers eagerly experiment with the new medium already, there exist relatively few scientific studies about the differences between classical filmmaking and filmmaking in 360 and VR.

We therefore present this study on cinematic narration in VR. In this we give a comprehensive overview of techniques and concepts that are applied in current VR films and games. We place previous research on narration, film, games and human perception into the context of VR experiences and we deduce consequences for cinematic narration in VR. We base our assumptions on a conducted empirical test with 50 participants and on an additional online survey.

In the empirical study, we selected 360-degree videos and showed them to a test-group, while the viewer's behavior and attention was observed and documented.

As a result of this paper, we present guidelines which suggest methods of guiding the viewers' attention as well as approaches to cinematography, staging and editing in VR.

Keywords: VR film · 360-degree video · VR storytelling · Cinematic narration

1 Introduction

Virtual Reality (VR) is an established technology, particularly in gaming applications. Now that the corresponding content and technologies are becoming accessible for a vast number of users, people start to consider VR as a new media form with a plethora of new possibilities for entertainment, industry, art, communication, tourism and much more. While VR primarily seems to be the perfect medium for games, filmmakers begin to explore it as a new medium to tell stories. This includes both, computer-generated VR

© Springer International Publishing AG, part of Springer Nature 2018
J. Y. C. Chen and G. Fragomeni (Eds.): VAMR 2018, LNCS 10910, pp. 184–201, 2018.
https://doi.org/10.1007/978-3-319-91584-5_15

experiences and filmed 360-degree films. However, it turned out that planning and shooting a film in 360 degrees does not work the way it does in normal movies. The viewer takes the place of the camera and can choose freely where to look. This brings a high risk that he might miss parts of the action because he focuses on something not relevant to the plot. Likewise, if the pacing is wrong, he can become either bored or completely overwhelmed by a scene. Many of the established techniques of filmmaking like editing or dolly-shots can even be distracting when applied to VR film. The established filmic language does not seem to work anymore when applied to VR and 360-degree films.

VR filmmakers are already eagerly experimenting with solutions involving rather artistic approaches, but there is little scientific research yet on those specific issues.

In the scope of this study we subsume filmed 360-degree films under the term VR film, although there are technical differences. We consider cinematic narration in VR as the toolset of methods and techniques, which enable the filmmaker to guide the viewer through the scene and the narrative. Hence, this study takes a comprehensive approach to the topic, putting the various aspects into context with each other. Initially, we determined six major challenges for cinematic narration in VR:

1. Guiding the viewers' attention to the relevant story elements
2. Choosing the role of the viewer between an active participant and a passive observer
3. Choosing the right place for the camera, the action and story elements and what consequences this has for seated viewers
4. Balancing spatial and temporal story density
5. Rethinking Framing
6. Rethinking Editing

We approached these challenges by examining already applied methods, comparing approaches in other media forms, conducting an empirical test with 50 participants, an online survey and by making connections to other fields of research. Section 2 briefly summarizes the related work on VR film and current challenges for VR filmmakers. In Sect. 3 we introduce guidelines for cinematic narration in VR that make it easier to deal with the challenges mentioned above. In Sect. 4 we present our user study and its results, which was conducted to verify the assertions of the guidelines.

2 Theoretical Background and Related Work

Research on the specific topic of cinematic narration in VR was rare until 2017. Since then, several studies have been published. The issue of guiding the viewers' attention has been examined in several studies. The effects and effectiveness of diegetic and non-diegetic attentional cues in VR have been compared and evaluated [2, 3]. Brillhart introduced the Probabilistic Experiential Editing (PPE) as an editing concept for VR film [4]. Reyes [5] discussed a "Screenwriting Framework for an Interactive VR Film", which provides the dramatic structure of the hero's journey in interactive VR and 360-degree films.

To get a better understanding of VR as a medium and how film can be implemented in it, it is useful to look at research in many other areas such as film, games, theatre, narratology and human perception. Therefore, the preceding study [1] made a broad examination of the related topics: The VRs high chance of creating a feeling of presence has been explored, based on the Two-Level Model of Spatial Presence, introduced by Wirth et al. [6]. This presence, in which the viewer locates himself in the scene, is one of VRs greatest strengths, but also one of the biggest challenges for storytelling in VR. If the viewer feels part of the scene, his role also needs to be considered in the story [1].

As he might feel and react like in a real-world situation, it can have a strong impact on his perception and interpretation of the VR scene. This is for example reflected by the effect of proxemics in VR. Depending on the zones of interpersonal distance in which a character is placed around the camera, it has direct emotional effects on the viewer [7]. Regarding proxemics, Pope recommended the use of theatre techniques for staging in VR [7].

Furthermore, when feeling presence, a viewer may expect more agency in the virtual environment. If this agency is restricted, like in a non-interactive 360-degree film, it can have a negative effect on the feeling of presence [8]. On the other hand, if agency is given i.e. in an interactive VR experience, it can become difficult for the storyteller to maintain the narrative structure. In game studies this is a much-discussed issue that high viewer/user agency and a pre-scripted narrative can contradict each other. Ruth Aylett coined this issue the "narrative paradox" [9].

3 Guidelines for Cinematic Narration in VR

Based on the research of related work and preceding studies, we approached solutions for our six initial challenges:

3.1 Guiding the Viewers' Attention to the Relevant Story Elements

A filmmaker cannot know for sure where a viewer is going to look. Generally, the VR experience should give the viewer the freedom to choose his viewing direction. Forcing the viewers' attention to a specific element destroys immersion, thus contradicting the great potential of VR. Despite this, a filmmaker needs to make sure that the story is not missed by the viewer. Fortunately, he can influence this by implementing attentional cues that guide the viewers gaze to the relevant parts of the scene. There are several methods to guide the viewers' attention. However, if an attentional cue is to be seen, it must be made sure that it is within the viewer's field of view (FOV). Combining different attentional cues and even distributing a surplus of cues in the scene can increase the chances of guiding the viewers' attention. In the user study, we focused on the following diegetic attentional cues:

- **Gazes.** Faces attract our attention. Therefore, glances of the characters can work as attentional cues. Gazes of one or more characters in a specific direction are most likely to be followed. This way they are useful to guide the viewer's attention to a place beyond his current FOV.

- **Motion.** Motion in a scene strongly attracts the viewers' attention. Less motion in the scene leads to a better recognition of individually moving objects. Motion is particularly efficient at attracting attention in the peripheral vision. If the camera is moving, chances are high that the focus of attention will stay on the direction of movement.
- **Sound.** 3D sound is highly effective for guiding the viewer's attention. Mono sound sources can make the viewer search for the sound source. Sound is especially effective, when combined with visual cues.
- **Context.** The story itself can affect the expectations of the viewer and thus also his gaze. If there is anticipation that something is about to occur with a certain scene element, then it will most likely attract and keep the viewer's attention. By arousing and/or belying expectations, context related cues can create suspense.
- **Perspective.** The space and perspective can guide the viewer's attention. Just like in paintings, parallel lines are usually followed with the gaze to a vanishing point. Large, salient objects are usually tried to be captured as a whole. Objects, very close to the viewer attract generally more attention than similar objects which are further away.

In the scope of this study, we did not examine all possible cues. Other important cues are contrast, lighting, signs and signals [1].

3.2 The Range of Viewer Roles. Active Participant or Passive Observer?

The role of the viewer has to be considered carefully in every VR and 360-degree film. The viewer takes the position of the camera so he does not look at the scene from outside but is actually *in* the scene. The role which a viewer plays in the scene is crucial for his or her experience of it. There are generally two possible situations:

1. The viewer is only an observer with no connection to the scene
2. The viewer is part of the scene

The two situations are quite distinct and have a huge impact on the experience. Therefore, a filmmaker needs to define the role of the viewer very clearly. Making the viewer part of the scene is what utilizes the full potential of VR, although there might be situations in which this is not wanted. Both concepts have pros and cons. The following table illustrates the consequences on the experience (Table 1).

Table 1. Features of active and passive VR experiences

Viewer is part of the scene	Viewer is observer
Active experience/"Lean Forward"	Passive experience/"Lean Back"
Interaction possible and expected	No interaction
High involvement	Lower involvement
High potential for a feeling of presence	Lower potential for a feeling of presence
Story might fade into background	Emphasis on narrative
More control for the viewer	More control for the storyteller

Most of the effects in the left and the right column contradict each other (c.f. Narrative Paradox). It is important to consider the advantages and disadvantages that come with the two different concepts. The strongest argument to make the viewer become part of the scene is the higher probability for a feeling of presence to occur.

3.3   Placing the Action and Story Elements

The positioning of the action is very important. To exploit the whole potential of the 360-degree space, action could be placed all over the scene. However, it needs to be considered that many viewers watch 360-degree movies while seated. The online survey illustrated that VR is expected to be as interactive as possible, but when it comes to (VR) film, people still seem to see it as a rather passive medium in which they sit back and consume, just like they are accustomed to with the classical lean back medium film.

Therefore, one should attempt to place primary story elements in the front of the scene, in relation to the initial viewing direction (IVD) or to the seating alignment respectively. The test results showed that the IVD is accepted as the "correct" viewing direction for both sitting and standing viewers, and the action is usually anticipated to begin there. Hence, the attention usually goes back to the IVD after the orientation phase, except when an attentional cue leads to a potential point of interest (POI) somewhere else (Fig. 1).

The figure above illustrates this concept [1]. In the front 180-degree, story elements can be placed at any time. The closer the elements come to the back (blind spot), the less they should stay there. Hence, the main events, relevant to the plot should mostly happen in the front. However, secondary story elements can and should be placed all over the scene. This way, standing viewers can enjoy the full potential of 360-degree spatial storytelling in VR, while seated viewers do not have to crane their necks to follow the plot.

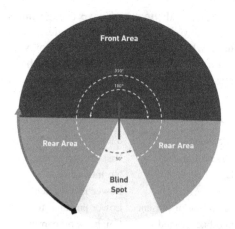

Fig. 1. Extended staging for seated VR-viewers

This concept is a compromise in favor of the seated viewer. It limits the creative possibilities in some situations. If a filmmaker wants people to experience his film while standing, for example because the narration needs him to walk around in the scene, it is recommended to give this information to the viewer prior to the experience.

However, placing story elements at the blind spot can be used in terms of narration, for example to surprise the viewer with elements he did not see before. Also, for standing viewers it can make sense to begin the experience in one direction and to begin the action in the opposite direction. The viewers have then already seen everything that is located in the starting direction and are less likely to return to it. This consequently increases their focus on the story elements in the new direction.

3.4   The Balance of Spatial and Temporal Story Density

In game design, environmental storytelling is a common term for a narrative that unfolds in the space of the scene, rather than being presented to the viewer in a linear fashion through time. Referring to VR experiences, Unseld coined the term *Spatial Story Density* [11] to define the amount of story elements that are arranged in the space of a scene simultaneously. We contrast Unselds spatial story density with the temporal story density, or simply the pace of the scene. We assume that a viewer can only follow a narrative sufficiently when temporal and spatial story density are aligned with each other.

Figure 2 illustrates this coherence: The blue bars represent primary story elements. It is assumed that all elements must be comprehended to understand the plot. The orange line represents the mental effort required by the viewer in order to comprehend the plot. With high temporal story density, narratives are fast paced, with high spatial story density, many narratives are happening simultaneously. Mental effort increases, when temporal or spatial story density is high. In the figure above, the viewers have more time to capture the story elements when they happen simultaneously. Temporal and spatial story density are separated in that scene.

Figure 3 shows the effect of excessive concurrent temporal and spatial storytelling during a moment of a scene. It becomes impossible for the viewer to keep track of all things happening around, the mental effort exceeds a certain threshold, and the scene

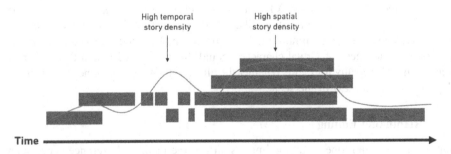

Fig. 2. Schematic representation of temporal and spatial story density during a VR-film. The blue bars represent story elements with any visual or auditory information, the orange line represents the viewer's mental efforts. (Color figure online)

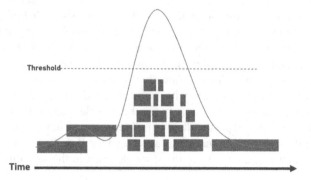

Fig. 3. Mental efforts accumulate and can exceed a threshold when spatial and temporal storytelling is too high.

just overwhelms the viewer. Consequently, the viewer is confused, misses some of the narrative elements and cannot comprehend the plot anymore.

Therefore, it is very important to design the narration with a balanced spatial and temporal story density, so that the viewer is neither bored nor suffers from sensory overload.

3.5   Rethinking Framing

VR covers 360 degrees of the scene, so the typical framing as in normal cinema is not possible anymore. The framing is determined by the FOV and the viewing direction. The latter is constantly changing with the viewer's head movement. The human FOV is usually confined by the human field of vision but current HMDs further limit the FOV to around 110 degrees. This mirrors approximately the binocular field of view in which we can perceive depth by means of stereopsis.

In VR, framing and camera position correlate with each other even more than in normal film. If the mise-en-scène cannot be changed flexibly around the camera, the choice of the camera position might be the only way to compose the image. In order to create a pleasing experience, it is advisable to stage the action around the camera. The influence of the distance between an object and the viewer/camera should always be to be considered. If a character in VR comes very close to the camera, this cannot be considered as a simple magnification, like a close-up. Instead, it has a direct effect on the viewer's experience. A filmmaker should be aware of proxemics when creating the experience. Closeness of virtual characters could, for example, frighten the viewer or make him feel empathy for them. Whether the effect will be positive or negative usually depends on the context of the scene.

3.6   Rethinking Editing

Jumps in space and time break the immersion and the feeling of presence, since such experiences do not exist in reality. Especially if the feeling of presence is intended in a VR film, it is preferable to avoid cuts.

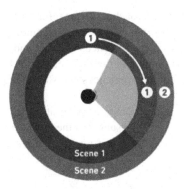

Fig. 4. Probabilistic experiential editing, according to J. Brillhart

However, there are techniques to guide the viewer more intuitively from one scene to another. Crossfades and fades to black are a much safer method for changing the scene. This way, the viewer can prepare for the change. However, they also have disadvantages as they slow the pace down and generally indicate a transition between two scenes.

We successfully tested Brillharts concept of probabilistic experiential editing (PPE): The most salient points of interests in two consecutive scenes should be aligned to present the viewer the next relevant element (Fig. 4): Element 1 is moving in the scene from left to right. The editor assumes that the viewer will follow element 1 with his gaze. After the cut to scene 2, the viewer is directly looking at element 2.

Although element 2 is presented to the viewer, he might still need to orientate in the new scene. Therefore, action relevant to the plot should not begin right at the beginning, even if the viewer already knows where the action would most likely begin.

Generally, orientation views weaken the initial attention to the POIs. Strong POIs that are closer to the viewer or in which an action is anticipated can suppress the orientation views to a certain degree. In order to increase the probability that a viewer looks at an in-point at the beginning of a shot, several in- and out-points can be placed in the shot. However, there should preferably be fewer out-points than in-points.

Since 2017, VR filmmaker have begun to use hard cuts more courageously. It can be assumed that people are getting more accustomed to cuts in VR and consider them less distracting and immersion breaking. In the end, this is also a matter of visual habit.

4   User Study

In order to verify the numerous assertions, which have been made in the previous chapter, we conducted an empirical viewer test with 50 test participants (TP) and an additional online survey with 88 online participants (OP). TP were 62% male and 38% female. Of the TPs, 64% were between 18 and 29 years old.

In order to additionally address more VR-experienced users, the online survey was posted in VR related social media groups. The average age of the OPs was older (51% between 30 and 49 years). The objective of the tests and survey was to clarify essential question concerning the attention, perception and comprehension of viewers during VR films, and thereby determine approaches to the afore-mentioned challenges of VR filmmaking. More precisely, this included methods of guiding the attention with sound, visual and context-related cues; the coherence of spatial and temporal story density; the importance of the orientation phase and the IVD; effects of PPE, effects of dolly-shots, differences of seated and standing experiences and story comprehension in scenes with multiple POIs.

As this research took a rather comprehensive approach to cinematic narration in VR, the aim was to integrate several issues into the test design. Furthermore, statistical data was collected to put the expected and unexpected results into a broader context.

4.1   Implementation

The main test consisted of six consecutive 360-degree videos, lasting seven minutes altogether. TPs experienced these on the head-mounted display (HMD) HTC Vive. They were chosen to analyze a number of different situations and to test related assumptions. The test video included only fragments of original videos which were freely accessible on YouTube.

The test had three parts. In the first part, viewers answered some general statistical questions. In the second part, they watched the videos. In the third part, they answered questions about their experience and their comprehension of the scenes. The whole test took approximately 20 to 30 min per participant.

While the viewers watched the videos, their FOV could be followed on a computer screen and the sound could be followed on extra headphones. This way, their attention and reaction to visual and auditory cues was monitored during the whole test. The

Table 2. The test video contained clips from these 360-degree films

Video	Title	Produced by
1	Strasbourg Cathedral[a]	Michael Gödde
2	Gladiatoren im Kolloseum[b]	Terra X Natur & Geschichte/ZDF
3	Invisible. Episode 2: Back in the Fold[c]	30 Ninjas
4	Resonance[d]	Jessica Brillhart
5	Through Mowgli's Eyes Pt. II: Cold Liars[e]	Disney Studios
6	HELP[f]	Google Spotlight Stories

[a]Gödde, Michael. "Strasbourg Cathedral". Produced by videoreality. 2016
[b]Terra X Natur & Geschichte. "360° Gladiatoren im Kolosseum". Produced by ZDF, 2016. Retrieved from https://youtu.be/QugGQIVgNJ
[c]Litwak, Michael. "Invisible – An Original VR Series. Episode 2: Back in the Fold". Produced by 30 Ninjas. 18. November, 2016. Retrieved from https://youtu.be/ M3FO3j2z5Tk
[d]Brillhart, Jessica. "RESONANCE. A Jump VR Video". Produced by Nick Kadner, 5. November 2015. Retrieved from https://youtu.be/qECnb4CT-9c
[e]Disney Movie Trailer "Through Mowgli's Eyes Part II: Cold Lairs - Disney's The Jungle Book" Youtube. Produced by Disney, 15. April 2016. Retrieved from https://youtu.be/ bUiP-iGN6oI
[f]Lin, Justin. "360 Google Spotlight Story: HELP". Produced by Google Spotlight Stories, 18. April 2016. Retrieved from https://youtu.be/G-XZhKqQAHU

Fig. 5. Screenshots of 360-degree films used in the test video. No. 1: video 1, no. 2+3: video 2, no. 3: video 3, no. 5+6: video 4, no. 7: video 5, no. 8: video 6

viewing direction could indicate the attention that a viewer paid to a specific POI. As the viewer's eye movement was not tracked during the test, the FOV only gave an approximate measurement of the viewer's attention. However, research has shown that the face pose follows, with only a minor delay, the eye's looking direction and is hence a reasonable indicator of the visual attention [10]. Especially in scenes in which different strong potential POIs could not be seen simultaneously in the FOV of the HMD, the estimation of the viewer's attention could be expected to be relatively precise.

The participants were divided into two groups. Group A was asked to sit on a simple chair with backrest (no swivel chair) during the first two videos and then to stand up for the remaining videos. Group B was standing from the beginning.

First, 37 true/false conditions were defined (i.e. a specific cue caused attention or did not). The TPs FOV was then observed and the results of these conditions were recorded.

These were then evaluated together with the answers to the 23 questions which were asked (Table 2 and Fig. 5).

4.2   Results

Seated and Standing Position, the Initial Viewing Direction and Its Effects on the Viewers' Attention

For VIDEO 1 and 2, the viewing direction and behavior in a seated and standing position was compared. The test results showed that the attention on a POI behind the viewer is 40% lower when viewers were sitting. In VIDEO 1, less of the seated participants looked around when they heard the voice of a woman standing next to the camera, while the standing participants tried to locate the voice with their view. Once spotted, more than twice of the standing participants were more likely to follow the position of the woman and kept the attention on her (Figs. 6 and 7).

Almost every TP looked up to the cathedral in front of the IVD. It seems that for structures that do not fit in the FOV, the viewer attempts to capture them as a whole. This effect can be used to guide the view through a scene.

In the intro of VIDEO 2 (wooden elevator into the arena), the FOV of both participants is mainly in the front 180 degrees in relation to the IVD. While all sitting participants were looking primarily to the front, this applied to only 72% of the standing participants. Even the standing participants who turned around, eventually turned back to their IVD, even though all sides of the elevator looked exactly the same. Both groups of participants expected the IVD as the "correct" direction in which the filmmaker had oriented them. Therefore, action is anticipated in front of the IVD, at least until any attentional cues prove otherwise. After the gladiators faded in, it became apparent that participants of group B changed their view to the back while viewers of group A mostly looked to the front. For a third of all participants a predominant viewing direction was not recognizable. At the climax of the video, when the emperor appeared at the tribune, far fewer sitting than standing viewers turned their head to the emperor or had already looked into his direction. So even the strong endogenous attentional cue that the gladiators gave (gaze and salutation) could not make half of the group A look into his direction.

While these results were generally expected, their distinctness was still surprising. Especially in the moment when the emperor appears, it was assumed that more seated viewers would have looked at him, despite the inconvenience of craning their neck. Most of test group A perceived the seated position as uncomfortable when they wanted to look around. Consequently, only 12% of this group preferred the seated position during the experience.

However, the first two videos were multiple POI scenes that required the viewer to look around. In contrast, most of the VR films produced today do not demand that the viewer turns to the back, so that sitting in a chair would not restrict him in any way. Consequently, the OPs who had more experience with VR films gave different answers. Only 12.6% preferred VR films when standing to 29.9% when sitting. For 56.3% of the OPs it depended on the film.

Slightly more TPs of group A disagreed (20%) or partially disagreed (36%) that the action should mainly happen in front of the viewer. Potentially the inconvenience of the seated position was not the main reason that they preferred to stand. Instead, the wish to explore the whole 360-degree in a VR experience could be a motivation to

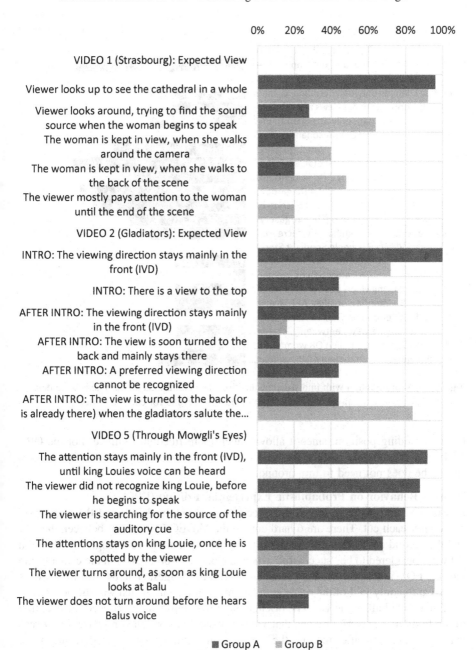

Fig. 6. FOV observation with divided acquisition for group A and B. The conditions on the y-axis were defined as true or false. The x-axis shows the percentage of positive results for each condition

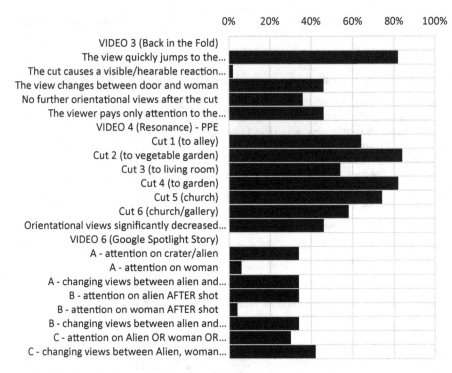

Fig. 7. FOV observation with undivided acquisition. The conditions on the y-axis were defined as true or false. X-axis shows the percentage of positive results for each condition

favor a standing position, since it allows much more freedom to move. For the OPs, 17.4% agreed and 58% partially agreed that the action should be in front of the viewer, so that he does not need to turn around.

Viewers Behavior on Probabilistic Experiential Editing (PPE)

In VIDEO 3 and 4 we observed the effects of hard cuts and PPE and the orientation phase after each cut. There are 6 hard cuts in the VIDEO 3. The shot between the first and the second cut is 18 s long whereas the other shots are 8–10 s long. The PEE of a cut was considered to be "successful" when one of the in-points was in the center of the viewers FOV after the cut. In the second cut after the longest shot, 84% of the viewers looked at the only POI of the scene at the moment of the cut, which was the best result.

For almost half of the viewers, orientation views significantly reduced the attention to the POIs. It was very obvious that viewers needed an orientation phase after every cut. Therefore, just after the cut, the viewers' attention stayed at the POI only for a moment, before they would begin to look around. When no other POIs were found and the whole scene had been explored, viewers turned their head back to the POI from the beginning. This worked best in shot 2, which had only one salient POI in the scene and the viewers had enough time to look around. Most viewers needed around 15 s before they moved their attention back to the POI. This was just the right timing for the cut to the next shot. In the other, shorter shots, viewers did not have enough time for this orientation phase and therefore often did not look at the intended out point at the moment of the cut. Nevertheless, shot 4 worked well, probably because the POI was relatively near and a possible interaction between the two people was attracting more attention. Therefore, viewers were more likely to suppress their orientation views in order not to miss an anticipated action. Hence the cut worked quite well, even if the shot was much shorter than the second one. Cut 5 still worked for 74% of the viewer, even though the preceding shot was short and the POIs were not very close to the viewer. This can be explained with two probable out-points (2 persons) and three in-points (3 persons). Therefore, the multiple in- and out-points increased the probability for this cut to work.

When interviewed after finishing the test, most of the viewers remembered the hard cuts in VIDEO 4 (78%) and VIDEO 3 (59%). The recognition of the cut in VIDEO 3 was surprisingly low, as it was the first hard cut of the experience. At least for two TPs this cut caused noticeable reactions of confusion, which might have been an indication of the breaking of the immersion. However, the low recognitions rather indicate that the cut was not perceived as negatively as expected.

84% of all respondents agreed or partially agreed that hard cuts have a negative effect on the VR experience. Only 5% and 14% did not agree or partially did not agree on that statement. There was no significant difference between the answers of TPs and OPs. That means that hard cuts generally seem to have a rather negative effect on the experience, even when PEE is applied. Although PEE can make the editing in VR much more pleasant for the viewer, the cuts are still perceived as immersion breaking.

Attention During Orientation Phase

VIDEO 5 tested the viewer's attention on a POI with or without an orientation phase. Therefore, we created different versions for each test group: Test group A saw the full length of the video, while for group B the first 17 s were cut out completely and the IVD was turned around for 180 degrees. This way, the viewers of group B saw King Louie right in the beginning, in which he immediately began to speak to them.

In effect, group A paid more attention to King Louie than test group B which did not have the orientation phase. Group B looked around while the giant ape was already speaking to them.

However, King Louie was still the strongest POI in the scene and therefore attracted most of the attention of all viewers. Nevertheless, the lack of time to orientate in the scene clearly weakened the attention to the POI which confirms the results of the previous videos. According to the viewers' attention, the 17 s orientation phase seemed to be a sufficient time to explore the scene and facilitates to keep focus on the action afterwards. The orientation time that viewers needed in VIDEO 4 principally confirms this result.

Still, the orientation phase depends on the complexity of the scene and the viewer himself. For the first VR film of the Oculus Story Studios, "Lost" (2015), director Saschka Unseld measured an optimal orientation phase of 40 s [11]. Although he referred to "Lost", it can be compared quite well with VIDEO 4, as both videos have no salient POIs during the orientation phase.

The gap between Unselds estimation and the test results could be partially explained by the increased VR experience of the test participants, as participants with a

198 M. Gödde et al.

lot of VR experience have proved to need less time for orientation. Especially TPs who have had more than 30 VR experiences before just needed a very short orientation phase. They turned the head around very quickly in the beginning, capturing the whole scene in just a few seconds. Those more experienced viewers usually turned their head back to the IVD already after 5 to 10 s and waited for the action to begin. This was a good indication that they finished their orientation phase, ready to concentrate on the action. Less experienced viewers moved their head much slower and therefore needed more time for the orientation phase or did not turn around at all.

In group A, which faced in the opposite direction to King Louie at IVD, 92% of the TPs mostly kept the IVD until they heard his voice. Therefore, 88% did not see him before he began to speak. When they heard his voice, most of them began to look for the source of the voice. Except for one participant, all viewers in group A found King Louie after a few seconds and turned around with their whole body, accepting the new direction with the primary POI as the new "front" direction. Those results basically confirm again the assumptions regarding the preferred orientation to the IVD as well as the importance of the orientation phase. Also, it proves that mono sound sources that attract the auditory attention of the viewer, make the viewer look around to find this sound source in most of the cases. However, with 3D sound the viewer would have most likely found King Louie much quicker as his voice could have been immediately localized in the scene.

Gaze Interpretation
The second difference in VIDEO 5 for group A was the muted first sentence of Balu, when the bear enters the scene behind the viewer. This way, only King Louie's angry gaze guided the viewer's attention to Balu. Group B instead heard Balu's first sentence simultaneously with the change of King Louie's gaze towards Balu. 96% of group B interpreted the auditory and visual cue correctly and immediately turned around to Balu. In group A, still 72% turned around to Balu, but only because they interpreted and followed King Louie's gaze to Balu without the auditory cue. However, the reaction of group A was significantly slower with a delay of 3 to 5 s. This seemed to be the time that was needed for most participants to interpret the endogenous cue of Louie's gaze. 28% of the participants in group A could not interpret King Louie's gaze in such a short time and did not turn around before Balu's voice appeared, which was 7 s after King Louie looked at Balu. Overall the test results show that gazes can be good endogenous cues but take a long time be interpreted when they come unexpectedly or out of the context of the scene. Likewise, auditory cues that cannot be localized can make the viewer look for the source of the audio. The combination of mono audio sources and gaze has a very high probability of directing the viewers gaze as intended. It proves the effectiveness of diverse attentional cues, especially when addressing multiple senses.

Interestingly, VIDEO 5 also illustrated the strong effect of proxemics in VR. The closeness of the giant ape left such a strong impression that when TPs were asked afterwards, they falsely remembered it as stereoscopic. Likewise, the stereoscopic VIDEO 4 had been perceived as monoscopic, since characters were staged further away from the camera. Although this was a purely subjective impression, it seems that the effects of the technical immersion are sometimes overrated.

Attention in Multiple POI-Scenes

VIDEO 6 had a fast paced narrative with multiple POIs: *An alien crashes down on earth like a meteorite. A woman approaches the crater and picks up a device from the ground. Accidentally she shoots at the alien with the device. The alien becomes aggressive, grows, and starts to chase the woman.* Here we examined the correlation of high temporal and spatial story density and its effects on plot comprehension.

Of the several POIs in the scene, two were important to the plot (woman and alien). Interestingly, all viewers focused on a waste bin, which the camera approached in the beginning. As the camera came closer it seemed to be a strong POI even though it did not have any relevance to the story. It was even more surprising that the fast-moving meteor crashing down on the street was not recognized by some viewers.

After the camera movement stopped, the viewers began to look around to orientate in the scene. More of the viewers focused on the alien (46%) than they did on the woman (14%). The rest of the viewers changed their view between woman and alien at least once. The strong focus on the alien can also be explained with the subtle dolly shot towards the crater. Therefore, more participants looked at the crater compared to the woman. The reactions seen on all camera movements confirmed that the viewer is most likely to face the direction of movement. At least 40% of the viewers recognized both alien and woman as relevant POIs. However, the most important moment for understanding the plot - when the woman picks up something from the street - was missed by most of the viewers as they were focusing on the alien at that moment as a much stronger POI. While focusing on the alien, viewers were unable to see the woman as she was clearly out of the FOV (110 degrees) (Fig. 8).

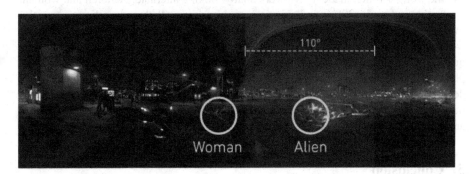

Fig. 8. The alien attracted more attention, so most of the viewers missed the short moment, when the woman picked up the object. (Source: Google Spotlight Story: HELP)

This test proved the importance of carefully planned temporal and spatial storytelling as well as how the FOV has to be taken into consideration when staging the action. More precisely, it has shown that two simultaneous POIs which are relevant for the plot need to be within the FOV of the HMD, as it cannot be expected that viewers will change their view between multiple POIs at the right moment or even at all.

Comprehension of Story
After the test videos, the participants were asked three specific questions on VIDEO 6
to evaluate their comprehension of the plot (Fig. 9).

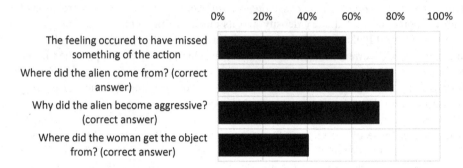

Fig. 9. Viewers comprehension of plot in VIDEO 6

The viewers who did not look at the woman at the important moment when she
picked up the object obviously did not recognize it. Consequently, not even half of the
TPs could answer a question about where the woman got the object from. This would
result in a poor comprehension of the story and plot. At least, 68% of the viewers
recognized that the woman shot a blue beam of light with "something" at the alien and
that it became aggressive because of that. The blue beam visually connected the alien
and the woman which made the viewers finally looking alternately at alien and woman.

In the end, only 20% of all viewers could answer all three questions correctly:
"Where did the alien come from? Why did the alien become aggressive? Where did the
woman get the object from?" 8% of the viewers could not answer any of those
questions. Therefore, the scene failed in the sense that viewers could not follow the
plot. VIDEO 6 is a good example of what can happen when temporal and spatial story
density is too high. Viewers cannot pay attention to several POIs that occur at the same
time or close together temporally. However, only 57% of the TPs felt to have missed
anything in the scene.

5   Conclusion

This study verified several methods which have already been used but not yet proven. It
also introduced new models, such as extended staging for seated VR-viewers and
examined the coherence between temporal and spatial storytelling.

In summary, it can be stated that many of the methods which have already been
applied intuitively by VR filmmakers or that have been developed through several
iterations can be confirmed as reasonable and successful. The results of the previous
chapters might be used as guidelines for VR filmmakers to help them deal with the
challenges of cinematic narration in VR. With no doubt, there is further research
necessary to get a deeper understanding of each particular challenge that comes with

VR filmmaking. Furthermore, we recognize that, as usage increases, not only is the production of VR content evolving, but so also is the viewer's use and perception of this content.

Therefore, future work on this topic might develop its ideas further, and increasingly independent from the context of established media formats.

In a direct comparison of established filmic techniques with the possibilities of VR film, the limitations of VR are still evident. Likewise, there are a plethora of new possibilities and techniques to tell stories in VR. It seems that from an artistic point of view, we do not necessarily need to find a replacement for every established filmic technique. Instead, VR filmmaker should also try to discover a completely new approach to narration in VR films. Ultimately, the real challenge lies not in finding a new way of editing, framing, or other established filmic tools, but in the creation of an unforgettable experience for the viewer which lets him immerse into a story and its virtual world.

References

1. Gödde, M.N.: Cinematic narration in virtual reality - rethinking film conventions in 360 degree. Master's thesis for Leadership in the Creative Industries, Hochschule Darmstadt - University of Applied Sciences, Germany (2017)
2. Rothe, S., Hußmann, H., Allary, M.: Diegetic cues for guiding the viewer in cinematic virtual reality. In: Proceedings of the 23rd ACM Symposium on Virtual Reality Software and Technology (VRST 2017) (2017)
3. Nielsen, L.T., Møller, M.B., Hartmeyer, S.D., Ljung, T.C., Nilsson, N.C., Nordahl, R., Serafin, S.: Missing the point: an exploration of how to guide users' attention. In: 22nd ACM Conference (2016)
4. Brillhart, J.: In the Blink of a Mind — Prologue.medium.com, 12 January 2016. https://medium.com/the-language-of-vr/in-the-blink-of-a-mindprologue-7864c0474a29#.v0gfq5v0x
5. Reyes, M.C.: Screenwriting framework for an interactive virtual reality film. In: Immersive Learning Research Network, Coimbra, Portugal (2017)
6. Wirth, W., Hartmann, T., Böcking, S., Vorderer, P., Klimmt, C., Schramm, H., Saari, T., Laarni, J., Ravaja, N., Gouveia, F.R., Biocca, F., Sacau, A., Jäncke, L., Baumgartner, T., Jäncke, P.: A process model of the formation of spatial presence experiences. Media Psychol. **9**, 493–525 (2007)
7. Pope, V.C., Dawes, R., Schweiger, F., Sheikh, A.: The geometry of storytelling: theatrical use of space for. In: CHI 2017, Denver (2017)
8. Burdette, M.: The swayze effect, 18 November 2015. https://storystudio.oculus.com/en-us/blog/the-swayze-effect/
9. Aylett, R.: Emergent narrative, social immersion and "storification". In: Proceedings of the 1st International Workshop on Narrative and Interactive Learning Environments, pp. 35–44 (2000)
10. Slaney, M., Stolcke, A., Hakkani-Tür, D.: The relation of eye gaze and face pose: potential impact on speech recognition. In: Proceedings of the International Conference on Multimodal Interaction, pp. 144–147 (2014)
11. Unseld, S.: 5 Lessons Learned While Making Lost. Oculus Story Studio, 15 July 2015. https://www.oculus.com/story-studio/blog/5-lessons-learned-while-making-lost/

Walking with Angest: Subjective Measures for Subjective Evaluation in a Walking Simulator Virtual Reality Game

Wilson Prata$^{(\boxtimes)}$, Juan Oliveira, and Paulo Melo

Sidia, Manaus, Amazonas, Brazil
{wilson.p, juan.braga, paulo.melo}@samsung.com

Abstract. The aim of this article is to present and discuss the methodology and the findings of a qualitative evaluation of a Virtual Reality (VR) game. The object of this article is the player satisfaction and the thematic proficiency of game 'Angest', developed by Black River Studio. The definition, particularities and challenges that the platform (Samsung Gear VR) and genre (walking simulators) imposed to this research are presented and discussed in the article, as well how they could benefit one another. The methodology was defined based on these particularities and given research questions. It is explained which references, apparatus and techniques of co-related fields (as HCI and game evaluation) was selected and the reason why. From the evaluation, it was possible to confirm the benefits of qualitative validation for this kind of genre and platform as well what should be used from standard user experience and player experience evaluation, what need to be adapted and what should be avoided.

Keywords: Virtual Reality · Walking simulators · Game evaluation

1 Introduction: Angest, a VR Walking Simulator

Playing a game is an interactive experience. Due to its highly interactive nature there are a series of inputs that the players address to the system. The system, by its turn, process all the players inputs, providing, as response, the outputs that the they should decode. Being able to give inputs means that the player has agency. Being an experience it means that it is more than just the sequence of the small events that compound it, as a narrative it's the sequence of the events that give meaning for the whole and for each of its steps, this characteristic can create a deep immersion in the experience. Because of these two aspects, the agency and the immersion, games can trigger strong social emotions. As any other media, while the person who is consuming it advance through the experience, it is possible that the events unfolded produces angry, happiness, sadness or a sense of belong. "Ultimately, I think the power of a game lies in its ability to bring us close to the subject. There is no other medium that has this power" [1].

The game genre is a key aspect for the immersion and evolvement of the player within the experience. Regarding the capability to construct an emotional bond between the player and the game characters, 'walking simulator' are gaining more and more popularity. A walking simulator is a genre of video game which lacks many of

© Springer International Publishing AG, part of Springer Nature 2018
J. Y. C. Chen and G. Fragomeni (Eds.): VAMR 2018, LNCS 10910, pp. 202–212, 2018.
https://doi.org/10.1007/978-3-319-91584-5_16

the traditional aspects of a game (such as a goal, win/loss conditions, any kind of game system to interact with) despite taking the form of a video game. Walking simulator are low pace games, covering topics about contemplation and exploration with some level of emotional evolvement from the player with the narrative [2].

The elements that defines if a game fits this category usually are too open and wide, what led to many different games being categorized as walking simulator. For that reason, some specialist even defends the term should be avoided [3]. However, as many terms in the mass culture, the term captures well the spirit of the experience despite its lacks of consistency. The game concept is not new, the first game as such date from the 1980's, developed for ZX Spectrum computers, with the title The Forest [4], but walking simulators are gain lots popularity in the recently years (2010's). Firewatch has sold more than 1 million copies [5] and Gone Home [6] have reached more than 250,000 downloads. Each and receive prizes and recognition from the game industry, particularly the specialized critic.

Walking simulators and Virtual Reality games have many common characteristics. Some of these similarities between the platform and the genre are: slow pace, immersive experiences and strong emotional bond. These elements are deliberated decided by the game designer, the professional responsible for defining all core elements of player experience and how well the game supports and provides the type of fun players want to have [7]. To do so, game designers had a set of tools that can be used to provide a good and immersive experience for the players: avatars, first person view, non-players characters and plot twists in the narrative are some of the most common used resources [8]. How successful a game can be in exploring these tools is correlated with the quality of the player experience. Since Virtual Reality is a computer-generated self-contained digital world, consequently, Virtual Reality in a game is another powerful resource for the game designer to provides a richer and deeper player experience for the player because the entire "world" that the game is taken place is under his/her control.

Furthermore, it is possible to say that even the strengths of the walking simulators and the Virtual Reality are so complementary that they obfuscate their weakness. For example, 'slow pace' is one of the main critic for walking simulators, but fast pace is one of the main challenges in VR because too fast pace leads to motion sicknesses, to avoid it, low pace experiences is a recommendation [9]. Other aspect is that walking simulators and VR are about immersion, the journey itself is more important than achieving a specific rank or beat an enemy [1]. Regarding the immersion, a deeper immersion is not dependent of hyper realistic graphics, some walking simulators make use of really simple 3D graphics called low-poly (from low number of polygons, consequently, low details and less hardware demand) and for VR it is an interesting option because its better rendered; high resolution graphics is a currently corner stone for VR performance. Besides been a performance improvement solution, low-poly is also an aesthetic, such as 8 bits games that started as a solution for technological constrains but became a deliberated choice for games. VR and walking simulators are about exploring a space and have an immersive experience, together and well combined they are strong resources for game designers develop meaningful player experiences.

Angest is a Virtual Reality game developed for Samsung Gear VR and distributed in the Oculus app store (Fig. 1). Samsung Gear VR is a headset in which some high-end Samsung mobile devices can be plugged in, transforming the device in a VR platform. Making use of the sensors of the mobile phone, such as accelerometer and gyroscope, it can provide a three degree of freedom VR experience (the user can see the all scenario that appear rendered in the three axes which simulate depth with high fidelity but it is not possible to walk in this scenario) [10].

Fig. 1. Screenshot of Angest.

Angest is a Virtual Reality game that has many of the elements that characterizes itself as a walking simulator. In the game, the player control Valentina, a cosmonaut that perform a series of ordinaries activities in a spaceship with the company/guidance/ vigilance of Konstantin, an artificial intelligent robot that interacts through voice and text information that appear in monitors fixed in different locations of the space- ship. Nonetheless, the game intentionally lacks lots of elements that normally com- pound the player experience as 'fun to beat obstacles', 'intrinsic reward', 'increase workload' and the premise that 'humans need to be challenged' [1]. Angest provide the opposite experience: there is no big obstacle, on the days that Valentina pass by on the spaceship there is nothing that imped or challenge her on her routine. The activities that are performed are intentionally boring and repetitive, no meaning or fulfillment felling can be extract from them. The narrative becomes more confusing while player advance on it and there is no skill to be mastered or any puzzle to be solved that can explain this confusion. During the game, the burden of a routine, its repetition and inevitability are not a fault or error in game design, in fact, they are exposed and explored as a narrative resource. More than choices the player is presented to open and wide questions that at first sight are addressed to the game character, Valentina, but are generic and intimate enough to be extended to the player.

The Angest particularities arouses some interesting issues. Since 'meaningful choices' is a well-known pillar of good game design, once the choices are not available for the player, do the other decisions in game design compensate this lack? If winning condition is a broadly used paradigm in the game industry, what about the player experience in a game that is not possible to win or to lose?... and for the research perspective, what is the definition of success in a game like this? All of these questions will be carefully addressed in the next item, methodology.

2 Constructing the Object and the Methodology

A game is an artefact, it means that a game is not a given thing, it is result of human practice. This practice itself can have a high or low degree of expertise, i.e., the level of domain of the skill necessary to perform a practice. A high degree of expertise is called proficiency. Concerning the practice of game development, we can point out two kinds of proficiency: 'structural proficiency' and 'thematic proficiency' [11]. The first, structural proficiency, is about the technical execution of the game: the performance of the software on a given hardware, the quality of graphics, absence of bugs, if the 'gulfs of execution and evaluation' [12] are consistent and if the game can sustain the 'magical circle' (the magical circle is a symbolic space, a context in which it is possible to blend fantasy and reality [13]). Structural proficiency is about the sharpness and capability of game development team to execute what was planned. The former, thematic proficiency, is about the quality of what was planned: gameplay, narrative, atmosphere, how the sound track is appropriate to game pace etc. Once we agree that it is necessary a well-done structure to sustain the "magical circle", structural proficiency could be comprehended as the structure that maintain the circle and thematic proficiency is about what is inside the circle. For the objectives here underlined, the evaluation will focus on the thematic proficiency of the player experience.

An evaluation consists on extracting the relation between two things. Those things are identified as variable, the control of certain variables to inquiry the relation and causality of those independent variables with dependent variables make clear the relation between them. When we talk about Game evaluation, the most commons variables are: the player satisfaction and pleasure in play the game. The evaluation itself is called 'playtest': an experience of playing a game to evaluate it structural and/or thematic proficiency.

To proper evaluate the player experience it is necessary to have, maintain and update a formalized research procedure to conduct the playtest [14]. The objective of a playtest is to highlight and make evident player's opinion and attitudes regarding the game being tested [15]. Playtest helps to validate if the player perception of the game corresponds to that what was planning by the game designer, it helps to check if this communication is fluid. To keep the research objectives pretty clear for the game development team, the researcher should make an document that summarizes all the issues regarding the game. This document is called 'research plan' and it describes the procures and the rationale behind the approach chosen for the playtest. To do so "research plan" must contain the research questions, the hypothesis and the overall methodology that was choose for this research.

2.1   Defining Research Questions

Defining research questions is the starting point of many researches. A research is conducted to answer the questions and doubts that the researches think is worth solving and reply. These questions help to clarify what is the challenge to be solved and why the research is being conducted, its object and what is the problem that need to be explained. Angest was developed by Black River Studio, the game division of Sidia, a Research and Development institute in Brazil [16]. The research was conducted by another division of Sidia, UX & Design, though the research was an in-house demand. Because the research team and the development team do not interact till the final playtest of Angest, we spent almost one week building an alignment to understand and keep clear all the doubts that should be addressed in playtest. The "clients" of the research were the game designer and game developer of Angest, thus it was conducted many rounds of interviews with the game designers and game producers in charge of the game and sporadic talks with other members of the development team.

Angest is a game that was planned and executed based on a series of assumptions that, by the perspective of the development team, justified the elaboration of the game. Exposing those assumptions was the first step to start the research plan. Many of them were related with the opportunity of walking simulators in a Virtual reality platform (as presented in item 2). Based on the decisions made for the game, the game designer and the producer wanted to confirm: (i) if the game fits in walking simulator game category for players that appreciate this game gender; (ii) if players are able to identify that the game has many ends and how does it motivate people to play the game again; (iii) if the game was deep enough to make the player reflect about his/her own life. With these clarification, it was defined that the test scope should addressed participants' perception of game style, value and quality; game playability (mechanics, immersion, interactions, etc.) and overall game satisfaction; consequently, other topics that impact on the player experience were keep out of scope, such as acquisition process (search, download, etc.), Game set-up (install, paring controller, etc.) and adherence for players out of the target player profile or game niche.

2.2   Defining Research Techniques

Research techniques are like tools that the researcher chose in order to solve the research problem. As exposed previously, in this walking simulator, the reflection and questioning of the subject's own condition, discomfort and anguish is part of the narrative. Heuristics are nor useful for walking simulators. The difficult aspect of evaluating walking simulators can be easily perceived when the researcher tries to apply a heuristic evaluation as the one proposed by Korhonen and Koivisto (2006) [17]. The game objective is not clear and, since it is not clear the end point or the victory conviction, tracking player progress is also complicated. Rewards, strategy and feeling of control (regarding structural proficiency) sometimes make no sense as well the questions related with repetitive, boring tasks or stagnation of the game. It implies that most of the legitimated and well-known game's evaluation methodology and techniques do not fit the need of the faced challenge here because the satisfaction that walking simulator players pursuit is not exactly the same the one that most of the games usually offer (explosions, beat an enemy, solve a puzzle, etc.) To select out tools we kept in mind that subject approaches work better to identify attitudes and preferences of gamers, consequently it was expected that the interview after the playtest would be the main instrument to answer the research questions.

2.3 About Player Profile

Recruiting participants was a central aspect for test success, a short questionnaire was developed to guarantee it. Besides social demographic questions, the main question was about the game style of the participant. Walking simulators are strong biases games, in other words, or people hate or people love it [3]. The recruiting questionnaire asked the favorite games of the potential participant and if he/she had played some walking simulators, these questions showed to be appropriate to validate the player profile. As expected, most of the players that like walking simulators included them in their top three favorite games. Another characteristic to be confirmed was 'previous experience playing VR', we didn't want non-VR players because the fascination with the technology should obfuscate some aspects and characteristics of the game. As a 'nice to have' we search for players that actively comment on forums and discussion groups about games, critical players that can be categorized as 'extreme users'.

After the interviews with the game development team it was clear that the evaluation should focus on player satisfaction, players' perception of game immersion, narrative and quality. In our research we had to take into account some aspects regarding the game playability and structural proficiency (mechanics, graphics, interactions, etc.) However, once the structural proficiency was considered as a secondary aspect for player satisfaction and most of its issues were validated by Sidia's Q&A team, we decided not focus so much on these technical issues. Based on that, we design a couple of question for the user after he/she finishes the game session, those are the questions: (i) what was your first impression of the game? (ii) how easy to understand was the game; was it intuitive, interesting and immersive? (iii) was the game becoming easier to play while you were advancing on it? (iv) there was something confusing or that was not clear for you? (v) what would you change in the game? (vi) what should be maintained in a hypothetic new release of the game? (vii) did you think that the game could have another ending? (viii) what parts of the game do you liked the most… and what do you liked least? (ix) would you play this game again, why?

2.4 Running the Playtest

The playtest was set in São Paulo, during three days of August of 2017 in a VR arcade (Fig. 2). We had 14 participants from which 12 had validated data, that number had been proof to be appropriated for a qualitative research with a homogeneous group [5]. All participants were gamers with more than 8 years of 'serious' gameplay. They have had previous experience with more than one game console, read reviews online and follow games news. Based on the request and details provide by the game development team, the participants sample were fully representative of the game target audience.

The playtest followed the overall structure of most of user validation tests: a moderator and a facilitator welcomed the participants; they were requested to sign a

Fig. 2. Playtest of Angest.

nondisclosure agreement form; the instructions were presented for the participants; they played the game; there was the debriefing and then each participant was thanked for its participation. As described before, the test focused on the thematic proficiency of the game, so it was decided to do not use the "think aloud" verbal protocol because it could break the "magic circle".

The planning, execution and report of the results took four weeks altogether. The methodological walkthrough was: (i) understand the challenge and define research questions; (ii) define the player profile; (iii) select methodologies; (iv) define a chronogram; (v) recruit participants; (vi) set-up playtest location, documentation and devices; (vii) run the playtest; (viii) collect the data; (ix) analyze the data; (x) partial report; (xi) final report and results presentation.

Until this point in this article we had presented and discussed the main issues from the items 'i' to 'vii'. In the next part, we are going to present the evaluation results and then discuss, based on our experience with Angest, the effectiveness of the research technique chosen, its weakness and strengths, when evaluating walking simulator VR games.

3   Findings

Here we are going to present the findings of the playtest as input to discuss the efficiency and efficacy of proposed methodological approach to proper respond how to evaluate a virtual reality game experience.

The responses given in the debriefing session were recorded for late being tabulated for the analysis of player experience. On average playtest sessions lasted 60 min. Maximum gameplay was 124 min, minimum was 22 min. From 20 participants, 10 finished the game during the playtest. The data from debriefing could be analyzed through a bottom-up or top down approach. In the first one, the categories of analysis were defined before the data consolidation (there are some categories in game evaluation that enables it approach). Due the intrinsic complexity of the game and the particularities of VR and walking simulators, it was decided to user a bottom-up categorization. Players comments were categorized in the following categories: The debriefing session was helpful to identify user satisfaction and to respond the research questions. There were no critical or major bugs in the playtest what justified the choice of evaluating the thematic proficiency with less focus on the structural proficiency. The players enjoyed the Russian retro futuristic atmosphere, the look and feel of the characters (Kostantin and Valentina) and the philosophic nihilist atmosphere. The sounds effects were an important element in the experience and player satisfaction as well.

The participants pleasure the scenario, interactions and the activity outside the spaceship. The movements in the game was by teleport points: the player was located in one point at time, he/she can't move around the scenario step by step, when he/she can move by gazing in some specific points that works as teleport anchors, the gaze has a loading, it fade-out and them fade-in in the new position. It was not high pleased by all the participants however it was not disappointing. In fact, it was a game design decision to avoid motion sickness, since no player reported it, the decision has been shown correct. In Aeroponics (a scenario of the game) the leaves grew in same sequence what is not the common behavior of a plant; when the player change water PH it doesn't change anything (the plants wouldn't die or grow faster). In VR, it is important that everything that look real and afford to behave as something in the real world should have to behave this way, if not, there should be a good explanation.

About gameplay, the was some minor problems. In players opinion, there was some information that was not explicit enough and it was not possible to retrieve the instructions from Konstantin. A dyslexic player informed that it was had trouble to read the 'russian-nish' typeface that was used to spaceship signalization. The storytelling was another good point of the game, the small hints about Valentina nature and the nightmares were well-used storytelling resources. Nightmares were like another virtual reality inside the virtual reality of the game, it was a good way to present new scenarios for a narrative that happens inside a spaceship. The tests that Valentina should perform during her routine were a good way to address the philosophical existentialist questions to the player. However, it's know that walking simulators are criticized for its low pace, but in Angest there were some critics about the narrative being too fast, the players also would like to have more logs to read and more tests to perform. Some players realize that the game has different ends based on the choices made in the test and the way that the interaction with Konstantin were build. According with the give feedback, it encourages most of the players to play the game again to confirm this assumption.

Immersion is a key feature in VR and in walking simulators and Angest had proof that explored it well. Samsung Gear VR is the least potent of the main commercial VR hardware. The processor of Gear VR is the mobile phone and even the most powerful ones are far behind of other VR computers or video games. Even so, there were lots of feedbacks saying that the game was as good as any other VR games and far better than the average VR mobile game. The overall evaluation of the game was positive, besides the problems with some instructions there were no complains. The doubts were about specific points in the narrative that were intentionally open to interpretation.

Nonetheless, the assumptions were not fully validated or refuted. About the first one, some of them need a more deeply research. Angest was clear recognized as a walking simulator, the participants really appreciated the graphics, sounds and the atmosphere of the game. The mechanics and the characters were much praised. The first interaction at the lab was the unique pain point but it didn't interfere in the engagement or immersion. Some users reported that they suppose that the game could have many ends and that the choices during the game could determine which will be the end. However, this point was not clear for all. The participants that had this guess reported that they probably will play the game again.

Now that the game had been released it is possible to confirm that most of the topics related to the thematic proficiency were high praised, even for those that don't appreciate the game itself, these players recognized that they were not the target profile and that the game was a niche game [19, 20]. The game has a score of 4.4 of 5 in Oculus play store. One objective aimed by the game development team was that through the game the player could reflect about his/her own life. Some players recognized that the questions were in fact addressed to them, but they did not reflect too much about it. Comments on Oculus store reinforce many of the findings presented here.

4   Conclusion and Next Steps

VR games evaluation is not a simple thing. It's not simple because it's not well-known. It's not well-known yet nor because it's complicated but because it's new. Although, there are many procedures that can be used from other areas as game evaluation and user experience evaluation to help in this effort. For example, as in most of the social science researches, the methodology used to evaluate our object (player satisfaction of the game Angest) was constructed based on research questions that identified by the research team together with the "client" (game development team). Most of the research questions and doubts were directly related with the player satisfaction and subjective perception of the plot and the overall experience. Besides that, there were identified other questions and issues that could impact the player experience. Other point that was stressed by the game development team was the category of the game, a walking simulator, and many choices in game design due to VR potentialities and limitations.

After the research questions were identified, the next challenge was to choose a methodology that could handle all these issues. The usage of a research document to organize the test, detail its structure and deliverables had been proved good enough to map the player satisfaction and to reply most of the doubts. The debriefing session was a key point and open questions design specific to the game proposal had worked well with the players. The feedback was natural and riche. The participants profile was very specific and the research focused on the thematic proficiency of the game, with this focus, the number of participants was adequate, as indicated by most of the bibliography about qualitative research. Because there are no clear, specific and dedicated categories to evaluate VR walking simulators, open questions are more indicated than closed questions. The experience of playing a deeper VR game provides complex emotions in the players and enables each one to construct its own perspective of that experience. That's why bottom-up analyses are recommended in this kind of evaluation.

The test set-up for VR games is another technical challenge, specially one running in Samsung Gear VR. The hardware sometimes overheats and shutdown the device, disturbing the experience and the test. It didn't happen in this playtest because of the quality of software but it is a common constrains. There was the possibility to cast the screen during the game session to a TV but it is not a simple set-up and there was concerns about hardware and battery performance. We decided to drop out this possibility to reduce the attrition in the experience.

The feedback from the development tem about the evaluation was positive. There was a lot of assumptions that could be confirmed and the report was used to justify some market and promotion decisions. The choice to develop a walking simulator for VR, a huge risk at first sight since walking simulator still niche games, had been confirmed as a good strategic decision. The comments on Oculus store and other specialized reviews where very similar and reinforced the research findings. The research also helped to set the expectation of game success to the high manager team.

This kind of research demands planning, organization and mainly the alignment between the development and the research team. It was extremely necessary that the research team understood the game proposal, mechanics and the intentions of its creators. VR is not as familiar as many other platforms as desktop and mobile but it is growing fast in many different areas, not only games. It is important that games and UX researches be prepared to deal with this technology and its characteristic and we hope that this article helps new VR researches to be prepared for it. Our perception is that when the object of research is a new challenge in a given field the first procedure is to return to the basis of the field, review its fundamentals and check how relevant they remain. In case, we selected techniques from the User Experience and from Game Design area. There is a double gain with this strategy, (i) first, however the basis of a field sometimes is not enough to exhaust all the doubts in a research, they are open and generic enough to enable the research to start to address the problem; (ii) second, it is possible to clarify how much the object of the research still belonging to that given field of knowledge and; (iii) if this relation is too weak, keep it clear the need of news approaches and methods. Human-computer interaction provides guidance and tools to start to approach any object that emerge from the interaction between a human and a computer. It's possible to apply it from classic computer desktop interactions to Virtual Reality and wearable devices. About the second and third topic, one clear example is the arise of other specific areas of the human-computer interaction in recent years, such as User experience and Player experience with focus on digital games. There are still relations between these new areas of knowledge and the one from where they emerged, they have a common ground at the same time that each one justifies itself as a proper research area due its particularities. The know-how of the former field is necessary for the new areas, yet it is not sufficient to solve the new challenges. Probably, in a near future, VR game evaluation will have it owns methods and apparatus. Till there, researches like this depurates legitimated methods and apparatus of co-related fields to help this construction.

References

1. Moyama, et al.: Games user research (GUR): our experience with and evolution of four methods. In: Isbister, K., Schaffer, N. (eds.) Game Usability: Advice from the Experts for Advancing the Player Experience. Elsevier Inc. (2008)
2. PC Games: Talking 'walking sims': The Chinese Room's Dan Pinchbeck on the pointlessness of the debate. https://www.pcgamesn.com/dear-esther/dan-pinchbeck-interview-are-walking-sims-games. Accessed 15 Jan 2018
3. Kill Screen: Is it time to stop using the term "walking simulator"? https://killscreen.com/articles/time-stop-using-term-walking-simulator/. Accessed 15 Jan 2018
4. Eurogamer: The origin of walking simulators. http://www.eurogamer.net/articles/2016-11-13-the-origins-of-the-walking-simulator. Accessed 15 Jan 2018
5. PC Gamer: Firewatch has sold more than one million copies. https://www.pcgamer.com/firewatch-has-sold-more-than-one-million-copies/. Accessed 15 Jan 2018
6. Engadget: Gone Home finds 250K sales, most on Steam. https://www.engadget.com/2014/02/06/gone-home-finds-250k-sales-most-on-steam/. Accessed 15 Jan 2018
7. Lazzaro, N.: The four fun keys. In: Isbister, K., Schaffer, N. (eds.) Game Usability: Advice from the Experts for Advancing the Player Experience. Elsevier Inc. (2008)
8. Rolling Stones: Why VR Is the Next Step for Walking Simulator Games. https://www.rollingstone.com/culture/news/vr-is-the-next-step-for-walking-simulator-games-w445685. Accessed 15 Jan 2018
9. Pocket Gamer: Why virtual reality's killer app is the walking simulator. http://www.pocketgamer.co.uk/r/Virtual+Reality/Oculus+Rift/feature.asp?c=67566. Accessed 15 Jan 2018
10. Samsung: Gear VR. http://www.samsung.com/global/galaxy/gear-vr/specs/. Accessed 15 Jan 2018
11. Gamasutra: The Two Kinds of Proficiency in Games, and the Two Kinds of Criticism. https://www.gamasutra.com/blogs/MatthiasZarzecki/20130227/187453/The_Two_Kinds_of_Proficiency_in_Games_and_the_Two_Kinds_of_Criticism.php. Accessed 15 Jan 2018
12. Norman, D.: The Design of Everyday Things: Revised and, Expanded edn. Basic Books, New York (2013)
13. Isbister, K.: How Games Move Us. iBooks (2017)
14. Nørgaard, M., Sørensen, J.R.: Organizational challenges for user research in the videogame industry: overview and advice. In: Isbister, K., Schaffer, N. (eds.) Game Usability: Advice from the Experts for Advancing the Player Experience. Elsevier Inc. (2008)
15. Isbister, K., Schaffer, N.: Game Usability: Advice from the Experts for Advancing the Player Experience. Elsevier Inc., New York (2008)
16. Black River Studio. http://blackriverstudios.net/angest/. Accessed 12 Jan 2018
17. Bernhaupt, R.: User experience evaluation methods in the games development life cycle. In: Bernhaupt, R. (ed.) Game User Experience Evaluation. HIS, pp. 1–8. Springer, Cham (2015). https://doi.org/10.1007/978-3-319-15985-0_1
18. Mandryk, R.: Physiological measures for game evaluation. In: Isbister, K., Schaffer, N. (eds.) Game Usability: Advice from the Experts for Advancing the Player Experience. Elsevier Inc. (2008)
19. Skarredghost: Angest review: a surreal experience for Gear VR. https://skarredghost.com/2017/09/27/angest-review-surreal-experience-gear-vr/. Accessed 12 Jan 2018
20. Mapinguari Nerd: Review: Angest – uma breve análise de tempo | memórias de um old gamer. http://mapinguanerd.com.br/angest-uma-breve-analise-de-tempo-memorias-de-um-old-gamer/. Accessed 12 Jan 2018

AI-Based VR Earthquake Simulator

Ryota Suzuki[1(✉)], Ryoki Iitoi[2], Yue Qiu[2], Kenji Iwata[1],
and Yutaka Satoh[1,2]

[1] National Institute of Advanced Industrial Science and Technology,
Tsukuba, Japan
ryota.suzuki@aist.go.jp
[2] Tsukuba University, Tsukuba, Japan

Abstract. We propose a novel AI-based VR earthquake simulator that can easily simulate an arbitrary real indoor environment. The user first scans any room using inexpensive RGBD sensors, such as Kinect sensors. The automatic model generator then detects objects in RGBD data using a deep-learning-based classification method and generates 3D models given appropriate physical characteristics, such as centroid and friction. In this manner, users can obtain appropriate content for earthquake simulation simply by scanning the room. The content can provide the user with a real experience in the event of an earthquake in the room.

Keywords: AI · Earthquake simulator · 3D reconstruction · VR
Deep-learning

1 Introduction

Huge destructive earthquakes regularly occur throughout the world. The U.S. Geological Survey reported that huge earthquakes, of magnitude greater than 7.0, occurred 164 times over the last ten years[1]. In Japan, a recent huge earthquake, which is known as the April 2011 Fukushima Earthquake, struck the east coast of Japan. Although the resulting tsunami devastated Fukushima, other areas, such as Tokyo, which were not hit by the tsunami, were damaged by the earthquake itself. Shelves were toppled, windows were broken, and traffic came to a standstill.

Earthquake simulators are very important for disaster prevention training, especially in earthquake-prone countries. Considering such circumstances, several systems that allow people to experience simulated earthquakes have been produced. In Japan, although an Earthquake simulation vehicle, which consists of a room and mechanism to physically simulate huge earthquakes, is well known, most people have little opportunity to take advantage of the simulation vehicle. With the recent growth of VR technology, several VR earthquake simulation systems have been proposed [1–3]. However, developing three-dimensional VR content for such systems is expensive.

Allowing people to experience a simulated earthquake in their own home is thought to be an effective means of clarifying potential risks and providing knowledge to avoid

---

[1] Searched by https://earthquake.usgs.gov/earthquakes/map/ (referenced in Jan. 15, 2018).

© Springer International Publishing AG, part of Springer Nature 2018
J. Y. C. Chen and G. Fragomeni (Eds.): VAMR 2018, LNCS 10910, pp. 213–222, 2018.
https://doi.org/10.1007/978-3-319-91584-5_17

dangers such as items falling on beds. Based on their experiences, people may then rearrange furniture to reduce potential dangers or make evacuation plans. As such, the development of a low-cost system with which users can construct high-quality 3D models of their surroundings is strongly desired.

We herein propose a novel AI-based VR earthquake simulator that can easily simulate arbitrary real indoor environments. Users can experience simulated earthquakes in VR rooms constructed by scanning users' rooms with low-cost RGB-D sensors. The rooms are reconstructed in VR space as several planes with high-resolution surface textures. Moreover, objects in the rooms are recognized by a recently proposed deep-learning based object detection technique and translated into 3D models. Finally, the system simulates earthquakes in the VR room in real time by applying a physics engine. In order to evaluate the system, we conducted a user experience experiment using VR earthquake content and found that users can experience earthquakes in their virtual rooms without feeling artificiality.

2 AI-Based VR Earthquake Simulation System

In this section, we explain the proposed AI-based VR earthquake simulation system. An overview of the system is shown in Fig. 1. The system process is executed as follows:

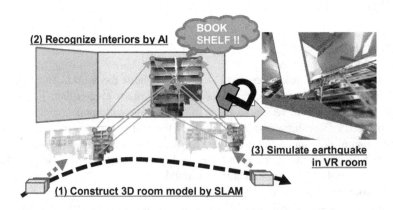

Fig. 1. Overview of the system.

1. Scan the entire room using a multi-RGBD sensor system.
2. Calculate the 3D point cloud of the room using the SLAM framework.
3. Separate the point cloud into planes.
4. Apply object detection to each texture of the constructed planes.
5. Project the reconstructed room via VR.
6. Simulate an earthquake by physical movement.

2.1   Scanning and Mapping

We use RGBD sensors, which are less expensive compared to other 3D scanners, such as LIDAR, to scan the entire room. Moreover, visual simultaneous localization and mapping (SLAM) is commonly used to obtain a 3D model using RGBD sensors [4]. However, since the angle of view is narrow, scanning the entire room is far more labor intensive. Furthermore, in the case of a room with few textures, since feature points such as SURF cannot be sufficiently observed, localization estimation via SLAM fails and a distorted map if generated. In order to address these problems, we developed a multi-RGBD sensor system, as shown in Fig. 2. By arranging calibrated RGBD sensors on the circumference, it is possible to simultaneously acquire all of the surrounding RGBD data. By moving through a room with the sensor and performing SLAM, it is possible to easily acquire the 3D space of the entire large room (see Fig. 3). In the present study, we use nine XTION sensors, the range of depth of which is up to eight meters, so that the sensors can sufficiently scan the indoor environment. As compared with the case of using a single RGBD sensor, the accuracy of localization estimation is improved, and hence point cloud data with less distortion can be obtained. The system also works outdoors in conditions of weak daylight and in areas that are not too wide for the sensors to capture depth data.

2.2   Interpretation into Planes

Although a dense undistorted point cloud can be acquired, the point cloud is insufficient for immersive interactive VR. The system must recognize the structure and shape of scanned rooms in order to enable proper physical simulation. The computational cost required for an interactive system to visualize numerous points is high. In order to deal with these problems, we implemented a framework by which AI interprets point cloud 3D space as planes.

First, meshes between locally nearest points are constructed as local planes, as shown in Fig. 4. The set of points to be connected was acquired from the connectivity of the original images when they were scanned. These planes were then reconstructed into global planes by applying a statistical plane estimation method considering the similarity between local planes based on the distances between the orientations and positions of the planes. Moreover, the texture of each plane was also created by merging partial RGB images corresponding to the plane. Pixels taken from nearby or in front of the plane at the time of scanning have priority with respect to selection. As a result, each of the walls, floors, and ceilings was automatically recognized as an unseparated plane with a texture, as shown in Fig. 5.

2.3   Object Detection

The methodology of interpreting the point cloud as planes mentioned in Sect. 2.2 enables AI to perform high-quality object recognition by applying a deep-learning framework. Recently, advances in deep learning, such as advances in two-dimensional image object recognition, have been realized. As a result, we can obtain unseparated textures of entire planes, to which high-performance deep-learning object detection can

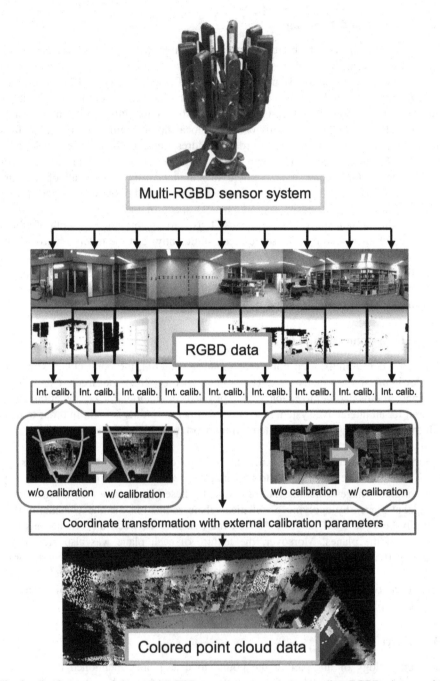

Fig. 2. Configuration of the multi-RGBD sensor system. A surrounding RGBD view can be acquired immediately so that the entire room can be localized and mapped easily without distortion.

(a) Feature point matching by RANSAC.

(b) SLAM result. The red line indicates the localization estimation of sensor trajectory.

Fig. 3. SLAM by multi-RGBD data. Loop closing is successful and the map is not distorted. (Color figure online)

be applied. In the present study, we use YOLO v2 [5], which is a state-of-the-art real-time object detector, to detect the interiors of items such as clocks, chairs, and books, as shown in Fig. 6.

3 VR Earthquake Simulation

The system can generate an interactive virtual room, which is a projection of a real room. The system then simulates earthquakes using a physics engine. Physical simulation is computationally expensive, which makes real-time operation difficult. However, in recent years, highly powerful graphics processing units (GPUs), which enable

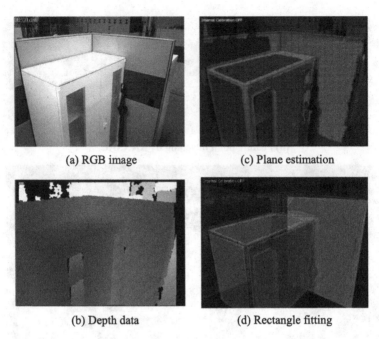

(a) RGB image   (c) Plane estimation

(b) Depth data   (d) Rectangle fitting

Fig. 4. Converting a point cloud into planes. Local planes are constructed from depth data, and global planes are then robustly estimated from these local planes.

Fig. 5. Recognition result of room structure. The entire room is reconstructed with high-quality textures.

Fig. 6. Example of a detection result for a reconstructed plane texture.

acceleration of general parallelizable calculations, have been produced. In the present study, we use the PhysX physics engine, which is maintained by NVidia.

In the simulation, we use real earthquake data measured by an accelerometer-type seismograph of the Japan Meteorological Agency[2]. In order to use the time sequential acceleration data in PhysX, we convert accelerations to displacements by applying an IIR filter that reflects the frequency response characteristics[3] [6] and then animate the floor plane. PhysX can simulate the propagation of energy from an earthquake to items on the floor.

4 Evaluation

We conducted an experiment to evaluate user experience associated with the proposed VR earthquake simulator. We evaluate the proposed system from the viewpoints of (i) the effectiveness of the reconstruction for providing a comfortable and immersive VR environment and (ii) the ability to frighten users using only visual cues. Based on the results of this experiment, we simulated a 3D VR earthquake, in which horizontal planes were automatically recognized as boxes or tables and were then made to topple onto the floor. Moreover, items that were recognized as "books" by the AI were made to topple to the ground when a strong earthquake was simulated (see Fig. 7).

---

[2] Open access available at http://www.data.jma.go.jp/svd/eqev/data/kyoshin/jishin/index.html (in Japanese) (last confirmed in Jan. 23, 2018).

[3] Program code for calculating IIR filter parameters available at http://www.mri-jma.go.jp/Dep/st/member/akatsuma/program_acc2seisogram.c (last confirmed in Jan. 23, 2018).

Fig. 7. Example of simulated scenes, in which a large degree of up/down translation of the floor can be observed.

4.1   Condition

We surveyed eight subjects, who were university students, technical fellows, or researchers who worked in the same office building every day, and were thus familiar with the constructed environment, allowing for an immersive virtual environment. The subjects reported various levels of experience with immersive VR.

In the present study, we use HTC Vive, a VR system that implements a head-mounted display (HMD) and its position tracker, and head direction and position can be reflected in VR space in real time.

During the experiment, the subjects experienced a simulation of the April 2011 Fukushima Earthquake. We used the data observed at Okeya Town, in Miyagi Prefecture, where the magnitude of the maximum acceleration was 479.1 cm/s^2. The parameters for calculating the IIR filter are as follows: the period of the seismograph is 6.0 s, the damping constant is 0.55, and the sampling interval is 0.01 s.

4.2   Protocol

First, we asked each subject to go into a room other than the room that was to be reconstructed. An HMD was worn by each subject while sitting on a fixed stool. A table was placed in front of the stool in order to secure each subject's initial body orientation, but we provided no instructions as to body or head orientation. Based on the initial orientation from the chair, a bookshelf was placed in the VR room so as to enhance the user experience. Before starting the simulation, we told the subject that we would stop the experiment whenever s/he reported any discomfort. After starting the experiment, the earthquake was simulated for approximately two minutes.

After the experiment, we asked each subject to answer a questionnaire with a seven-point scale (see Table 1). Table 2 shows the questions contained in the questionnaire. The reason for the response to each question was also asked to be provided in the form of free comments.

4.3   Result

The questionnaire results are shown in Fig. 8. Most of the subjects were in agreement on all questions. The results of Q1 and related comments, such as "The room seemed familiar." or "The room seemed neither realistic nor fictional." indicate that the proposed method was capable of constructing high-quality 3D spaces that people were

Table 1. Seven grades for each question.

7	Definitely agree
6	Agree
5	Somewhat agree
4	Neutral
3	Somewhat disagree
2	Disagree
1	Definitely disagree

Table 2. Questions posed in the questionnaire.

Q1	Did the 3D environment seem realistic while not shaking?
Q2	Did you feel that the shaking of the room was realistic?
Q3	Had you considered earthquake countermeasures in your daily surroundings before the experiment?

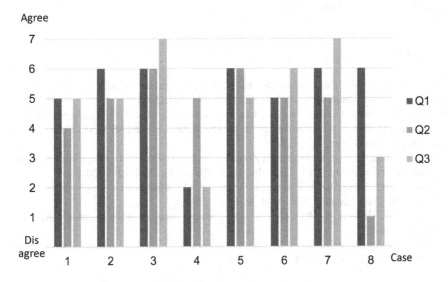

Fig. 8. Questionnaire results.

used to seeing in daily life. The results of Q2 and related comments, such as "The shaking and changing of view felt realistic" or "That was what I feel unpleasant during a real earthquakes", indicate that the system could properly simulate earthquakes and that the VR space did not adversely affect the simulation of the earthquake. However, the response of subject #8 to Q2 was "definitely disagree", and the subject commented that "The quake was slow. It seemed as if the camera were shaking." There are several causes to be considered: (i) the original earthquake consisted of primarily long-period wave components, (ii) very-short-period waves were filtered and were converted from accelerations to displacements, and (iii) camera positions in the VR system were fixed with respect to the HMD and were not influence by the earthquake. Item (i) indicates that the subject felt as if they were experiencing a real earthquake. Item (ii) could be solved by adding extra-short-period waves. Item (iii) could also be solved by applying a physical human head model to the physical simulation. Items (ii) and (iii) can be easily implemented in the proposed system.

5   Conclusion

We proposed a novel earthquake simulation system that can easily simulate arbitrary, real, indoor environments by using AI technologies. The system can recognize and reconstruct real 3D spaces and project them into VR spaces into which users can become immersed and interact with. We developed a system for scanning an indoor environment and reconstructing the environment by planes with high-quality textures and recognize interiors on the textures by applying deep-learning object detection. A physical simulation of an earthquake was performed in the reconstructed VR space. The proposed system can be extended to various kinds of VR experiences that reflect and reconstruct real circumstances.

References

1. Li, L., Zhang, M., Xu, F., Liu, S.: ERT-VR: an immersive virtual reality system for emergency rescue training. Virtual Reality **8**(3), 194–197 (2005)
2. Sinha, R., Sapre, A., Patil, A, Singhvi, A., Sathe, M., Rathi, V.: Earthquake disaster simulation in immersive 3D environment. In: Proceedings of the 15th World Conference on Earthquake Engineering, p. 9 (2012)
3. Gong, X., Liu, Y., Jiao, Y., Wang, B., Zhou, J., Yu, H.: A novel earthquake education system based on virtual reality. IEEE Trans. Inf. Syst. **E98-D**(12), 2242–2249 (2015)
4. Taketomi, T., Uchiyama, H., Ikeda, S.: Visual SLAM algorithms: a survey from 2010 to 2016. IPSJ Trans. Comput. Vis. Appl. **9**(16), 11 (2017)
5. Redmon, J., Farhadi, A.: YOLO9000: better, faster, stronger. arXiv preprint arXiv:1612. 08242 (2016)
6. Katsumata, A.: Recursive digital filter with frequency response of a mechanical seismograph. Q. J. Seismol. **71**, 89–91 (2008). (in Japanese)

Immercity: A Curation Content Application in Virtual and Augmented Reality

Jean-Daniel Taupiac[1,2], Nancy Rodriguez[1,2(✉)], and Olivier Strauss[2]

[1] Capgemini Technology Services, Bayonne, France
[2] LIRMM, University of Montpellier, Montpellier, France
{jean-daniel.taupiac,nancy.rodriguez,
olivier.strauss}@lirmm.fr

Abstract. When working with emergent and appealing technologies as Virtual Reality, Mixed Reality and Augmented Reality, the issue of definitions appear very often. Indeed, our experience with various publics allows us to notice that technology definitions pose ambiguity and representation problems for informed as well as novice users.

In this paper we present Immercity, a content curation system designed in the context of a collaboration between the University of Montpellier and CapGemini, to deliver a technology watch. It is also used as a testbed for our experiences with Virtual, Mixed and Augmented reality to explore new interaction techniques and devices, artificial intelligence integration, visual affordances, performance, etc. But another, very interesting goal appeared: use Immercity to communicate about Virtual, Mixed and Augmented Reality by using them as a support.

Keywords: Virtual Reality · Augmented Reality · Curation content

1 Introduction

The Montpellier Laboratory of Informatics, Robotics and Microelectronics (LIRMM) and Capgemini Company work together on a PhD project which focuses on the study Virtual, Augmented and Mixed Reality environments for training. In this context, one of the first difficulties encountered was to communicate about these technologies definitions. Indeed, it soon became clear that definitions posed understanding, ambiguity and representation problems as well for informed than novice interlocutors.

It seemed interesting, in the scope of this project, to disseminate a technology watch destined for colleagues, partners and customers. Today, content curation is principally made on specialized websites and blogs, social or business-social networks as Twitter [1] or LinkedIn [2] as well on dedicated platforms and tools as Scoop-it [3] or Paper.li [4].

Thereby, by seeking to find a way to diffuse the technology watch in an original manner, we conceived a multi-technological application which manages the idea of communicating on these technologies by their use. Our system, **Immercity,** aims to centralize information from the technology watch within a unique 3D representation, a city. By interacting with each building, the user has access to a particular kind

© Springer International Publishing AG, part of Springer Nature 2018
J. Y. C. Chen and G. Fragomeni (Eds.): VAMR 2018, LNCS 10910, pp. 223–234, 2018.
https://doi.org/10.1007/978-3-319-91584-5_18

information (news, scientific papers, videos), the city becoming in this way a metaphor of a blog or website main menu. The city 3D representation is available in the Virtual and Augmented Reality clients by using a web browser or by installing an application on a smartphone. This multi-technological aspect supports the communication main objective with a secondary one: illustrate differences between these technologies.

In this paper, we introduce our work in progress regarding the development of Immercity. We introduce the general principle of the application and we detail the prototypes as well as our work concerning visual cues for selection and navigation. Finally, we present the first experiment we have run and discuss the results obtained and the improvement perspectives they bring.

2 Background

In the context of this work, it seems important to remind that an Augmented Reality system respects three essential rules [5]:

- Combine real and virtual
- Interact in real time by an interactive way
- Be recorded in 3 dimensions.

Augmented Reality aims to complete the user perception by adding virtual information. Mixed Reality refers to a continuum connecting physical world to virtual world, including therefore two aspects [6]: Augmented Reality and Augmented Virtuality, which consist of enriching virtual world by adding real elements.

[7] propose a technical definition of Virtual Reality as *a scientific and technical field exploiting information technologies and material interfaces in order to simulate in a virtual world the performance of 3D entities which are in interaction in real time, amongst themselves and with one or several users in a pseudo-natural immersion through sensorimotor channels.*

By relieving previous works [8, 9] extends this definition by determining a fundamental principle, the "perception, cognition, action" loop: in any Virtual Reality application, the user is in immersion and interaction with a virtual environment. He perceives, decides and acts in this environment.

As far as we know, the idea of communicate by these technologies in this specific use case has not been exploited yet. However, some interesting initiatives designed to communicate on these technologies by example exists, like the VENTURI [10] system. One of the studies of this project aims to understand what users think about a new concept of AR gaming by using several prototypes.

Curation means to collect and organize resources with value added by an expert in order to lead to greater understanding and insight of information. The Information Visualization domain provides some examples of collection presentation in Virtual Reality. In their CyberNet project, Dos Santos et al. [11] implemented a city metaphor for NFS data visualization. The advantages highlighted by the authors are that a city implies a natural hierarchy (districts, blocks, streets, and buildings) which allows interesting possibilities for hierarchical visualization.

Sparacino et al. [12] designed City of News, an immersive and interactive web browser. It is a dynamically growing urban landscape where information, i.e. URL's content, is mapped on skyscraper's frontages. The city is organized in urban quarters and each quarter is linked to a specific thematic. It also evolves and grows organically through exploration: by following a link, the user causes a new city-element creation. Sparacino et al. [13] have early developed Hyperplex, an environment for browsing digital movies. They are structured within a multi-dimensional virtual inhabited building. Each room of the building is associated with specific topics. When a movie content is selected, the background change dynamically by transforming itself according to the content.

In Immercity application, the city is a collection of collections: the buildings are not supposed to represent an information but a collection of information organized by type.

3   The Immercity Application

3.1   Use Cases

As stated before, Immercity aims to be a multi-technological application. Indeed, the targeted users range from Capgemini co-workers to the company partners and customers. Furthermore, the system has to take into account that it can be used in a fixed environment on the workplace as in a mobile context for use on exhibition or conferences.

Following this aspects, several uses cases has been defined for Immercity:

1. On a web browser, the application would allow to display a 3D perspective view of the city and to access the information.
2. In Virtual Reality, the user, equipped with a Cardboard, could explore the city in order to access the information.
3. In Augmented Reality, it would be possible to bring out a 3D model of the city from a visual tag representing its 2D plan. This visual marker, limited in size, can be placed on the back of a business card. The user could then use this tag in order to download the application, and to see the city emerge on 3D.
4. In Mixed Reality, the user visualizes the city which would appear over a planar surface of his environment, or over the same visual tag used in Augmented Reality. He would use his hands to interact with the different objects of the scene. *At present time the Mixed Reality development has not yet started.*

3.2   The 3D City Representation

By interacting with each building, the user would access to the different information available in the technology watch. We choose to link six key buildings to the different kind of information, by their semantics and common use (**Error! Reference source not found.**):

- The School, in which we find information about the different definitions and concepts.

- The Kiosk, presenting the last news on Virtual, Augmented and Mixed technologies.
- The Supermarket, containing a catalog of existing devices, and supporting comparison based on their characteristics.
- The Library, offering access to scientific papers
- The Cinema, giving access to videos and demonstrations.
- The house, allowing to access user's preferences and bookmarks (Fig. 1).

Fig. 1. Immercity key buildings

We choose to place key buildings near each other to increase their visibility and ease exploration of content. Furthermore, it was necessary to find a way to highlight key buildings in order to ease their identification by the user. We discuss these visual cues in the Sect. 3.4.

Prototypes for our three first use cases (cf. Sect. 3.1) have been realized via Unity3D [14], on an eight weeks sprint [15]. The aim was to confirm the technical feasibility of this kind of application. For the city modeling, we choose to keep a low realism level and enhance visual appealing by using a cartoon graphic style.

3.3   Web Browser Prototype

The web browser prototype allows to display a perspective 3D view of the city in a web browser by WebGL (Fig. 2) and to select a building by a mouse click. A fixed camera has been positioned in order to visualize the set of key buildings.

To easily identify key buildings, they are surrounded with a halo which changes its color when the mouse hovers over the building. A tooltip with the name of the building is displayed in the same time.

3.4   Virtual Reality Prototype

The Virtual Reality prototype offers an immersive visualization to users equipped with a cardboard device. It used the Google VR SDK [16] for Unity3D to define the stereoscopic view (Fig. 3).

Fig. 2. Web browser view

Fig. 3. Virtual Reality prototype

To allow navigation while being compatible with different kinds of cardboard devices, we use a visual pointing method. This avoids using cardboard specific physical buttons. The cursor supporting selection and navigation included in the Google VR SDK consists in a small reticle which became wider when it is over an interactive object (Fig. 4).

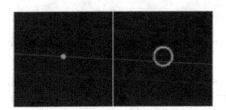

Fig. 4. Google VR SDK cursor

This cursor shows however some limits. During the unit tests, it seemed important to have an indicator of the time needed to point an object before its activation. We suppose that novice users could not directly understand that they have to point for a time in order to be transported to the building. We modified the cursor in order to add a second circle, indicating the loading time necessary for triggering the action (Fig. 5).

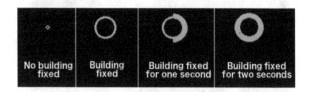

Fig. 5. Immercity cursor

As indicated above, the user is conducted to the building she has selected but she has the possibility of change her direction. The moving method was implemented through the A* Pathfinding API [17]. This library allows to define a graph of allowed footpath in the Unity3D scene (Fig. 6) and then to move from a point to another. This allows us to respect some rules for example to use the crosswalks. The path is calculated according to the A* pathfinding algorithm, which find the short path between the position of the user and the chosen destination.

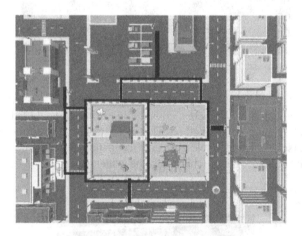

Fig. 6. Allowed paths (in blue) definition (Color figure online)

As in the web browser prototype, we defined a way to highlight key buildings in order to allow the user to recognize them. It consists in positioning a highlight effect over or in front of each key building (Fig. 7).

3.5   Augmented Reality Prototype

In the Augmented Reality prototype, the city is displayed on top of a 2D marker. It has been implemented using Vuforia SDK [18], a library allowing to rapidly creating Augmented Reality applications on Unity3D (Fig. 8).

Fig. 7. Highlighting key buildings

Fig. 8. Augmented Reality prototype

Users can interact with buildings in two different ways. The first one, which seems more intuitive, involved a simply tap on the building. In the second one, we integrate the same cursor than in the Virtual Reality prototype. Key buildings are highlighted in the same way as in the Virtual Reality prototype.

One of the main problems of this prototype concerns the visual marker quality, which will be placed in the back of a business card. The initial idea was to use the city's 2D plan, but this lightly contrasted image has only a few features (detectable points) and obtained a low reliability indication from Vuforia (2/5).

To add more features points we choose to insert a QRCode in the middle of the card. Even if the number of detectable points increased, detection was not robust and the city model was easily lost when the camera explore the peripheral zones of the city where the QRCode is not visible. A satisfying solution was found by drawing the entire marker in black and white and by integrating directly several QRCodes in the city map (Fig. 9). This kind of marker has numerous features, uniformly distributed across the image which allows recognition even when the entire marker is not visible. Therefore it obtained a 5/5 reliability indication from Vuforia.

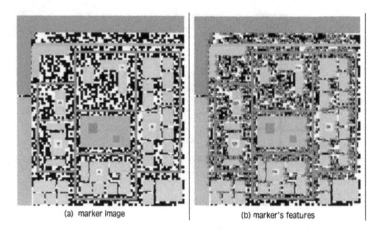

(a) marker image   (b) marker's features

Fig. 9. Visual marker for the AR prototype

4 Experiments and Results

The goal of our experiment was to analyze the user's reactions to prototypes and to assess the validity of the visual cues implemented: highlight of key buildings in the Augmented Reality (AR) and Virtual Reality (VR) prototypes, and the visual cursor supporting navigation for the Virtual Reality prototype.

Therefore, we wanted to verify the following hypothesis:

1. In Virtual Reality, users should prefer to use the loading cursor than the simple one included in the Google VR SDK;
2. In Virtual Reality, users should prefer to directly interact with key buildings more than with highlights;
3. In Augmented Reality, users should find useful the presence of highlights on key buildings.

We didn't include the Web browser prototype in the experiment, its functionalities being covered for the AR and VR prototypes.

4.1 Context and Procedure

The experiment took place in the Capgemini office of Bayonne. The panel consisted of 37 persons, mainly Capgemini employees (90%), 70% men. A majority of them (59%) occupy technical posts (Developer or Technical head). Their age varies from 21 to 59 years old, for an average of 36 years old and with an important part of 20–30 years old (48%). Finally, it is interesting to specify that, for most of them, it was their first experience in Virtual Reality (68%) and Augmented Reality (70%).

Experiments were made on a Samsung Galaxy S7 smartphone and, for the VR prototype, using the Samsung Gear VR (v1) headset.

In order to verify our hypothesis, we have defined four test sets for the VR prototype, one for each combination of cursor and highlights:

1. Simple cursor and pointing on highlights
2. Simple cursor and pointing directly on buildings
3. Loading cursor and pointing on highlights
4. Loading cursor and pointing directly on buildings.

Each participant tested the two prototypes and one combination of the test sets: 1 and 4, or 2 and 3. For the AR prototype only two test sets were implemented, with highlights enabled or disabled. In order to balance the tests, the proposed test sets were alternated from one subject to another.

Two experimental procedures have been defined. In the first one, the VR prototype integrating one test set was tested for about five minutes. Then we asked the user to cite the key buildings she has been identified. After a brief presentation of key buildings, we asked the user to move towards a specific building. This task was repeated once using a different test set. Finally, the AR prototype was tested. In the second procedure, users tested the AR prototype for about 3 min. As before, we asked the user to cite the key buildings she has been identified before a brief presentation of key buildings. Then we asked the user to select a specific building. After activation/deactivation of highlights, the task was repeated. Finally, the VR prototype was presented.

Even if exchanges was directed by a questionnaire (based of the Group Presence Questionnaire [19]), we encouraged subjects to freely discuss during and after the whole procedure in order to collect their impressions and suggestions.

4.2   Virtual Reality Results

Analysis of results allows us to validate our first hypothesis, it is necessary to provide a loading time indicator. On the 27% of subjects which experienced difficulties in finding the way to move, 70% of them had a test set with the simple cursor. This tendency is confirmed when we analyze the preferences expressed by the subjects (Fig. 10). Furthermore, 24% of the subjects express the interest to have a loading time indicator, independently of the cursor type they experienced.

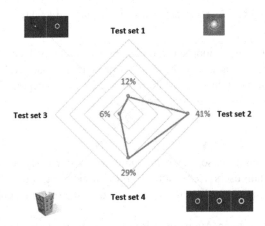

Fig. 10. Users preferences in Virtual Reality

Among the subjects having experienced difficulties in finding the way to move, 80% of them had a test set where it was necessary to select the building directly. Nevertheless, we can notice that subject preferences are rather balance on this point. Indeed, some of them questioned highlights on other criteria (aesthetics, practicality, positioning or visual overload). Nevertheless, this result doesn't allow us to confirm our second hypothesis.

A large part of users (41%) described the prototypes as "fun" and "exciting" but a substantial part of them was not comfortable with the travel technique proposed. The fact of impose a path has not been appreciated (49%), they want to being teleported (22%), move by themselves (14%), stop the movement (14%) or fly (3%). Future research is needed to address these difficulties.

4.3   Augmented Reality Results

In Augmented Reality, the main aspect analyzed for this work concerns the highlight of key buildings. During discussions, 44% of the subjects confirmed the interest of the highlights, independently of the test set they have experienced. Subject preferences are showed in Fig. 11.

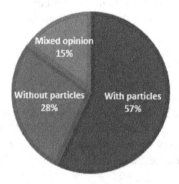

Fig. 11. Users preferences in Augmented Reality

Nevertheless, it seems important to underline that all the subjects having preferred the solution without highlights explained that it brought a visual overload. An animated solution, lighter and more discreet would probably be well accepted. We consider then than our third hypothesis can be validated.

4.4   Perspectives

The interest of a loading cursor has been confirmed in our study. However, it slightly lacks visibility; certain users needed a time before noticing it. It could be interesting to emphasize the loading cursor by a different color than the original cursor on which it is inserted.

As well in Virtual as in Augmented Reality, the necessity of highlighting the key buildings was underlined. By taking into account the results of the experiments, as well as the users remarks and suggestions, it could be interesting to position a "real" animated element floating on top every key building instead a visual effect. In the style of a sign on roof, this animated element would indicate the building by an icon. These elements will allow us to improve the application interaction. Future work will allow users to be able to access to the information, in the form of web pages at the first place, when they interact with a key building.

5 Conclusions

This paper presents Immercity, a content curation application in Virtual and Augmented Reality allowing to structure and share information by using a 3D city.

Prototypes were developed in order to validate the visual cues and pointing implemented, which allows users to identify and move towards key buildings.

The results of our experiments provide insights about the interest and usage of the visual cues for selection and navigation tasks. Future research needs to confirm these results by studying the particular design characteristics which contribute to a more intuitive interaction with the city elements.

References

1. Twitter homepage. http://twitter.com. Accessed 01 Feb 2018
2. LinkedIn homepage. http://linkedin.com. Accessed 01 Feb 2018
3. ScoopIt homepage. http://scoop.it. Accessed 01 Feb 2018
4. Paper.li homepage. http://paper.li. Accessed 01 Feb 2018
5. Azuma, R.: A survey of augmented reality. Presence: Teleoper. Virtual Environ. **6**(4), 355–385 (1997)
6. Milgram, P., Kishino, F.: A taxonomy of mixed reality displays. IEICE Trans. Inf. Syst. **77**, 1321–1329 (1994)
7. Arnaldi, B., Fuchs, P., Tisseau, J.: Traité de la réalité virtuelle, 1st edn, vol. 1 [Virtual Reality Treaty]. Les presses de l'Ecole des Mines de Paris (2003). (in French)
8. Fuchs, P., Moreau, G., Berthoz, A.: Traité de la réalité virtuelle volume 1: L'Homme et l'environnement virtuel, 2nd edn [Virtual Reality Treaty: Human and virtual environment.]. Les presses de l'Ecole des Mines de Paris (2006). (in French)
9. Fuchs, P.: Les casques de réalité virtuelle et de jeux vidéo [Virtual reality and video games headsets], Les presses de l'Ecole des Mines de Paris (2016). (in French)
10. Genevès, P., Layaïda, N., Michel, T., Razafimahazo, M.: Mobile augmented reality applications for smart cities. ERCIM News 98, 45–46 (2014). Special theme: Smart Cities
11. Dos Santos, C.R., Gros, P., Abel, P., Loisel, D., Trichaud, N., Paris, J.-P.: Mapping information onto 3D virtual worlds. In: Information Visualization, pp. 379–386 (2000)
12. Sparacino, F., Davenport, G., Pentland, A.: City of news. In: Ars Electronica Festival, pp. 8–13, Linz, Austria (1997)
13. Sparacino, F., Wren, C., Pentland, A., Davenport, G.: HyperPlex: a world of 3D interactive digital movies. In: IJCAI Workshop on Entertainment and AI/Alife (1995)
14. Unity3D homepage. http://unity3D.com. Accessed 01 Feb 2018

15. Masseport, S.: Prototypage d'une application pluri-technologique en réalité virtuelle et augmentée. [Prototyping a multi-technological application in virtual and augmented reality]. Internship report, Bachelor Engineering in Computer Science, University of Montpellier (2016). (in French)
16. Google cardboard homepage. http://developers.google.com/vr/discover/cardboard. Accessed 01 Feb 2018
17. A* project homepage. http://arongranberg.com/astar/front. Accessed 01 Feb 2018
18. https://developer.vuforia.com/. Accessed 01 Feb 2018
19. Schubert, T.: The sense of presence in virtual environments: a three-component scale measuring spatial presence, involvement, and realness. Zeitschrift für Medienpsychol. **15**, 69–71 (2003)

VAIR Field - Multiple Mobile VR Shooting Sports

Masasuke Yasumoto[1]([✉]) and Takehiro Teraoka[2]

[1] Faculty of Information Technology, Kanagawa Institute of Technology,
1030 Shimo-ogino, Atsugi, Kanagawa 243-0292, Japan
yasumoto@ic.kanagawa-it.ac.jp
[2] School of Media Science, Tokyo University of Technology, 1404-1 Katakura,
Hachioji, Tokyo 192-0982, Japan
teraokatkhr@stf.teu.ac.jp

Abstract. VAIR Field is a mobile virtual reality (VR) system that enables multiple players to play a battle game with multiple mobile devices. By tracking the mobile devices' positions and detecting their rotation and movement, VAIR Field displays images viewed from each player's position on their displays like a head-mounted display (HMD). VAIR Field enables players to immediately play with the VAIR Gun and VAIR Bow without needing instructions. It also enables children under 13 to safely play VR or augmented reality (AR) games because it does not require a HMD. We compared our new VAIR Gun and BOW with a HTC Vive controller, the initial VAIR Gun, and our previous electric bow interface. The new VAIR Gun and BOW mostly realize VAIR Field's concepts of user-friendliness for children, sports-like play, and "feel of things."

Keywords: Tangible interface · Design · VR

1 Introduction

Head-mounted displays (HMDs) offer virtual reality (VR) gaming that exploits visual and auditory senses. For example, "The VOID" [1] is a large-scale VR attraction that enables players to play games while walking around a wide area. However, using HMDs can lead to problems including VR sickness or discomfort due to compression of the head, and HMDs are often not sanitary due to sweat when used by large numbers of people. Also, children under the age of 13 are recommended not to use HMDs as wearing them may cause health problems.

VR devices utilizing senses other than visual and auditory senses have also been developed. Nakagaki's Linked-Stick [2] is a stick-based device that can mimic the motion of someone else using a stick-like tool; for example, a conductor, a baseball batter, and a swordsman. Striker VR [3] is a gun-type device that

---

T. Teraoka—Presently with Department of Computer Science, Faculty of Engineering, Takushoku University.

J. Y. C. Chen and G. Fragomeni (Eds.): VAMR 2018, LNCS 10910, pp. 235–246, 2018.
https://doi.org/10.1007/978-3-319-91584-5_19

can recreate the feeling of shooting a gun. Electric bow interfaces [4,5] use a real Japanese bow with the installation projector or real bows with the mobile laser projector. Moreover, there is also a pregnancy experience system that enables a user to affect the virtual fetus's behavior with gentle or violent movements [6].

We have developed VAIR Field, a mobile VR system that enables multiple players to play a battle game with smartphones. As we prioritize user-friendliness for children, VAIR Field uses smartphones not HMDs to display images since smartphones are lightweight and easy to handle. This allows players to look around and avoid obstacles while handling their device, so they can safely move around without hesitation while they are playing. However, VAIR Field cannot superimpose images of guns and swords on the controller or replace walls and obstacles in rooms with forests or outer space.

Considering these things, we developed VR shooting games that involve using infrared guns, BB bullets, and paint bullets for VAIR Field. In VAIR Field, gun-like and bow-like devices can be used that combine a smartphone, a positional tracking sensor, and a server integrating them. By using VAIR Field, we can implement VR or augmented reality (AR) shooting games with multiple players without HMDs as shown in Fig. 1.

In this paper, we describe VAIR Field and its devices: a new VAIR Gun and VAIR Bow. We also compare the new VAIR Gun and VAIR Bow with the initial VAIR Gun and our previous electric bow interface.

Fig. 1. Depiction of playing VAIR Field

2   VAIR Field

2.1   Concept

VAIR Field is based on three concepts. The first is user-friendliness for children. Thus, it does not use a HMD, which can cause health problems and is often unhygienic. Also, children tend to treat devices roughly, so the device must be robust and difficult to break. Moreover, it must be sufficiently safe to use.

The second concept is sports-like play. VAIR Field is not just a technical demonstration but also needs to offer high quality in terms of appearance, accuracy, response speed, and handleability. Especially, players can be expected to improve their shooting ability by physically handling the VAIR Gun and VAIR Bow.

Finally, the third concept is "feel of things." This means something that physical objects possess the right temperature, feel, hardness, weight, ease of use, and affordance. The VAIR Gun and Bow require sufficient affordance to enable players to understand how to immediately handle them. Of course, interactions such as recoil and reaction when using VAIR devices are also important. For example, the VAIR Gun should be shaped so that the player can understand immediately how to grasp and shoot without instructions and should feel stable, have the right weight balance and hardness, and be comfortable to touch. Also, the VAIR Gun should produce recoil and sound after shooting.

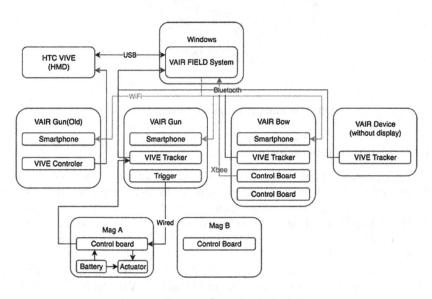

Fig. 2. System flow of VAIR Field

2.2 System

Figure 2 shows the system flow of VAIR Field. VAIR Field consists of a server combining the two VAIR devices (VAIR Gun and VAIR Bow), a HTC Vive tracker, and a Windows Server. Each device consists of the HTC Vive tracker and a smartphone. We use the HTC Vive tracker, which is the best positional tracking sensor, to make VAIR Field sufficiently scalable that multiple players can play. This tracker cannot be used without HTC Vive (which is a HMD), so VAIR Field needs to connect to Windows to access HTC Vive.

Figure 3 shows a minimum floor plan for playing VAIR Field. Multiple players can play with the VAIR devices in any room meeting the requirements of this minimum plan.

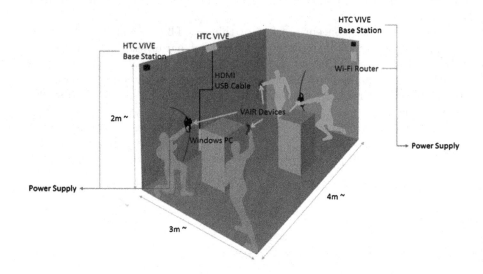

Fig. 3. Minimum floor plan for using VAIR Field

2.3   Registering Obstacles

As shown in Fig. 3, a player's has more potential tactics when there are obstacles and walls than when playing in an open space. In fact, such obstacles are also used in competitions such as games using infrared guns and bows with archery tabs. VAIR Field also utilizes obstacles. Although VAIR Field cannot yet perfectly recognize and synchronize with obstacles, it can register existing obstacles in advance.

For example, by inputting data of a real object's position and scale to the VAIR Field, the object can be used as an obstacle in VR space (Fig. 4). When a player hides behind the object, he or she can hide behind the obstacle in VR space and can play in a shooting fight using realistic tactics. Since the real space is clearly visible in the mobile VR, a player can safely run around, which is impossible with a HMD.

Therefore, VAIR Field enables players to move in a sports-like way much more freely than VR using a HMD.

2.4   Displaying Other Players

Figure 5 shows a screen displayed on a smartphone while playing VAIR Field. The opposing player is displayed as a blue pin in the dashed red circle. We

Fig. 4. Positional synchronization of virtual and real objects

Fig. 5. Screen in play. (The blue pin in the dashed red circle is another player.) (Color figure online)

measured the distance to the screen from a player's eyes when the player stretches his arm forward. We calculated the viewing angle so as to display the scale correctly. However, since the screen of the smartphone is small, the viewing angle becomes too narrow, and it is difficult for the player to understand what is happening in the surrounding area. Therefore, we set the viewing angle slightly wider, so it is hard to say whether the screen displays images that are sufficiently realistic.

3   VAIR Device

3.1   VAIR Gun (Old)

Figure 6 shows the initial VAIR Gun, which uses a HTC Vive controller for tracking its position. Also, its trigger is the controller's trigger. This gun uses the controller, so its system flow is slightly different from that of the current VAIR Gun.

Fig. 6. Initial VAIR Gun

First, the initial VAIR Gun uses the controller's positional tracking sensor and trigger information. After being sent via Bluetooth, the information is input to VAIR Field software in Windows via the HTC Vive headset. This software, built by Unity, uses the server client model of network games and Windows functions as a server. Each smartphone's client software, also built by Unity, connects to the server via Wi-Fi and then performs pairing with the controller. Next, by using the pairing information, the server sends information received from the corresponding controller and game information to the smartphones via Wi-Fi. Finally, by using their information, rendering is done on each smartphone.

This framework is scraped out of aluminum alloy (a6061) for physical robustness, it is sandblasted for a satin finish, and the grip part is painted lacquer on walnut. The upper parts are molded with a 3D printer and painted to look like metal, and the muzzle that fixes the parts is a screw made of aluminum alloy (a5052).

Using these components, this initial gun is designed to imitate a real gun. However, some parents who saw and tested the gun at the Taipei Game Show

2017 claimed that they did not want their children to have it because this device looked too realistic. Therefore, this initial gun is not currently used for VAIR Field.

Fig. 7. Current VAIR Gun. (The center is a model for iPhone.) (Color figure online)

3.2   VAIR Gun (Current)

Figure 7 shows the current types of VAIR Gun, which have a science fiction-like appearance and do not look like real guns. However, their forms enable players to recognize easily that they are gun-like devices. These guns use the HTC Vive tracker as a positional tracking sensor, so their trigger functions are independent. Because their magazines and main bodies are separated, players must exchange the magazines when reloading. Hence, if the magazines are not loaded, the guns cannot shoot bullets.

As shown in Fig. 7, there are three types of magazines: red, silver, and black. The magazines have different numbers of bullets with different power and automatically change the viewing angle when loaded. For example, the red magazine contains few bullets with high power, like ammunition for a sniper rifle. Also, when the red magazine is loaded, the viewing angle is automatically zoomed in, enabling the player to shoot more precisely, like a sniper.

These magazines are loaded and released by imitating the exchange mechanism of a real gun's magazine. As shown in Fig. 8, there is a release lever on the left rear part of the device, and by pushing this, the magazine lock is released and the magazine can be pulled out. The magazine can be pushed in and pulled out from the back of the device, locking is automatically applied by pushing in the magazine, and bullets are loaded.

Fig. 8. Current VAIR Gun and magazines. (Press the lever on the left rear side to release the magazine. By pushing in a magazine from behind, it is automatically locked and loaded with bullets.)

The magazine (i.e., Mag A in Fig. 2) contains a battery, an actuator, and a control board. In other words, this part is the main body of the VAIR Gun. To identify each magazine, its ID is electronically set in the control board. The magazine contains a pogo pin and a pogo pin receiver. When the magazine is loaded, the pogo pin and its receiver are connected. After connecting them, the magazine's ID information is sent to the server of the Vive tracker via Bluetooth. At the same time, the trigger is connected to the magazine. When the player pulls the trigger, the information is transmitted to the inside of the magazine, the actuator is activated immediately upon receiving the trigger, and a reaction that varies depending on magazines is generated. Then, this information is sent to the Vive tracker, which then sends the same information as well as information of position and angle to the Windows PC via Bluetooth. After this processing, this current gun operates in the same way as the initial gun.

Most parts of the VAIR Gun were produced by using 3D printers, so there are few metal parts. Compared with the initial gun in Fig. 6, the new gun has about three times as many parts but is 100 g lighter. It also has a standard Picatinny rail and can be equipped with not only an iron site but also a commercially available dot site. Moreover, it can be customized, such as by attaching a cowl (Fig. 9). The parts that hold a smartphone can be easily reattached, so players can attach any smartphone such as an iPhone, iPod Touch, and Android.

Fig. 9. Fully equipped VAIR Gun. (Spare magazines can be stocked inside the cowl.)

3.3   VAIR Bow

The VAIR Bow (Fig. 10) is a bow-like device that has a similar basic structure to the VAIR Gun. It consists of the rims, strings, dampers, and stabilizers of a real bow. It uses the Vive tracker as a positional sensor and can also attach any smartphone. The best feature is that the shooting intensity depends on the amount the string is pulled.

Fig. 10. VAIR Bow and depiction in use

The grip consists of an aluminum alloy (a 6061) sandwiched between wood. The upper uses parts output by a 3D printer. Four strain gauges are affixed on the aluminum alloy just under the upper rim. They constitute a Wheatstone bridge circuit and measure distortion of aluminum. It can calculate the amount of force applied when a player pulls the string. The value of the distortion is passed through the amplification circuit and is sent to the Arduino Fio. Then, by using Xbee, the information is sent to a Windows PC via Wi-Fi. However, since a standard Windows PC cannot receive Xbee, it connects to a USB Xbee receiver.

The VAIR Bow uses the Vive tracker as a positional sensor and the Arduino Fio for the input information separately, so its structure is complicated. Although the bow weighs 4.5 kg, it is still not lightweight enough for children under 13. Therefore, VAIR Bow needs to be lightened and its structure improved.

4   Comparison

Table 1 shows specifications of four devices using the Vive controller or tracker and our previously developed 3rd Electric Bow. Compared with a general-purpose Vive controller, the initial VAIR Gun (Old) using it has basically the same performance and is heavier because of the added exterior. For the initial and current VAIR Guns, the strength of the trigger cannot be adjusted by changing the tracking sensor from the Vive controller to the Vive tracker. However, the current VAIR Gun is built so that trigger strength does not need to be changed.

Table 1. Comparison of specifications of devices using Vive controller or tracker, and previous work. (* means the weight without a smartphone.)

	HTC Vive controller	VAIR Gun (Old)	VAIR Gun	VAIR Bow	3rd Electric Bow
Position tracking	Vive controller	Vive controller	Vive tracker	Vive tracker	9-axis sensor
Display	None	Smart-phone	Smart-phone	Smart-phone	Mobile laser projector
Standalone	No	No	No	No	Yes
Simultaneous use	2	2	15	15	1
Shape	General purpose	Real handgun	Not real handgun	Real archery	Real archery
Weight	202.9 g	533.6 g*	357.1 g*	919.5 g*	1697.0 g
Strength	Yes	Yes	No	Yes	Yes
Magazine	No	No	Yes	No	No
Aiming	None	None	Iron sight or Dot sight	None	None
Recoil	Vive	Vive	Solenoid	Natural	Natural

On VAIR Field, up to two controllers and 15 trackers can be used with wireless per a set of Vive. Of course, if there are multiple sets, the numbers of controllers and trackers increase accordingly. The current VAIR Gun is about one-third lighter than the initial one because it mainly uses resin parts. Moreover, when using the current VAIR Gun, a player can exchange magazines and handle it like a real gun because the player can aim at a target with a real site.

Furthermore, the current VAIR Gun has three types of magazines. The red and silver magazines that have the recoil mechanism weigh 106.3 g and 84.5g, and the black magazine that does not weighs 14.6 g. The weight of the current VAIR Gun (357.1 g) in Table 1 includes the medium magazine weight of 84.5 g. Without this magazine, the VAIR Gun weighs 272.6 g, about half as much as the initial VAIR Gun (533.6 g). When playing, the weight of the smartphone is added.

Comparing the bows, the VAIR Bow can track positional information better than the 3rd Electric Bow [5], which can detect only rotation. For displaying images, all VAIR devices use a smartphone whereas the 3rd Electric Bow uses a mobile laser projector. The 3rd Electric Bow displays images on the wall, so its screen is larger than that of a smartphone. Since the 3rd Electric Bow's viewing angle of projection is not very wide, the player does not feel the difference in screen size between images.

The 3rd Electric Bow projects images onto a wall, so multiple people cannot use it in the same space at the same time. It contains a PC, a projector, and a battery, so it can work as a standalone device. However, it is so heavy (about 1697g) that a player has difficulty using it for a long time. On the other hand, the VAIR Bow weighs less than 1 kg without a smartphone. When an iPhone 7 is attached to the VAIR Bow, it weighs 1057.5 g. The VAIR Bow is about one-third lighter than he 3rd Electric Bow, so it is comparatively lightweight.

5   Conclusion

From the comparison of specifications, we conclude that the new VAIR Gun and Bow mostly realize VAIR Field's concepts of user-friendliness for children, sports-like play, and "feel of things." However, the space in which Vive can be used is too narrow for multiple people, so tracking in a wider space needs to be achieved. In the future, we plan to enable more people to use VAIR Field at the same time.

References

1. The Void. https://www.thevoid.com/
2. Nakagaki, K., Inamura, C., Totaro, P., Shihipar, T., Akikyama, C., Shuang, Y., Ishii, H.: Linked-Stick: conveying a physical experience using a shape-shifting stick. In: Proceedings of the 33rd Annual ACM Conference Extended Abstracts on Human Factors in Computing Systems, CHI EA 2015, pp. 1609–1614. ACM (2015)
3. Striker VR. https://www.strikervr.com/

4. Yasumoto, M., Ohta, T.: The electric bow interface. In: Shumaker, R. (ed.) VAMR 2013. LNCS, vol. 8022, pp. 436–442. Springer, Heidelberg (2013). https://doi.org/10.1007/978-3-642-39420-1_46
5. Yasumoto, M., Teraoka, T.: Electric bow interface 3D. In: SIGGRAPH Asia 2015 Emerging Technologies, SA 2015, pp. 11:1–11:2 (2015)
6. Kosaka, T., Misumi, H., Iwamoto, T., Songer, R., Akita, J.: "Mommy Tummy" a pregnancy experience system simulating fetal movement. In: ACM SIGGRAPH 2011 Emerging Technologies, SIGGRAPH 2011, pp. 10:1–10:1 (2011)

Industrial and Military Applications

Command and Control Collaboration
Sand Table (C2-CST)

Bryan L. Croft[✉], Crisrael Lucero[✉], David Neurnberger[✉], Fred Greene[✉],
Allen Qiu[✉], Roni Higgins[✉], and Eric Gustafson[✉]

Space and Naval Warfare Systems Center Pacific, San Diego, USA
{bryan.croft,crisrael.lucero,david.neurnberger,fred.w.greene,allen.qiu,
roni.higgins,eric.a.gustafson1}@navy.mil

Abstract. A Command and Control (C2) display system using the
Microsoft HoloLens and the Intelligent Multi-UxV Planner with Adaptive Collaborative Control Technologies (IMPACT) has been developed as a demonstration of a new advanced user interface. This allows
for human-to-human-to-machine collaboration for situational awareness,
decision making, and C2 planning and execution of simulated multi-unmanned heterogeneous autonomous vehicles. The advanced user interface allows multiple operators to collaborate across a shared holographic
sand table and control multiple vehicles. Multiple networking frameworks
were used to offload the computation of vehicle autonomy and planning algorithms to allow the HoloLens to run efficiently for an improved
user experience. Additionally, the concept of pseudo-classified information filtering allows for tiers of classification levels for each HoloLens user
derived from a 'need-to-know' classification basis.

Keywords: Command and Control · Augmented reality
Mixed reality · Microsoft Hololens · User interfaces
Natural user interface · Gaze · Gesture · Voice · Unity3D
Collaboration · Classification filtering

1 Introduction

Human interface improvements in the presentation, understanding, and collaboration for C2 systems can achieve better situational awareness, decision making
and effective interaction. Human-autonomy teaming requires tri-collaboration of
human-to-human-to-machine as humans collaborate with each other and autonomy simultaneously. Additionally, a new concept in shared visualization is created where multiple classification levels exist within the same virtual space. A
shared virtual environment with means to filter levels of classification or function
has wide application yet serious concerns of information spillage from one classification level to the next. The pros and cons of such a multi-level classification
approach was well suited for an augmented reality-based interface.

J. Y. C. Chen and G. Fragomeni (Eds.): VAMR 2018, LNCS 10910, pp. 249–259, 2018.
https://doi.org/10.1007/978-3-319-91584-5_20

The C2 system selected for evaluation of the human-machine interface was the Intelligent Multi-UxV Planner with Adaptive Collaborative/Control Technologies (IMPACT) [1]. IMPACT was built to demonstrate agility in tactical decision making, mission management, and control with key elements for enabling heterogeneous unmanned vehicle (UxV) teams to successfully manage the "fog of war" with its inherent complex, ambiguous, and time-challenged conditions. Applied research for IMPACT was based on supervisory control and the machine learning of tactics that combine flexible play-calling, bi-directional human-autonomy interaction, "global" cooperative control algorithms, and "local" adaptive/reactive capability.

The Microsoft HoloLens is an Augmented Reality device which has a see-through lens to the real world upon which computer graphics are overlaid. The operator of this device can interact via gaze, gesture and speech while visualizing the virtual C2 based scene in any defined presentation space. This new modality of user interface provides the premise for the investigation of the effectiveness of such human-machine interface as add-ons or replacement for existing C2 human-machine interfaces.

2   Background

2.1   Mixed Reality in the Military

Advances in mixed reality has grown remarkably in the past few years due to the commercialization of the technology. The concepts behind the technology have been around for quite some time such as the Virtual Fixtures Platform [2] developed at the U.S. Air Force Armstrong Laboratory in the early 1990s. SSC Pacific and Naval Postgraduate School were involved with virtual reality for a project called CommandVu [3–5]. CommandVu was utilized for Marine Corp platoon mission development and training within a virtual environment and a mixed-live fire demonstration at 29 Palms, California. More recently the Battlespace Exploitation of Mixed Reality (BEMR) Lab [6] has been evaluating, integrating and exploiting commercial mixed reality technology for adaptation into a virtual world's battlespace. The goal is to reduce associated costs and risks when bringing the mixed reality technology and capability to the warfighter. The intent of the goal is to increase effectiveness, efficiency, collaboration, innovation, battlespace visualization and speed to response and pace of evolution in decisions making and situational awareness.

2.2   Microsoft HoloLens

The Microsoft HoloLens is a commercial-off-the-shelf, self-contained holographic computer which enables engagement with digital content and interaction with holograms superimposed on the real world [7]. The device is an adjustable-fit headset that uses a visor to display virtual, augmented, and mixed realities (VAMR) to the end user. The headset consists of a self-contained Windows 10 computer system with multiple sensors for advanced optics and holographic computing. A special holographic processing unit (HPU) was designed specifically for VAMR.

Interaction with the holograms displayed through the HoloLens is based on gaze, gesture, and voice [8]. The hologram elements are overlaid as computer graphics onto the view of the real world. The collaboration aspect allows multiple users to have synchronous shared experiences for presentation, collaboration, and interaction, while at the same time, the view of real world surroundings is maintained to allow spatial orientation within the environment and visual ques from users in the same room from their own perspective of the shared environment. This collaborative environment is considered an innovation in the realm of a more natural human interface.

2.3 IMPACT

The IMPACT system is a C2 prototype platform for centralized supervised control of multiple simulated autonomous unmanned vehicles [1,9,10]. Research related to IMPACT was to demonstrate how a single human can provide supervisory control of many unmanned vehicles through the fusion of several autonomous agents and the autonomy associated with the unmanned vehicles working in concert to achieve missions in an uncertain and changing environment. The underlying goal of the IMPACT initiative was to invert the applied ratio of human operators to autonomous vehicles [11]. The operator manages missions through a "play calling" approach where the operator is supported by autonomous agents in performing these tasks. This concept, designed and implemented with a tri-service set of research teams from the Air Force Research Lab (AFRL), SPAWAR Systems Center (SSC) Pacific, Army Research Lab (ARL) and Naval Research Lab (NRL).

3 Technical Approach

C2-CST application connects the IMPACT system with one to many augmented reality display systems. The virtual environment represents the information in the IMPACT system as a virtual sand table. The IMPACT system contains a component called the HUB, which permits the exchange and flow of data via standardized formats thus allowing external applications the ability to communicate with IMAPCT. A computer placed in between the HoloLens and IMPACT runs a Unity3D application along with the Photon server which functions as the middle tier and permits the communication brokering between IMPACT and the HoloLens.

This section covers the architecture, environment, scene creation, communications via ZeroMQ, the Photon Unity Networking server, the Mixed Reality Toolkit for Shared Experiences, the classification filtering of visualized data, and the simplified Play Workbook interface to the C2 IMPACT system. The C2-CST project provides a start into a new and rich area in human user interfaces for

Command and Control systems. The design for the prototype and experiment is extensible and scalable.

3.1 Architecture

Most visualization-based systems generally do not have sufficient computing power required for both the processing of C2 related information and providing a real-time visualization and human interaction of that C2 information. With this in mind, the architecture was comprised of three core components, which as designed and implemented provide the necessary support to achieve the underlying goals and overcome the obstacles for such a system. These three core components are:

- The IMPACT system, which was designed to reside on one to many computer systems and provide many services such as vehicular autonomy, supervisory control, planning algorithms, path determination, resource allocation, unmanned systems sensor control, and a simulated environment to provide test scenarios.
- The Unity workstation is a separate computer system with the Unity3D toolset and Unity Photon Server installed. This workstation via the Unity interface acts as the communications mediator between the IMPACT system and the HoloLens devices. This communications mediation and added computational capability, offloads the HoloLens devices and allows them to work best as visualization and interaction tools of the C2 information in the virtual sand table.
- The HoloLens devices and their associated APIs and frameworks support the new approach in visualizing and interacting with C2 information and other users embedded within the same holographic environment.

The C2-CST architecture permits the processing of C2 information and the updating of that information to be handled by more powerful computing system than that provided by the HoloLens. The HoloLens can therefore focus on visualization and interfacing to the C2 data that gets represented as a holographic advanced interface.

The C2-CST system communicates bilaterally with the IMPACT system using the ZeroMQ network communications framework that connects to the IMPACT centralized HUB component [12]. With the HUB communications pipeline based on ZeroMQ, the logical choice for interchange of information to C2-CST was to utilize ZeroMQ as the networking communications protocol. ZeroMQ is an asynchronous messaging library which can be utilized for concurrent applications as a messaging library based on sockets while providing a message queue. ZeroMQ can also run without a dedicated message broker. This allows for a many-to-many connection amongst the connection endpoints.

The Unity workstation is the second core component to C2-CST architecture. The component provides a middle tier connection between IMPACT and the HoloLens interface. The Unity workstation uses Photon Unity Networking

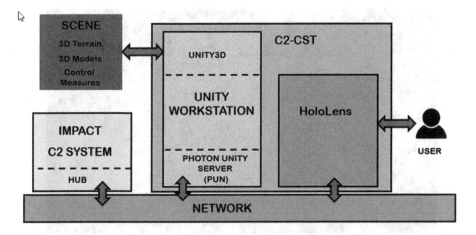

Fig. 1. C2-CST architecture diagram

(PUN) as a server which is a third-party package for Unity3D developed by Exit Games [13] for multiplayer games. The Photo Unity Server has a load balancing API which matches "players" to shared sessions and transfers messages synchronously in real-time between these connected "players" (users). The "players" in the case of C2-CST can be considered to be each of the individuals using a HoloLens device that shares the same holographic environment. The Unity workstation with the Photon Unity Networking adds the support for the shared environment which essential given the intended collaborative use of the C2-CST system (Fig. 1).

3.2 Environment - Scene Creation

The military expression of a "sand table" usually refers to a terrain model used in support of military planning and wargaming. This definition essentially applies to the C2-CST system, but more specifically to C2 planning and execution (Fig. 2).

The HoloLens holographic environment utilizes the Unity3D development tool to support the development of the interface as well as building the environment for the holographic scene. For IMPACT, the designated default scenario is a base force protection mission over an assumed Air Force base and surrounding region. The map within IMPACT was created for the HoloLens holographic scene in Unity3D. The air base in the scenario is fictitious in its representation for both IMPACT and C2-CST but provides a very suitable and realistic representation for the simulated environment. Within Unity3D a third-party terrain tool builder called World Composer [14], provided the means to generate to scale the 3D realistic terrain for the C2-CST "sand table" display.

Fig. 2. C2-CST sand table display within the HoloLens

3.3 C2-CST Communications

The communication flow between IMPACT and the C2-CST system must also pass through the Unity workstation which acts as a mediator and supports the computational offload for the HoloLens devices (Fig. 3).

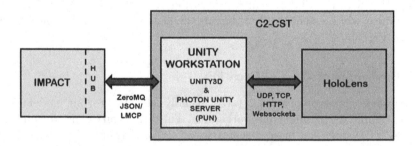

Fig. 3. C2-CST connections and communications design

C2-CST communications utilize the ZeroMQ asynchronous messaging library which is an open-sourced network communications framework for distributed messaging [12]. IMPACT's centralized HUB component distributes all its messages to each component connected to the HUB. The two messaging patterns used throughout the entirety of IMPACT, and by extension, to C2-CST are:

– Pub-Sub: The first messaging pattern is the Publish-Subscription model, allowing the HUB to publish every message it receives to a port. All services and components subscribe to the HUB's IP and port to receive messages and filter the desired messages to read based on the header information.

– Push-Pull: The second messaging pattern is the Push-Pull model, which allows all the services to push messages to the HUB's IP and port to be distributed to each end user. The HUB receives these messages by pulling from its port and publishes the message out.

3.4 Shared Experiences via Mixed Reality Toolkit

The Mixed Reality Toolkit is an open-source collection of scripts and components intended to accelerate development of applications targeting the Microsoft HoloLens and Windows Mixed Reality headsets [15]. The Mixed Reality Toolkit was developed by the Microsoft Corporation and is necessary for the C2-CST application to have both collaboration and sharing capabilities. The stacked layer consists of the C2-CST application on top of the Mixed Reality Toolkit for Unity, which in turn rests on top of the Windows 10 UWP (Mixed Reality APIs) (Fig. 4).

HoloLens Stacked Layer for C2-CST

Command and Control Collaboration Sand Table (C2-CST)

Mixed Reality Toolkit - Unity   **Mixed Reality Toolkit**

Mixed Reality Toolkit

Windows 10 UWP (Mixed Reality APIs)

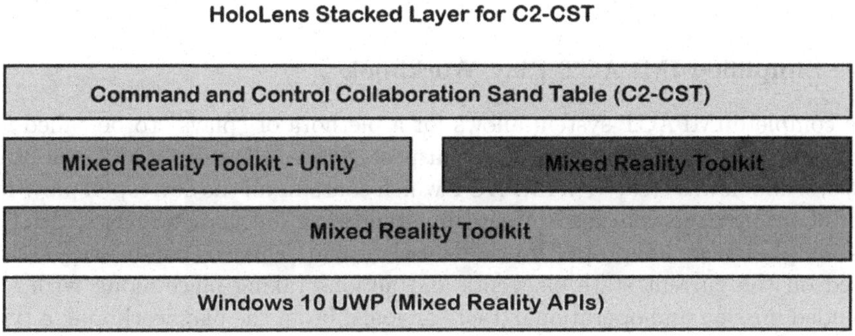

Fig. 4. Microsoft HoloLens stacked layer API

This allows multiple HoloLens users to communicate and stay in sync seamlessly in real time. This communication can occur within the same location or with users in remote locations. When the first HoloLens joins the Unity workstation scenario via the Photon Unity Server it utilizes the 'anchor' for configuration and registration to the virtual sand table. Thus, as each subsequent HoloLens joins the session it is synchronized to the holographic environment with that anchor and allows them to share the exact same virtual experience.

3.5 Classification Filtering of a Shared Visualization

The classification filtering of a shared visualization is an extension to shared experiences based on the Mixed Reality Toolkit. In the basic shared experience all HoloLens users in that session share the exact same scene or scenario and the same set of information is available to each user in that session. Classification filtering changes from the globally shared set of information to various subsets of non-shared information. The goal for C2-CST was to determine if such an environment could be useful and still protect against the spillage of classified information from one level to the next.

The C2-CST system handled the classification levels by filtering data between each HoloLens headset via a distinct configuration. This configuration is set on the Unity workstation and when the scenario is run and a HoloLens connects, that particular HoloLens receives a specific filtering configuration. This is displayed in the filtering toolbar. In a real-world system such configuration would be restricted and purposely assigned based on the end user's classification. For this development effort, the Unity workstation user can select a different filtering level for each specific HoloLens that joins the session. In this design there are five filters:

(1) Complete information access and control (2) Ground, air, and sea vehicle information access (3) Ground and air vehicle information access (4) Ground vehicle access (5) No access.

A simplistic approach was taken to classification filtering which leaves a lot of room for research, exploration and experimentation in classification filtering.

3.6   Simplified IMPACT Play Workbook

The complete IMPACT system allows for a plethora of "plays" to be called for various tasks such as Point/Area/Line inspect, Shadow Hostile, or Overwatch. A play workbook was created in IMPACT which contains all the developed plays for a set of autonomous vehicles to create an intended action that correlates with the mission plan or an adaptation to that mission plan. This is a conditional action based on the current state of events and actions taking place along with the intended mission and operational/tactical goals. From the play workbook a type of play is selected and is generally followed by a target location and its intended target or goal. IMPACT application-level autonomy supports the determination of solution sets for accomplishing the specified play (Fig. 5).

Fig. 5. The full capabilities of a play within the IMPACT system

In the C2-CST version of play-calling, HoloLens users have a very simplified play workbook. Instead of selecting the type of play and then the location, the HoloLens users gaze is set to the intended location for the play task to be accomplished, then an air tap gesture is used to bring up the simplified workbook for selection of the desired play. The initial design was primarily intended for point inspect plays consistent with this simplified interaction for play calling (Fig. 6).

Fig. 6. Simplified play calling in C2-CST only allows for point inspects across different vehicle types

The simplified play calling capability within the C2-CST interface is a prime example of how the IMPACT interface could be extended as mixed reality interface. As the scenario and environment are shared and users collaborate on intended courses of actions, the C2-CST holographic user interface allows not only this collaboration but the execution of decisions from that collaboration via play calling. The C2 interface changes from a single user, single interface to a multi-user shared interface where collaborative decisions and actions can take place. The intended human evaluation of C2-CST was also designed to discover the value of execution of play calling from a HoloLens especially in a shared virtual environment.

4   Conclusion and Future Work

The C2-CST project provided an opportunity to examine a new user interface for C2 systems. C2-CST leveraged the Microsoft HoloLens API and associated capabilities to provide a unique user interface based on current state of the art COTS mixed reality technology. The IMPACT application based on human supervisory control of multiple unmanned autonomous systems and collaboration with in-application autonomous agents was utilized as the baseline C2 system for the evaluation. Comparison of the HoloLens mixed reality interface to that of the nominal IMPACT interface provided the fundamental components of the study for human motor processing, perception and cognition. The HoloLens device offered a new paradigm in user interface of mixed reality using gaze, gesture and voice with a unique holographic environment overlaid on the user's view of the real-world surroundings.

C2-CST created unique features of a shared collaborative holographic environment as well as permitting a filtered classification on information displayed in that environment. C2-CST leveraged several capabilities to permit an immersed collaborative environment. These capabilities are also possible for remote users.

The following describes areas of the C2-CST project that could use further research, development and experimentation:

- Voice-based Interaction: The IMPACT system allows automated task generation and play calling through a chat box interface as well as some operator-to-operator communications over the chat box interface. A voice-based interface was not included into the C2-CST project goals, non-the-less, the HoloLens also has a speech recognition and speech command-based API to allow this additional user interface action to occur. The middle tier of C2-CST could process and translate HoloLens voice input to an acceptable format to go across the IMPACT HUB and be processed in IMPACT. The reversal of this voice communication is also possible. Voice could play a significant role in user interface improvement to advanced user interfaces for C2 systems and as such should be considered in future efforts.
- Comprehensive Human Subject Matter Testing: For any new or revised operational or tactical application, subject matter experts and end user feedback is essential to understanding the level of utility and improvement need for existing or systems still in the early design stages. The human evaluation feedback for new advanced user interfaces has been on overreaching purpose of C2-CST.
- Remote Collaboration: Remote collaboration is built in as part of the HoloLens system. This proves very beneficial in C2 systems in cases where collaboration regarding C2 information for mission planning or execution may come from disparate locations such as a ship at sea and a land-based command center. HoloLens provides the means to allow this remote collaboration via a networked connection. Within that environment the remote participants appear as virtual avatars. These HoloLens capabilities are ideal for C2 related remote collaborations.

References

1. Coronado, B., Gustafson, E., Reader, J., Lange, D.S.: Mixing formal methods, machine learning, and human interaction through an autonomics framework. In: Proceedings of the 2016 AAAI Fall Symposium Series (2016)
2. Rosenberg, L.B.: The use of virtual fixtures as perceptual overlays to enhance operator performance in remote environments. Technical report AL-TR-0089, USAF Armstrong Laboratory (1992)
3. Zyda, M.J., Pratt, D.R., Monaham, J.G., Wilson, K.P.: NPSNET: constructing a 3-D virtual world. In: Proceedings of the 1992 Symposium on Interactive 3-D Graphics, March 1992
4. Cohen, P.R., Johnston, M., McGee, D., Oviatt, S., Pittman, J., Smith, I., Chen, L., Clow, J.: QuickSet: multimodal interaction for simulation set-up and control. Report from center for human computer communication, Oregon Graduate Institute of Science and Technology (1997)
5. Clarkson, J.D., Yi, J.,: LeatherNet: a synthetic forces tactical training system for the USMC commander. In: Proceedings of the Sixth Conference on Representation. Institute for Simulation and Training Technical report IST-TR-96-18, pp. 275–281 (1996)
6. Smalley, D.: BEMR: A New Reality for the Future Force. Armed with Science The Official US Defense Department Science Blog, December 2015
7. Microsoft HoloLens. https://www.microsoft.com/en-us/hololens
8. Furlan, R.: The future of augmented reality. IEEE Spectr. 5(6), 21 (2016)
9. Gutzwiller, R.S., Lange, D.S., Reeder, J., Morris, R.L., Rodas, O.: Human-computer collaboration in adaptive supervisory control and function allocation of autonomous system teams. In: Shumaker, R., Lackey, S. (eds.) VAMR 2015. LNCS, vol. 9179, pp. 447–456. Springer, Cham (2015). https://doi.org/10.1007/978-3-319-21067-4_46
10. Lange, D.S., Verbancsics, P., Gutzwiller, R., Reeder, J.: Command and control of teams of autonomous units. In: 17th International Command and Control Research and Technology Symposium (2012)
11. Cummings, M.L.: Operator interaction with centralized versus decentralized UAV architectures. In: Valavanis, K.P., Vachtsevanos, G.J. (eds.) Handbook of Unmanned Aerial Vehicles, pp. 977–992. Springer, Dordrecht (2015). https://doi.org/10.1007/978-90-481-9707-1_117
12. Distributed Messaging. http://zeromq.org
13. Photon Unity 3D Networking Framework SDKs and Game Backend. https://www.photoengine.com/en/PUN
14. World Composer. http://www.terraincomposer.com/worldcomposer
15. Mixed Reality Toolkit Unity. https://github.com/Microsoft/MixedRealityToolkit-Unity

CAE/VR Integration – A Qualitative Assessment of Advanced Visualization for Interactive Conceptual Simulations (ICS) in Industrial Use

Holger Graf[1]([⊠]) and André Stork[2]

[1] Virtual and Augmented Reality, Fraunhofer IGD,
Fraunhoferstraße 5, 64823 Darmstadt, Germany
holger.graf@igd.fraunhofer.de
[2] Interactive Engineering Technologies, Fraunhofer IGD,
Fraunhoferstraße 5, 64823 Darmstadt, Germany
andre.stork@igd.fraunhofer.de

Abstract. One of the key driving technologies for a better communication, representation, interaction, and visualization of design and engineering data has been Virtual Reality (VR). The idea of Interactive Conceptual Simulations (ICS) combines real-time interaction and visualization in a turn-around loop with the CAE simulation. However, the automation of the processes between the changes of the domain and the resulting simulation requires update rates within min 30 Hz, in order to remain interactive, not blocking the CG engine redrawing the update. Here, the overall simulation requires an advanced CAE process chain from model import, model manipulation, simulation results generation and visual preparation. Although many publications have been addressing the CAD/VR and only few the CAE/VR process chain, one might assume that endeavors for this are regarded as unnecessary, as a tidy showcase with a low-level quality visualization would be sufficient for engineers. This paper will object this hypothesis by presenting the results of a qualitative validation based on industrial use of our established VR environment for ICS. It follows the methodology and complements the quantitative analysis presented in earlier work providing the results of a qualitative assessment of engineers for our established VR based ICS post-processing unit (IDEFix – Immersive Data Explorer for CAx Integration).

Keywords: Immersive data explorer · VR/CAE integration · CAE simulation

1 Introduction

Computer Aided Engineering methods have influenced the PDP significantly. Popular application areas include structural mechanics (e.g. stress analysis, dynamic analysis, modal analysis, kinematics) and computational fluid dynamics (analysis and validation of fluidal behavior). Following an analysis step, engineers are getting an insight into material characteristics or physical properties. Those are described by numerical values of some kind of physical quantities (e.g. pressure, stress concentration, deformations,

© Springer International Publishing AG, part of Springer Nature 2018
J. Y. C. Chen and G. Fragomeni (Eds.): VAMR 2018, LNCS 10910, pp. 260–271, 2018.
https://doi.org/10.1007/978-3-319-91584-5_21

velocities) that are available at discrete points within space. Nevertheless, computer engineering methods are complex and resource intensive, consuming significant computational power and time, thus leading to long and cost intensive analysis processes. On the other hand, the demand for shortening the time intervals within the product life cycle is crucial to remain competitive.

The potential of VR for post-processing of engineering/manufacturing data raised also hopes to deploy this advanced man machine interface for conceptual simulations that might become interactive (ICS) using advanced real-time interaction techniques within the CAE domain [1, 2].

Here, several endeavors for coupling VR systems to manufacturing and product development management systems have been realized in the past. [3] presents the state of the art on a VR coupling to DES systems. The coupling has been mainly driven by ideas to complete the smart factories idea and its overall value chain from production lines, logistics and monitoring of machine states. [4] presented a comprehensive literature survey of VR research within the product development since the 90's and showed, that VR technology has been mostly applied to design reviews and assembly tests of products based on a VR/CAD integration. Research endeavors for an integration of VR within the computer-aided engineering (CAE) domain, however, remained very little. Based on the number count of publications the authors stated *"... This likely means that we can only achieve relatively little profit by applying VR to CAE. The application of VR technology has been considered unnecessary in CAE: relatively simple visualization provided enough support to make decisions [...]"*, [4].

Therefore, we have conducted a user evaluation study with industry using our developed solution called IDEFix (Immersive Data Explorer for an CAx Integration) in order to object this hypothesis and aim to present a series of results which we obtained in cooperation with CAE engineers. We started our analysis with a quantitative analysis that was presented in [5]. Here, we were showing that the use of advanced and integrated 3D interactive pre-/post-processing facilities based on VR, might lead to a faster assessment of the analysis results (down to minutes and seconds compared to in-house COTS[1]) and thus could shorten the turn-around cycles for analysis and re-analysis. Finally, several engineers estimated to shorten down their engineering workflow by several days. Here, a clear benefit of the proposed solutions could be shown. However, as not only timing has been seen as important to the engineers, the fulfillment of their requirements as well as the efficiency, clarity and stimulation of the environment has been regarded as important aspects as well.

Thus, aim of this paper is to present the results, we obtained from the engineers for the use of IDEFix within industrial use and complement the quantitative analysis results by qualitative aspects the environment was able to deliver. As a consequence, the paper shows how stimulating the use of VR was for the engineers and how the quality of the environment lead to a higher acceptance of new technology at their workplace.

---

[1] COTS – Commercial off-the-shelf tools like MSC.Nastran, ANSYS Fluent, PERMAS.

2 Methodology

The validation sessions we have been conducting addressed dedicated workflows of engineers using ICS. A taxonomy of ICS can be found in [2]. We were setting up the hybrid desktop (see Fig. 1) in which the engineer was capable of using legacy systems as well as our VR tools for model preparation, model simplification, simulation and analysis (IDEfix). The validation sessions were conducted over a total period of four months within a first tier OEM (ZF)[2], Airbus and CSTB[3], covering the requirements from automotive, aerospace and urban planning departments. As in-house COTS-tools MSC.Patran/Nastran, PERMAS, IDEAS-NX, ANSYS Fluent were used.

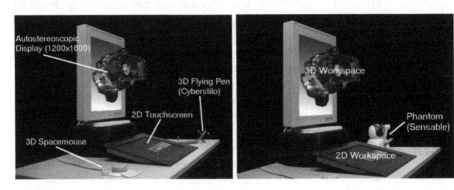

Fig. 1. Hybrid desktop combined with optical tracking system and different 6DOF input devices.

2.1 Participants

In total 15 test subjects delivered feedback. The group of test subjects comprised experts from two engineering domains, 6 from engineering analysis and 3 from urban planning, as well as 6 graduate students. Several graduate students have been involved in the final assessment of the user interface concepts being application and VR novices, yet with a dedicated background in computer science. Due to the complexity of the system and realized functionalities a "real world effect" of the developed framework can only be proven in real engineering environments. Thus, the main objective of acquiring "on-site expertise" was threefold:

1. An installation on-site allowed an involvement of more test subjects with a strong computational engineering background in order to deliver more reliable and competent feedback on the realized functionalities.
2. Testing new immersive functionality being available at desktop working places returned on how the test subjects reacted to hybrid system configurations enabling

---

[2] ZF – ZF Friedrichshafen, www.zf.de.

[3] CSTB – Centre Scientific et Technologie du Batiment, France, www.cstb.fr.

immersive 3D analysis as well as performing pre-/post-processing tasks, and if this technology was held to be beneficial to their daily work in terms of user interaction and performance.

3. The validation sessions showed, if the system features were understood and easy-to-use for the test subjects. In addition, diverse sessions showed where the framework needed improvement and which new functionality is deemed useful developing in order to enhance ergonomics and workflow aspects.

2.2 Questionnaires and Instruments

We developed dedicated questionnaires for different aspects of the validation sessions. The intention was to collect qualitative as well as quantitative data during each validation session. The focus of the questionnaires has been designed for completeness and availability, level of integration, as well as suitability of the workplace concept. Usability issues related to the design of the interaction metaphor were also raised yet being limited to ergonomic acceptance. The questionnaires were composed of multiple choice questions providing predefined, alternative answers. Several questions were formulated as statements. The answers to these questions were given as a range of multiple choices enabling a mapping for a qualitative assessment on a scale from $0...2$, $0...3$, and $0...4$, indicating the degree of conformance ($0 =$ none, $2/4 =$ fulfilled; $0 =$ not useful at all, $3 =$ useful). The test subjects should fill in a questionnaire according to the test cases and scenarios. The preliminary questionnaire consists in its first part of 5 questions, which helped building up a user profile, analysing skills, habits and software used until now, as well as to evaluate the degree of familiarity with VR environments and their share of usage during daily work routines. 25 questions did cover the new workplace, ergonomics, as well as the hybrid user interface. For the analysis of these parts, the reader should be referred to [5]. The second questionnaire aimed at collecting the information on the available functionality, its clarity, efficiency, and fulfilment with respect to the requirements. Here, the different aspects needed to be assessed during the validation schedule and tasks ($1 =$ not available, $2 =$ poor, $3 =$ satisfactory, $4 =$ good, $5 =$ very good). Also comments in free-text format could be provided whether the functionality required some refinements, enhancements or suggestions for an improvement.

2.3 Test Cases

Three test cases from each domain had to be examined and analyzed: A small and medium sized model to verify the entire process chain within solid mechanics applications, and a large model to experience the current limits of the approach and to check the post-processing capabilities within the hybrid desktop, see [5]. For the qualitative validation the engineers had to accomplish the following task list for each model:

- Import mesh with results from external solver
- Change visualization options
- Display and evaluate principal stresses
- Display displacements and animate

Table 1. Qualitative assessment of IDEfix – Visualization

"Clarity" (c)	Descriptives	Std. Error	"Efficiency" (e)	Descriptives	Std. Error
Visualization Modes	M(9) = 3,67 V(9) = 0,333 SD(9) = 0,577	,333	Visualization Modes	M(9) = 4,33 V(9) = 1,333 SD(9) = 1,115	,667
Scalar Fields	M(9) = 4	,0	Scalar Fields	M(9) = 4,33 V(9) = 0,333 SD(9) = 0,577	,333
Vector Fields	M(9) = 3,67 V(9) = 1,333 SD(9) = 1,155	,667	Vector Fields	M(9) = 3,67 V(9) = 1,333 SD(9) = 1,155	,667

"Consistency" (cs)	Descriptives	Std. Error	"Fulfilment" (f)	Descriptives	Std. Error
Visualization Modes	M(9) = 3,67 V(9) = 0,333 SD(9) = 0,577	,333	Visualization Modes	M(9) = 4 V(9) = SD(9)=0	,0
Scalar Fields	M(9) = 4,33 V(9) = 1,333 SD(9) = 1,155	,667	Scalar Fields	M(9) = 3,67 V(9) = 0,333 SD(9) = 0,577	,333
Vector Fields	M(9) = 3,33 V(9) = 2,33 SD(9) = 1,58	,882	Vector Fields	M(9) = 3,67 V(9) = 1,333 SD(9) = 1,155	,667

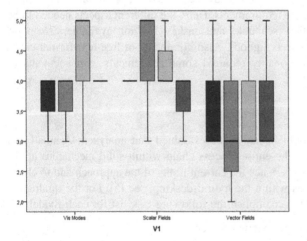

X_i(not available, poor, satisfactory, good, very good) $\rightarrow$ $X_i \in \{1,2,3,4,5\}$, $i \in \{c,e,cs,f\}$

- The overall visualization modes were perceived as good, thus being in line with the functionality provided by in-house COTS-tools
- The clarity of the display of scalar fields has been perceived as good, whereas the display of the vector fields was perceived as satisfactory. This might be due to the used glyph metaphors deployed for the vector fields which get quickly unclear in larger data sets.
- In general the end users were satisfied with the achieved visualization/display modes reaching a high level of consistency compared to their COTS-tools as well a good perception of fulfillment for their needs.
- Some quotes of the free-text fields:
  - *"The visualization of the results is very fast, view manipulations with displayed results as well. View manipulations with results could be performed with both tools in nearly the same speed. Switching between geometry display and between different analysis models (CAD/complete model/submodels/wireframe/shaded/results) is in the VR environment much faster (seconds compared to minutes)" (Airbus)*

- Solve local mesh (re-simulate)
- Post-process sub-/local model (use freely definable cross section and element probes, based on a laser beam metaphor 'glued' to the virtual interaction device)
- Compare refinements and result sets

As task for the qualitative assessment, the user had to evaluate on the clarity, availability, efficiency and fulfilment of the requested functionality within the VR component. For the automotive and the aerospace domain the implemented modes for visualization and interaction have been similar.

2.4   Analysis

Several experiments conducted by the test subjects were modelled as discrete random variables. The realizations of a random variable are called random variates. Thus, let Ω be a probability space and E a measurable space. The random variables $X_i : \Omega \rightarrow E$, $i = 1 \ldots l$, model a stochastic process on Ω, with $X_i^{-1}(A) \dot{=} \{\omega | X(\omega) \in A\}$, $A \subset E$. For l observations $X_i(\omega) = x_{i,n_i}$, $i = 1, \ldots, l$. of samples with size $n = n_1 + \ldots + n_l$ the realizations (variates) are x_{i,n_i}. For the analysis of returned feeback by the test subjects the software suite SPSS of IBM was used in order to derive the descriptive statistics of several modelled variables. The results have been analyzed according to the descriptives: mean (M), variance (V) and standard deviation (SD). For the qualitative assessment the variables $X_i : \Omega \rightarrow E, E = \{1, 2, \ldots, 5\}, \Omega =$ ("not available", "poor", "satisfactory", "good", "very good") reflect on "clarity (c)", "efficiency (e)", "consistency (cs)" as well as "fulfilment of demands (f)" of the developed solutions. Here, the consistency reflects on the need of the functionality to be competitive to in-house COTS-tools. The mark "good" mirrors the same level of possibility provided by typical working tools, "very good" being superior to the traditional way. The efficiency reflects on the need of the functionality to allow the engineer to quickly get to an assessment of the problem areas or the overall mock-up. The higher the mark the faster he could accomplish his task.

Table 2. Qualitative assessment of IDEFix – Interaction

"Clarity" (c)	Descriptives	Std. Error	"Efficiency" (e)	Descriptives	Std. Error
Interaction	M(9) = 4,33	,667	Interaction	M(9) = 4,67	,333
	V(9) = 1,333			V(9) = 0,333	
	SD(9) = 1,155			SD(9)= 0,577	
Navigation	M(9) = 4,33	,667	Navigation	M(9) = 5	,0
	V(9) = 1,333			V(9)=SD(9)=0	
	SD(9) = 1,155				
Areas of	M(9) = 4,33	,333	Areas of	M(9) = 3,67	,882
Interest	V(9) = 0,333		Interest	V(9) = 2,333	
	SD(9) = 0,577			SD(9) = 1,528	

"Consistency" (cs)	Descriptives	Std. Error	"Fulfilment" (f)	Descriptives	Std. Error
Interaction	M(9) = 3,33	,667	Interaction	M(9) = 4,33	,333
	V(9) = 1,333			V(9) = 0,333	
	SD(9) = 1,155			SD(9) = 0,577	
Navigation	M(9) = 4,33	,667	Navigation	M(9) = 4	,577
	V(9) = 1,333			V(9) = 1,0	
	SD(9) = 1,155			SD(9) = 1,0	
Areas of	M(9) = 4,33	,333	Areas of	M(9) = 3,33	,333
Interest	V(9) = 0,333		Interest	V(9) = 0,333	
	SD(9) = 0,577			SD(9) = 0,577	

X$_i$(not available, poor, satisfactory, good, very good) → X$_i \in$ {1,2,3,4,5}, i $\in$ {c,e,cs,f}

- The interaction modes were overall perceived as very good, thus raising expectations for more advanced modes of traditional functionality provided by COTS-tools. Thus, the fulfilment of demands shows a tendency to "only" a good assessment.
- The navigation possibilities within/with the mock-up have been perceived as "very good" ($q_{X_i 75}$ = 5, $\forall i$) being superior to current in-house tools for their workflows.
- The efficiency to define dedicated areas of interest was satisfactory as only limited functionality by two selection mechanism (sphere, box) had been realized. A further drawback has been identified as the imprecise positioning using any kind of interaction device.
- In general the interaction modes were seen as comparable to current tools in the diverse engineering domains. Some tasks could be accomplished much faster at the expense of precision.
- Some quotes of the free-text fields:
  - *"Model manipulation is very good and very useful. Picking is a little more difficult. We need more practice" (CSTB).*
  - *"The handling of the housing is done with the tracker. Moving and rotating the object is very intuitive" (ZF).*
  - *"It is very good that the size of the model (model scale) and the spatial distance can be adjusted independently of one another" (ZF).*
  - *"The object in hand metaphor is very interesting and very intuitive to manipulate the object. But it is sometimes difficult to hold the object avatar in one hand and the pen in the other hand: small movements and tiredness can make very precise tasks very difficult" (CSTB).*
  - *"About manually defining areas of interest: It is not very easy to exactly position the pen at a desired node/element with the pen. Highlighting of selectable members would help more" (Airbus).*

3   Results

This section provides the comprehensive analysis of the results we obtained as part of the feedback and collected questionnaires by the engineers.

3.1   Visualization

Visualization options were realized to switch between several visualization modes such as nodes, wireframe, lighted surface, Gouraud shading. Further on, the display of scalar fields and vector fields were essential in order to be competitive to in-house COTS-tools (Table 1).

3.2   Interaction

For the interaction, the general functionalities in view of mock-up manipulation (rotation, zooming, translation), picking or navigation modes, such as walk/fly through or the possibilities to manually define the areas of interest (i.e. selection boxes) had to be marked. A mark "very good" mirrors the perception of being advanced to current COTS-tools (Table 2).

Table 3. Qualitative assessment of IDEFix – Post-processing

"Clarity" (c)	Descriptives	Std. Error	"Efficiency" (e)	Descriptives	Std. Error
Animation	M(9) = 4,50	,500	Animation	M(9) = 3,67	,667
	V(9) = 0,500			V(9) = 1,333	
	SD(9) = 0,707			SD(9) = 1,155	
Iso Surfacing	M(9) = 4,0	,0	Iso Surfacing	M(9) = 4,50	,500
	V(9) =			V(9) = 0,500	
	SD(9)= 0			SD(9) = 0,707	
Comparing	M(9) = 3,50	,500	Comparing	M(9) = 4,0	1,000
Results	V(9) = 0,500		Results	V(9) = 2,000	
	SD(9) = 0,707			SD(9) = 1,414	
Define CP	M(9) = 3,33	,333	Define CP	M(9) = 3,33	,667
	V(9) = 0,333			V(9) = 1,333	
	SD(9) = 0,577			SD(9) = 1,155	
Apply CP	M(9) = 4,0	,577	Apply CP	M(9) = 4,0	1,000
	V(9) =			V(9) = 3,000	
	SD(9)= 1			SD(9) = 1,732	
Data Probing	M(9) = 4,0	,577	Data Probing	M(9) = 4,33	,667
	V(9)= SD(9)			V(9) = 1,333	
	= 1			SD(9) = 1,155	

"Consistency" (cs)	Descriptives	Std. Error	"Fulfilment" (f)	Descriptives	Std. Error
Animation	M(9) = 3,67	,667	Animation	M(9) = 3,33	,333
	V(9) = 1,333			V(9) = 0,333	
	SD(9) = 1,155			SD(9) = 0,577	
Iso Surfacing	M(9) = 4,50	,500	Iso Surfacing	M(9) = 4,50	,500
	V(9) = 0,500			V(9) = 0,500	
	SD(9) = 0,707			SD(9) = 0,707	
Comparing	M(6) = 4,0	1,000	Comparing	M(9) = 3,50	,500
Results	V(6) = 2,000		Results	V(9) = 0,500	
	SD(6) = 1,414			SD(9) = 0,707	
Define CP	M(9) = 3,67	,333	Define CP	M(9) = 3,67	,333
	V(9) = 0,333			V(9) = 0,333	
	SD(9) = 0,577			SD(9) = 0,577	
Apply CP	M(9) = 4,0	,577	Apply CP	M(9) = 4,0	,577
	V(9)=SD(9)=1			V(9) =SD(9) = 1	
Data Probing	M(9) = 4,33	,333	Data Probing	M(9) = 4,0	,577
	V(9) = 0,333			V(9) = SD(9) = 1	
	SD(9) = 0,577				

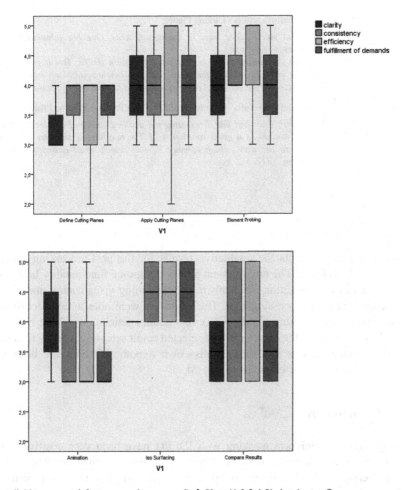

X_i(not available, poor, satisfactory, good, very good) → $X_i \in \{1,2,3,4,5\}$, $i \in \{c,e,cs,f\}$

- Several functionalities with respect to the post-processing capabilities were perceived as "good" being comparable to in-house COTS-tools.
- Main advantage as stated by several experts is the tight coupling of simulation/mesh refinement and the post-processing of the results. Post-processing functionality is comparable to available tools, some modes such as the application of cross cutting or data probing are perceived superior to current tools due to the easy way of interaction. However, they have been lacking of some precision as the evaluation of the "define cutting plane" shows where only satisfactory results could be achieved.
- The fulfillment of the demands was in average marked as "good". Except the animation which only achieved satisfactory marks.
- As very positive statement, the experts were satisfied with the speed of interactivity thus generating high "efficiency" values. Some quotes of the free-text fields:
  - *"The overall response times in the VR environment are excellent! In no situation we have encountered waiting times, which where not acceptable. Of cause, our 3 test models have been small or medium sized, but in comparison to COTS Post-processor (MSC.Patran) no drawback has been found. MSC.Patran and IDEfix have both been tested on the same hardware (Intel PC, Nvidia Gforce graphics board)" (Airbus).*

- Post-processing of analysis results - Cutting Plane:
  - *"Easy and much faster than in traditional tools. One big advantage of the VR environment!" (Airbus).*
  - *"Defining the cutting plane is very intuitive within IDEfix. But it is not possible to define the exact position of the plane. Within GLview you always have to define the exact position of the cutting plane which is not so fast but more precise" (ZF).*

- Post-processing of analysis results - Element Probing (Laser Probing/Volume Probing):
  - *"In general: easy and fast. Presenting the detailed values of a selected element in a separate window is a good solution. [...] The handling of the pen does not give a feedback to the user, which element he will select, when activating the selection mechanism" (ZF).*

3.3   Post-processing

The following presents the qualitative results for the post-processing functionalities provided by IDEFix. The environment allows traditional functionality being conducted using advanced interaction mechanism, i.e. combining visualization and interaction to an enhanced post-processing tool. The engineers were able to conduct data probing, mock-up cutting (cutting planes (CP)), or visualize animations of the resulting vector fields. Furthermore, the comparison of selected result sets should allow the engineers to review former results and thus dismiss own hypothesis about the behavior of the mock-up at specific local areas (Table 3).

4   Conclusion

In general the engineers working with IDEFix have been very positive. The system provides a dedicated framework, which has been designed to closely fit defined engineering needs. The system offers an effective and intuitive dissemination platform for analysis results, especially to non-technical personnel. The speed of performing variations of the CAD/CAE model in real-time has been perceived as excellent.

For the qualitative analysis, the performing engineers within the different disciplines were satisfied about the system set-up. The ease of the system incorporating state-of the art VR technologies by providing an intuitive GUI (3D with the pen, or 2D with a touch screen) was mentioned as another advantage. Several post-processing methods, intuitive visualisations, manipulations, interaction (stereo vision, tracked pen, spacemouse, tracked artefacts) have been perceived as being powerful leading to time savings during result exploration. Although some of the post-processing functionalities had its bottlenecks especially with smaller models in which traditional COTS tools still seem to be preferred, the overall assessment for utility, efficiency and stimulation has been high.

To wrap up the quantitative and qualitative assessment, several evaluations have shown, that using advanced and integrated 3D interactive pre-/post-processing facilities based on VR, might lead to a faster assessment of analysis results in the CAE domain.

Several new techniques for conceptual simulations proved to allow an engineer being concentrated on smaller problems and being faster and more efficient with the interaction modes for interactive exploration. Further on, the qualitative assessment supports our hypothesis that there is a real benefit for VR integrated CAE environments, IF and only IF several processes and stages of the engineering workflows are integrated and if fast interaction methods on an analysis mock-up can be provided to the engineers.

As mentioned in [5] the involved engineers evaluated the VR-based hybrid desktop as an easy to use and intuitive access technology. This motivates our work in order to object the hypothesis of Choi et al., that only small and tidy visualisations might be sufficient for an engineering analysis. We have shown, how engineers could benefit from new and integrated simulation methodologies integrated into advanced front ends such as VR.

References

1. Graf, H., Stork, A.: Enabling real-time immersive conceptual cae simulations based on finite element masks. In: Proceedings of the ASME World Conference of Innovative VR, (WINVR 2011), Milan, Italy (2011)
2. Graf, H., Stork, A.: Virtual reality based interactive conceptual simulations. In: Shumaker, R. (ed.) VAMR 2013. LNCS, vol. 8021, pp. 13–22. Springer, Heidelberg (2013). https://doi.org/10.1007/978-3-642-39405-8_2
3. Turner, C.J., Hutabarat, W., Oyekan, J., Tiwari, A.: Discrete event simulation and virtual reality use in industry: new opportunities and future trends. In: IEEE Transactions on Human-Machine Systems, vol. 46, no. 6, December 2016
4. Choi, S.S., Jung, K., Do Noh, S.: Virtual reality applications in manufacturing industries: past research, present findings, and future directions. Concurr. Eng.: Res. Appl. 23(1), 40–63 (2015)
5. Graf, H., Stork, A.: CAE/VR integration – a path to follow. In: Proceedings of the European Conference on Modelling and Simulation (ECMS 2017), Budapest, Hungary (2017)

Augmented Reality and Mixed Reality Prototypes for Enhanced Mission Command/Battle Management Command and Control (BMC2) Execution

Michael Jenkins[(✉)], Arthur Wollocko, Alessandro Negri, and Ted Ficthl

Charles River Analytics, Cambridge, MA 02138, USA
mjenkins@cra.com

Abstract. This work provides an overview of three prototype augmented reality (AR) applications developed for the Microsoft HoloLens with the intention of exploring the strengths and weaknesses of AR for supporting planning and decision making–specifically, within the domain of US Army Mission Command and Battle Management Command and Control (BMC2) execution. We present each prototype application accompanied by the target audience from whom we sought feedback, key features of the application, and technical goals we hoped to achieve, demonstrate, and evaluate. Findings with respect to AR strengths and weaknesses, framed around the technical goals of each of the AR applications, are then presented to begin to shed light on limitations and opportunities of the state-of-the-art in AR hardware, and the potential to support Mission Command and BMC2 stakeholders. This material is based upon work supported by the Communications-Electronics Research, Development and Engineering Center (CERDEC) under Contract No. W56KGU-18-C-0002. Any opinions, findings and conclusions or recommendations expressed in this material are those of the author(s) and do not necessarily reflect the views of CERDEC.

Keywords: Military · Virtual reality · Mixed reality · Augmented reality
Situational awareness · Design · Visualization · BMC2 · C2 · AR
VR · MR · XR

1 Introduction

Mission Command (MC) is a core principle and philosophy of the US Army, and all Commanders must master MC to be successful across a variety of Battle Management Command and Control (BMC2) missions and operational situations. Maintaining effective MC is a focus of numerous Army training courses and events. Army Doctrine Reference Publication 6-0 is dedicated entirely to MC [1]. The Army is simultaneously supporting and advising global counterinsurgency (COIN) missions while pivoting towards the future, which will focus on BMC2 and expeditionary operations and Major Combat Operations (MCO) in megacities and Anti-Access Area Denial (A2/AD) domains. Developing technology to support MC BMC2 has been a cornerstone of Army

© Springer International Publishing AG, part of Springer Nature 2018
J. Y. C. Chen and G. Fragomeni (Eds.): VAMR 2018, LNCS 10910, pp. 272–288, 2018.
https://doi.org/10.1007/978-3-319-91584-5_22

R&D efforts over the past decade. In 2013, driven by explicit Joint Urgent Operational Needs (JUONs), the Communications-Electronics Research, Development and Engineering Center (CERDEC) Intelligence and Information Warfare Directorate (I2WD) began a three-year, MC-focused Technology Enabled Capability Demonstration (MC TECD) to demonstrate next-generation technology that could support MC within existing Army architectures, such as the Distributed Common Ground System-Army (DCGS-A). MC remains a key driver of R&D, training, and study across the Army, as evident by the 2015 Army Warfighting Challenges [2], numbers 9 (Improve Soldier, Leader, and Team Performance) and 19 (Mission Command Execution) being directly relevant to MC enhancement.

MC is a complex topic with diverse elements, applicable to multiple echelons of command and mission types. For example, MC is applicable in Battalion and Brigade Tactical Operations Centers (TOCs) where Commanders and their staff execute the full Military Decision Making Process (MDMP) [3] and wargame courses of action (COAs) for lethal engagements in force-on-force missions. It is also applicable in Company Command Posts, where leaders execute similar doctrinally defined processes to support stability operations with socio-cultural sensitivities in megacities. The theory (e.g., ADRP 6-0) and practice of MC both emphasize the importance of Commanders establishing and maintaining situational awareness (SA) to conduct effective MC, and detailed visualization of relevant information in the external environment is a critical contributor to that SA. However, given the diverse array of information required to support all of the varieties of MC, it is difficult to characterize the specific information required to support MC.

In recent years, Augmented Reality (AR) technologies have supported users in a variety of commercial applications to enhance SA and support decision making when reasoning over complex and even uncertain information. Applications include mechanical maintenance, architecture, gaming, collaboration and remote social interaction, and navigation and information display for vehicle operation. These commercial applications have been the primary drivers of AR technology to date, and DoD-relevant AR based technologies are only beginning to emerge (e.g., simulated trainers for platforms that are expensive to run, such as training Air Force F-35 pilots). To date, no widely adopted AR approaches have been developed to support MC or BMC2, despite the fact that the capabilities afforded by AR technologies have a natural relevance to the MC/BMC2 domain.

To begin to address this gap as part of a US Army funded effort (Contract No. W56KGU-16-C-0043), we first conducted a scoped AR trade study, focused on characterizing: (1) the state-of-the-art in AR input and output (I/O) hardware; (2) existing and past applications of AR relevant to MC/BMC2; (3) gaps in understanding with respect to how AR can be effectively applied to support human decision-making processes and other cognitive-based tasks; and, (4) extraction of critical research priorities within the AR domain that are needed to drive development of effective AR-based MC/BMC2 support capabilities. We then conducted focused Work Domain Analysis [4, 5] to correlate the most promising AR technologies to MC/BMC2 execution tasks most likely to benefit from AR-driven support given the limitations and affordances of current and near-future AR technologies. Leveraging the outputs of these research tasks, we generated proof-of-concept AR capability prototypes, designed explicitly to: (1) illustrate current COTS technology capabilities and limitations; (2) demonstrate the potential for AR technology to be applied to support different aspects of MC/BMC2; and (3) inform the design of a human subjects research (HSR) experimental plan to explore critical dimensions of AR performance relevant to MC/BMC2 applications. This paper provides an overview of three of the resulting proof-of-concept AR capability prototypes that were developed and informally evaluated by representative end users via basic prototype demonstrations. For each prototype, we provide details on the intended target audience, key features the prototype sought to highlight, technical goals the prototype sought to achieve, and key findings that resulted from both the development of the prototype and targeted demonstrations of these limited scope capabilities to representative end users.

2 Background

The introduction of new technology has shown that increased computerization and hardware capabilities does not guarantee improved human-computer system performance [6–8]. Poor use of technology can result in systems that are difficult to learn or use, create additional workload for system users, or in the extreme, result in systems that are more likely to lead to catastrophic errors (e.g., confusions that lead to pilot error and fatal aircraft accidents). In most cases, AR falls into this class of novel technology, where a lack of fundamental understanding with how to effectively apply it results in misuse (leading to the negative performance results mentioned above) and eventually abandonment (noting that aviation HUDs are one of the few exceptions as a result of decades of continued investment into the effective design, application, and deployment of AR HUDs). To avoid this abandonment, there are critical knowledge gaps that must be understood if the AR field is to continue to trend upward through the design, development, and deployment of novel AR applications that provide benefits within the context of targeted use cases. This is especially true for the military and MC/BMC2, as military applications will be among the more challenging to address and are likely to receive little support by way of defining guidelines for effective design of AR capabilities from the consumer sector (which is likely to be driven by the entertainment, gaming, and lifestyle industries in the near-term). To begin to characterize these gaps, and build a foundation of knowledge in AR design guidance specific to MC/BMC2 applications, the three prototype AR applications were used to elicit feedback from representative end users, to promote an iterative approach to AR capabilities design founded on vetting proof-of-concept capability value and exploring HCI aspects of how to effectively design those capabilities with promise.

3 Proof-of-Concept AR MC/BMC2 Support Interfaces

The following sections provide an overview of three proof-of-concept AR prototypes designed to demonstrate a range of AR capability strengths and weaknesses for MC/BMC2 support. Section 3.1 describes a terrestrial battle space visualization. Section 3.2 describes a distributed training common operating picture (COP). Section 3.3

describes a user-defined operating picture (UDOP) for space situation awareness (SSA). For each prototype, we provide details on the intended target audience, key features the prototype sought to highlight, technical goals the prototype sought to achieve, and key findings that resulted from both the development of the prototype and targeted demonstrations of these limited scope capabilities to representative end users.

3.1 Terrestrial Battle Space Visualization

The terrestrial battle space visualization provides an AR terrain visualization designed to provide Commander and staff with general awareness of the battlefield for planning, rehearsal, and mission oversight and execution. The target audience for the demonstration was a mix of active duty and civilian expert MC researchers and practitioners, with additional demonstrations presented to our team's internal SMEs (including a retired Army Colonel and Major), our funding Sponsor, US Army CERDEC, and a number of industry and military personnel at the 2016 Inter-service/Industry Training, Simulation, Education Conference (I/ITSEC) who visited the Charles River exposition hall booth. These demonstration recipients were instructed to provide feedback not only on the potential utility of a AR geospatial display, but also to focus on the viewability of the symbology, the scene, and their ability to extract information from graphically encoded elements of the AR visualization. Key features and technical goals for this prototype are provided below, followed by Figs. 1, 2, 3, 4, 5 and 6 providing screen capture examples of the concepts the AR prototype was designed to illustrate. Key findings from demonstrating these prototype capabilities then follows.

Fig. 1. AR view of large scale (200 × 200 km) terrain using 2D MIL-STD symbols to indicate partial Corps level deployment, illustrating the difficulty in reading 2D content due contrast, resolution, and view perspective issues.

Key Features of the Prototype. With the goal of exploring a range of AR visualization perception issues for MC/BMC2 key features of the prototype included: (1) representation of a large scale terrain area with 3D topology (200 × 200 km) explore ability to extract precision positioning and movement information and provide Corps level battlefield awareness; (2) representations of units with both symbolic 2D, symbolic 2.5D, and ecological 3D forms to enable comparison between forms; (3) ability to dynamically shift levels of perspective from Corps level overview to squad level boots-on-the-ground details to explore context switching and ability to explore details on demand; (4) visualization of terrain sensor coverage to explore understanding of area-encoded symbology; and (5) representation of units at varied scales to explore the impact of mixed scale elements.

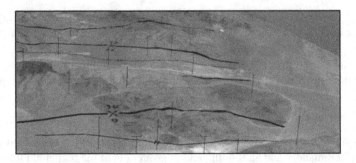

Fig. 2. AR view of large scale (200 × 200 km) terrain using 2.5D MIL-STD symbols (achieved by elevating them above the terrain as markers), illustrating readability issues that result from poor rendering resolution of the HoloLens.

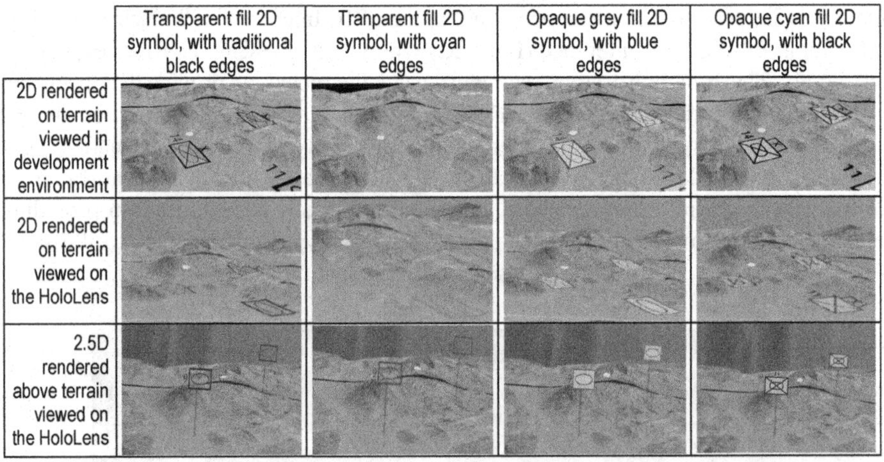

	Transparent fill 2D symbol, with traditional black edges	Tranparent fill 2D symbol, with cyan edges	Opaque grey fill 2D symbol, with blue edges	Opaque cyan fill 2D symbol, with black edges
2D rendered on terrain viewed in development environment				
2D rendered on terrain viewed on the HoloLens				
2.5D rendered above terrain viewed on the HoloLens				

Fig. 3. Renderings for MIL-STD symbology to illustrate the difference in resolution from the AR development environments (top row) to AR platform views (2nd/3rd rows, acquired on the HoloLens), and the impact of different visual features on saliency of 2D symbols (yellow dot indicates gaze position). (Color figure online)

Technical Goals. From a technical perspective, our goals with the prototype were based on a desire to explore both the human-computer interaction (HCI) and AR platform elements of the overall AR experience. Specific goals the prototype was designed to support included demonstration of the: (1) challenges of simply converting 2D display formalisms (i.e., traditional desktop information displays) to a 3D AR information display; (2) potential for AR to visualize additional integrated data layers due to the added dimensionality; (3) potential of AR to offer dynamic and configurable semi-immersive and immersive information displays; (4) selected AR platform (i.e., the Microsoft HoloLens) graphical power limits; (5) rendering disparities shifting from a software development process to end AR deployment using modern AR development tools; and (5) limits of AR for geospatial visualization due to challenges of mixed-scale to support ecological model representation.

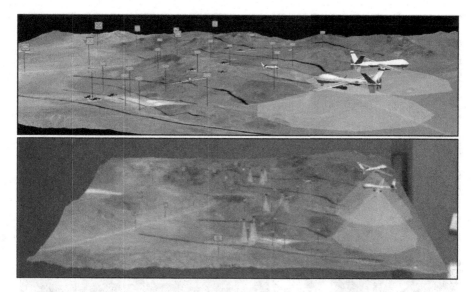

Fig. 4. AR scenes illustrating issues of scale when using ecologically valid models; e.g., the Global Hawk models are scaled up for readability, making them approximately 15 km in length if referenced based on the terrain scale.

Fig. 5. AR scene illustrating issues with referenced-based scaling whereby showing a 10-story building, person, and MRAP vehicle to scale with the terrain result in significantly diminished saliency and discernability even with a relatively close up view of the scene.

Key Findings. The Terrestrial Battle Space Visualization prototype was presented to the Army MC experts, our team's internal SMEs (including a retired Army Colonel and Major), our funding Sponsor, US Army CERDEC, and a number of industry and military personnel at the 2016 Inter-service/Industry Training, Simulation, Education Conference (I/ITSEC) who visited the Charles River Analytics exposition hall booth.

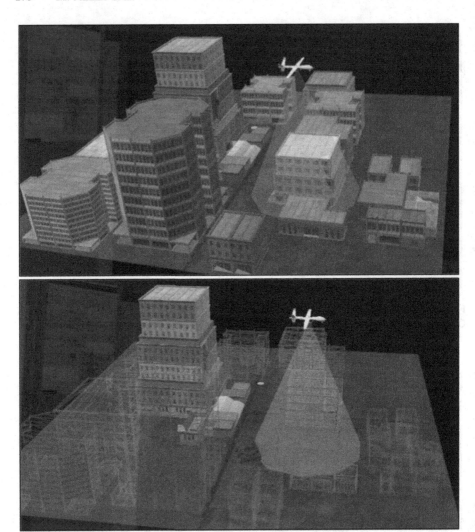

Fig. 6. AR scene showing a small-scale urban environment (left) that resulted in run-time performance issues on the HoloLens along with a similar scene utilizing a rendering strategy to reduce GPU load (right).

Our goal of explicitly demonstrating AR capability strengths and weaknesses was emphasized to ensure viewers with operational backgrounds did not focus on the accuracy or completeness of the represented battle space and instead were calibrated to our key features and technical goals. Table 1 summarizes these findings.

3.2   Distributed Training Common Operating Picture (COP)

The Distributed Training COP provides an AR mission state overview visualization that indicates the position, status, and other characteristics of multiple distributed

Table 1. Key findings resulting from the AR terrestrial battle space visualization prototype.

ID	Finding
TBS-1	Representation of even basic elements (e.g., MIL-STD symbology, fire control phase lines, waypoint markers) is not a straightforward task—perceptual saliency is impacted by symbology graphical elements (e.g., color, transparency, line weight, scale), viewing environment (e.g., room lighting, dynamic background (ex. people walking past your FOV), background consistency), and viewer perspective (e.g., pose and orientation of the viewer with respect to the position of the AR virtual scene and overlaid symbology elements)
TBS-2	Ecological symbology (i.e., using 3D models representative of actual assets) resulted in multiple scaling issues resulting in a need for mixed-scale and mixed-symbology content. Example issues included: (1) entity overlap when in close proximity on medium and large scale terrain maps preventing visibility and unit type, status, and precise location/formation extraction; (2) inability to track multiple entities across a wide area due to FOV limitations; (3) inability to discern unit type or status when true-scaled to terrain; and (4) inability of the HoloLens to render large numbers of high fidelity entity models when combined with other graphically intensive scene elements
TBS-3	Visualizing 2D or topology-overlaid geospatial data layers (e.g., via KML) results in knowledge gaps due to inability of viewer to see the complete terrain scene from a combination of the limited FOV and terrain and entity viewing obstruction based on the position and orientation in the physical room of the viewer relative to the virtual scene
TBS-4	Microsoft HoloLens experienced frame rate lag when rendering complex models (based on the number of polygons in the entity surface mesh) or large quantities of simple models, with dynamic elements exacerbating this issue
TBS-5	Examples of potential benefits over traditional 2D, screen-based geospatial displays seems to primarily result from the potential ability to better visualize spatiotemporal information related to: (1) dynamics of the battle space (e.g., shifting view scales, changing viewing perspective); and (2) visualization of volumetric intangible information (e.g., ISR sensor coverage, EMF spectrum/signal propagation, weaponry effect trajectories, ranges, and impact area, COA coordinated phase lines and temporally dependent symbology)

entities participating in a mixed live, virtual, and constructed (LVC) training event. The target audience for this prototype capability was the US Air Force personnel and researchers, in addition to our team's internal SMEs, and a number of industry and military personnel who participated in a limited scope LVC training event which incorporated this demonstration capability during the 2016 Inter-service/Industry Training, Simulation, Education Conference (I/ITSEC). For the I/ITSEC limited scope LVC event, USAF personnel and USAF contractors participated in a variety of roles to simulate a flight mission, conducted using a simulated ground station, aircraft flight simulators, and live aircraft flying at a controlled training site. For participating live and simulated aircraft, their position, status, and other characteristics were shared using the distributed interactive simulation (DIS) framework, which was integrated into the Distributed Training COP prototype to enable live and dynamic entity updating. Key features and technical goals for this prototype are provided below, followed by Figs. 7, 8, 9, 10 and 11 providing examples of the concepts the AR prototype was designed to illustrate. Key findings from demonstrating these prototype capabilities then follows.

Fig. 7. AR scene illustrating textual and dynamic video information being associated with an entity (F-35) based on its position as indicated via a DIS update, integrating DIS and GIS data.

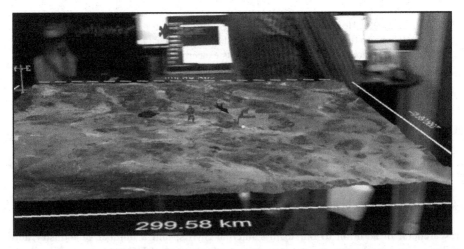

Fig. 8. AR scene representing a live training exercise involving two fighter jets, two ground vehicles, and a joint terminal air controller, demonstrating issues with saliency when viewing against an inconsistent background, and issues with non-referenced based scaling.

Key Features of the Prototype. The key features of this demonstration prototype were primarily focused on demonstrating technical capabilities and limits of the AR platform (i.e., the HoloLens) in comparison to traditional display platforms (i.e., desktop or laptop computers). As a result, the key features of the demonstration included: (1) integration with the Modern Air Combat Environment (MACE) scenario

Fig. 9. AR scene exploring viewability of content under different lighting conditions, readability of text, and the ability to script events (i.e., the attack event on the left) via the MACE scenario framework.

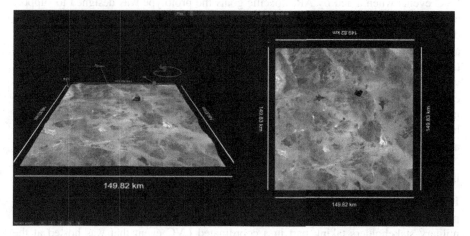

Fig. 10. Desktop rendering of the 3D visualization showing playback of recorded missions, illustrating the ability to capture and record AR contents, and the increased readability and saliency of content when viewing on a desktop display/with a solid black background and zero content transparency.

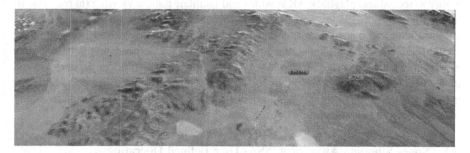

Fig. 11. Rendering from a leaned in position with high resolution terrain, illustrating issues of scale as evident from the convoy of 5 vehicles moving towards the building are nearly indistinguishable from terrain features, and enhanced text readability when coupled with a solid and contrasting background.

software to illustrate the ability to allow a third-party service to script AR visual content in real time; (2) integration with the distributed interactive simulation (DIS) protocol to illustrate the ability to both tie into standardized ontologies and to support LVC event integration; (3) ability to support asset-level drill down for details on demand to explore human-computer interaction (HCI) mechanisms, specifically gaze-based and gesture-based inputs, for interacting with AR content; and, (4) integration with geospatial information system (GIS) terrain data to explore processing limitations of the HoloLens with respect to the ability to access and render high resolution terrain maps.

Technical Goals. From a technical perspective, our goals with the prototype were based on a desire to explore networking and dynamic content capabilities on the HoloLens, and potential benefits to spatiotemporal awareness during dynamic live LVC events when aided by AR. Specific goals the prototype was designed to support included demonstration and exploration of the: (1) ability to network the HoloLens to drive dynamic AR information displays in real time; (2) ability to record and playback a sequence from an AR environment (e.g., to support after-action reviews (AARs)); (3) ability to wirelessly stream a primary user's AR content view to third-parties via a web-browser (e.g., show what the AR user sees on a tablet); (4) limitations of using ecologically valid objects that result from reference-based scaling issues (as identified in our first prototype characterized in Sect. 3.1); (5) performance of speech and gesture based interactions in a real-world environment with a high degree of both visual and auditory noise (i.e., the I/ITSEC exposition hall); (6) readability of text in AR; and, (7) issues with communication between co-located AR-equipped and non-AR equipped individuals.

Key Findings. The Distributed Training COP prototype was presented to USAF personnel and researchers at the 2016 I/ITSEC event, along with other industry and military stakeholders taking part in a coordinated LVC event that was hosted at the conference. We also show the demonstration to industry collaborators and our team's internal SMEs. Our goal with this prototype was to enable demonstration of networking capabilities of the HoloLens and the ability to dynamically and in real-time interface with third-party networked services to drive AR content. In addition, we explored the ability to record and playback AR sessions and facilitate remote viewing (in response to the communications issues we observed with our first prototype), and to present text legibly and in a manner that facilitated readability from any viewing position (accomplished via colored panels that rotated to always be perpendicular to the user's gaze, upon with text was placed). While this prototype was used to support a coordinated LVC event, it was not a critical capability to the overall event goals and was instead included to facilitate exploration of these goals. Table 2 summarizes the findings from the demonstrations of the prototype.

3.3   Space Situation Awareness (SSA) User Defined Operating Picture (UDOP)

The SSA UDOP provides the ability to arrange a set 2D and 3D information displays within an AR virtual environment. This configurable approach allows users to

Table 2. Key findings resulting from the AR distributed training COP visualization prototype.

ID	Finding
DTC-1	Ecologically valid symbology representation issues persisted due to the difference in scale between terrain and models resulting in issues such as false entity overlap (e.g., two jet models overlapping wings when flying in formation, visually indicating a crash that is false) and inability to extract precise location and targeting information due to the large area entities covered on the terrain
DTC-2	High resolution terrain from standard GIS system crippled HoloLens performance, requiring custom down-sampling to reduce the resolution to a level where the HoloLens could perform at adequate levels and stream network data to drive dynamic display components
DTC-3	3D models of different entities within the simulation required mesh optimization to reduce impacts on HoloLens GPU to enable rendering of multiple concurrent entities during the LVC event
DTC-4	Text rendering required additional graphical enhancements to facilitate readability in visually noisy environments. The addition of a solid background with contrast to the viewing environment background scene significantly improved text readability; however, text also had to be dynamically oriented to the user's gaze to prevent situations where users had to physically walk around the AR scene to read different text elements
DTC-5	Speech-based interactions were ineffective due to inability of novice users to quickly memorize available commands, in addition to ambient noise interfering with microphone signal pickup (when conducting tests within the I/ITSEC conference venue)
DTC-6	Gesture-based interactions were effective once trained; however, prolonged device use with gesture-based interactions can become fatiguing due to the requirement to hold one's directly in front of one's head so that HoloLens cameras can detect the gesture motion. Gesture-based interactions were also limited to only two-gestures due to HoloLens limitations and visual background noise in the physical environment interfered with gesture detection (e.g., individuals walking past the AR scene in the aisleway of the I/ITSEC demonstration site)
DTC-7	Networking capabilities worked relatively well for isolated discrete data transmissions; however, streaming data (e.g., video) resulted in system lag unless a dedicated Wi-Fi network was established for networking (e.g., the native I/ITSEC expo hall Wi-Fi was insufficient to run networked demonstrations in real-time)

configure a workstation tailored to their information needs to support different users working collaboratively on a mission. The target audiences for the demonstration was the US space enterprise BMC2 expert practitioners and our team's MC/Army BMC2 SMEs, in addition to opportunistic audiences including military audiences and a number of industry collaborators and DoD customers of Charles River Analytics. Demonstration audiences were instructed that the goal was not to critic the information for its relevance to space operations support, but to evaluate the ability to interact with and configure AR content within their physical space. Key features and technical goals for this prototype are provided below, followed by Figs. 12, 13 and 14 providing screen capture examples of the concepts the AR prototype was designed to illustrate. Key findings from demonstrating these prototype capabilities then follows.

Fig. 12. AR scene illustrating issues of digital occlusion (i.e., a satellite is not viewable as it is located behind the earth) and 2D text readability requirements (i.e., the 2D text panel must continuously adapt its orientation to remain perpendicular to the user's gaze).

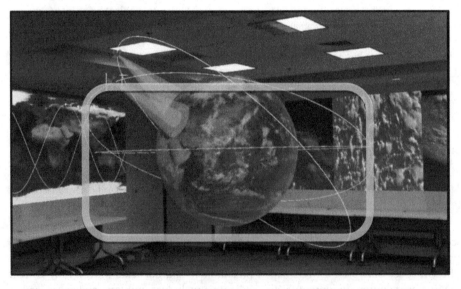

Fig. 13. AR scene illustrating the unconstrained AR space and the ability for the user to place different 2D and 3D AR content displays throughout their real-world location (i.e., AR information panels are located to the left and right of the central 3D earth visualization), and illustrating (via the yellow box added to the image above) the approximated HoloLens FOV (versus the fully rendered scene shown in the image). (Color figure online)

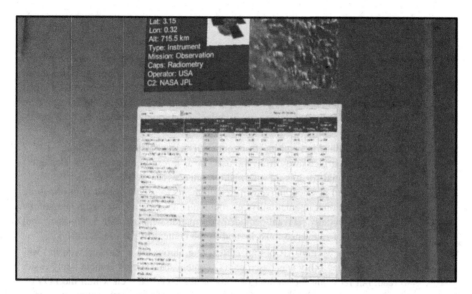

Fig. 14. AR scene illustrating readability issues of rendering dense 2D text in AR from a third-party source (in this case a website with tabular data) with the Microsoft HoloLens.

Key Features of the Prototype. The key features of this demonstration prototype were focused on exploring more interaction mechanisms and allowing users to self-configure AR virtual content within their physical environment. As a result, the key features of the demonstration included: (1) support for gaze-, speech-, gesture-, and controller-based interactions; (2) ability to scale, position, and orient AR content; (3) inclusion of 2D visual, 2D textual, and 3D visual content for placement in the AR virtual environment; and (4) an unconstrained AR space with which to configure a custom virtual environment.

Technical Goals. From a technical perspective, our goals with the prototype were based on a desire to explore AR interactions and user-driven AR information environment configuration. Specific goals the prototype was designed to support included demonstration and exploration of the: (1) multiple modes of interaction, including gaze, speech, gesture, and controller options; (2) visualization methods for displaying 2D visual and textual/tabular content; (3) readability of large volumes of text (i.e., more than the brief labels and phrases seen in the above prototypes); (4) ability for users to define their AR content arrangement; and (5) potential for AR content occlusion and beyond-FOV content presentation.

Key Findings. The SSA UDOP as demonstrated for US space enterprise BMC2 expert practitioners and our team's MC/BMC2 SMEs, in addition to military audiences and a number of industry collaborators (e.g., Cubic) and DoD customers (e.g., ARL) of Charles River Analytics. In addition, the prototype is still undergoing development to as part of a larger multimodal SSA UDOP capability prototype. Findings from these demonstrations informed the design of this multimodal framework that mixes AR displays with traditional screen-based displays to overcome many of the issues

Table 3. Key findings resulting from the AR SSA UDOP prototype.

ID	Finding
SSA-1	Speech and gesture interactions pose a challenge for novice users who need to learn both what commands are possible and when the system will accept them; however, after learning basic commands, users were able to effectively utilize both for limited AR interaction that did not required repetitive inputs (e.g., gesture interactions were frequently used to configure the environment, which only needs to be done once initially during setup)
SSA-2	Information occlusion resulting from either 3D visualizations that present information on a face away from the user, or as a result competing AR elements results in potential for missed information, unnecessary search (i.e., lost efficiencies), and physical movement requirements to access occluded information. Providing additional interactions (e.g., rotation controls) combined with symbology to indicate potentially relevant occluded information helps to address this issue, but determination of relevance must be tied to the context of the user's task
SSA-3	Text readability for non-AR-optimized text (e.g., browsing a standard website) was challenging as legibility was based on: (1) content scale (larger content being easier to read, but reducing the amount of content that could be seen within the FOV); (2) viewing angle (off-center angles greater than $\sim 15°$ resulted in text being too blurred to read); (3) distance (related to scale, with normal website text requiring users to be $< \sim 3$ feet from content when presented at approximately native scale (i.e., replicating a computer monitor's dimensions)); and (4) AR and background contrast (with greater contrasts from virtual backgrounds and/or the physical environment background increasing readability)
SSA-4	Limited HoloLens FOV severely limits the ability to monitor multiple AR content displays as users need to either scale down the content to fit within the FOV, largely resulting in the content becoming unreadable, or frequently adjust their position and view to scan between different content displays and check for updated or relevant content
SSA-5	User workstation configuration was unique as different users configured the AR content in different manners, e.g., different users replicated traditional multi-monitor workstation setups, configured a room-scale workspace with different content grouped in different areas of the room, utilized different vertical and horizontal content areas (e.g., some users placed content above or below level line of sight), etc. In addition, users preferred different scale content, with some users scaling content up for distance viewability, sacrificing FOV content coverage, and others scaling down content to maximize FOV coverage, but requiring more movement and adaptation to increase readability as required
SSA-6	Controller plus gaze-based interactions were preferred as it provided a means to accurately and quickly select content (via gaze) and then activate actions (via controller buttons) without risk of the system failing to register or incorrectly registering a user's input (which was often the case with gesture and speech inputs). Interactions that replicated traditional expectations (e.g., resizing content by selecting and dragging corners) was intuitive and allowed more efficient user interactions

identified with current AR state-of-the-art. Table 3 summarizes the findings from the demonstrations of the prototype.

4 Conclusions

Three prototype AR applications were developed to facilitate feasibility demonstrations and illicit feedback from representative users of the MC and BMC2 domain. All three prototypes provided geospatial visualizations combined with additional information display formalisms within the AR virtual environment. Each of the three prototypes was designed with specific features and technical goals in order to evaluate AR strengths and weaknesses, given the state-of-the-art in AR viewing and interaction capabilities (i.e., the Microsoft HoloLens). While a number of findings specific to each prototype's intended goals were identified, the lack of consistent findings and guidance for AR content design reinforced the need for HCI design standards for this evolving modality. Feedback from multiple demonstration events highlighted the need to consider not only the hardware properties (e.g., resolution, processing power, field of view), but also the viewing environmental characteristics (e.g., lighting, noise, ambient visual noise, dimensions), the user's characteristics (e.g., height, visual acuity, familiarity with AR gesture interactions) and preferences (e.g., preferred content arrangement), and the intended benefits AR is anticipated to produce (vs. creating a similar 3D visualization for a traditional screen-based display).

For MC/BMC2, the primary anticipated benefit appears to be visualization of area or volumetric content (e.g., sensor coverage zones, weaponry range, trajectory, and blast zone) and spatiotemporal factors that continually update (e.g., fire control phase lines). In addition, as AR is a new modality to most individuals, there is no standard for configuration of AR content to support decision making. However, many users revert to what they know, replicating a traditional multi-monitor workstation setup versus taking advantage of AR's flexibility with respect to room-scale content deployment. This may be an artifact of hardware limitations (e.g., the minimal field of view of the HoloLens). In addition, many potential benefits of AR may stem from its ability to support more interactive, and immersive collaboration; however, this was outside the scope of the goals of the supported prototypes for the most part. The findings presented in this paper were collected informally via hands-on demonstrations, from users who are representative of the military users who are anticipated to benefit from AR MC/BMC2 capabilities. However, simply translating content designed, with intention, for 2D computer displays into an AR virtual scene offers little perceivable benefit and due to the many issues that accompany this type of uniformed transformation, are likely to contribute to AR application abandonment. For this reason, there remains a need for a standard HCI guidance framework for AR information display design.

Acknowledgements. This material is based upon work supported by CERDEC under Contract No. W56KGU-18-C-0002. Any opinions, findings and conclusions or recommendations expressed in this material are those of the author(s) and do not necessarily reflect the views of CERDEC.

References

1. Odierno, R.T.: Army Doctrine Reference Publication (ADRP) 6-0: Mission Command. Department of the Army, Headquarters (2012)
2. United States Army Capabilities Integration Center (ARCIC): Army Warfighting Challenges. Department of the Army (2015)
3. Odierno, R.T.: Army Doctrine Publication (ADP) 5-0: The Operations Process. Department of the Army, Headquarters (2012)
4. Schraagen, J.M., Chipman, S.F., Shalin, V.L. (eds.): Cognitive Task Analysis. Psychology Press, Kentucky (2000)
5. Rasmussen, J., Pejtersen, A.M., Goodstein, L.P.: Cognitive Engineering: Concepts and Applications. Riso National Laboratory (1991)
6. Roth, E.M., Malin, J.T., Schreckenghost, D.L.: Paradigms for intelligent interface design. In: Handbook of Human-Computer Interaction, 2nd edn, pp. 1177–1201 (1997)
7. Woods, D., Sarter, N., Billings, C.: Automation surprises. In: Salvendy, G. (ed.) Handbook of Human Factors and Ergonomics, 2nd edn. Wiley, Hoboken (1997)
8. Woods, D., Dekker, S.: Anticipating the effects of technological change: a new era of dynamics for human factors. Theor. Issues Ergon. Sci. 1(3), 272–282 (2000)

Helmet-Mounted Displays to Support Off-Axis Pilot Spatial Orientation

Stephanie Kane$^{(\boxtimes)}$ and Ryan M. Kilgore

Charles River Analytics, Cambridge, USA
skane@cra.com

Abstract. Aerial refueling is one of the most demanding and dangerous activities faced by pilots. To monitor refueling, pilots must focus for long periods of time while looking up and outside the aircraft ("off-axis"), a more difficult task than focusing forward in the direction of flight ("on-axis"). To address these challenges, we designed a set of augmented reality display strategies for head-mounted displays (HMDs) that support pilot spatial orientation during off-axis activities, such as refueling. These display strategies include extending traditional on-axis displays (e.g., pitch ladders) for the off-axis context and designing new displays that convey critical information specifically tailored for the off-axis context. In this paper, we present our overall approach and a subset of concepts to address these needs. We also describe plans for formal evaluations.

Keywords: Cockpit displays · Spatial orientation · Augmented reality

1 Background

Aerial refueling is one of the most demanding and dangerous activities faced by pilots. Even under high visibility conditions with clear skies, refueling is a complex perceptual challenge—pilots must maintain their flight profile with respect to the tanker while monitoring tanker refueling operations. Air crews must maintain aircraft control with high precision, under tight physical safety envelopes, against the backdrop of accurately perceiving and appropriately responding to moving connection points with the fuel tanker. Under these challenging conditions, the pilot must work hard to communicate with the tanker, navigate into the tanker's slipstream and stabilize the aircraft, and then perform a detailed spatial alignment task as they lineup with the boom. Even under high visibility conditions with clear skies, refueling represents a complex perceptual challenge. This complexity is further compounded under reduced visibility (e.g., night, adverse weather) where naturally available and compelling perceptual cues specifying relative orientation and motion through space are degraded.

Many displays attempt to overcome the loss of natural sensory cues by taking critical state information and presenting it digitally over foveal vision displays. However, this format, frequently presented as text or display bugs on scales, is only insufficiently compelling to compete with other "strong-but-wrong" preattentive sensory cues as it must be visually extracted, translated, and interpreted, which is a cognitive, but not perceptual task. As such, these display-mediated cockpit cues do not

© Springer International Publishing AG, part of Springer Nature 2018
J. Y. C. Chen and G. Fragomeni (Eds.): VAMR 2018, LNCS 10910, pp. 289–297, 2018.
https://doi.org/10.1007/978-3-319-91584-5_23

support direct ecological perception and response. For this reason, such mediated displays do not support direct, *ecological* perception and response [1].

Furthermore, during refueling operations, pilots must focus for long periods of time while looking up and outside the aircraft ("off-axis"), a more difficult task than focusing forward in the direction of flight ("on-axis"), as seen below in Fig. 1. When looking off-axis, pilots cannot see traditional cockpit displays (e.g., attitude indicators) or virtual heads-up displays (VHUDs) that contain key orienting representations. Because refueling operations frequently occur during sustained, banked turns, pilot difficulty perceiving this continued roll can lead to spatial disorientation phenomena, such as "the leans."

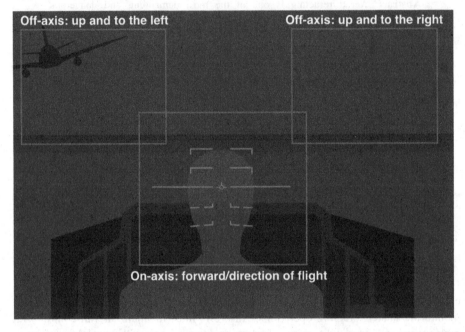

Fig. 1. During refueling pilots are primarily focusing off-axis (up and to the left) during refueling and traditional on-axis cockpit displays are outside of the pilot's view

Given these challenges, display solutions are required to improve pilots' accurate perception of their orientation and movement during precision maneuvers in challenging visual environments, particularly in supporting pilots' spatial orientation during aerial refueling.

2   Approach

Our approach began with a formal work domain analysis. As part of this effort, we performed a set of knowledge elicitation (KE) sessions with a team of pilot subject matter experts (SMEs), including Navy and Air Force pilots. During these knowledge elicitation sessions, we discussed a broad range of topics related to aerial refueling operations, spatial disorientation, cockpit symbology conventions, potential displays to support pilot understanding of aircraft attitude during refueling events, and the many complicating factors from environmental conditions and operational considerations that compound spatial orientation challenges. These interviews incorporated sets of scenario-based walkthroughs which were used for the SMEs to "talk-aloud" through key control tasks, interactions, and task sequences.

One key element contributing to spatial orientation challenges during aerial refueling is sub-threshold maneuver rates and sustained banked turns. During refueling, the pilot must constantly work to maintain an optimal position on the tanker. These maneuvers are typically small in magnitude, with bank angles of 40° or less with pitch between −5 and 5°. This constrains the operational problem to consider smaller roll and pitch rotations for effective display design. To effectively support spatial disorientation, pilots need displays that reminds them that they are in sustained banked turns, which is not readily detected by the vestibular system and contribute to the occurrence of spatial disorientation. Further compounding the spatial orientation challenges is that the pilot refueling and the entire group formation may need to maintain their position with respect to the tanker. Because of this operational aspect, aircraft may not necessarily enter level flight to align with the entire formation when finished refueling the aircraft, a key consideration for when designing *directive* displays providing control guidance to the pilot. In contrast, our preliminary approach under this effort has been focused on providing *descriptive* information displays that describe the spatial environment to the pilot.

A key orienting element for pilots is the horizon line as enables the pilot to understand aircraft attitude (e.g., pitch and roll) when visibility is good. In poor visibility, the pilot leverages aided vision capabilities to understand aircraft attitude and monitor position relative to the horizon. However, the pilot looks off-axis during refueling, so normal attitude displays (e.g., artificial horizon, pitch ladders) are not visible. When visibility is poor (e.g., at night, bad weather), there is little visual information about aircraft attitude, and the pilot must attend to the tanker's director lights to maintain optimal refueling position.

Another key orienting element for pilots includes pitch ladders. Pitch ladders are a traditional on-axis display that provide the pilot with roll and attitude information, but are not displayed when the pilot looks off-axis during aerial refueling. Pitch ladders show aircraft pitch using a series of lines distributed at equal intervals parallel to the horizon. Pitches above the horizon are typically represented with a pair of solid L-shaped lines, with the short end of the L pointing towards the horizon. Pitches below the horizon are typically represented with a pair of dashed L-shaped lines, with the short end of the L pointed towards the horizon. Line pairs below the horizon become increasingly angled with each step away from the horizon. The horizon (neutral pitch) is visually differentiated from other pitches with longer lines that are not L-shaped. When visibility is poor, pilots increasingly rely on pitch ladders to understand aircraft climb, descent, and roll.

While pitch ladders are a critical on-axis display, simply placing the traditional pitch ladder display so it appears when pilots are looking off-axis would be misleading as the pitch ladder display elements no longer map to physical real-world element. For example, in a simple addition of the pitch ladder to the off-axis context, the horizon line display would no longer act as a digital horizon line that maps the physical location of the horizon line in the world. Instead, the horizon line would be an abstract representation of the horizon line displayed from the on-axis perspective.

3 Design Concepts

To address these challenges, we designed a broad set of augmented reality display strategies for head-mounted displays (HMDs) that support pilot spatial orientation during off-axis activities, such as refueling. We explored a range of potential design solutions, both extending traditional pitch ladder displays for the off-axis context and designing new displays that convey critical information specifically tailored for the off-axis context.

Our first set of display strategies extends traditional pitch ladder representation symbology. We explored utilizing a range of display methods to show that the pitch ladder is no longer mapped to the physical pitch in the pilot's focus area, but instead conveys the information about the direction of flight for the aircraft. These methods included modifying the location/size of the pitch ladder, varying the styling and rendering of the pitch ladder (background border, line thickness, etc.), chaining multiple rendering methods together (e.g., both altering location and background style), and removing aircraft and current path indicators.

For example, Fig. 2 shows one design concept that employs traditional pitch ladder symbology, but uses a smaller size, background color, and explicit placement to distinguish it from traditional on-axis pitch ladders. The placement of this display is at the side of the VHUD nearest to on-axis—if the pilot looks off-axis to the left, it appears on the right side of the VHUD; if the pilot looks off-axis to the right, it appears on the left.

As another example, Fig. 3 below shows a "minimal" variation on traditional pitch ladders for level flight. In this example, the aircraft indicator remains, with only the horizon line is provided for a reference during level flight. The representation has also moved from the center of the screen to the right of the screen to further encode that this is an off-axis display concept, not a traditional on-axis pitch ladder. Figures 4 and 5 show two other examples with a slight roll and slight pitch up and slight pitch down variations.

We also explored a range of display concepts for display forms that convey critical aircraft orientation information using new visual forms. These display strategies were designed around key information relationships that integrate new display capabilities with aiding information to more effectively support spatial orientation and control inputs. When implemented in a clumsy fashion, poor visual-cue design and data-organization strategies require significant pilot cognitive resources to compensate, creating an explicit design opportunity to turn these currently *cognitive* tasks into natural *perceptual* tasks that free the pilot's attentional resources.

To address these design challenges, we applied mature ecological interface design (EID) techniques [2–4] to develop these design concepts. EID is an approach to perceptually grounded interface design that was developed specifically to address the challenges of cognitive work within highly constrained physical systems, such as pilot

Fig. 2. Extended off-axis pitch ladder design. The pilot is looking off-axis, up and to the left. This design extends the traditional pitch ladder by removing aircraft/route indicators, changing the location/size of the pitch ladder by reducing the size and placing it in the lower right corner, and employing a background for additional cueing that this pitch ladder represents on-axis information.

Fig. 3. "Minimal" extension to traditional pitch ladders for off-axis context indicating a slight roll

Fig. 4. "Minimal" extension to traditional pitch ladders for off-axis context indicating a slight pitch up and slight roll

Fig. 5. "Minimal" extension to traditional pitch ladders for off-axis context indicating a slight pitch down and slight roll

control of aircraft in flight. We used established EID design techniques to develop a variety of display sets that maximize the perceptual availability of these critical and integrated information sources to pilots. Figure 6 shows a subset of example display concepts that explore representations for depicting the horizon line, altitude, and roll. In these examples the altitude is represented by a vertical bar and the horizon line is represented immediately beneath it.

Fig. 6. New off-axis pitch ladder design. Key orientation information (roll and altitude) is encoded in graphical formats within the off-axis context with the altitude represented by the vertical bar and horizon line by the horizontal line directly beneath it.

As part of this approach we explored both egocentric and exocentric representations. Across the visual forms, we also explored a range of conditions with subset of graphical elements maintained static positions for reference points while other graphical elements were dynamic and changed over time.

4   Prototyping and Demonstration

As these designs evolved, we prototyped a subset of promising display approaches to prototypes of increasing fidelity and detail, both to support our own internal iterative review and incremental design process, as well as to support critical evaluations with our team of pilots. We explored a range of augmented reality prototyping options, such as commercial off-the-shelf (COTS) see-through augmented reality helmets, which can support head-tracking displays capabilities. Head-tracking is particularly critical for this effort to sense the transition between on-axis and off-axis displays, such as when the pilot is looking up outside of the cockpit to manage refueling activity.

For our preliminary proof-of-concept prototype we leveraged the Microsoft HoloLens augmented reality device [5] as a primary hardware prototyping platform due to its rich, out-of-the-box support for head-tracking and rapid integration with our in-house flight simulation environment. However, one challenge of note with the HoloLens is the limited field of view. Using these prototypes, we performed initial cognitive walkthroughs and informal evaluations of our display methods and preliminary prototypes with a team of pilots.

5 Conclusions and Future Work

This paper describes a set of preliminary design strategies to support off-axis spatial orientation for pilots during refueling. As part of this effort, we performed preliminary evaluations with subject matter experts on a set of pitch ladder extensions and new visual displays for the off-axis contexts. Based on the results of these evaluations, both methods show promising methods of conveying critical information in off-axis context. Next steps would include medium fidelity testing on both approaches and formal evaluations with representative users.

Key areas of additional investigation include exploring the effectiveness of transition between on-axis and off-axis orientation and display strategies and methods to facilitate effective transition. For example, consideration such as animations, timing, motion relative to the pilot's head movement may impact awareness between on-axis and off-axis displays. Another area of investigation includes identifying the impact of effectiveness on refueling task and efficiency of interpreting spatial information. Finally, another broader area of investigation is exploring how these off-axis cockpit displays can work in isolation or in coordination with information displays across other modalities (e.g., auditory displays).

We are currently designing a formal, human-in-the-loop experimental plan to investigate the effectiveness of both these displays and transitions between on- and off-axis orientation. In particular, we plan to identify the impact on pilot interpretation of spatial orientation during intensive off-axis mission tasks, such as aerial refueling. Our research plan will test a set of display strategies and investigate their effects on performance for maintaining a manual tracking tasks similar to those for maintaining a long, sustained turn during aerial refueling, and visually-intensive secondary tasks (e.g., watching for changes in a visual display). We will examine a number of metrics to assess performance and spatial orientation.

This research will provide insight into the basic and fundamental question of how we can better understand, develop, and design effective displays for supporting pilots in on- and off-axis contexts. By examining the effect of on-axis and off-axis HMD strategies on users' task performance and spatial orientation, we will be able to better understand and develop displays that effectively support pilots in both contexts. Our research will shed light on whether there are effects inherent to wearing HMDs, or whether the different physical viewing orientation of a HMD may differentially affect the user. This research is critical for a variety of applications, including military and medical operations; as well as general gaming entertainment use. We believe the results from this study will inform domain-specific displays as well as more broadly augmented reality displays.

Acknowledgements. This material is based upon work supported by the Navy under Contract No. N68335-15-C-0158. Any opinions, findings and conclusions or recommendations expressed in this material are those of the author(s) and do not necessarily reflect the views of the Navy.

References

1. Gibson, J.: The Senses Considered as Perceptual Systems (1966)
2. Burns, C.M., Hadjukiwicz, J.: Ecological Interface Design. CRC Press, Boca Raton (2004)
3. Kilgore, R., St-Cyr, O.: The SRK inventory: a tool for structuring and capturing a worker competencies analysis. In: Proceedings of the Human Factors and Ergonomics Society Annual Meeting, vol. 50, no. 3. SAGE Publications, Thousand Oaks (2006)
4. Kilgore, R.M.: Formalizing display development in ecological interface design: the form comparison matrix. In: Proceedings of the Human Factors and Ergonomics Society Annual Meeting, vol. 51, no. 4. SAGE Publications, Thousand Oaks (2007)
5. Microsoft HoloLens. https://www.microsoft.com/en-us/hololens. Accessed 08 Mar 2018

Augmented Reality Views: Discussing the Utility of Visual Elements by Mediation Means in Industrial AR from a Design Perspective

Jens Keil[2]($\boxtimes$), Florian Schmitt[1]($\boxtimes$), Timo Engelke[2]($\boxtimes$), Holger Graf[1]($\boxtimes$), and Manuel Olbrich[1]($\boxtimes$)

[1] Fraunhofer IGD, Darmstadt, Germany
{Florian.Schmitt,Holger.Graf,Manuel.Olbrich}@igd.fraunhofer.de
[2] Visometry GmbH, Darmstadt, Germany
{Jens.Keil,Timo.Engelke}@visometry.com

Abstract. In this paper we present and discuss common visual elements in Augmented Reality which create a distinct information context while presenting them in either video- or optical-see-though setups, and which align with the promise of AR being able to bridge the gap between real world objects and the digital information space about them.

Reflecting on nowadays common elements with these premises in mind, we collected and categorized a variety of visual elements, e.g. annotation & labels, visual highlights, assisting visual aids and trans-media elements. Focusing on industrial AR applications, we discuss their suitability in terms of mediation and communication goals, instead of technological and implementation considerations.

In doing so, we seek to identify the currently most relevant visual elements and discuss the deployed meaning that can be created in utilizing these elements for a informed and successful communication. From there we introduce a first framing meta-model that on the one hand helps clarifying the mediation strength of these elements and on the other enables to reflect their suitability on a more strategic level.

Keywords: Adaptive and personalized interfaces
Human centered design · Information visualization · Interaction design

1 Introduction

In the 1920s, Otto Neurath among others formulated the idea, that one should use images to make impression and introduced with Isotype a graphic system in order to make data understandable to a broad, non-informed and probably non-educated audience through data visualization means (cf. [13]). Ever since, VR and AR visualizations are seen as such utilities that, by mixing and blending reality with overlaid annotations and information, create such clear, unambiguous views. Especially in industrial application, such as maintenance, production

© Springer International Publishing AG, part of Springer Nature 2018
J. Y. C. Chen and G. Fragomeni (Eds.): VAMR 2018, LNCS 10910, pp. 298–312, 2018.
https://doi.org/10.1007/978-3-319-91584-5_24

or training, this is not only crucial but regarded as the key advantage and added value of AR and mixed reality technology. However, even with the third AR wave and technology push from Smartphones in 2007, PokemonGo and Hololens in 2015, and ARKit in 2017, AR apps and prototypes stick to rather simple superimposition that present 3D data merely affixed on reality, or worse eventually block or occlude it. By doing so, they are showcasing technological improvements instead of focusing on communication and mediation aspects or the creation of a clear and consistent information context. In that sense, AR visuals are presented in reality but are often hardly or not at all connected to it.

With AR tracking technology in mind that is capable track objects precisely (e.g. via vision based techniques such as [17]), information can be presented precisely spatially positioned at an object of interest and enables to use tracking technology e.g. for a discrepancy check. Consequently, this enables both: to add complementary information to such target objects (e.g. 2D annotations or 3D graphics), and to employ these objects during visualization, e.g. by digitally highlighting parts of a machinery.

Ideally such techniques allow the user to focus on the content and the perception of an augmented or extended reality. It needs a visual language and an idea on how to strategically use visual elements to convey information appropriately. In this paper we are going to discuss such AR elements in the context of industrial use cases.

Through a bottom up approach, we present a collections of elements that we've seen useful throughout industrial AR projects, such as (a) communication of a novel product's main features, (b) task- and procedure-based maintenance support, (c) spatially located and aligned expert information.

Having a background of around 10 years in the field, up until today we found a coherent system or classification during the design phase missing, of how AR is utilized to (ideally) convey information of such industrial apps. But we think it is needed in order to create a distinct information context while presenting visual overlays in either video- or optical-see-though setups. With ARs ability to display information that is relevant to a context at hand, i.e. a situation or a task users perform, the imperative hypothesis is that ARs eases a users cognitive transfer performance through distinct visuals that guide the eye and the user thereby. Hence, visual elements ideally come in an appropriate visual form, and at best supplement mediation approaches.

We discuss the state of AR visual elements and aim at answering which visual elements are available and what to gain from them in terms of mediation and communicative goals, besides technological issues, which have been intensively addressed in literature until now.

2   Related Work

We've been looking into mediation and visualization techniques in AR with a bottom-up approach, using various publication sources, from research to public project documentations on the web and our own experience and work. A sound collection can nowadays be found in [18], which focuses on visualization techniques on technical level, detailing algorithmic and implementation details rather than focusing on application and use case. However, it identifies and describes the most relevant recent visual elements. Looking into the latter, at least the work of Xu [14] is relevant. The paper introduces and describes pre-patterns as an systematic attempt for visuals and interaction alike, but is focusing primarily on AR games.

The work of [15] and our study around [16] have illustrated, that there is a strong need for a smart view management and an informed usage of visual elements for information presentation in AR, and, that such presentations can benefit from camera- and motion-controlled interactions. Ideally, such techniques allow the user to focus on the content and the perception of an augmented or extended reality.

A formalized framing, or more concretely standardization, has also a vast history in the area. Many groups try to formalize information models and data structures as well as semantics in the data modeling for the AR-related usage of content. AREL was one of the first efforts, which was a propitiate declaration driven by the private organization Metaio. Today, NIST [20] and AREA [21] are driving such efforts, especially in terms of industrial utilization.

3 Visualizations and Visual Elements in AR

In industrial cases, we think AR evolves its potential especially in MRO scenarios (Maintenance, Repair, Overhaul) as it enables the superimposition of maintenance instructions and assisting information. Self-evidently the usage of AR should be meaningful without increasing the inherently complexity of maintenance tasks in industrial environments. Due to information density, there's a necessity to adapt users perceptional limitation by adaptive visualizations and this should be considered in the design process of AR applications. However, as Grasset et al. [15] summarize various visualization techniques for AR have been proposed, but adaptive visualization techniques are still poorly studied in AR. Although this is a common methodology in disciplinary fields like geographic information system and cartography. To some extent this transfer is considered on a technological level by some approaches, f.e. by Julier et al. [11] who proposed filtering methods to reduce information overload and visual clutter or by adaptive visual aids by Webel et al. [10] where the strength of information changes dynamically.

With such a goal in mind, we collected and identified different visual elements with a focus on mediation quality instead of technical feasibility. The aim is to describe, categorize and organize visual elements in such a way that we are able to discuss their suitability for different tasks and mediation levels in industrial AR cases. With such a canvas, the idea is to derive a template or tool box of common visual AR elements and with a set of design criteria to (visually) guiding the user's focus and attention by e.g. virtually highlighting elements of a physical object, or through adaptive annotations.

3.1   Common Visual Elements

In AR on smartphones, tablets or glassware like HoloLens, one can consider several layers, which compose an overall perceptual impression for a user: one is the real surrounding, either perceived by video-see-through or optically, second is the 3D world or AR space, where superimposed 3D renderings appear aligned to real objects, and third is the 2D or semi-3D screen space, which typically holds traditional, non-AR UI elements which stick on screen, even if the device is moved around.

3.2   Annotations and Labels

Appearances: By definition, annotations are spatially dependent components, which anchors an object and have to be registered to the real world or spatially independent components not contained in the real world [12]. While these could be any graphical element with usage from navigation in AR up to maintenance information, we see mainly textual labels are frequently used. From here, three major forms appear useful: (a) icon-like, bill-boarded pointers, which are directly centered in the anchor position, (b) twin-elements of (2D or 3D) labels with leader lines that connect the label to the anchor - these elements can be either in the 3D or the 2D screen space, a relative position to the object or with a fixed position in screen space. Either way, the leading line as the anchor point will move and appear sticky to its origin at the object and thereby maintain a visual connection of the two. Sometimes, pointer annotations also behave like targets that trigger events or reveals more details once activated.

Usage: On a mediation level, we tend to treat annotations and labels in our understanding like real world extending elements, which add additional contextually useful information without the need of this information to otherwise fit to the augmented object in visual terms (e.g. in contrast to a visually highlighted part of a target object). Those elements are nowadays heavily used and popular in AR browsers, like Layar, Wikitude or YELP Monocle. They act as visual proxies, with either a descriptive labeling role or a link to detailed information, for instance linking a Wikipedia entry to visually recognized book or sight, where the link is presented as an AR-icon.

3.3   Highlights

Appearances: Being able to precisely track objects with edge tracking, by means of a target object's 3D model, enables to visually highlight parts or entire objects in an highly fitting and convincing visual way through the use of its shape. Highlights can also be animated, e.g. smoothly fading from none to the highlighted color while being slightly transparent so to not occlude the real part with the rendering entirely. When the geometry or shape of an element isn't available, pointer or other proxy geometry can be used as an indicator or highlighting element instead.

Usage: While such proxies are technically close to annotations, on an mediation level, they serve a different purpose. Instead of extending reality, they rather emphasize it, just like a text marker would. Geometrically-fitting highlights make parts or objects stand out and catch attention, which is even enhanced when animated. Highlights not only lead attention, they can also be used as a selection indication during AR-selection techniques, where real physical objects become digitally select-able through the AR view.

3.4   Assisting Visual Aids: Helper and Guiding-Geometry

Appearances: Within this category we summarize supplemental visual elements, like arrows and other pointers, guideline elements or metaphorical indicators, like Torch-Light or Magic Lens (cf. [5]) effects, that are basically composed of 2D or 3D sprites or geometry and that refer to or are anchored to particular points-of-interest at the target object. Like Highlights, they can be animated too. Such elements can either appear in the AR space only, e.g. be fixed to their anchor position, or like the lead line of annotations and labels, be connected to the screen space in some way (e.g. as in [19]).

Usage: Again, such elements are close to annotations in technical terms. But in contrast to the latter or highlights they communicate stronger meaning by their own means. The way we see them used, they basically serve as marker, links and container for textual content within the AR space. In contrast to highlights, visual aids not only shallowly emphasize elements on a target object or a points-of-interest in the view. Instead, their shape and motion (when animated) itself suit a communication goal, for instance to clear a screwing direction, or to emphasize caution and attention on otherwise missed details during assemblies users would otherwise not pay attention to. Magic Lenses are a special case, as they typically come with a distinct visible bounding box that visually set the superimposition apart from the rest of the scene. In doing so, such elements draw attention but also are one way to cope with visual clutter - which is considered a notorious problem of information display in AR (cf. [18]).

3.5   Additive Elements: XRay

Appearances: XRay visuals uncover hidden, occluded or otherwise impercepti-ble or structures, e.g. a car's engine underneath a closed hood. The illusion is created by artificially removing occluding parts from real world objects, as if looking through solid matter. Literature defines such visualizations as comprised by phantom or occlusion geometry, or a ghosting render technique that enables themselves to occupy, clip or occlude the real objects in areas, where the "look-behind-the-curtain" effect should happen, while keeping or introducing addi-tional geometry as depth cues in order to support the depth perception. Espe-cially the ghosting technique with shape outlines or transparent outer hulls aim to reveal enough of the XRay objects underneath (cf. [6]) to be comprehensible, while keeping/preserving major structural elements of the occluder, i.e. the physical object, in order to preserve valuable depth cues to understand the presented AR-view.

Usage: On an meditation level, we can think of such add-ins as an enrichment of reality, as they reveal spatial and semantic relationships between hidden and visible objects. In that sense, they are not only a sole extension, but create meaning immediately within the viewing context in AR. Examples are the revelation of pipes in the ground or a cable tree inside a car that through superimposition communicate the meticulous network-like character, while visually help to find and identify e.g. connecting control-units during a diagnose phase (rendering the prior physical dismantling unnecessary).

3.6   Additive Elements: Explosion Diagrams

Appearances: AR explosion diagrams are a quite common visual element in industrial AR. Originated in technical illustrations, such elements are used to present object assemblies at the real physical counterparts in such a way that it becomes possible to memorize and reassemble the object mentally and to show relations, assembly steps and the structural layering of parts. In literature (cf. [18]), these elements are often addressed as spatial manipulation.

Usage: The goal is to stimulate the user cognition process of creating a mental model of complex objects (cf. [10]). Likewise to the former elements, such visuals can be seen as additional layer, where virtual representation enriches the current scene. The challenge, however, is to ensure, that the virtual element coherently co-exist with the real one, i.e. not generate clutter or ambiguity, or mutual occlusion between virtual and real that hinders the mediation strength. Connected to interaction, explosions not only convey structural assembly hierarchies, they can also be treat as extending, linking elements, e.g. in case of the tires-breaking system of car, each part could be connected to a replacement part catalogue.

3.7   Trans-Media Material

Appearances: As a category of its own, we can think of trans-media material that can be of any form, from 2D to 3D sprites or video footage, which is superimposed into the user's view and still aligned to the target object and viewing context. For instance historical 2D photo material, or the virtual recoloring of historical art pieces and statues belong in this category. Depending on the used material, not all media per sé meet AR requirements: while 3D models suite rather well, because they can be augmented and viewed perspective- and view independent, 2D and 2.5D images or videos might be not. Therefore, through the use of a ghost-like, bill-boarded presentation, such media can very well be integrated into the AR view as it allows to be sticky relative the target object or within the surrounding, while not appearing odd or misplaced, once users move the device.

Usage: In AR terms and those of our understanding, such visuals are again an enrichment of reality. But in contrast to the prior visual elements, they suite the wish for creating high immersion imagery, without necessarily much more meditation or communicative aspects. For instance in the area of heritage and tourism, the restitution of a broken temple would belong to such a classification. Ghost-like presentations typically won't block or occlude real world elements, as they are rendered transparently; in doing so, they usually also come with an appealing aesthetics, that metaphorically-speaking give augmented objects literally a digital aura. Such visuals works as a whole: they don't necessarily proxy or encode information in a visualization manner.

4 Discussion

4.1 Debriefing the Visual Elements

Summing up the common elements already reveals that some have become such a commodity in its usage that we can assume them as quasi-standard elements which are both, well elaborated and useful.

This especially concerns labels and annotations as they belong to the most important AR elements in industrial applications. We think this is mainly because they are easy to generate in technical terms. However, they are also one of the most challenging elements, because their misuse can easily produce clutter and ambiguity instead of being of assistance.

Next to annotations, highlights (Sect. 3.3) and what we refer to as assisting visual aids (Sect. 3.4) belong to the category of elaborated visual elements, too. Especially contour-bound highlights allow to visually stand out, while being appealing and unobtrusive at the same time (Fig. 2b+d). However, if the highlighted elements are too small, they can easily be overseen or not recognized. Here, visual aids that are complementing or acting as highlights are of huge help, as they can overcome such shortcomings (Fig. 2a).

Other categories, like XRay or explosion diagrams are less clear to grasp. In terms of their composition they are comprised of several media elements to such and extend, where not single elements, but rather the whole picture suits a communicative purpose; be it more or less only to give a whole picture, like in the case of virtual restitution. However, we think such visuals only add value if they align and integrate into the real view well enough, at least to some degree. For instance, maintaining depth perception of Xray blendings is rudimentary in order to frame and conceive the AR view. Either by using appropriate occlusion geometry (cf. Fig. 4c) or other visual cues, such as ghostings of the outer hull of a target object, enable to deliver a coherent AR presentation.

In term of trans-media material – which builds the visually richest and, if well done, most appealing superimposition elements – interaction can enhance the experience beyond the point of sole presentation-only. For instance, with Magic Lenses the superimposed content is not visible all-at-once, thereby encouraging the user to move the device so to explore the overlaid content that becomes incrementally visible by doing so (cf. Fig. 1d), which presents a Xray of a rocket's interior in a Magic Lens). However, the better the visuals are fused and integrated into the real scene, the more credible and convincing the AR impression and

Fig. 1. Examples for annotation and label types (left to right): (a) situated icons linking to online references of the sights [23], (b) pointer indicators as hints to further information, (c) lead lined labels with contextual expert information, (d) Magic Lens and lead-lined labels, which in contrast to the prior are sticky in the right-handed screen space.

Fig. 2. Range of highlighting elements (left to right): (a) semi-transparent, circular indicator enclosing the point-of-interest, (b+c) shape and geometry-based yellow highlight make target objects protrude [22], (d) highlight as selection indicator: similar to the prior, the object's contour is used as highlight boundary, here interactively triggered at the target object through a gaze-technique. (Color figure online)

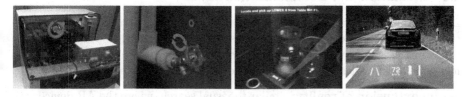

Fig. 3. Types of helper and guidance geometry (left to right): (a+b) circular arrow-like overlays communicating working directions on a machinery. (c) Superimposed guidelines on a see-through-device as a leading tool during assemblies [19]. (d) Red sickle-shaped element indicating the distance control's preceding target in a head-up display [25]. (Color figure online)

immersion will become (cf. Fig. 5, where the shape in (a) is almost seamlessly blended, while the video in (d) is merely pinned at a building's blank wall). In order to connect information precisely and clearly to objects, it is a necessity (Fig. 3). We think this is also true for the type of AR apps common for today, where with SLAM and visual odometry – as used by ARKit and HoloLens – media is superimposed and placed into reality like holograms: they rely on the AR illusion and appear to exist in reality, but in contrast to above must not be any further related or connected to objects in it.

Fig. 4. Range of XRay, explode and ghost-like visuals (left to right): (a) revealing sub-surface infrastructure with XRay visuals, and (b) with ghostings [24]. (c) XRay with semi-transparent cover structure of the target object's shell. (d) Interactive explosion diagram revealing a breaking system's topology.

Fig. 5. Examples of trans-media as visual overlays in AR. (a) One of the first AR-based restitution of the ruins of the Acropolis in Archeoguide [1]. (b) 2D restitution of a Medusa relief and (c) a recoloring of a maiden statue in CHESS [2]. (d) Historical video overlay superimposed in-situ in the Berlin Wall App [26].

4.2 Mediation and Communication Goals

Looking into literature around AR visuals and visualization techniques reveals that at first developers and AR app designers need to decide what they want to do in the AR view and what they want to achieve with it. With the prior mentioned visual elements in mind, we identified three major aspects:

(a) **an extension of reality:** similar to visual search, where the AR device acts gap-bridging between physical and virtual via a "point-and-show" or "show-and-tell" metaphor: the added-value then lies in the ease of connecting digital info to the target objects, which would otherwise require users to manually search e.g. online. Interaction with the device and the visuals help to sort, filter or ease access of information and fuse them by utilizing annotations and labels as visual elements. Thereby, real objects are linked-with or linked-to complementary digital information immediately. This creates a quick and unobtrusive experience that nicely bridge the physical/digital gap.

(b) **an emphasis of reality:** by highlighting or otherwise emphasizing relevant parts. Doing so, helps identifying and focusing on important aspects. For example during a step-by-step maintenance procedure, highlighting frankly lead users to focus on the machinery parts-of-interest at the current step. Or, they indicate its virtual selection or activity at the target object. Another aspect, which we see relevant in this context, but won't be discussed in detail here, is working the other way around by diminishing reality in order to emphasize an AR view and to lead the eye. In video-see-through AR, this basically means manipulation and filtering the video, at simplest turn irrelevant information in the video-acquired reality gray, while relevant information stays colored.

(c) **an enrichment of reality:** where augmenting rich visuals allows user to immerse in the AR view and create a picture as-a-whole. In our sense, going back step-wise from photo-realistically depiction to explosion diagrams, ghost-like add-ins or XRay visuals, such techniques are more than a extension or emphasis, but allow to reveal the invisible, restore, reconstruct or mix real and virtual quite vividly, enable to depict different temporal states of the target-object or scenery – but in technical terms take also more effort to create.

In terms of industrial application, an additional aspect leads into the element's usage during authoring. Here, elements which can easily be created automatically and deliver quick-encoded information are likely preferred over (what we collected under) trans-media elements. The latter typically rely on time-intense manual creation work during the media production phase. Talking to industrial leads, automatized authoring is seen as a key element during the design and authoring phase of industrial AR maintenance systems.

Another huge topic is whether is it possible to transfer the often dense traditional information into AR views at all – or, more precisely, to find metrics to which degree such information should be transferred into AR. On tablets and smartphones, we nowadays see many UI concepts that not only rely on sole AR presentations, but combine state-of-art 2D UI dialogues with AR visuals. While this appears appropriate at first, in research related to the CHESS project [2] we found that the more (2D) UI elements in screens space exist, the less attention is given to the AR space. In a more recent follow-up evaluation with 40 students, who took our demonstrator from [3], all participants stated that this takes already effect, even if only a small amount of additional UI elements are visible: In the minute people need to cope or touch UI elements while holding the AR device up, they tend to immerse less in the AR view and to loose the impression of the media "existing" in reality.

Our identified visuals and categorizations ground on the core promise of mixed reality to bridge the gap between real world objects and the digital information space about them. In that context, two central questions arise: are these elements working well? And, to which extend do they suite as mediation elements? Especially for the latter, we see the question closely connected to possible interactions (e.g. while annotations and labels might visually be less intriguing aesthetics compared to more compelling renderings, in terms of UX and interaction they are so relevant, because of the prior mentioned show-and-tell principles). Although we can't cover interactivity in AR and with UI elements in more detail here, we think it is an essential element that goes hand in hand with AR visuals in terms of our discussion regarding mediation and communication adequacy.

5   Proposing a Consistent Model

5.1   The AR Visualization Cube

Identifying the taxonomy of the common visual elements as a holistic view has
exposed that manifold concepts of visualization techniques have been investigated and proposed for augmented reality applications. Especially in complex
maintenance scenarios, AR should assist the user on the accomplishment of his
tasks by only showing the currently relevant information. Therefore superimposing unfiltered information leads to ambiguities and disturb the user's focus. The
approaches in this paper and our work in this field have shown that there is a
strong necessity to progress the core visual elements into an adaptive manner.
This includes a multifaceted consideration of adaptive visualization techniques,
where the strength of superimposed information changes dynamically through
means of interaction techniques (cf. [16]).

As mentioned before, we see very similar demands to visualizations in AR
to visualization techniques in geographic information systems and cartography.
MacEachren [4] introduced a model called 'the cartography/visualization cube',
which defines visualization in terms of map use, conceptualized it into three
dimensions (user, task and interactivity). Synoptically, this model splits the map
usage into visualizing/exploring the unknown and communicating the known.
This model is an appropriate way to describe visualizations for information mediation on maps and we think, due its similarities (in terms of interactivity and
modality), it is transferable to AR visualizations (Fig. 6).

Against MacEachrens 'cartography cube', our approach defines visualizations
in terms of usage in AR applications. As quintessence, the diagonal axis describes
the effort which needs to be expended to transfer/generate knowledge for the

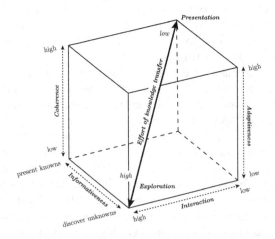

Fig. 6. 'AR visualization cube', transferred from visualization cube defined by
MacEachren [4].

respective visualization. Thereby this effort depends on the amount on informativeness (scale between discover unknown & present known) and on the level of interaction as a ratio of exploration. In other words, with less informativeness and a high degree of interaction the information extraction need to be done by a sophisticated process of exploration. As opposed to this, the communication of aggregated and pre-processed information significantly decrease the effort of knowledge transfer.

5.2   Applying the Cube

The cube's principle can be illustrated at the example of annotations. Extending objects by annotations and labels should ideally create an added value and discreetly give the user a hint about additional context, without distracting the user's attention. It should be noted, however that displaying multiple, excessive, unfiltered visual elements (i.e. annotations or labels) at once, leads to information overload and ambiguities affected by occlusion or visual clutter. Furthermore, they tend to appear visually incoherent with regard to the target object they are connected to and become illegible and impend to interact with (cf. [16,18]). Considering our model, therefore unfiltered visualizations unveil less information and a sophisticated exploration process is required to gain insights. This could not only interrupt the users perception but even worse could unintendedly lead to wrong conclusions. Looking beyond AR, this visual impairment is also well known in cartography and is solved by generalization methods, which allow the simplification of map contents by deriving the information density in relation to the level-of-detail (LOD) [9]. Even adaptive rendering has been poorly studied in AR [15], however there are several approaches for filtering and ordering techniques [11]. Particularly for annotations, the effort of knowledge transfer can be decreased by spatial, knowledge-based, or combined filtering methods [7], as they enable the possibility for decomposing the information density and keeping the visual coherence by only showing the relevant information.

Fig. 7. Unfiltered [8] vs. proximity- and angle-sensitive clustered annotations.

With regard to e.g. adaptive annotations, this paradigm facilitates user-centric spatial- & motion driven interaction methods in AR. By connecting superimposed annotations and other content to motion-based interaction and to camera-acquired targets, the information density can be intuitively controlled by proximity. In a simplified scheme, this can be illustrated in (cf. Fig. 7, as the level-of-detail of information presented is influenced by the distance/proximity and the angle to the tracking target. In order to clarify the view through a meaningful filtering and thereby reducing the cognitive load to the users, the motion-driven and the user controlled adaptive behaviour of the visuals encourages the user's perception and improves mediation strength. We see that this effect and trade-off of exploration to presentation is also true for the majority of the before mentioned visual elements (especially for indicative visualization rather then complementary/supplementary ones like XRay, explosion diagrams or trans-media material). Applicable on each of the presented common visuals in AR, we think our conceptional 'AR visualization cube' is an appropriate and consistent model and a start to describe visualization and their requirements in regards to Augmented Reality as well as implications on interaction.

6   Conclusion and Future Work

In this paper we collected common visual elements in AR in terms of mediation and communication aspects, especially focusing on industrial use cases, with ARs core promise in mind of being able to bridge the gap between real world objects and the digital information space about them. Reflecting on today's common elements taken from public sources, literature and own experience, we categorized and discussed their suitability regarding mediation and communicative goals instead of technical and implementation considerations. In doing so, we have introduced (a) three mediation principles, namely extend, emphasize, enrich, and (b) the 'AR visualization cube', a framing meta-model that on the one hand helps clarifying the mediation strength of these elements and on the other enables to reflect on their suitability on a more strategic level.

While we see high relevance in shifting attention from technology to application of AR visual elements as visualization-based aids during industrial usage and similar mediation-intense cases, we also see the need for further investigation. Especially in terms of assessing the performance of AR visuals and their suitability regarding didactic and physiological models of cognition, a deeper formal investigation would contribute to the discussion (Webel et. al. [10] started to do so, but was focusing on maintenance based AR training).

As a result of this paper we raise the question of a visual language or at least a toolbox or framework of visual strategies in terms of communication and mediation aspects, since we found appropriate guidelines missing. With our presented model and the idea behind it to link the topic of AR visualization to other, more elaborated disciplines such as geo-visualization, we aim to contribute to the discussion without being complete or having considered all possibilities.

References

1. Vlahakis, V., et al.: Archeoguide: first results of an augmented reality, mobile computing system in cultural heritage sites. In: Proceedings of the VAST Conference on Virtual Reality, Archeology, and Cultural Heritage (2001)
2. Katifori, A., et al.: CHESS: personalized storytelling experiences in museums. In: Mitchell, A., Fernández-Vara, C., Thue, D. (eds.) ICIDS 2014. LNCS, vol. 8832, pp. 232–235. Springer, Cham (2014). https://doi.org/10.1007/978-3-319-12337-0_28

3. Keil, J., Engelke, T., Schmitt, M., Bockholt, U., Pujol, L.: Lean in or lean back? Aspects on interactivity & mediation in handheld augmented reality in the museum. In: EGCH Eurographics Workshop on Graphics and Cultural Heritage (2014)
4. MacEachren, A.M., Taylor, D.R.F.: Visualization in Modern Cartography, vol. 2. Elsevier, New York City (1994)
5. Bier, E.A., Stone, M.C., Pier, K., Buxton, W., DeRose, T.D.: Toolglass and magic lenses: the see-through interface. In: Proceedings of the ACM SIGGRAPH Conference on Computer Graphics and Interactive Techniuqes (1993)
6. Feiner, S., Seligmann, D.D.: Cutaways and ghosting: satisfying visibility constraints in dynamic 3D illustrations. Vis. Comput. **8**, 292–302 (1992)
7. Götzelmann, T., Hartmann, K., Strothotte, T.: Agent-based annotation of interactive 3D visualizations. In: Butz, A., Fisher, B., Krüger, A., Olivier, P. (eds.) SG 2006. LNCS, vol. 4073, pp. 24–35. Springer, Heidelberg (2006). https://doi.org/10.1007/11795018_3
8. Camba, J., Contero, M., Johnson, M.: Management of visual clutter in annotated 3D CAD models: a comparative study. In: Marcus, A. (ed.) DUXU 2014. LNCS, vol. 8518, pp. 405–416. Springer, Cham (2014). https://doi.org/10.1007/978-3-319-07626-3_37
9. Bereuter, P., Weibel, R.: Real-time generalization of point data in mobile and web mapping using quadtrees. Cartogr. Geogr. Inf. Sci. **40**, 271–281 (2013)
10. Webel, S., Bockholt, U., Keil, J.: Design criteria for AR-based training of maintenance and assembly tasks. In: Shumaker, R. (ed.) VMR 2011. LNCS, vol. 6773, pp. 123–132. Springer, Heidelberg (2011). https://doi.org/10.1007/978-3-642-22021-0_15
11. Julier, S.J., Baillot, Y., Brown, D., Lanzagorta, M.: Information filtering for mobile augmented reality. IEEE Comput. Graph. Appl. **22**(5), 12–15 (2002)
12. Wither, J., DiVerdi, S., Hoellerer, T.: Annotation in outdoor augmented reality. Comput. Graph. **33**, 679–689 (2009)
13. Hartmann, F., Bauer, E.K.: Bildsprache: Otto Neurath Visualisierungen. In: Facultas Verlags- und Buchhandels AG (2006). ISBN-10: 3-7089-0000-6
14. Xu, Y., Barba, E., Radu, I., Gandy, M., Shemaka, R. Schrank, B., Tseng, T., MacIntyre, B.: Pre-patterns for designing embodied interactions in handheld augmented reality games. In: Proceedings of the IEEE ISMAR International Symposium on Mixed and Augmented Reality - Arts, Media, and Humanities (2011)
15. Grasset, R., Langlotz, T., Kalkofen, D., Tatzgern, M., Schmalstieg, D.: Image-driven view management for augmented reality browsers. In: Proceedings of the IEEE ISMAR International Symposium on Mixed and Augmented Reality (2012)
16. Keil, J., Zoellner, M., Engelke, T., Wientapper, F., Schmitt, M.: Controlling and filtering information density with spatial interaction techniques via handheld augmented reality. In: Shumaker, R. (ed.) VAMR 2013. LNCS, vol. 8021, pp. 49–57. Springer, Heidelberg (2013). https://doi.org/10.1007/978-3-642-39405-8_6
17. Seo, B.-K., Wuest, H.: A direct method for robust model-based 3D object tracking from a monocular RGB image. In: Hua, G., Jégou, H. (eds.) ECCV 2016. LNCS, vol. 9915, pp. 551–562. Springer, Cham (2016). https://doi.org/10.1007/978-3-319-49409-8_48
18. Schmalstieg, D., Hoellerer, T.: Augmented Reality: Principles and Practice. Addison-Wesley, Boston (2016). ISBN-10: 0-321-88357-8
19. Henders, S., Feiner, S.: Augmented reality in the psychomotor phase of a procedural task. In: Proceedings of the IEEE ISMAR International Symposium on Mixed and Augmented Reality (2011)

20. National Institute of Standards and Technology NIST: Focus: Augmented Reality for Standards Development. http://www.nist.gov/publications/focus-augmented-reality-standards-development. Accessed Feb 2018
21. Augmented Reality for Enterprise Alliance. http://thearea.org/. Accessed Feb 2018
22. Courtesy of Metaio (2015)
23. Courtesy of Wikitude (2011)
24. Courtesy of Bentley (2012)
25. Courtesy of Continental Automotive GbmH (2014)
26. Courtesy of Augmented Traveler (2014). https://www.youtube.com/watch?v=HlbA7G8V3jA. Accessed Feb 2018

Usability Evaluation for Drone Mission Planning in Virtual Reality

Yifei Liu, Nancy Yang, Alyssa Li, Jesse Paterson, David Mcpherson,
Tom Cheng, and Allen Y. Yang[✉]

UC Berkeley, Cory Hall Room 337, Berkeley, CA 94720, USA
{yifei.liu, nancy_yang, alyssa_li, jesse.r.pat,
david.mcpherson, tcheng96}@berkeley.edu,
yang@eecs.berkeley.edu

Abstract. There has been a lot of research conducted on human-robot inter-action (HRI) with drones as well as human-computer interaction (HCI) with virtual reality (VR). However, little work was done on VR as HRI, even less for VR and drones in particular. In this paper, we evaluate the usability of VR interfaces used to control drones through working with UC Berkeley's Immersive Semi-Autonomous Aerial Command System (ISAACS) project, which experiments with new ways for humans to interact with drones in a VR environment. Our experiment setting focuses on the drone mission planning phase and on creating an onboarding experience for new users. We develop a usability evaluation framework for the ISAACS VR system, and use this framework to conduct two iterations of user testing and prototyping with a human-centered design process.

Keywords: Drone · UAV · Virtual reality · HCI · Usability evaluation
User interface

1 Introduction

Although VR is not a new technology, recent industrial buy-in and consumer uptake finally makes VR-based applications practical and affordable. As its hardware becomes more affordable and ergonomic, the VR market likely will continue to grow rapidly. Because VR places the user in a highly immersive environment, understanding its usability as an interface is crucial in the success of developing good VR experience.

Yet, many user experience professionals who are mostly familiar with designing for 2D interfaces often find that VR presents a challenging front. Designers and researchers have to consider how users perceive the virtual world, how to enable intuitive inter-actions, prevent motion sickness, and design and iterate on a VR application. With all the attention given to VR, there is currently still a lack of a standard usability standards when evaluating VR interfaces.

The first three authors contributed equally to this work.

© Springer International Publishing AG, part of Springer Nature 2018
J. Y. C. Chen and G. Fragomeni (Eds.): VAMR 2018, LNCS 10910, pp. 313–330, 2018.
https://doi.org/10.1007/978-3-319-91584-5_25

We believe that good VR design must start with a good understanding of both technology as well as human perception. Our current study to advance this understanding focuses on the drone mission-planning phase, as that is a key use case for an intuitive robot command and control system. In particular, we focus on building an onboarding experience for new users who would need more guidance.

2 Literature Review

HCI researchers have proposed several frameworks separately on human robotics interaction with drones and human computer interaction in VR. Germani et al. [4] proposed a schema that included four HCI main actors (tasks, human, equipment, and external worlds), where their metrics were divided into usability metrics and presence metrics. Murtza et al. [5] came up with 9 virtual reality heuristics, including synchronous body movements, physical space constraints, immersion, glitchiness, switch between real and virtual world, cord design, headset comfort, mental comfort, and user interface design. Norman's classic framework of the seven stages of action [3] evaluated the usability based on the goal formation, three execution stages, and three evaluation stages. Since we are particularly interested in understanding how people perceive information and execute goal-oriented tasks in a step-by-step on-boarding experience, we adopt Norman's classic seven stages of action to assess the perception and execution level of each task.

3 Metric Framework

Below is the metric framework that we develop based on Norman's seven stages of action model (Table 1).

The usability questions we investigate are:

- How easily can users tell what actions are possible?
- How easily can users perform specific tasks?
- How easily can users tell if the system is in a desired state?

We adopt Norman's four design principles [3] for improving the VR interface:

1. visibility: a user can tell the state of the system and alternatives for action;
2. good conceptual model: there is consistency in presentation of operations and results;
3. good mapping: there is a clear relationship between actions and results, and between controls and effects; and
4. feedback: the system provides full and continuous feedback on the results of users' actions.

Table 1. Usability framework

Goal formation stage	Fly semi-autonomous drone in VR
Execution stage	
Make a plan	Create a flight mission plan in VR
Specify action sequence	1. Navigate the map
	2. Plan a flight mission
	2.1. Select a drone
	2.2. Add/edit a waypoint
	2.3. Complete a flight plan
Perform the actions	- Successfulness
	- Error proneness
	- Efficiency
	- Satisfaction
Evaluation stage	
Perceive what happened	- Immersion
	- Navigation
	- Interaction
Interpret what happened	- Comfort
	- Intuitiveness
	- Consistency
	- Clarity
Compare to the goal	Completion level (0–4)

4   Usability Evaluation

Based on our framework, we further develop our usability evaluation metrics. Table 2 is a summary of the heuristic evaluation.

Table 2. Evaluation metrics

Perceive	
Immersion	
Visual	e.g. Do the UI elements have appropriate sizes and shapes?
Audio	Does the audio have appropriate volume?
Haptic	Is there any haptic feedback (such as vibration)?
Navigation	
Flow	Does the user flow follow logical sequence of the user?
Change of State	Does the UI have a clear change of state?
Animation	Does the motion have constant velocity without acceleration/deceleration?
Interaction	
Input	Does the experience start automatically or based on a timer?
Output	Does the UI respond appropriately to the user action?
Interpret	
Comfort	Are the objects placed in a comfortable proximity to the player?
Intuitiveness	Can the user discover the controls as needed?
Consistency	Is the language used consistent in the system?
Clarity	Does the text writing clearly convey the meaning?

5   Usability Testing Process

Each usability test takes about 30–40 min per person, where we start with learning about a user's background experience in VR prior to the testing. During the test, we have the participants verbali their thoughts as they move through the user interface. This is a simple but effective method to discover what the user is thinking during the interaction and if there are any usability problems or confusion. At the same time, we also observe their performance and record notes and scores based on their performance. After testing, we ask the user to fill out two surveys. The first survey asks the user about their age, background in VR and drone flying, and how they evaluate their performance in the testing session. The second survey conducts the heuristic evaluation by comparing the interface against our defined usability principles (see Table 2). Based on the heuristic evaluation we conduct internally, we choose the questions that applied in this context and gather feedback on immersion, navigation, interaction, comfort, intuition, consistency, and clarity. We also record all testers' virtual and physical interactions so we could compare and analyze their performance. All participants will be asked to complete the tasks listed below:

User Tasks

1. Set up a drone.
2. Set the first waypoint.
3. Adjust the height.
4. Modify the waypoint.
5. Add a waypoint on an existing route ("middle waypoint").
6. Complete a flight route.
7. Remove a drone.

After the usability test, we then interview the testers for qualitative feedback on what went well and what did not.

6   First Round Usability Testing

For the first round of user testing, we test the original prototype which does not come with any onboarding tutorial to guide the user. The user is instructed to follow the step-by-step instruction from the facilitator. There are also no controller tooltips on the Oculus control to indicate how each button functions. In the starting steps, the user has to click on the joystick to retrieve the laser in order to begin tasks (Fig. 1).

6.1   Demographic

In this round, we have invited six participants between 19–29 years old with various background in VR and drone flying experience (Table 3).

6.2   Problems Identified

From the user testing, we define 4 simulated problems.

Fig. 1. First version that we user tested with.

Table 3. Demographic data from 1st round user testing.

Participants	6 participants
Any experience with VR/any experience with drone	1. No; Yes 2. No; No 3. No; No 4. Yes; Yes 5. Yes; No 6. Yes; No
Age range	19–29 years-old

Add Waypoints
Without the controller tooltip, it was confusing for the user to start this task. In our design, the user need to start with adding a drone and then they would need to hover over the drone and click on button B to see the waypoint-adding option. It was not very intuitive. Most users thought they could click anywhere to start adding a new waypoint.

Adjust Height
After adding a waypoint, the waypoint would still be floating. The user can move their hands up and down to adjust the height before clicking on the button B again to finalize selecting the location. However, many users sometimes may double click and accidentally set the waypoint right after it was added. Due to the latency, the user would not notice they could make changes and moved on to the next task (Fig. 2).

Modify Waypoints
In the system, there are no visual cues to indicate how to modify waypoints. Prior to modifying waypoints, the users have to rely on the laser beam to select and click on objects for intended actions. However, they will not be informed that they could modify waypoints by holding and dragging them.

Fig. 2. Not enough visual feedback on adjusting the height.

In addition, once the user accidentally set the waypoints to the ground, it could be difficult to modify them. Sometimes, these waypoints are set on the tables or outside of the area that the user could physically approach and modify (Fig. 3).

Fig. 3. Once the waypoint was set on the ground, user sometimes could not physically reach to modify.

Add Mid-waypoints
To add a mid-waypoint, the user needs to click on the route in between two waypoints, click on button B again to add. The visual feedback on whether they are interacting with the waypoint or the route is unclear to indicate this interaction, which would lead to confusion.

Finally, in this version, there is no opportunity to remove waypoints. When the user sometimes tries to explore this function, they may accidentally add waypoints. Not being able to remove the waypoints is frustrating among all users (Fig. 4).

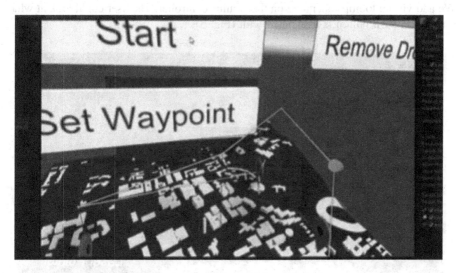

Fig. 4. There's no remove waypoint option in the menu.

7 Second Round Usability Testing

After revising the system based on the feedback from the first round of user testing, we conduct a new round of testing.

7.1 Demographic

In the second round, we invite six participants aged from 24–34 years old with diverse backgrounds in VR and drone flying (Table 4).

Table 4. Demographic data from 2nd round user testing.

Participants	6 participants
Any experience with VR/any experience with drone	1. Yes; No
	2. No; No
	3. No; No
	4. Yes; No
	5. Yes; Yes
	6. Yes; Yes
Age range	24–34 years-old

7.2   Changes

We make four main changes for this round of testing.

Adding Tooltips
We add virtual tooltips anchored on the Oculus controller. The user could look at what interaction each button is associated with (Fig. 5).

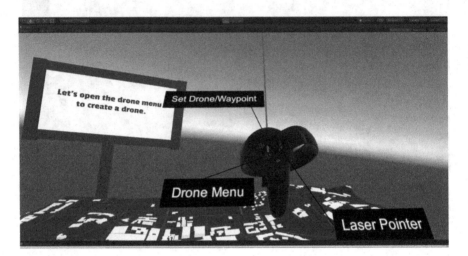

Fig. 5. Adding tooltips on the controller to indicate what interactions the buttons are associated with

Onboarding Tutorial
We also add a step-by-step tutorial so the user could follow the instruction on the board. Once they complete a task, the board will display the next step of the task. The purpose is to guide them through the planning task and be more familiar with the controls (Figs. 6 and 7).

Fig. 6. Adding onboarding step by step instruction.

Fig. 7. Following the instructions user will complete the tutorial with a complete mission planning.

Minimizing Control

In the first version, we used 5 buttons on the controller (Fig. 8). In this version, we remove the use of button B to decrease the memory load and learning curve of the user (Table 5).

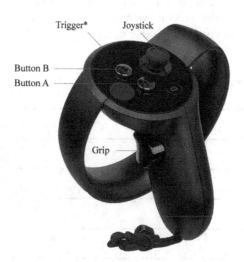

*Not showed in the picture

Fig. 8. Oculus controller buttons that are used in our VR prototype.

Table 5. Controls for version 1 and version 2

	1st Version	2nd Version
Laser Beam	Joystick On Click	Joystick On Click
Menu	Button A	Button A
Select	Trigger	Trigger
Modify Waypoint	Grip	Grip
Add Drone	Button B	Trigger
Add Waypoint	Button B	Trigger
Add mid-waypoint	Button B + Button B	Trigger + Trigger
Number of Controls	5	4

Visual Cues

We used 4 colors on the laser beam in the first version and the color mapping was not very clear to the user. In this version, we remove yellow in the system to have a more intuitive use of color as visual cue (Table 6).

Table 6. Visual cues on version 1 and version 2.

	1st Version	2nd Version
Select		
Add Drone		
Add Waypoint		
Adjusting Height		
Modifying Waypoint		
Error		

8   Results

To evaluate the usability of the system, we take a holistic approach comprising of: (1) data collected during testing, (2) a post-interview questionnaire, and (3) heuristic evaluation form for our internal team as well as a shorter version for users.

User Metrics
Table 7 shows the results collected from the user tests, based on these 7 user tasks. We select the following metrics to evaluate for each task:

Table 7. Overall test results

Tasks	Task Complexity	Session 1 Average Completion Score	Session 2 Average Completion Score	Diff (Avg. Completion Score)	Session 1 Average Error Rate	Session 2 Average Error Rate	Diff (Avg. Error Rate)	Session 1 Avg Time Taken	Session 2 Avg Time Taken	Diff (Avg. Time Taken)
Add a drone	4	3.17	3.00	-0.17	3.29	1.88	-1.42	2:19:30	2:00:00	-0:19:30
Add a new waypoint	4	3.33	3.00	-0.33	1.96	1.79	-0.17	1:27:50	1:32:30	0:04:40
Adjust the height	2	2.00	2.83	0.83	0.67	0.50	-0.17	0:27:10	0:27:10	0:00:00
Modify an existing waypoint	3	3.00	3.00	0.00	3.89	3.78	-0.11	2:36:00	2:27:20	-0:08:40
Add a middle waypoint	3	2.83	3.17	0.33	1.72	2.22	0.50	1:40:00	1:32:10	-0:07:50
Complete a flight route	2	4.00	3.50	-0.50	0.58	0.39	-0.20	0:21:30	0:23:40	0:02:10
Remove a drone	2	4.00	3.50	-0.50	0.33	0.92	0.58	0:33:30	0:31:20	-0:02:10

Completion Score: The completion score (0–4) is a measurement of how successful the user was at accomplishing the task, with or without assistance. 0 indicated that the user failed the task. 1 indicated that the user partially completed the task with facilitator's assistance. 2 indicated that the user partially completed the task without assistance. 3 indicated that the user completed the task intended with assistance. 4 indicated that the user completed the task intended without assistance.

Number of Errors: Errors can be either slips ("fat finger"), mistakes, or user interface problems. Errors can occur more than once per user per task. We counted the number of errors occurred, even if it was the same error occurring multiple times, because that is an indication that the system lacks adequate feedback for user errors.

Error Rate: The Error Rate calculation takes the total number of errors divided by the task complexity, which we've defined as the number of steps it takes to accomplish a task (e.g. number of clicks using the hand controller). The calculation for Error Rate is intended to convert errors into a proportion based on the opportunity for errors, with the idea that some tasks, especially those that are longer or more complex, will have more opportunities for users to make mistakes. This is partly borrowed from the concept used for THERP (Technique for Human Error Rate Prediction).

Time to Completion: The time it took for a user to complete a task (either fully or partially).

9 Survey Results

Figure 9 shows the results from the post-interview questionnaire provided to users to capture subjective experience and perception.

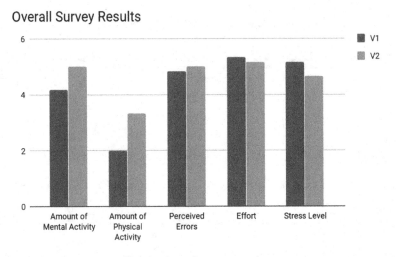

Fig. 9. Overall survey results.

Insights from User Metrics and Survey

Error rates have decreased for 70% of the tasks and Time to completion is shortened by 31 s for completing all tasks. However, we did receive mixed results for the Completion Score. After some reflection, we should conclude that this was likely due to a mix of factors: a small sample size of 12 participants with varying previous experiences in VR. In addition, since we provided an onboarding tutorial in VR during round 2, less instructions were given by the testing team, which suggests that the tutorial could be more explicit.

We found that error rates have improved for 5 out of the 7 tasks when an interactive onboarding tutorial were added, and participants reported lower stress levels and effort in round 2. This indicated that the onboarding tutorials helped reduce errors in almost all of the tasks. However, we did not find significant improvement in completion score, and the participants' self-reported physical and mental activity were higher in round 2. This suggests that the onboarding tutorial could be more explicit - it is not sufficient for a tutorial to just tell users what to do. It is equally important to show them how to do it.

Comparing Test Results Based on Prior VR Experience

To dive deeper into the metrics, we split the results above and compared the results between participants with and without VR experience.

Table 8. Test results with VR experience

Tasks	Task Complexity	Session 1 Average Completion Score	Session 2 Average Completion Score	Diff (Avg. Completion Score)	Session 1 Average Error Rate	Session 2 Average Error Rate	Diff (Avg. Error Rate)	Session 1 Avg Time Taken	Session 2 Avg Time Taken	Diff (Avg. Time Taken)
Add a drone	4	3.33	3.00	-0.33	2.17	1.25	-0.92	1:30:00	1:21:40	-0:08:20
Add a new waypoint	4	3.67	3.00	-0.67	2.25	1.33	-0.92	1:37:40	0:54:40	-0:43:00
Adjust the height	2	3.50	3.33	-0.17	0.50	0.50	0.00	0:24:40	0:19:40	-0:05:00
Modify an existing waypoint	3	3.00	3.00	0.00	5.00	2.44	-2.56	2:20:40	1:29:00	-0:51:40
Add a middle waypoint	3	3.00	3.33	0.33	1.11	1.33	0.22	0:54:40	1:24:00	0:29:20
Complete a flight route	2	4.00	3.20	-0.80	1.17	0.68	-0.48	0:30:40	0:28:20	-0:02:20
Remove a drone	2	4.00	3.20	-0.80	0.67	0.17	-0.50	1:02:40	0:11:20	-0:51:20

Table 9. Test results with no VR experience

Tasks	Task Complexity	Session 1 Average Completion Score	Session 2 Average Completion Score	Diff (Avg. Completion Score)	Session 1 Average Error Rate	Session 2 Average Error Rate	Diff (Avg. Error Rate)	Session 1 Avg Time Taken	Session 2 Avg Time Taken	Diff (Avg. Time Taken)
Add a drone	4	3.00	3.00	0.00	4.42	2.50	-1.92	3:09:00	2:38:20	-0:30:40
Add a new waypoint	4	3.00	3.00	0.00	1.67	2.25	0.58	1:18:00	2:10:20	0:52:20
Adjust the height	2	1.00	2.33	1.33	0.83	0.50	-0.33	0:29:40	0:34:40	0:05:00
Modify an existing waypoint	3	3.00	3.00	0.00	2.78	5.11	2.33	2:51:20	3:25:40	0:34:20
Add a middle waypoint	3	2.67	3.00	0.33	2.33	3.11	0.78	2:25:20	1:40:20	-0:45:00
Complete a flight route	2	4.00	3.20	-0.80	0.00	0.10	0.10	0:12:20	0:19:00	0:06:40
Remove a drone	2	4.00	3.20	-0.80	0.00	1.67	1.67	0:04:20	0:51:20	0:47:00

Table 8 shows the results comparing round 1 and round 2 for participants with prior VR experience, while Table 9 shows the results for participants without prior VR experience.

For participants with prior VR experience, the results showed a decrease in time taken per task and error rates for 6 out of 7 tasks, which could be attributed to the consistency in visual cues and decrease in control inputs. However, we also found a decrease in completion scores for 5 tasks, which is likely due to the lack of explicit instructions in the onboarding tutorial.

For participants without prior VR experience, we found that error rates and time taken per task increased from round 1 to round 2. Compared to the results above, it is unsurprising that participants without any prior VR background are less equipped to complete the tasks on their own without a tutorial to show them how to do it.

10 Heuristic Evaluation

We conduct heuristic evaluation on our VR prototype internally. We also ask participants to self-report their overall experience in our prototype using a smaller subset of questions.

Internal
Figure 10 below shows the data collected when our team conducted a heuristic evaluation comparing rounds 1 and 2. Our internal heuristic evaluation revealed improvements in navigation, consistency, and intuitiveness. This is in-line with our initial hypothesis that adding an on-boarding tutorial would improve navigation, and minimizing control inputs would improve consistency and intuitiveness (Table 10).

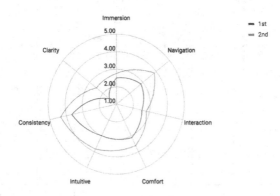

Fig. 10. Internal heuristic evaluation

User Testing
Figure 11 below shows the data collected from user testing with a subset of heuristics. Users reported better results for intuitiveness and navigation, and less positive results for comfort and interaction. While we only tested this on a small sample size of users,

the data is still in line with what we found during the user testing phase, where users reported inconsistent interactions when changing a waypoint versus adding a middle waypoint.

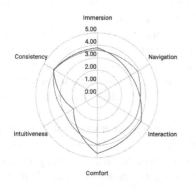

Fig. 11. Heuristic evaluation from users.   **Fig. 12.** Heuristic evaluation comparison.

Final Version

After the second round of user testing, we added some enhancements for the final version: opting to turn on the laser team pointer by default, and making the map bigger. Figure 12 shows the final heuristic evaluations chart done by our internal team, which revealed improvements in navigation, consistency, and intuitiveness. This is in-line with our initial hypothesis that adding an on-boarding tutorial would improve navigation, and minimizing control inputs would improve consistency and intuitiveness.

Table 10. Minimizing control process in the system.

	1st Version	2nd Version	**Latest Version**
Laser Beam	Joystick On Click	Joystick On Click	**On by Default**
Menu	Button A	Button A	Button A
Select	Trigger	Trigger	Trigger
Modify waypoint	Grip	Grip	Grip
Add Drone	Button B	Trigger	Trigger
Add Waypoint	Button B	Trigger	Trigger
Add Mid-waypoint	Button B + Button B	Trigger + Trigger	Trigger + Trigger
Numbers of Controls	5	4	3

11   Usability Testing Insights

From two rounds of user testing, we synthesized our research into four key findings:

First, a step-by-step tutorial which walks users through an entire mission planning process is crucial in helping new users performed better. The tutorial helped to decrease the error rate and the completion time in 70% of the assigned tasks.

Second, as situational awareness is important during flights, minimizing input controls would help to decrease the error rate as it prevents cognitive overload. By using the same control button for a similar function instead of two control buttons, it helps reduce the learning curve for new users and makes it easier for them to remember the controls while experimenting with a new interface. (See Table 8 which shows the final version after two rounds of prototyping.)

Third, mission planning tools in VR should also have more interactions that imitate the real world, such as grabbing and dragging. Participants reported improved satisfaction, immersion, and intuitiveness when they discovered that that they could physically reach out, grab a waypoint, and then drag it to their desired location. Having interactions that is intuitive would be helpful in actual drone-flying situations.

Lastly, it is important for the VR system to provide immediate feedback and visibility for any system state changes during mission planning, as this would minimize any guessing on how the system works, which always leads to frustration and could potentially cause errors during the flight. In our example, during the second round of testing, the time to completion for adding a new waypoint increased from the first round. Even though we provided instructions to teach them what to do, we likely were not specific enough in our instructions. The users then started trying to guess the state of the system and how it works, which took them longer to complete the task and generally caused more frustration.

12   Future Work and Conclusion

Both usability testing and heuristic evaluation show that we could reduce users' confusion and perceived ambiguity in our VR prototype by further improving the clarity of users' status and providing more user controls in future iterations. First, based on the feedback received during our user testing sessions, we would like to enable users to remove waypoints, and build a consistent interaction between changing waypoints and creating a middle waypoint. Second, we plan to allow users to save a particular mission, and to record the process for future playback. From our initial research of existing 2D applications for drones, we would also add a pre-takeoff checklist and display safety concerns, such as height, incompatibility alerts, safety checks, and warning the user if the mission would exceed battery time. Finally, from our review of existing VR usability literature, we believe that adding audio and haptic feedback would provide a more immersive experience for the users. We hope to continue working with the ISAACS Human Interfaces team to conduct user studies on a larger scale to discover new ways of improving humans' interactions with drones in a VR environment.

In addition to feature improvement, we believe that there is potential application for drone planning in VR.

1. Drone videography: we believe that there is a need for drone videography planning in a VR environment. From our interviews, planning for drone videography is currently either done via 2D apps, such as on the iPad, or using more basic techniques such as eyeing the landscape or looking over Google Earth. VR would provide a more intuitive way of planning their mission, as well as more control over the specific route, allowing videographers to preview shots and prevent accidents that would exceed safety height limitation.
2. Agriculture: farmers and agriculture professionals could use the system to monitor crop health or assess drought conditions.
3. Disaster management: disaster management experts could use the system to create a flight path that monitors cleanup progress and evaluates potentially dangerous areas.
4. Real estate and construction: Real estate and construction professionals could use the system to survey a property or monitor progress on a new development project.
5. 3D mapping: companies such as drone deploy are already using drones for 3D environmental mapping to create 3D models and high-resolution maps. The system could increase the level of immersion and intuition by allowing users to plan and save their missions in VR.

As the gap between virtual and physical worlds shrink in the use of VR with robotic systems like drones, usability become more complicated to evaluate. This paper provides a framework to address usability needs for a specific action sequence within the drone mission-planning phase, combining quantitative and qualitative analysis as well as heuristics to capture a comprehensive view of a subjective experience.

Acknowledgements. We would like to thank James O'Brien and the Berkeley ISAACS team for their guidance and support on this project, as well as the UAV at Berkeley club for introducing us to the world of drone flying. The project was supported in part by a Philippine-California Advanced Research Institutes (PCARI) grant.

References

1. Intel. Ground Control Station Users' Feedback (2016). http://dronecode.github.io/UX-Design/Research/GCSUsersFeedback.pdf
2. Jerald, J.: The VR Book: Human-Centered Design for Virtual Reality. ACM Books, New York (2015)
3. Norman, D.A.: The Design of Everyday Things. MIT Press, Cambridge (1988)
4. Germani, M., Mengoni, M., Peruzzini, M.: Metrics-based approach for VR technology evaluation in styling product design. Proc. ASME Des. Eng. Tech. Conf. **5**, 1325–1339 (2009). https://doi.org/10.1115/DETC2009-86228
5. Murtza, R., Monroe, S., Youmans, R.J.: Heuristic evaluation for virtual reality systems. In: Proceedings of the Human Factors and Ergonomics Society 2017 Annual Meeting (2017)
6. VR Oxygen. VR Heuristic Evaluation Tool (2017). https://vroxygen.com/VRheuristics-tool-open.html
7. Peshkova, E., Hitz, M., Kaufmann, B.: Natural interaction techniques for an unmanned aerial vehicle system. Pervasive Comput. IEEE **16**, 34–42 (2017). ISSN 1536-1268

8. Cauchard, J.R., Zhai, K.Y., Spadafora, M., Landay, J.A.: Emotion encoding in human-drone interaction. In: 2016 11th ACM/IEEE International Conference on Human-Robot Interaction (HRI), Christchurch, pp. 263–270 (2016). https://doi.org/10.1109/hri.2016.7451761
9. Jankowski, J., Grabowski, A.: Usability evaluation of VR interface for mobile robot teleoperation. Int. J. Hum.-Comput. Interact. 31(12), 882–889 (2015). https://doi.org/10.1080/10447318.2015.1039909
10. Nguyen, L.A., Bualat, M., Edwards, L.J., et al.: Virtual reality interfaces for visualization and control of remote vehicles. Auton. Robots 11, 59–68 (2001). https://doi.org/10.1023/A:1011208212722
11. KZero. Number of active virtual reality users worldwide from 2014 to 2018 (in millions). In: Statista - The Statistics Portal (n.d.). https://www.statista.com/statistics/426469/active-virtual-reality-users-worldwide/. Accessed 13 Mar 2017
12. System Reliability Center. Technique for Human Error Rate Prediction (THERP). https://src.alionscience.com/pdf/TechHumErrorRatePred.pdf

Cyber Vulnerability: An Attentional Dilemma

Joseph B. Lyons[1], Mark A. Roebke[2], Philip Bobko[3(✉)],
and Craig A. Cox[4]

[1] Air Force Research Laboratory, WPAFB, Dayton, USA
joseph.lyons.6@us.af.mil
[2] Air Force Institute of Technology, Dayton, USA
mark.roebke.ctr@afit.edu
[3] Gettysburg College, Gettysburg, USA
pbobko@gettysburg.edu
[4] Air Force Life Cycle Management Center, Dayton, USA
craig.cox.1@us.af.mil

Abstract. Cyber security remains an ominous task for the military. Generating awareness of some cyber challenges is daunting, yet aspects of cyber vulnerabilities are often ambiguous to everyday operators. Many of these challenges have been documented in prior papers. The current effort focused on two studies which describe levels of general awareness of cyber challenges among students (a typical age range for entry-level military operators). The studies asked participants to evaluate aerial images and to determine if the images had been degraded. Following a positive degradation identification, participants were asked to list the reason for the perceived degradation by drawing from a set of four options. The option related to cyber attack was proportionally used much less than the others, even in the context of an explicit experimental prime to motivate cyber awareness and vulnerabilities. The implications for these results for interactions with autonomous systems are discussed.

Keywords: Cyber security · Trust in automation · Suspicion · Military

1 Introduction

Autonomous/robotic systems represent a significant portion of the future for Department of Defense (DoD) and civilian technologies. Human users of such systems can often interact with these platforms at great distances, improving reach, adaptability, and effectiveness of human-machine systems. Yet, inherent in these interactions is the notion of information security, as these technologies rely on digital links to command and control systems, human operators, and cloud-based networks. As a result, these systems may be susceptible to cyber attacks. Many scholars suggest that the most vulnerable link in the cyber security domain is the human operator/user of technology. These vulnerabilities may exist for a variety of reasons, as discussed below. The current paper will discuss two studies, each with relevance to cyber-related vulnerabilities. These studies, which were conducted as part of an effort to validate trait measures of suspicion, revealed an interesting pattern of low awareness of cyber threats.

A recent paper [1] reviewed the literature surrounding the construct of suspicion. They defined state suspicion as a "*simultaneous* state of cognitive activity, uncertainty,

© Springer International Publishing AG, part of Springer Nature 2018
J. Y. C. Chen and G. Fragomeni (Eds.): VAMR 2018, LNCS 10910, pp. 331–340, 2018.
https://doi.org/10.1007/978-3-319-91584-5_26

and perceived mal-intent about underlying information" from an external agent [1, p. 493]. Suspicion may be a key factor motivating operators to critically evaluate and question a particular stimulus. Yet little is known about baseline rates of suspicion during military oriented tasks such as image evaluation.

Intelligence, Surveillance, and Reconnaissance (ISR) analysts are often asked to exploit and examine imagery, full motion video, signals intelligence, and other forms of intelligence and to determine the presence of various objects, people, or actions. This information comes from a variety of sources (i.e., collection assets) and may be subject to variations in quality, timeliness, and pedigree – all of which can influence an analyst's trust of the information [11]. These perturbations, in quality for instance, can be associated with either innocuous or perhaps pernicious causal mechanisms. For example, poor quality imagery may be driven by a bad sensor, unfortunate weather conditions, bad signal strength, or a low-quality information source. In addition, there are also potential malicious actors in the world who are constantly seeking to gain an advantage of US operations across the world. As such, intelligence may be subject to groups seeking to deny or disrupt ISR data, resulting in poor quality intelligence. Cyber attacks on ISR platforms are a very real threat to our military.

In the domain of cyber security, human errors and or vulnerabilities are often cited as the primary threat to cyber resilience. Estimates suggest that most known cyber-related breaches can be attributed back to human error [5, 9]. This is an interesting trend given that cyber awareness campaigns are common in society and cyber breaches are often highly publicized. Data breaches in the public and private sectors appear with alarming regularity. In the military, cyber awareness training is standard, as are mechanisms to both thwart cyber attacks (e.g., network firewalls) and policies to reduce cyber breaches (e.g., behavioral policies of DoD users). Yet, cyber breaches do occur and the frequency of cyber attacks are on the rise versus on the decline. Researchers and cyber professionals are left pondering – why are cyber attacks both so prominent and effective given a populace that *should* be aware of cyber threats?

The answers to the above questions are as diverse as they are ambiguous. Some researchers note the extreme challenges faced by cyber operators. As noted by [13], cyber operators must deal with a combination of high cognitive workload, poor user interfaces, and aids that tend toward high false alarm rates. High false alarm rates could result in distrust over time as operators discount guidance from such tools [10]. Thus, given the right tools, training, and work context, cyber operators may be more effective at addressing cyber-related challenges. However, others suggest that types of cyber-attack make all of the difference in terms of understanding human responses and vulnerability. In an empirical paper by [4], cyber attacks were categorized according to five factors: (1) well-known and overt attacks [e.g., a computer or software crash], (2) low and slow attacks (which includes errors that may be common among operators) [e.g., the mouse is unresponsive or sluggish, the internet is unusually slow], (3) common errors that are not perceived to be the fault of the user [e.g., printer errors], (4) perceptual/memory errors [e.g., objects on the screen randomly appear or disappear], and (5) evidence of tampering or remote control of the computer [e.g., additional text is inserted in emails or posts]. The authors conclude that the low and slow attacks may be most pernicious to operators, as these attacks may be the least likely to be detected [4]. The reasons why they may be less detectable by operators are because these attacks may not violate what the operators view as normal system behavior, and they may not be consistent with mental models of cyber attacks (which may be more evident in the overt attack, common error attacks, and tampering attacks). This is unfortunate because the vast majority of cyber security research is geared toward technology solutions and applications (e.g., network intrusion detection sensors, algorithms, aid designs) rather than understanding the human vulnerabilities associated with the cyber domain [12]. Considerably more research is needed to fully understand human behavior in the context of cyber challenges. It is in this context, on the cusp of human suspicion for/human awareness of cyber attacks, the current paper investigated the propensity of individuals to perceive that a cyberattack event had occurred.

1.1   Participants

Participants engaged in an image degradation analysis task. There are two studies discussed in this paper. Study 1 had one hundred and nine participants from a Midwestern university. The average age was 20 (SD = 4) and the sample was 62.4% female. Study 2 had one hundred and six participants from a Midwestern university with the same general demographics as Study 1. All participants were above the age of 18 and the study was approved by the Air Force IRB prior to data collection.

Fig. 1. Sample of degraded image

1.2 Design

The participants were asked to view 80 images and to determine if the images were "degraded" or "not degraded". In reality, 70 of the 80 images were degraded to the same degree (i.e., the number of pixels degraded for all degraded images was the same). The other ten images were not degraded at all. An example of a degraded image can be found in Fig. 1. Notably, while 70 of 80 images were systematically degraded, they were degraded only in so far as to motivate suspicion at a just-noticeable difference. Hence some 'degraded' images were likely be viewed as non-degraded. The authors piloted the 70 degraded images with an independent sample to ensure that some but not all of the participants would evaluate the images as degraded, signifying a just-noticeable difference subject to individual differences. In fact, in our first study. the image in Fig. 1 was perceived as degraded by 49% of the respondents, while 51% did not identify it as degraded. If participants believed an image was degraded, they were simply asked to choose a rationale for why they thought the image was degraded from the following list of options: weather interference, sensor malfunction, signal weakness (i.e., lack of signal strength), or cyber attack.

1.3 Apparatus and Materials

A Java-based interface was used for the study (see Fig. 2). Participants were shown an image and asked if they believed the image was degraded or not. If the participant noted a degradation in the image, they were asked to choose why they thought the image was degraded using the above a priori list of possible causes. The level of degradation was determined by the interaction of two methods. First, the percentage of pixels in an image that are changed can be adjusted, with a higher percentage causing more degradation. Second, the 24 bits that determine a pixel's color can be adjusted systematically. Each additional bit that is changed of the 24 will cause the pixel's color to change more dramatically. The joint effect of changes across these two variables determined the total amount of corruption in an image.

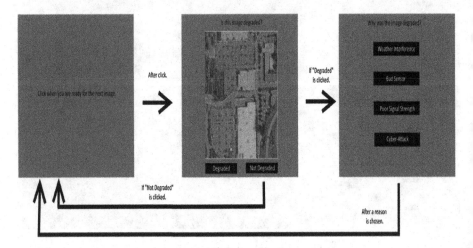

Fig. 2. Example of the experimental platform.

1.4   Procedure

Study 1. As part of a larger study on suspicion, participants provided informed consent and were given instructions for the task. In the task instructions, participants were told that the images in the study might be degraded and that their task was to determine which ones were degraded. Participants were also told that aerial images could be degraded for multiple reasons including: weather conditions, sensor quality/performance, network strength/quality, or cyber attacks (e.g., hacking). More specifically, they were told: "weather conditions can reduce visibility and cause turbulence for aircraft taking pictures, reducing image quality. The sensors taking the pictures may not be performing optimally, or may need maintenance, reducing image quality. The network strength at a given time and space may be low, making it more difficult to send a high-quality image, reducing image quality. Outside groups may attempt to purposively disrupt the electronical signals (cyber-attack), reducing image quality. Finally, the larger the distance between the target and the camera, the more likely the picture is to look grainy and fuzzy. Your task will be to view a set of images, then decide if each image is degraded or not. If you think an image is degraded, we will ask you to identify the possible cause of that degradation. One factor - distance from target, will be held constant, meaning that all of your images will come from a distance that is approximately the same."

Study 2. The second study was modified to heighten cyber awareness. Specifically, the task instructions were prefaced by the following statement, "Cyber warfare is of great concern to the U.S. Air Force and our current experimental project reflects that concern. The Wall Street Journal reported back in 2009 that it is possible for hackers to hack into image feeds from military aircraft, which could influence the quality of images that are transmitted to drone operators. On the other hand, when taking such pictures from the air, there are other, unintentional factors that can influence the quality of the picture. In general, when a picture appears to be of lower quality than expected it might be considered to be "degraded" and, regardless of cause, poor quality images may reduce the effectiveness of military missions." Participants were then given the normal task instructions as in Study 1. Then, participants were told that the results of this study **"will be of vital importance to imagery and cyber analysts"**. All other aspects were identical between studies 1 and 2. The images were identical and the four categories of degradation causes were the same.

2   Results

2.1   Study 1

Participants perceived, on average, that 53 (66%) of the images were degraded. The actual rate was close to 90% (70 of 80) suggesting that there were some ambiguities in the degradation perception, as expected. None of the non-degraded images were perceived as degraded. The results from Study 1 (see Fig. 3) demonstrated that when participants viewed an image as degraded, cyberattack was the least likely explanation provided for the degradation. Only 7% of the degraded images were believed to be due

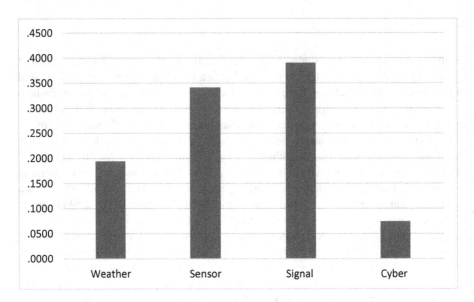

Fig. 3. Proportion of degraded image explanations for study 1.

to cyberattack – relative to 20% weather, 34% sensor issues, and 39% signal strength. Thus, Study 1 evidenced a low base rate for cyber attack attributions when participants were asked to explain degraded images.

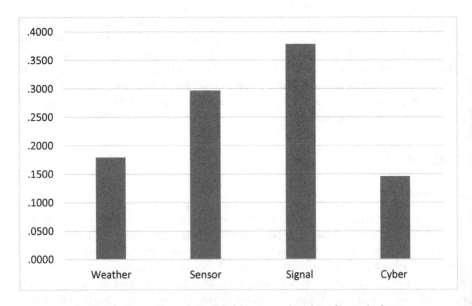

Fig. 4. Proportion of degraded image explanations for study 2.

2.2   Study 2

Study 2 sought to prime cyber awareness by telling participants that cyber attacks were prominent in Air Force operations and that this study was designed explicitly to examine perceptions of cyber attacks. Other than the differences in the initial instructions/priming, the remaining methods were identical to Study 1. Results from Study 2 (see Fig. 4) demonstrated that the priming increased the cyber attack rationale to 15% (versus 7% in Study 1; a statistically significant increase, $p < .05$), yet it was still low relative to the other explanations (weather 18%, sensor issues 30%, and signal strength 38%). Participants perceived, on average, that 50 (63%) of the images were degraded. Once again, none of the non-degraded images were perceived as degraded.

3   Discussion

Human awareness of cyber-related vulnerabilities are often not well understood. Cyber attacks remain a significant threat among businesses, public organizations, and the military and humans are often believed to be the weakest link in the cyber security equation. As a result, researchers have called for additional research to better understand the role of humans in cyber-related phenomena [4, 12]. The current studies sought to better understand individuals' propensity to attribute suspicious events to a cyber attack relative to other possible causes.

Study 1 demonstrated that individuals were quite reluctant to attribute potential image degradation to a cyber-related attack relative to attributions for weather, sensor problems, or poor signal strength. There are at least two potential reasons for this. First, participants may have believed that a cyber attack would manifest itself differently in the context of aerial images. For instance, similar to the overt attacks discussed in [4], participants may have believed that a cyber attack in an aerial image context may have resulted in the loss of the image in totality whereas a partially degraded image may be attributed to more common/familiar causes such as sensor issues and signal strength. Given the ubiquity of cell phones, it is highly likely that most individuals have encountered a bandwidth limitation at some point in their lives. This explanation is consistent with the mental models hypothesis posed by [4] which highlights the potential dangers of low and slow methods. "In the presence of a cyberattack, users' propensity to become suspicious will be dependent on their mental models of the system. Users will only likely identify cyber attacks that (1) violate their expectations of the system's normal behavior and (2) fit into a well-informed mental model that attributes such occurrences to cyber attacks rather than to human error or 'finicky' computers" [4, p. 30]. Given that there was no training involved before the experiment began, in the context of a degraded image, people may be more accustomed to having problems with sensors and bandwidth than in thinking about cyber vulnerabilities.

Second, it is possible that the participants did not believe that a cyber attack was likely given that this was an experimental context versus a natural interaction or actual work context. That is, perhaps actual military operators would be more vigilant of cyber-related threats in operational domains. Thus, the current study paradigm needs to be examined in the context of actual operators using tasks/platforms where real stakes are involved. It is interesting however, that the sample was drawn from an age range that would be typical of many entry-level military operators.

Study 2 sought to intentionally prime individuals to think about cyber attacks to overcome the low base rates of cyber attack attributions from Study 1. Participants in this study were explicitly told to think about cyber attacks, to be aware that cyber attacks were possible, and that the current study was explicitly designed to support operators in the cyber domain. The added cyber emphasis was successful in doubling the cyber attributions relative to Study 1. However, cyber attributions remained the lowest category for participants, despite the successful priming. Participants were still twice as likely to attribute a degraded image to a faulty sensor or to poor bandwidth. It is clear that participants' mental models of what could cause a degraded image were not consistent with the notion of a cyber-related event, but were rather associated with bandwidth and sensor performance. Future research might examine the concept of mental models of cyber threats in an image context (as well as other contexts) to see if concepts such bandwidth and sensor problems are more familiar/accessible to individuals when considering threats to the image quality. It is also possible that a different degradation method would differentially influence suspicion. For instance, the degradation technique applied to the current images was applied in a systematic and uniform fashion to the images – meaning each part of the image had the same level of degradation. Degradation of a portion of the image may have motivated greater suspicion as that may be more inconsistent with common issues such as bandwidth limitations and sensor problems which may impact the whole image versus a portion of it.

3.1 Implications

The collective study results have implications for cyber awareness training, as well as the concept/design of interactions with future autonomous systems. Designers of cyber awareness training should be encouraged that increasing awareness of cyber-related vulnerabilities increases cyber-related attributions when humans encounter stimuli they view as suspicious. However, two points are notable. First, as shown in Study 1, individuals' baseline levels of cyber awareness are insufficient to motivate cyber-related attributions. In other words, it might be ill-advised for cyber trainers to hope that individuals will be sensitive to cyber events based on awareness of public threats and vulnerabilities. That is clearly not the case as evidenced by the low base rates found in Study 1. Second, cyber trainers should not solely hope that by priming cyber awareness, individuals will be sufficiently sensitive to cyber-related threats unless those threats are well-aligned to individuals' mental models of threats in that context. It is quite possible that if other explanations are more familiar to individuals, they will attribute suspicion to those factors rather than to cyber-related factors.

The current results are also interesting from the perspective of human-machine interaction. Similar to the commercial and public sectors, autonomous systems are believed to be an important aspect of future military operations [2, 3]. One of the grand challenges associated with autonomous systems is certifying the trustworthiness of these systems given that their behavior may change over time as a result of machine learning [7]. As discussed in [7], transparency needs to be injected into the design, training regime, and operator interfaces to facilitate appropriate reliance on novel systems. Transparency refers to the set of methods to foster shared awareness and shared intent between humans and machines [6]. Shared awareness and shared intent will help to facilitate aligned mental models between humans and autonomous systems which should aid human operators in understanding cyber-related vulnerabilities associated with the autonomous system. Given that human interactions with autonomous systems will be dependent on data links, software interfaces, and may involve distributed operations, cyber vulnerabilities will likely be present. Interestingly, operational pilots note concerns of cyber attacks for technologies that include greater autonomous capabilities relative to those that are more automated [8]. It is possible that 'low and slow' attack vectors will be even less salient to human operators for autonomous (relative to simply automated) technologies, because the autonomous systems may be less understood and predictable to operators. Thus, the performance of operators can be enhanced by future research and design solutions that enable human operators to have accurate mental models of the technology and the cyber-related vulnerabilities of that future technology.

References

1. Bobko, P., Barelka, A.J., Hirshfield, L.: The construct of state-level suspicion: a model and research agenda for automated and information technology contexts. Hum. Factors **56**, 489–508 (2014)
2. Defense Science Board (DSB) Task Force on the Role of Autonomy in Department of Defense (DoD) Systems. Office of the Under Secretary of Defense for Acquisition, Technology, and Logistics, Washington, DC (2012)
3. Defense Science Board (DSB) Summer Study on Autonomy. Office of the Under Secretary of Defense for Acquisition, Technology, and Logistics, Washington, DC (2016)
4. Hirshfield, L., Bobko, P., Barelka, A.J., Costa, M.R., Funke, G.J., Mancuso, V.F., Finomore, V., Knott, B.A.: The role of human operators' suspicion in the detection of cyber attacks (2015)
5. IBM. The 2013 IBM Cyber Security Intelligence Index (2013)
6. Lyons, J.B.: Being transparent about transparency: a model for human-robot interaction. In: Sofge, D., Kruijff, G.J., Lawless, W.F. (eds.) Trust and Autonomous Systems: Papers from the AAAI Spring Symposium (Technical Report SS-13-07). AAAI Press, Menlo Park (2013)
7. Lyons, J.B., Clark, M.A., Wagner, A., Schuelke, M.J.: Certifiable trust in autonomous systems: making the intractable tangible. AI Mag. **38**, 37–49 (2017)
8. Lyons, J.B., Ho, N.T., Van Abel, A.L., Hoffmann, L.C., Eric Fergueson, W., Sadler, G.G., Grigsby, M.A., Burns, A.C.: Exploring trust barriers to future autonomy: a qualitative look. In: Cassenti, Daniel N. (ed.) AHFE 2017. AISC, vol. 591, pp. 3–11. Springer, Cham (2018). https://doi.org/10.1007/978-3-319-60591-3_1
9. Ponemon Institute. 2013 Cost of Data Breach Study: Global Analysis (2013)
10. Rice, S.: Examining single and multiple-process theories of trust in automation. J. Gen. Psychol. **136**, 303–319 (2009)
11. Veinot, B., Anders, S., Dominguez, C.: Identifying dimensions of trustworthiness in analyst's operational environments. Technical report delivered to the Air Force Research Laboratory (2013)

12. Vieane, A., Funke, G., Gutzwiller, R., Mancuso, V., Sawyer, B., Wickens, C.: Addressing human factors gaps in cyber defense. In: Proceedings of the Human Factors and Ergonomics 2016 Annual Meeting, pp. 769–772 (2016)
13. Vieane, A., Funke, G., Mancuso, V., Greenlee, E., Dye, G., Borghetti, B., Miller, B., Menke, L., Brown, R.: Coordinated displays to assist cyber defenders. In: Proceedings of the Human Factors and Ergonomics 2016 Annual Meeting, pp. 344–348 (2016)

Trust in Autonomous Systems for Threat Analysis: A Simulation Methodology

Gerald Matthews[1(✉)], April Rose Panganiban[2], Rachel Bailey[2], and Jinchao Lin[1]

[1] Institute for Simulation and Training, University of Central Florida, Orlando, FL, USA
{gmatthews, jlin}@ist.ucf.edu
[2] Air Force Research Laboratory, Wright-Patterson AFB, OH, USA
{april_rose.fallon, rachel.bailey.8.ctr}@us.af.mil

Abstract. Human operators will increasingly team with autonomous systems in military and security settings, for example, evaluation and analysis of threats. Determining whether humans are threatening is a particular challenge to which future autonomous systems may contribute. Optimal trust calibration is critical for mission success, but most trust research has addressed conventional automated systems of limited intelligence. This article identifies multiple factors that may influence trust in autonomous systems. Trust may be undermined by various sources of demand and uncertainty. These include the cognitive demands resulting from the complexity and unpredictability of the system, "social" demands resulting from the system's capacity to function as a team-member, and self-regulative demands associated with perceived threats to personal competence. It is proposed that existing gaps in trust research may be addressed using simulation methodologies. A simulated environment developed by the research team is described. It represents a "town-clearing" task in which the human operator teams with a robot that can be equipped with various sensors, and software for intelligent analysis of sensor data. The functionality of the simulator is illustrated, together with future research directions.

Keywords: Autonomous systems · Trust · Threat detection · Simulation
Cognitive processes

1 Introduction

1.1 Autonomy in the Military Context

The US military will increasingly rely on autonomous systems to perform actions currently delegated to human Warfighters, including detection of explosives, reconnaissance and surveillance, and support of combat operations. Such systems include robots and unmanned vehicles capable of independent situation analysis, decision-making and action, under some level of human monitoring and control. The US Air Force envisages autonomous systems making contributions to a range of operations [1]; we focus here especially on intelligence, surveillance, and reconnaissance (ISR). One realization of the Air Force vision is the "Loyal Wingman" concept, a

© Springer International Publishing AG, part of Springer Nature 2018
J. Y. C. Chen and G. Fragomeni (Eds.): VAMR 2018, LNCS 10910, pp. 341–353, 2018.
https://doi.org/10.1007/978-3-319-91584-5_27

scenario involving collaboration between a manned fighter platform and one or more Unmanned Autonomous Systems (UASs) with capabilities for locating and possibly attacking targets without full-time human direction. Autonomy may minimize cognitive load on the pilot, and protects the mission against jamming of communications between the pilot and the UAS.

Unmanned systems are especially suitable for "dull, dirty and dangerous" missions [2], including monitoring for threat. Consider, for example, a soldier at a vehicle checkpoint tasked with identifying possible insurgents. Use of a robot to detect hazardous materials such as explosives traces or radiation is within current capabilities. Advancements in machine intelligence will enhance robot functionality. For example, it might utilize infrared cameras to determine if the vehicle's body panels had been altered to hide contraband, a determination that requires complex inferences from sensor data. Robots will also acquire increasing abilities to analyze human beings for threat. Analysis of facial emotion and body posture can indicate fear and aggressive intentions, whereas off-the-body sensors will detect physiological responses such as autonomic arousal. For example, eye tracking methodologies show promise for detecting insider threat behavior at a computer workstation [3]. Effective use of such strategies requires more than advanced sensor technology. Psychophysiological responses do not map onto human behavior and emotion in a simple one-to-one manner [4]; they must be interpreted insightfully with some understanding of context, requiring "intelligence" on the part of the robot. For example, the Transportation Security Administration (TSA) has a pilot Behavior Detection and Analysis (BDA) program, which seeks to identify suspicious passenger behaviors at airports. However, behaviors alone may not be sufficiently diagnostic to be practically useful; analysis of the context for the behavior may be necessary to distinguish a fearful terrorist from a person afraid of flying.

An intelligent threat detection system would be of great value to the military and security services, through augmenting human capabilities, relieving human personnel of the tedious work of evaluating mostly harmless civilians, and physically removing humans from the potential dangers of close contact with those who are far from harmless. However, human oversight will remain critical. That is, threat detection and neutralization will require collaborative decision making between a human and an intelligent system. The robot or other autonomous agent must maintain and update threat evaluations based on its own sensors, communication with other team-members, and inference mechanisms.

1.2   The Importance of Trust

Teaming with autonomous systems places a burden of trust on the human operator [5]. Some degree of trust is essential to capitalize on the functionality of the autonomous system, but the operator must also remain alert to possible system errors, requiring careful calibration of trust. In the security context, human oversight is necessary to detect threats beyond the machine's detection capabilities, given the diversity of threats that may occur. It is also important to reduce "false positive" threat determinations which may waste resources and antagonize civilian populations.

There is a large human factors literature on trust [6, 7], which increasingly refers to human-robot interaction [8, 9]. Issues of automation misuse, disuse, and abuse [PR] broadly apply to autonomous as to other mechanical systems. A meta-analysis of trust in human-robot interaction [8] found that system performance characteristics including reliability, false alarm rate, and failure rate were more strongly related to trust than other robot attributes, or human and environmental characteristics.

Existing research provides only limited guidance for optimizing trust in autonomous systems operations [5]. A key issue is that enhancements in machine intelligence will change operator perceptions of functionality in complex ways, impacting trust in the process. On the one hand, greater intelligence will improve the machine's capabilities, enhance its ability to accommodate contextual factors, and improve its communications with the human operator. Generally, these capabilities should enhance trust. On the other hand, the downside of machine intelligence is that the bases for analysis and decision become increasingly complex and hard to communicate, and diagnosis of machine error is correspondingly difficult. Operators may also have faulty assumptions about machine intelligence that interfere with trust calibration. Thus, findings from trust research based on conventional automation may not generalize to autonomous systems.

1.3 Current Aims and Scope

Limitations of current research suggest a need for new methodological approaches to understanding the factors that impact operator trust in autonomous systems [5]. This paper describes some of the factors that require investigation, and describes a novel simulation methodology for determining how characteristics of the autonomous system, the operating environment, and operators themselves may influence trust. The methodology focuses on threat analysis as a specific context in which a human operator teams with an autonomous system. Specifically, the methodology aims to simulate interactions with an autonomous robot possessing sensors for various types of threat stimuli, as well as the capacity to analyze sensor data intelligently.

2 Trust in Autonomous Systems: Research Challenges

2.1 Facets of Trust

Trust is a complex construct with multiple facets and determinants [6]. Furthermore, it is a concept that comes from the social psychology of interpersonal relations, and its generalization to trust in machines is uncertain. In human factors research on trust in traditional automation, perceptions of competence predominate [9].

Qualities such as technical competence, reliability and understandability are readily applicable to machines [10]. Human-human trust also depends on additional factors - benevolence and integrity complement ability (competence) in one well-known model [11]. Such factors imply a self-motivated agent, perceptions that are unlikely to apply to simple automated systems, such as a vehicle cruise control. However, autonomous systems may be perceived as possessing a limited kind of personhood [12], implying that human-centered models of trust may become increasingly applicable.

Emotional as well as cognitive processes are also critical for human-human trust, which is influenced by the simple preference of liking or disliking the other person, a preference generated automatically with little cognitive effort [13]. Emotional aspects of trust are also shaped by longer-duration deliberative processes, e.g., a person might initially dislike a new coworker but come to appreciate their contributions over time. Simple automation elicits emotions associated with competence, such as frustration at repeated failures, or contentment with satisfactory performance. However, perceptions of machines as person-like agents open up the range of possible emotional responses, including socially-infused emotions. The person might experience disappointment or pride in the machine's performance, or guilt over failing to support it effectively.

2.2 Demand Factors and Trust

The advent of machine intelligence increases the range of demands potentially experienced by the operator, with implications for trust. Generally, as interacting with the machine becomes more demanding, trust is likely to deteriorate, as costs of machine management become perceived as higher than benefits of the machine's contributions to the mission [14]. Demands and trust may also be linked reciprocally; failure to calibrate trust optimally is likely to increase demands. Under-trust means that the human must take on more work, unnecessarily; over-trust will eventually lead to a mission failure due to machine error which the human must responsibility for mitigating.

Table 1. Challenges of autonomy and their performance impacts.

Challenge	Examples	Demands of autonomy	Performance vulnerabilities
Cognitive	• Sensor malfunction • Machine goal management error • Cyber attack	• Additional cognitive demand	• Attentional overload • Knowledge-based errors • Mode errors
Social	• Mis-perceptions of autonomy • Failure to support machine (human is poor team-mate) • Perceived lack of support (machine perceived as poor team-mate)	• Maintaining shared situation awareness • Appropriate back-up behavior • Function allocation	• Impaired shared situation awareness • Lack of team cohesion • Negative attitudes to machine
Self-regulation	• Stress from uncertainty and overload • Loss of perceived self-efficacy	• Overload • Managing feedback from machine (explicit or implicit)	• Diversion of attention • Disruption of executive control

Table 1 lists multiple sources of demand characteristic of interactions with autonomy [14]. The greater complexity of autonomous systems relative to traditional automation may impose higher demands on the operator. They may also increase operator uncertainty; for example, fault diagnosis becomes more difficult if it is unclear whether the fault is in a sensor or in the machine software. Demands may also be exacerbated by uncertainty over the machine' intentions [8]; in the military context, the operator might wonder whether unusual behavior was the result of the machine being hacked by a cyber-adversary. High cognitive demands and uncertainty may influence trust via the operator's assessment of machine competence; a machine that behaves unpredictably may not be deemed trustworthy.

Increasing autonomy also raises the scope for "social" interaction, as the machine graduates from tool to team-mate [15]. Team operations require not only coordination of actions to accomplish mission goals, but also teamwork behavior such as mutual performance monitoring, providing back-up, and leadership [16]. Lack of trust impairs teamwork, potentially leading to issues such as breakdown of a shared situational awareness and cohesion in performance [17]. Conversely, perceptions of poor team-work by the machine – for example, if it fails to back-up the human as anticipated - will damage trust. Finally, interacting with an autonomous system may increase self-regulative demands, as the human is forced to evaluate their own competence as an operator. Increased cognitive and social complexity may make it difficult for the human to gauge if he or she is actually performing competently, potentially causing stress which may disrupt information-processing [14]. An officer commanding troops understands the importance of effective leadership – but what constitutes leadership of a team of autonomous systems? In some cases, the system may have the capacity to adapt its behavior according to its evaluation of the human's capabilities, i.e., adaptive automation [18]. The downside of this facet of machine intelligence is that the human may feel denigrated if the machine's actions signal that it perceives the human as incompetent.

3   Drivers of Trust in Autonomous Systems for Threat Analysis

Trust in autonomous systems may be influenced by novel demand factors, in addition to established drivers of trust associated with machine performance and reliability [9]. Salient demand factors will be somewhat context-dependent, varying with the functionality of the specific autonomous system, and the operational challenges faced by the human-system team. We discuss the factors that may be important in the threat detection and analysis context, which define research priorities.

3.1   System Characteristics

Simple devices for threat detection include sensors for radiation or toxic chemicals. Future systems will add to these capabilities in various ways including novel sensors such as lidar-based detection of threats in 3-D space. They will also include sensors to detect psychologically relevant human responses such as facial emotions and autonomic arousal, coupled with software that can distinguish, for example, harmless expressions of frustration from purposeful aggression. Human operators may find it hard to trust advanced and/or unfamiliar detection and analysis capabilities. It may be especially hard to trust a machine that makes psychological judgments.

Future autonomous systems will also differ from conventional automation in regard to communication abilities. Current systems provide essentially a passive read-out of information, and the human must gauge its credibility and whether it is actionable. Autonomous systems will be able to also deliver confidence ratings, background information and transparency messages [19] that illuminate the reasons for its analysis, potentially increasing cognitive demands. Future systems may also have action capabilities, potentially including autonomous search for possible threats, calling for human or machine back-up to deal with a threat, or in some cases direct actions such as bomb disarming. Such capabilities will increase "social" needs for effective teaming and appropriate trust calibration.

3.2   Environmental Characteristics

Threat detection in military and security contexts takes place in a variety of operating environments, differing in the challenges that they pose. In some cases, the environment may be generally safe, and threats rare, such as scanning people attending a sports event for traces of explosives. In other settings, the ability of the machine to improve over human threat detection may be critical. In the military context, threats may be hard to identify, due to the increasingly asymmetric nature of combat; for example, insurgents seek to blend in with civilians and change tactics frequently. Future threat identification will increasingly require information fusion [20], i.e., analysis of multiple cues provided by different information sources, often under time pressure. For example, the machine might analyze immediate emotional cues along with information about a suspect's social media postings, credit card purchases, and phone records. Multiple cue integration, perhaps including "big data" methods, may threaten transparency, even if such functionality is included; it may not be feasible to explain the machine's analysis to the human, placing a particular burden on trust.

3.3   Operator Characteristics

Human operators differ considerably in terms of the personal characteristics they bring to autonomous system interactions, such as level of understanding of information technology. Inexperienced operators may be vulnerable to misleading depictions of artificial intelligence in popular media. Various psychological factors associated with propensity to trust humans have been identified, but the extent to which they generalize to trusting autonomous systems is unclear, especially as the social behaviors that influence trust may be interpreted differently when executed by an artificial system.

Operator characteristics can be represented as mental models, in this context, the person's internal representation of the machine's capabilities and limitations [15]. In fact, two types of mental model are relevant. First, people will have pre-existing mental models of what artificial system capabilities are. Barriers to trust include beliefs that machines cannot interpret human behaviors, or that machines cannot be relied upon as team-mates. Second, people will have a more narrowly focused model of machine-functioning in the context of the current mission's goals [17]. Training should accomplish realism in the mental model, but representations may nevertheless be biased by pre-existing conceptions of machine intelligence and by other characteristics such as personality. For example, in a UAS study, highly conscientious individuals appeared to prefer their own agency to reliance on automation under high demands [21].

3.4 Research Implications

We have identified multiple factors that may impact the operator's trust in an autonomous threat detection system, such as a robot or UAS. From previous research [8, 9] we can anticipate that factors such as perceived competence of the machine will impact trust, but system autonomy raises novel issues. Will the operator trust the machine's ability to infer threat from complex data sources, including psychophysiological data? Will the operator trust the machine to interpret threats emanating from challenging operational environments, such as insurgents actively aiming to disguise their intentions? Will the operator's trust be swayed by personal characteristics, such as pre-existing beliefs about intelligent machines, attitudes to technology, and knowledge of information technology?

The questions just framed point primarily to the role of cognitive demands in shaping trust, i.e., whether the operator can effectively cope with the increased complexity of working with an intelligent machine. However, in extended interaction scenarios, social and self-regulative demands may also factor into trust. Operators must determine the extent to which they will treat the machine as a team-mate capable of autonomous action, and the extent to which they trust their own judgment in managing the machine. Research on complex, realistic threat-detection scenarios may be necessary to answer such questions. Next, we describe a simulation platform that will be used in our research.

4 Simulation Use and Current Methodology

4.1 Unreal Engine for Research

Video game platforms are a favored tool for training purposes due to their versatility, elevating them to the status of "Serious games." [22]. Anecdotally, many military members report playing video games, supporting efforts to enhance training delivered through serious games. Younger Soldiers have greater gaming experience than older ones [23], so that gaming exposure is likely to increase in the future. The stimulating design of these systems may be naturally motivating for individuals [23] who regularly play video games. Serious games allow for the delivery of complex, situation-based information for the purpose of training due to the ability to program many environments and scenarios with multiple users. Using these features of serious games, researchers can examine decision-making, performance and subjective response in more realistic environments than traditional laboratory settings.

Gaming environments can be easily programmed for simulation of different complicated tasks from simple flight to dynamic exploration of a simulated environment. Unity and Unreal Engine 4 (UE4), by Epic Games, are popular game engines. The current study made use of UE4 due to its availability and ease of use. UE4 is a free downloadable gaming environment that is easily customizable. Objects for scenes can be purchased online and altered within the studio. Agents for simulation can be made in 3D modeling software such as make human (www.makehuman.org) or blender (www.blender.org) with animations created in software such as Mixamo (www.mixamo.com). Additionally, agents can be scanned into the designed environment and animated with commercial off-the-shelf software [24].

Scripting of levels can be done within UE4's editor using a node-based system called Blueprint shown in Fig. 1. Additionally, programming can be supplemented or done entirely using C++ and there is an abundance of tutorials for use of UE4 on YouTube and at the UE4 website (https://docs.unrealengine.com). The UE4 editor allows for programing of elements such as game rules, conditions, camera perspective, player control, weapon system controls, trigger events, and randomized or procedurally-generated props within the game [22]. Sound can also be added for atmosphere.

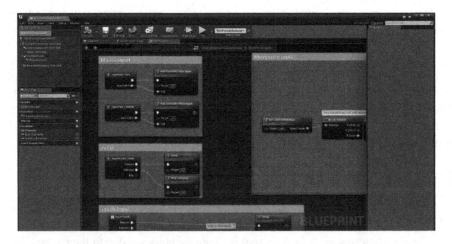

Fig. 1. Picture of UE4's node-scripting system.

4.2   Design of the Task

The current task was designed as a "town-clearing" task where a participant plays the role of a Soldier patrolling a small city with a robot partner to determine if threat activity is present. Participants are told that they are clearing a path through the town for a SWAT team to travel and must ensure that the areas along this path are safe. The robotic partner is armed with multiple sensors which it uses to make its own determination of the area's potential for threat. The type of cue used by the robot is manipulated. In one condition, the robot makes its judgement of the scene (see Fig. 2) using physical cues in the environment, such as a potential fire threat based off of thermal readings. In another condition, the robot partner makes a psychological inference from sensor readings, such as using thermal cameras to determine suspicious stress response in agents in the scene.

"I indicate possession of unknown metal objects. Metal objects match outline of weapons. My assessment of the scene is threat.

Fig. 2. Example of scene and robot judgement using physical sensor information.

Scene threat is manipulated to be low, medium, or high based on the number of suspicious objects, individuals and their qualities, and the condition of the buildings in the area. In low threat scenes buildings are new, one suspicious object is planted in the scene, and 1 out of 3 individuals seem angry. In medium threat scenes, buildings are slightly rundown and painted in the modeling software to appear dirty but without disrepair (no boarded or broken windows). There are also 2 suspicious objects such as a discarded duffle bag or package and 1 or 2 individuals appear upset and have angry or violent gestures. In the high threat scenes, the buildings appear in disrepair with broken or boarded windows and entrances or windows. Suspicious objects are higher in number. These include fire or smoke in the scene, and old package or random canisters next to each other (to hint at the possibility of explosives). Individuals in the high threat scenes appear ready to fight or riot; more individuals exhibit angry gesturing motions. Agents are carefully modeled to remove any social biases which may influence threat cues. There is an even representation of light, medium and dark complexion agents. Additionally, age is controlled in each complexion type so that an even number of individuals under and over 40 is drawn.

The robot is quite reliable so its evaluations are generally congruent with the scene. Cases where the robot's evaluation is discrepant may be especially important for assessing trust, and the person's willingness to trust the robot over their own senses.

After viewing the scene and robot evaluation, the participant uses Likert scales to answer various questions indicative of trust, beginning with an overall evaluation of threat (Fig. 3). Participants then rate the extent to which the robot's assessment is psychological in nature (Fig. 4). This rating tests if participants discriminate between the qualitatively different types of threat assessment that the robot makes, which may impact trust. Participants also rate their confidence in their robotic partner's judgement, and in its action recommendations. That is, there are two ratings of trust to test whether people are inclined to trust robot situation analysis more than choice of action. In further instantiations, the robot will in fact take autonomous action. Bias may be evident in any of these ratings.

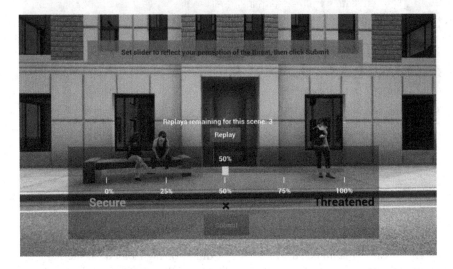

Fig. 3. Participant threat evaluation screen.

Initial studies will evaluate the extent to which trust in the robot is impacted by level of perceived threat, as well as the nature of the threat cue, i.e., whether analysis of sensor data identifies a physical or psychological threat. The role of individual difference factors related to the person's mental model for robot capabilities will also be assessed. Subsequently, the simulation will be utilized to explore trust in more complex, dynamic scenarios in which the robot has increased scope for acting autonomously.

5   Simulation Use - Future Directions and Challenges

The simulation methodology outlined in the previous section is intended to provide a platform for multiple studies that can address different aspects of trust in autonomous systems. In outline, specific research issues include the following:

- *Cognitive factors.* In addition to manipulating the reliability of the robot, studies may manipulate specific sources of cognitive demand on the operator, such as sensor and software failures, or a suspected cyber attack.
- *Social factors.* With more complex scenarios, the teaming aspects of autonomy may be brought to the fore. For example, the human and robot might be called upon to

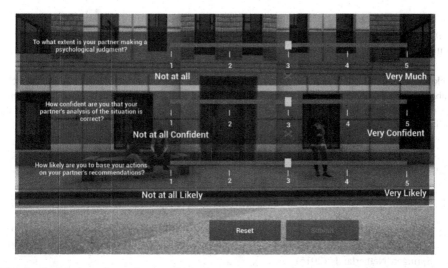

Fig. 4. Participant ratings of type of judgment and trust in robot's threat evaluation and action recommendation.

evaluate threat in different scenes, and communicate with one another to maintain shared situation awareness.

- *Self-regulative factors.* Scenarios can be developed in which the mission ultimately fails, either due to human or robot error. Attribution of blame, and the extent to which the human assumes responsibility for robot errors can be investigated.
- *Dynamic scenarios.* The simulator is currently configured to have the participant evaluate a series of independent scenes, but it might also be programmed to support an ongoing narrative in which a mission unfolds over time. Dynamic scenarios may be used to investigate factors influencing trust repair following a robot failure.
- *Mitigating factors.* It is likely that research can identify a variety of contexts in which trust in the robot is mis-calibrated, whether too high or too low. Further studies can investigate how to mitigate suboptimal trust. One focus is training, and how to optimize acquisition of a realistic mental model of robot capabilities. Another focus is robot design to elicit appropriate trust. Design features include the appearance of the robot, including the extent of anthromorphism, and the extent to which it provides transparency into the sources of its evaluations. Effective robot communication is also a focus for design efforts. For example, synthetic speech and displays of human-like emotion might support effective trust calibration.

Efforts to understand trust in the context of human interaction with autonomous systems are in their infancy. Systematic empirical work is necessary to determine the main influences on trust, beyond system competence and performance. Various challenges remain, including generalization of results from simulated to real environments. The role of contextual factors remains to be explored; can findings in the threat analysis scenario be generalized to other types of human-robot teaming mission? Results may also generalize to civilian contexts for autonomous systems including healthcare and manufacturing and service industries. Possible moderator effects of operator characteristics such as gender, cultural background, computer knowledge, and motivation remain to be explored. However, the increasing functionality and immersiveness of simulated environments provides a methodology for sustained research on trust and autonomy.

Acknowledgement. The authors gratefully acknowledge support from US Air Force Research Laboratory and US Army Research Laboratory. The views and conclusions contained in this document are those of the authors and should not be interpreted as representing the official policies, either expressed or implied, of AFOSR or the US Government.

References

1. Endsley, M.R.: Autonomous Horizons: System Autonomy in the Air Force - A Path to the Future. Office of the Chief Scientist, Washington, DC (2015)
2. Valavanis, K.P., Vachtsevanos, G.J.: Future of unmanned aviation. In: Valavanis, K.P., Vachtsevanos, G.J. (eds.) Handbook of Unmanned Aerial Vehicles, pp. 2993–3009. Springer, Netherlands (2015)
3. Matthews, G., Reinerman-Jones, L., Wohleber, R., Ortiz, E.: Eye tracking metrics for insider threat detection in a simulated work environment. In: Proceedings of the Human Factors and Ergonomics Society Annual Meeting, vol. 61, pp. 202–206. SAGE Publications, Los Angeles (2017)
4. Matthews, G., Reinerman-Jones, L., Abich IV, J., Kustubayeva, A.: Metrics for individual differences in EEG response to cognitive workload: optimizing performance prediction. Pers. Individ. Differ. **118**, 22–28 (2017)
5. Chen, J.Y., Barnes, M.J.: Human–agent teaming for multirobot control: a review of human factors issues. IEEE Trans. Hum.-Mach. Syst. **44**(1), 13–29 (2014)
6. Lee, J.D., See, K.A.: Trust in automation: designing for appropriate reliance. Hum. Factors **46**(1), 50–80 (2004)
7. Parasuraman, R., Riley, V.: Humans and automation: use, misuse, disuse, abuse. Hum. Factors **39**(2), 230–253 (1997)
8. Hancock, P.A., Billings, D.R., Schaefer, K.E., Chen, J.Y., De Visser, E.J., Parasuraman, R.: A meta-analysis of factors affecting trust in human-robot interaction. Hum. Factors **53**(5), 517–527 (2011)
9. Schaefer, K.E., Chen, J.Y., Szalma, J.L., Hancock, P.A.: A meta-analysis of factors influencing the development of trust in automation: implications for understanding autonomy in future systems. Hum. Factors **58**(3), 377–400 (2016)
10. Madsen, M., Gregor, S.: Measuring human-computer trust. In: Proceedings of the 11th Australasian Conference on Information Systems, vol. 53, pp. 6–8 (2000)
11. Mayer, R.C., Davis, J.H., Schoorman, F.D.: An integrative model of organizational trust. Acad. Manag. Rev. **20**(3), 709–734 (1995)
12. Waytz, A., Cacioppo, J., Epley, N.: Who sees human? The stability and importance of individual differences in anthropomorphism. Perspect. Psychol. Sci. **5**(3), 219–232 (2010)
13. Giner-Sorolla, R.: Affect in attitude: immediate and deliberative perspectives. In: Chaiken, S., Trope, Y. (eds.) Dual-Process Theories in Social Psychology, pp. 441–461. Guilford Press, New York (1999)
14. Matthews, G., Reinerman-Jones, L., Barber, D., Teo, G., Wohleber, R., Lin, J., Panganiban, A.R.: Resilient autonomous systems: challenges and solutions. In: Resilience Week (RWS), pp. 208–213. IEEE (2016)

15. Phillips, E., Ososky, S., Grove, J., Jentsch, F.: From tools to teammates: toward the development of appropriate mental models for intelligent robots. In: Proceedings of the Human Factors and Ergonomics Society Annual Meeting, vol. 55, pp. 1491–1495. SAGE Publications, Los Angeles (2011)

16. Salas, E., Sims, D.E., Burke, C.S.: Is there a "big five" in teamwork? Small Group Res. **36** (5), 555–599 (2005)

17. Ososky, S., Schuster, D., Phillips, E., Jentsch, F. G.: Building appropriate trust in human-robot teams. In: AAAI Spring Symposium: Trust and Autonomous Systems, pp. 60–65. AAAI Press, Menlo Park (2013)

18. Teo, G., Reinerman-Jones, L., Matthews, G., Szalma, J., Jentsch, F., Hancock, P.: Enhancing the effectiveness of human-robot teaming with a closed-loop system. Appl. Ergon. **67**, 91–103 (2018)

19. Lyons, J.B.: Being transparent about transparency. In: Sofge, D., Kruijff, G.J., Lawless, W.F. (eds.) Trust and Autonomous Systems: Papers from the AAAI Spring Symposium, pp. 48–53. AAAI Press, Menlo Park (2013)

20. Hall, D.L., Jordan, J.M.: Human-centered information fusion. Artech House, Norwood (2010)

21. Lin, J., Wohleber, R.W., Szalma, J.L., Ruff, H.A., Calhoun, G.L., Funke, G.J.: Cognitive overload, stress and automation utilization: a simulation study of multiple Unmanned Aerial System (UAS) operation (submitted for publication)

22. Ortiz, E., Reinerman-Jones, L., Matthews, G.: Developing an insider threat gaming environment. In: Nicholson, D.D. (ed.) Advances in Human Factors in Cybersecurity, pp. 267–277. Springer International, New York (2016)

23. Orvis, K.A., Moore, J.C., Belanich, J., Murphy, J.S., Horn, D.B.: Are soldiers gamers? Videogame usage among soldiers and implications for the effective use of serious videogames for military training. Mil. Psychol. **22**(2), 143–157 (2010)

24. U.S. Department of Defense, Air Force Research Laboratory: Rapid 3D prototyping & rigging for animation: Challenge problems and resources (2015)

Mxr Framework for Uncertainty Based Explanation for Uncovering Adversarial Behavior

Adrienne Raglin[1(✉)], James Michealis[1(✉)], Mark Dennison[2],
Andre Harrison[1(✉)], Theron Trout[1(✉)], and James Schaffer[2]

[1] Army Research Laboratory, Adelphi, MD 20783, USA
{adrienne.j.raglin.civ,james.r.michaelis2.civ,
andre.v.harrison2.civ,theron.t.trout.ctr}@mail.mil
[2] Army Research Laboratory, Playa Vista, CA 90094, USA
{mark.s.dennison.civ,james.a.schaffer20.civ}@mail.mil

Abstract. Mixed Reality (MxR) technologies have previously been explored in
military applications oriented towards supporting both individual situational
awareness and team collaborations. Ongoing technological advances in MxR
have expanded its potential usage by military analyst teams to view, digest, and
evaluate information from multiple data sources for uncovering adversarial
behavior. Towards facilitating improved situational awareness, MxR is a
promising medium for explaining patterns in data to uncover vital information.
By extension, analyst collaborations conducted using MxR may further enhance
collaborative decision making techniques used in military settings. In general,
explanations provide summarizations or descriptive information that supports
conclusions, depending on the desired level of abstraction. However, explanations that summarize information may not always preserve the underlying
uncertainty present in the data. This work proposes a fused reason-based
explanation technique for MxR that may help bring clarity to data where patterns may be unexpected, potentially revealing adversarial behavior.

Keywords: Explanations · MxR · Collaboration · Reasoning
Decision making · CSCW · Provenance · C4ISR

1 Introduction

Computer-Supported Cooperative Work (CSCW) systems aim to utilize information
and computer technology to allow distributed collaboration and to enhance collaboration for collocated members [1]. Under time-sensitive conditions, such as those
presented in military analyst operations, CSCW systems have faced challenges with
robustness in supporting remote collaborations as opposed to in-person approaches [2].
Effective support for future C4ISR operations, expected to rely upon the expertise of
dispersed forces coordinating under potentially high Operational Tempo (OPTEMPO),
requires the development of next-generation collaborative platforms capable of supporting both real-time interaction and seamless integration of available information.

J. Y. C. Chen and G. Fragomeni (Eds.): VAMR 2018, LNCS 10910, pp. 354–368, 2018.
https://doi.org/10.1007/978-3-319-91584-5_28

In CSCW systems, collaborators must often transition back and forth from a collaborative work space into their own work environment [3]. In typical face-to-face interactions, these transitions are often seamless and frequent. However, most elements of distributed collaboration environments (email, chat rooms, text messaging, video conferencing, or application sharing) have defined boundaries between collaborative and personal work areas that can negatively impact the collaborative process [3, 4]. Additionally, most methods of distributed collaboration support only a limited number of communication methods relative to the multiple modalities of communication that collocated collaborations can support [5].

Recent advances in Mixed Reality (MxR) technology shows promise in addressing existing challenges facing collaborative analyst tasks, potentially reducing or eliminating the communication and collaboration impairments caused by distributed collaborations. Collaboration using MxR systems can allow distributed members to interact with other members in a collaborative environment as if they were all collocated. MxR can also enhance face-to-face collaboration by associating digital information to physical objects in the collaborative space. This digital information can then be interacted with, manipulated, and altered in place of or in response to edits of physical objects. MxR is also largely a sandbox under which most existing collaborative tools can be added, allowing each user or the group to use the tools that best serves the decision making task. The user customized views of MxR systems also allows all of the members to experience the same collaborative space, but what each member sees can be tailored for each member of the group allowing them to focus on information of interest to them blending their own interpersonal workspace with the collaborative one.

Towards advancing the state-of-the-art in CSCW for military intelligence analysis, this work proposes a fused reason-based explanation technique for MxR that may help bring clarity to data where patterns may be unexpected, potentially revealing adversarial behavior. This technique is presently being developed around an MxR infrastructure under development by the U.S. Army Research Laboratory (ARL), and represents an ongoing line of research.

In the next section of this paper we present relevant work within the fields of explanation, mixed reality, and ontologies as they relate to CSCW. In Sect. 3 we discuss our concept for collaborative explanation utilizing uncertainty within an MxR system. In Sect. 4 we provide an overview and references of our custom collaborative environment in MxR. Finally, in Sect. 5 we provide a brief conclusion to discuss the relevance and importance of this system.

2 Background

Historically, methods for collaborative knowledge generation have been explored from an interdisciplinary perspective, with a strong emphasis on education-centric research. Work by Jakubik [6] supports the idea that collaborative knowledge creation can enhance understanding of knowledge spaces by individual contributors, by establishing awareness of participant roles and motivations. In an alternate effort by Goos et al. [7], the process of exploring reasoning and viewpoints of group participants helped in clarifying and justifying both information and applied analysis. Research on education methodologies by Hmelo-Silver et al. [8] discusses how collaborative knowledge building and analysis can be prompted through group questioning and collaborative construction of answer explanations. Similarly, research by Masters [9] presents "ExplaNet", a CSCW infrastructure aimed at explanation-based knowledge sharing. By design, ExplaNet is driven by an instructor posing questions about a domain of interest to students, which in-turn are answered by students through supporting explanations of their reasoning. In turn, students were able to collectively review explanations provided by their peers. Experimentation applied to evaluate ExplaNet demonstrated benefits for student in information retention and performance across lessons.

In Pikes' "Scalable Reasoning Systems" [10], visual analysis services that captured insight used reasoning artifacts. The reasoning artifacts are the information used in the analysis; with "tags" that shows their associations. As this process moves forward hypothesis are formed. In addition, a reasoning graph is used, confidence values and values that indicate the strength of the reasoning relationships are assigned to the hypothesis by the analysts.

Likewise, research on MxR systems has borrowed from a variety of disciplines, ranging from Computer Science to Human-Computer Interaction and organizational psychology [11]. On the use of MxR is to support C4ISR analyst tasking, a selection of relevant research efforts are presented below.

2.1   Explanation Usage in Computer-Supported Cooperative Work

Within the fields of Computer and Information Science, explanation methods date to foundational work on expert systems (e.g., MYCIN) [12], which on their own constitute a growing research agenda. In this context, system generated explanations are designed with trust, transparency, and persuasion in mind [13, 14]. For the purposes of this work, explanations are considered within the scope of Computer Supported Cooperative Work (CSCW) systems [1, 3], and aim to convince collaborative analysts of specific viewpoints. As such, explanations are viewed in this work as sets of assertions or statements that clarify and make understandable the data about the common operating environment, backed by: (i) pedigree/provenance about known facts; (ii) reasoning over facts about the world; and (iii) extrapolations about potential supporting facts. Here, a common concern for explanation usage lies in quantifying and managing uncertainty of information.

Provenance is important in collaborative environments for both scientific [15] and visual analytics [16]. Analysts and other decision makers are interested in both calculation (algorithmic) and data provenance [17]. Many desktop-based workflow systems have been proposed (e.g., [18–20]) that help manage complexity in environments where disparate analyses are synthesized into a single trace of knowledge. It is common for these systems to present node-link diagrams of related concepts, support the generation of scatterplots and other visualizations. Systems also attempt to help manage differences in notation between analysts, by automatically mapping concepts from each analyst's workspace onto a global model.

For decision making tasks, a need to account for uncertainty in available information is well-established in prior research. As reflected in [21], while decisions made by individuals may be the best given available information, any uncertainty surrounding that supporting information can remain of concern. More specifically, potential regret over an incorrect decision can impact how decision makers process available information.

Within the scope of C4ISR research, explanation techniques accounting for information uncertainty have been previously explored in the domain of adversarial reasoning. Under the U.S. Air Force's Adversarial Intent Inferencing (AII) program [22], which investigated techniques for information fusion to infer and predict adversarial behavior, explanation of predictions was considered a key function. The steps necessary for generating candidate explanations required: "information about the adversary's current actions and inferences about the adversary's motivations." Within the AII framework, descriptive and predictive probabilities were generated to highlight potential adversarial behavior. In related work, algorithmic and behavioral game-theory have been used to computationally express adversarial behaviors in systems [23]. Although this approach focuses on scheduling it has been applied to multiple tasks. In general, these algorithms are used to reveal "weaknesses of predictability" that could lead to vulnerabilities that adversaries can exploit or as an attribute of the adversaries.

2.2 Applications of Mixed Reality

Although many aspects of MxR are open research questions, numerous studies have attempted to examine its potential in improving visualization and learning of disparate data sources and easing multi-user collaboration. While not yet conclusively demonstrated, MxR may be well positioned to improve the efficiency and effectiveness of CSCW situations through improved spatial reasoning, immersion, and telepresence.

Usage of 3D vs 2D Environments in Analysis and Problem Solving. A study by Donalek et al. [24] reported that in a waypoint drawing task, subjects who viewed the environment in an Oculus Rift HMD performed with less distance and angle errors than those who viewed the environment on a 2D desktop monitor. [25] created an immersive virtual environment where Twitter data was overlaid atop real geography to improve the experience for analysts. The authors claimed that this MxR environment enhanced situational awareness, cognition, and that pattern and visual analytics were more efficient than on traditional 2D displays.

A study by [26] measured performance differences among subjects who had to complete a paper folding task after viewing information on a 2D desktop monitor or through an augmented environment. Subjects showed a higher cognitive load index when learning in 2D vs 3D, as measured by the ratio of frontal theta power over parietal alpha power. This indicated that information transfer was significantly easier when the data was viewed in an MxR environment. Other work has shown that the perception of one's virtual body and hands is also a critical feature when performing cognitively demanding tasks, such as memorization, when done in a virtual environment [27]. This decreased cognitive load may be related to the fact that humans are "biologically optimized" to perceive in 3D [24]. However, it is still an open research question as to which immersive mediums (VR, AR, MR) are best for improving user decision making across content domains.

Utility of Immersive Environments. The feeling of immersion in MxR environments may be supported through the use of technologies like the Myo armband[1], which can allow the user to manipulate virtual data points with naturalistic gestures. A recent study by [28] compared the effectiveness of immersive AR (HoloLens) and tablet VR to traditional desktop use by measuring completion time and error for various point cloud estimation tasks. They found that the immersive AR environment was best for tasks involving spatial perception and interactions with a high degree of freedom, such as with tangible user interfaces. In fact, using a 3D stereoscopic display has been shown to increase task performance by 60% [29, 30]. As MxR technologies evolve, these systems will need to support interactive actions like scaling, selection of sub-spaces, and navigation [31, 32]. It is also critical that these systems seamlessly integrate with existing workflows in order for them to be effectively utilized [33].

Telepresence in Cooperative Tasks. The costs associated with travel, building workspaces, and modifying them to meet evolving mission demands are often road-blocks to collaboration. These problems can potentially be mitigated through MxR technology. Recently, Fairchild and colleagues built a VR telepresence system which allowed scientists in Germany and the U.K. to collaborate remotely on data from Mars missions in real time [5]. The system tracked gaze, interpersonal distance, and facial expressions to maximize the scientists' nonverbal communication, allowing for more natural interactions. Some collaborations would have been impossible if MxR tech-nology were not implemented. For example, Gardner and Sheaffer [34] created a system called GraphiteVR, which allows multiple users to visualize high-dimensionality social media data and manipulate it in real time. AR has also been used successfully during remote collaboration to add world-stabilized text annotations over video that was played back live in 3D [35].

Information Retention in Analysis Tasks. In addition to collaboration, working with complex tasks in MxR environments has recently been shown to improve user per-formance and information retention. For example, individuals who manipulated visu-alized social media data in a fully-immersive and motion-tracked virtual environment reported that they learned more about the data than when it was viewed in a traditional setting [36]. Other studies have shown that overlaying virtual information [37] can dramatically improve performance and task engagement [38]. MxR can also be used to overlay information or even the virtual hands from one user to another, to help them better visualize a problem or navigate through a complex scenario [39]. For example, an analyst at a forward operating base in fully-immersive VR could assist a dismounted solider by highlighting known threat locations relative to his/her current viewpoint and display that information on a tablet or through an augmented reality overlay.

---

[1] https://www.myo.com/.

2.3 Integration of Cyber/Web-Based Content in Mixed Reality Systems

Increasingly, ISR operations are becoming reliant upon internet and web-based information sources [40]. Support for integration of these cyber-based information sources within MxR infrastructures represents a potential line of future research, complementing and enhancing the collaboration process of the analysts. Here, a short review is provided on how semantics-based technologies have previously been applied to support web-based content ingestion and reasoning in MxR platforms.

Ontologies, which provide formal representations of domain knowledge, can be used to formally structure and integrate content for information management systems. Towards supporting content integration, ontology-based techniques have previously been investigated across a collection of Augmented Reality applications. Two common themes of these efforts center on navigation through open areas (e.g., [41–43]) and visual inspection of artifacts in the real world (e.g., [43–46]). In both cases, ontologies are defined to support linking of information in the Augmented Reality system (e.g., points of interest) with information from outside sources. For example, Aydin et al. [44] defines a service for presenting historical information on buildings through time-specific 3-dimensional renderings and supplemental information on relevant events and persons. Likewise, Ruta et al. [41] investigated methods for assisting persons with physical disabilities in navigating through buildings, through the incorporation of outside information about building floor plans.

An additional benefit to semantic technologies lies in their capacity to support content personalization and filtering. In the Ruta et al. building navigation service [41], information on route selection is based in-part on user profiles that formally define the nature of a user's disability (e.g., if the user is wheelchair-bound, do not suggest paths involving stairs). Similarly, Ramón et al. [43] explore Augmented Reality applications for assisted living scenarios, guiding users through routine tasks (e.g., selection of medication from a cabinet) based on knowledge of their medical state (upcoming appointments, dosing schedules).

Based on these efforts, incorporation of semantic technologies into MxR systems for collaborative decision making appears to show promise. This is reinforced by recent user studies [46] which investigated user engagement in Augmented Reality environments. However, additional user studies are needed to establish this, based on the needs and requirements of military analysts.

3 The ARL Collaborative Environment for MxR (ACEMxR)

To support C4ISR intelligence analysis methods, such as the one proposed earlier, the U.S. Army Research Laboratory (ARL) is actively developing the ARL Collaborative Environment for MxR (ACEMxR). ACEMxR leverages a collection of Commercial off the Shelf (COTS) technologies, including the Unity Engine[2] for supporting MxR application development. In-line with military usage requirements, ACEMxR aims to ensure a variety of design objectives:

---

[2] https://unity3d.com/.

- **Confidentiality:** to prevent access to data by those not authorized to receive it.
- **Reliability:** to provide confidence that a transmitted message will reach its destination.
- **Integrity:** to ensure that the message received is free of unauthorized alterations and tampering.

A brief discussion is provided below on supporting technologies featured in ACEMxR, with additional details provided in [50].

Network Communications. One common mechanism for achieving acceptable levels of network security requirements is through the use of encrypted mesh networks. To support these requirements within ACEMxR, the Open Virtual Private Network (OpenVPN) protocol was selected based on its broad acceptance in the commercial networking space and its ability to transport UDP packets; the latter being necessary to establish a shared MxR environment using the Unity Engine's standard networking features. To support collaborative MxR applications, ACEMxR provides support for the deployment of collaboration servers which integrate input from both sensor feeds and individual analyst workspaces. In turn, secured communications are employed to facilitate data transmission across collaboration servers, enabling integration of multiple analyst teams across distributed locations. As detailed here, the ACEMxR communications architecture is illustrated in Fig. 1.

Instrumentation and Telemetry Capture. The ACEMxR infrastructure incorporates instrumentation and telemetry capture backed by Elasticsearch, Logstash, and Kibana (ELK). Collectively these capabilities are called an ELK stalk. Elasticsearch is a NoSQL database engine designed for large data analytics and machine learning. Logstash is a modular and configurable data import engine. It includes an extensive array of data input, filtering, and output plugins. This makes it suitable for collecting experimental data in environments composed of heterogeneous systems and data formats. Kibana is a web application that provides access to powerful querying and analytical tools as well as data visualization and graphing tools.

User Interface/Application Support. ACEMxR aims to support a collection of MxR analytics applications, based on usage of COTS software including the Unity Engine for 3D application development. Analysts using ACEMxR-hosted applications are expected to utilize virtual reality (VR) headsets such as Oculus Rift or HTC Vive. Due to the limitations in the current state of the art of true Mixed and Augmented Reality systems, such as Microsoft Hololens, ACEMxR presently focuses on approaches for simulating the MxR experience in VR. As existing MxR technologies mature, both in speed and reliability, corresponding adjustments to ACEMxR are anticipated.

4 An Approach for Collaborative Explanation Generation and Presentation

Towards advancing the state-of-the-art in collaborative systems for military intelligence analysis, a fused reason-based explanation technique for MxR is presented to aid in bringing clarity to data where patterns may be unexpected. This technique is presently

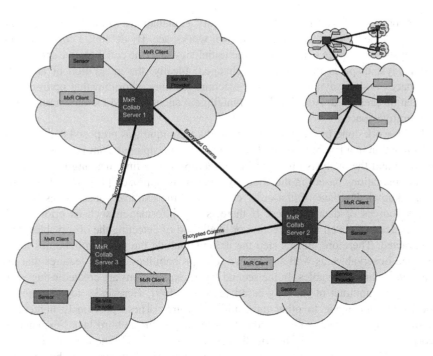

Fig. 1. ACEMxR communications architecture.

being developed around an MxR infrastructure being developed by the U.S. Army Research Laboratory (discussed in Sect. 4), and represents an ongoing line of research. Following an introduction to the technique, an illustrative usage scenario is provided.

4.1 Components of the Technique

The goal of providing explanations in an MxR environment is to aid in the decision-making process. In this example as it has been throughout this paper we focus on the case where the decision makers are military analysts. In this section we pose one possible approach as an initial concept to generate and present explanations into MxR.

Our concept is to form explanations from tactically relevant data generated by analysts equipped with MxR devices. In addition, the explanations will be presented and evaluated by the analysts in MxR.

The MxR framework is a secure mesh network providing secure connectivity between analysts, allowing multiple analysts to collaborate in unison. In the MxR framework, individual analysts will have their own workspaces as well as access to the joint collaborative space. For simplicity moving explanation information into the collaborative space is done iteratively. When an analyst wishes to modify the explanation information in the collaborative space they request permission to modify and the explanation information remains in a pending state until voted on by the other analysts in order to make it permanent.

The process of generating the uncertainty explanations from the different data sources is done by each analyst in their own workspace. By default, a combination of the analysts' workspace is injected, as the initial view into the collaborative space. Only if an analyst disputes this view is it changed. Ideally, the integration of all of the workspaces is done dynamically by a machine learning algorithm that optimizes the information presented. Additionally, an intelligent agent will aid the moderation of the collaborative space.

In the work done by Raglin and Harrison, a technique was proposed that generates an explanation in a layered manner [47]. Initially, data captured from various sources is presented and the analysts highlight the observables they find meaningful. In the first layer, explanations based on the abductive reasoning approach [48] are initially used. Here, a knowledge base of first-order clauses and the extracted observables from the various sources of data are used. If there is any information such as prior or joint probabilities associated with detection or likelihood of detecting the observables it will be extracted. Therefore, in this step the axioms include the prior probabilities for the identified observables as well any known joint probabilities and the features that may be linked to the observables. In the second layer, explanations are created using vector space representations of analogy-based reasoning [49]. Here links to the identified observations are made to other unidentified features. These previously unidentified features are considered as new candidate observables. In the third layer, explanations incorporate an uncertainty of information (UOI) measure [47]. The idea of this UOI is to account for any uncertainties such as constraints or ambiguities within the data. The UOI can be influenced or tailored by the pedigree or provenance of the data. This pedigree or provenance can include but is not limited to the original source of the data, the reliability of the source, and the time sensitivity of data.

After this layer, connections are made between data and adversary actions, behaviors, or decisions. Information from intelligence reports will be used as a filter to highlight any connection of objects, terms, or features between the observables and the report. This information will be integrated back into the knowledge base with links to the observables. For simplicity these links will be based on connections from the intelligence data and the extracted observables.

Next, multi-layered candidate explanations from each analyst are injected into the collaborative space, potentially overlaid on the data from these multiple sources in the MxR environment. Analysts collectively review these candidate explanations. Ultimately, selecting the "best" or generate a fused explanation based on the collective assessments of the group.

4.2   Sample Scenario

This section uses a sample scenario to present a walk-through of the techniques described in Sect. 4.1. This scenario was generated in the MxR environment discussed in Sect. 4.1. In the MxR, the avatars represent the military analysts and the wall panels display information in the virtual collaborative workspaces. The three military analysts are examining information to determine the likelihood of an ambush attack by the adversary in city Y along route X. Each analyst specializes in one of the three modalities of information, Analyst A specializes in text and linguistics, Analyst B

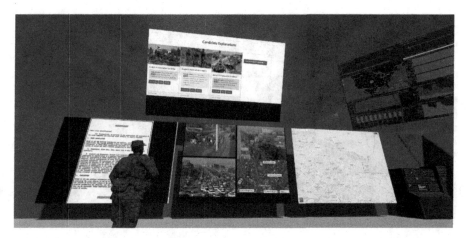

Fig. 2. Individual analyst workspace. The three larger panels display information and the single overhead panel displays the explanation(s) generated by the analyst.

specializes in image processing, and Analyst C specializes in geographical maps. Figure 2 shows an individual virtual workspace which includes a text file, several images, and a map. For this scenario each analysts uses the same information, focusing on the information that they specialize in. In the first step the analysts select key observables from the sources of information:

- **Analyst A (HUMINT report) observables:** Names of four people of interest, one person involved in two previous attacks, and the locations of the previous attacks.
- **Analyst B (Archived image) observables:** Three people of interest and two associated vehicles highlighted in the image.
- **Analyst C (Map of Area of Operations) observables:** Pinpoints of the location of the two previous attacks and the locations of both vehicles spotted in an unusual location.

Second, using the observables each analyst generates a set of candidate explanations and selects one explanation that will be pushed to the joint collaborative workspace:

- **Analyst A:** Ambush attack in Y at X likely with UOI = 75 because the other three individuals may be in jail or out of the city.
- **Analyst B:** Ambush attack in Y at X likely with UOI = 65 because three of the individuals are shown together in the image location in the image requires confirmation due to possible corruption in repository database.
- **Analyst C:** Ambush attack in Y at X likely with UOI = 50 because this site is the same area where vehicles used during the attacks have been sighted.

For this scenario the same information is in each of the individual workspaces and the collaborative workspace. It is in this joint collaborative workspace that the agreed upon explanation is generated:

Fig. 3. Collaborative analyst workspace with Analyst D submitting additional imagery information for review.

Joint Explanation: ambush attack in Y at X likely with UOI = 50 because there is an overlap of the people of interest in the same area and the sighting of the vehicles used during the attacks are have been mapped and determined to be just outside the city.

Figure 3 shows Analyst D joining the collaboration with additional information that can be considered to reduce the uncertainty tied with the identification of the people of interest and lowering the UOI. The information from Analyst D:

Analyst D: Updated imagery helps identify the fourth person, it is confirmed by Analyst A.

Figure 4 shows the joint collaborative workspace. For this scenario this view is used to finalize the joint explanation.

Fig. 4. Updated collaborative analyst workspace. The four large front panels display information and the large side panel displays the finalized joint explanation generated by the analysts.

Updated Joint Explanation: Ambush attack in Y at X likely with UOI = 35 because there is an overlap of the people of interest in the same area where vehicles used during previous attacks have been mapped to be just outside the city, imagery confirms identification of all the individuals.

This sample scenario focuses on generating and presenting the explanation in MxR to support collaborative decision making, there are many issues that need to be addressed. These issues include but are not limited to visualization of the information, facilitation of the collaboration, as well as integration of data and explanations. Ideally, the MxR space will allow a real-world view from an operator in the field. The analysts in our scenario in VR could be looking at that beamed data and using AR to relay information back to the operator. This would make for a scenario where all levels of, MxR, VR-AR-Reality, are present. This future capability would also add to other issues to address.

5 Conclusion

Many decision rules in artificial intelligence and machine learning are based on the mean or median of a distribution of supporting input data, but very often factoring in the variance around that data is essential to making better decisions. Also, any subsequent decisions a secondary decision system makes may also need the variance of the current decision that was just made. This frame of reference is analogous to the aims of this paper as we have proposed a system to factor in the uncertainty of supporting information into a joint decision-making processes and subsequent explanations of collaborative analyst tasks. This is the newest element within our MxR framework that allows DoD and non-DoD assets to securely collaborate within an MxR space for distributed decision-making objectives. We believe that MxR may be the environment where the fast pace of military analyst operations can be done effectively, due to its support for multiple modalities of communications, its improved sense of telepresence and immersion, and its ability to ingest and interact with both physical and digital information.

References

1. Mills, K.L.: Introduction to the electronic symposium on computer-supported cooperative work. ACM Comput. Surv. **31**(2), 1 (1999)
2. McGee, D.R.: Augmenting environments with multimodal interaction (2003)
3. Ishii, H., Kobayashi, M., Arita, K.: Iterative design of seamless collaboration media. Commun. ACM **37**(8), 83–97 (1994)
4. Billinghurst, M., Kato, H.: Collaborative mixed reality. In: Proceedings of the First International Symposium on Mixed Reality, pp. 261–284 (1999)
5. Fairchild, A.J., Campion, S.P., Garcia, A.S., Wolff, R., Fernando, T., Roberts, D.J.: A mixed reality telepresence system for collaborative space operation. IEEE Trans. Circ. Syst. Video Technol. **27**(4), 814–827 (2017)
6. Jakubik, M.: Experiencing collaborative knowledge creation processes. Learn. Organ. **15**(1), 5–25 (2008)

7. Goos, M., Galbraith, P., Renshaw, P.: Socially mediated metacognition: creating collaborative zones of proximal development in small group problem solving. Educ. Stud. Math. **49** (2), 193–223 (2002)

8. Hmelo-Silver, C.E., Barrows, H.S.: Facilitating collaborative knowledge building. Cogn. Instr. **26**(1), 48–94 (2008)

9. Masters, J., Madhyastha, T., Shakouri, A.: ExplaNet: a collaborative learning tool and hybrid recommender system for student-authored explanations. J. Interact. Learn. Res. **19**, 51–74 (2008)

10. Pike, W., Riensche, R.: The scalable reasoning system: lightweight visualization for distributed analytics a case study in law enforcement. IEEE Symp. Visual Analytics Sci. Technol. **8**, 71–84 (2009)

11. Costanza, E., Kunz, A., Fjeld, M.: Mixed reality: a survey. Hum. Mach. Interact. **5440**, 47–68 (2009)

12. Aamodt, A.: Explanation in case-based reasoning – perspectives and goals (2005)

13. Häubl, G., Murray, K.B.: Preference construction and persistence in digital marketplaces: the role of electronic recommendation agents. J. Consum. Psychol. **13**(1–2), 75–91 (2003)

14. Pu, P., Chen, L., Hu, R.: A user - centric evaluation framework for recommender systems. In: Proceedings of 5th ACM Conference on Recommender Systems - RecSys 2011, pp. 157–164 (2011)

15. McPhillips, T., Bowers, S., Zinn, D., Ludäscher, B.: Scientific workflow design for mere mortals. Futur. Gener. Comput. Syst. **25**(5), 541–551 (2009)

16. Brennan, S.E., Mueller, K., Zelinsky, G., Ramakrishnan, I.V., Warren, D.S., Kaufman, A.: Toward a multi-analyst, collaborative framework for visual analytics. In: IEEE Symposium on Visual Analytics Science and Technology 2006, VAST 2006 - Proceedings, pp. 129–136 (2006)

17. Simmhan, Y.L., Plale, B., Gannon, D.: A survey of data provenance in e-Science. SIGMOD Rec. **34**(3), 31–36 (2005)

18. Oinn, T., et al.: Taverna: a tool for the composition and enactment of bioinformatics workflows. Bioinformatics **20**(17), 3045–3054 (2004)

19. Altintas, I., Berkley, C., Jaeger, E., Jones, M., Ludascher, B., Mock, S.: Kepler: an extensible system for design and execution of scientific workflows. In: Proceedings of the 16th International Conference on Scientific and Statistical Database Management, pp. 423–424 (2004)

20. Gotz, D., et al.: HARVEST: an intelligent visual analytic tool for the masses. In: Proceedings of the First International Workshop on Intelligent Visual Interfaces for Text Analysis, pp. 1–4 (2010)

21. Bell, D.E.: Regret in decision making under uncertainty. Oper. Res. **30**(5), 961–981 (1982)

22. Santos, H.: Adversarial intent inference for predictive battlespace awareness, no. AFRL-IF-RS-TR-2005-378 (2005)

23. Tambe, M., Jain, M., Pita, J.A., Jiang, A.X.: Game theory for security: key algorithmic principles, deployed systems, lessons learned. In: 2012 50th Annual Allerton Conference on Communication, Control, and Computing, Allerton 2012, pp. 1822–1829 (2012)

24. Donalek, C., et al.: Immersive and collaborative data visualization using virtual reality platforms. In: IEEE International Conference on Big Data, pp. 609–614, October 2014

25. Moran, A., Gadepally, V., Hubbell, M., Kepner, J.: Improving big data visual analytics with interactive virtual reality (2015)

26. Dan, A., Reiner, M.: EEG-based cognitive load of processing events in 3D virtual worlds is lower than processing events in 2D displays. Int. J. Psychophysiol. **122**, 75–84 (2016)

27. Steed, A., Pan, Y., Zisch, F., Steptoe, W.: The impact of self-avatar on cognitive ability in immersive virtual reality. In: IEEE Virtual Reality Conference, pp. 67–76, March 2016

28. Bach, B., Sicat, R., Beyer, J., Cordeil, M., Pfister, H.: The hologram in my hand: how effective is interactive exploration of 3D visualizations in immersive tangible augmented reality? IEEE Trans. Vis. Comput. Graph. **24**(1), 457–467 (2018)

29. McIntire, J.P., Havig, P.R., Geiselman, E.E.: What is 3D good for? A review of human performance on stereoscopic 3D displays. In: SPIE Defense, Security, and Sensing, May 2012, p. 83830X (2012)

30. McIntire, J.P., Liggett, K.K.: The (possible) utility of stereoscopic 3D displays for information visualization: the good, the bad, and the ugly. In: 2014 IEEE VIS International Workshop 3DVIS, pp. 1–9 (2014)

31. Olshannikova, E., Ometov, A., Koucheryavy, Y., Olsson, T.: Visualizing big data with augmented and virtual reality: challenges and research agenda. J. Big Data **2**(1), 1–27 (2015)

32. Spicer, R.P., Russell, S.M., Rosenberg, E.S.: The mixed reality of things: emerging challenges for human-information interaction, p. 102070A (2017)

33. Bellgardt, M., Pick, S., Zielasko, D., Vierjahn, T., Weyers, B., Kuhlen, T.W.: Utilizing immersive virtual reality in everyday work. In: 2017 IEEE 3rd Workshop on Everyday Virtual Reality, pp. 1–4 (2017)

34. Gardner, M.R., Sheaffer, W.W.: Systems to support co-creative collaboration in mixed-reality environments. In: Liu, D., Dede, C., Huang, R., Richards, J. (eds.) Virtual, Augmented, and Mixed Realities in Education. SCI, pp. 157–178. Springer, Singapore (2017). https://doi.org/10.1007/978-981-10-5490-7_9

35. Gauglitz, S., Nuernberger, B., Turk, M., Höllerer, T.: In touch with the remote world. In: Proceedings of 20th ACM Symposium on Virtual Reality Software and Technology - VRST 2014, pp. 197–205 (2014)

36. Royston, S., DeFanti, C., Perlin, K.: A Collaborative Untethered Virtual Reality Environment for Interactive Social Network Visualization. arXiv preprint arXiv:1604.08239 (2016)

37. Frank, J.A., Kapila, V.: Mixed-reality learning environments: integrating mobile interfaces with laboratory test-beds. Comput. Educ. **110**, 88–104 (2017)

38. Dascalu, M.-I., Shudayfat, E.A.: Mixed reality to support new learning paradigms. In: 2014 18th International Conference on System Theory, Control and Computing, pp. 692–697, October 2014

39. Huang, W., Alem, L., Tecchia, F., Duh, H.B.L.: Augmented 3D hands: a gesture-based mixed reality system for distributed collaboration. J. Multimodal User Interfaces, 1–13 (2017)

40. Hurley, M.M.: For and from cyberspace: conceptualizing cyber intelligence, surveillance, and reconnaissance. Air Sp. Power J. **26**(6), 12–33 (2012)

41. Ruta, M., Scioscia, F., Ieva, S., De Filippis, D., Di Sciascio, E.: Indoor/outdoor mobile navigation via knowledge-based POI discovery in augmented reality. In: Proceedings of 2015 IEEE/WIC/ACM International Joint Conference on Web Intelligence and Intelligent Agent Technology, WI-IAT 2015, pp. 26–30 (2016)

42. Vert, S., Vasiu, R.: Integrating linked open data in mobile augmented reality applications - a case study. TEM J. - Technol. Educ. Manag. Inform. **4**(1), 35–43 (2015)

43. Hervás, R., Bravo, J., Fontecha, J., Villarreal, V.: Achieving adaptive augmented reality through ontological context-awareness applied to AAL scenarios. J. Univers. Comput. Sci. **19**(9), 1334–1349 (2013)

44. Aydin, B., Gensel, J., Genoud, P., Calabretto, S., Tellez, B.: Extending augmented reality mobile application with structured knowledge from the LOD cloud. In: CEUR Workshop Proceedings, vol. 1075, pp. 21–27 (2013)

45. Walczak, K., Rumiński, D., Flotyński, J.: Building contextual augmented reality environments with semantics. In: Proceedings of 2014 International Conference on Virtual Systems and Multimedia, VSMM 2014, pp. 353–361 (2014)
46. Kim, H., Matuszka, T., Kim, J.-I., Kim, J., Woo, W.: Ontology-based mobile augmented reality in cultural heritage sites: information modeling and user study. Multimed. Tools Appl. **76**, 26001–26029 (2017)
47. Raglin, A., Harrison, A.: Adversarial reasoning with an uncertainty of information measure for military centric decision making. In: Next-Generation Analyst V. International Society for Optics and Photonics (2018)
48. Gordon, A.S.: Commonsense interpretation of triangle behavior, pp. 3719–3725
49. Summers-Stay, D., Voss, C., Cassidy, T.: Using a distributional semantic vector space with a knowledge base for reasoning in uncertain conditions. Biol. Inspired Cogn. Archit. **16**, 34–44 (2016)
50. Trout, T., et al.: Networked mixed reality (MxR) infrastructure for collaborative decision-making. In: International Society for Optics and Photonics (2018)

Human-Agent Collaborative Decision-Making Framework for Naval Systems

Maria Olinda Rodas[✉], Jeff Waters, and Cheryl Putnam

Space and Naval Warfare Systems Center Pacific, San Diego, CA 92103, USA
maria.rodas@navy.mil

Abstract. This work provides an overview of a future human-agent collaborative decision-making framework to be developed for naval systems using an augmented reality platform. We present the basic concept behind the framework, key features of the application, and some details about a future proof of concept prototype that will demonstrate and evaluate the concept against a baseline design.

Keywords: Military · Virtual reality · Mixed reality · Augmented reality
Decision optimization · Provenance · Data visualization · Design
C2 · Innovation

1 Introduction

Increasingly, humans collaborate with intelligent and autonomous agents to meet military objectives [1]. The support of these agents is often used to acquire and analyze information, make decisions and plan future actions [2]. However, lack of trust is often mentioned as the main critical barrier to transition successful intelligent and automated agents into the military [3]. The concept of trust is often determined by three main factors: (1) the reliability of the agent; (2) the self-confidence of the human operator; and (3) the workload required for the task [4]. Often, intelligent agents are perceived as untruthful, not necessarily because they are unreliable, but because they are unable to adequately communicate their rationale to human operators [5].

Increasing trust in the intelligent agent via increasing reliability is crucial to avoid the "crying wolf effect"; however, helping the human operator to adequately calibrate trust in the agent is vital given that most intelligent agents will always be flawed (i.e., not designed for all requirements and therefore unreliable in some occasions) [6, 7]. This paper describes an effort to develop a human-agent decision-making collaboration framework to enable effective communication and trust calibration between intelligent agents and human's operators.

2 Background

A key objective of the U.S. military is to achieve Information Superiority for enabling sound and timely decision-making [8]. As part of the planning process, military personnel must make informed decisions, solve complex problems, and ultimately

J. Y. C. Chen and G. Fragomeni (Eds.): VAMR 2018, LNCS 10910, pp. 369–376, 2018.
https://doi.org/10.1007/978-3-319-91584-5_29

accomplish assigned missions. Decisions are critical as they drive actions which have impact that drive further decisions [2]. The consequences of a decision ripple through command structures driving more decisions of more organizations and entities which can be catastrophic if based on the wrong decision.

In the past these informed decisions were made without any support, while currently military personnel are making decisions with the support of intelligent and automated agents. While these technologies are meant to support humans in making faster and more efficient decisions; the current reality is that they are unable to effectively provide support because they fail to establish trustworthy relationships with the humans. Furthermore, they fail at providing humans with the supporting information in a way that will enhance their decision-making process. This involves providing information in a way that allows human operators to adequately weigh that information while making further decisions. In some cases, such as in the Automatic Target Recognition (ATR) technologies, human operators are forced to make blind decisions only considering yes or no answers on the part of the autonomous agent. In other such intelligent agents that make autonomous planning of optimal Unmanned Vehicle routes, the agent provides a course of action but again without any explanation on the algorithms rationale.

Most intelligent and automated agents still lack the adequate transparency critical to allow understanding of their rationale. There is the assumption that to make automation algorithms such as those of the ATR technologies transparent to human operators, the technologies must be able to communicate their purpose, process and performance [9]. Based on that assumption, researchers at the Army Research Laboratory developed the Situation Awareness-based Agent Transparency model (SAT) to explain aspects of SA that affect trust. The SAT model includes variables such as the agent's purpose (goal), process (intentions, progress), performance (constraints), reasoning process, projection of future state and limitations [10] to increase agent transparency and therefore overall trust in the agent. The same researchers showed the implementation of this SAT model during a human-agent teaming mission for multi-robot management demonstrating how transparency increased trust in agents without increasing the human operator's workload [11].

Understanding the decision-making process of intelligent and autonomous agents is not enough to ensure a successful collaboration between the two. Human operators must also be able to interact with the agents to allow further calibration of trust. Decision-making explanations by agents have shown to successfully calibrate trust in human-agent interactions allowing the agent to provide the right type of information to the humans [12, 13].

3 Problem Formulation

Several types of autonomous agents, such as those used in ATR and automated mission planning, are currently utilized in the Navy to make decisions at lower levels of command such as the Unmanned Vehicle (UV) operator level. UV Operators make decisions which form the basis for critical planning decisions made at higher levels of command, posing a critical risk to mission success if early decisions are faulty.

Adequate trust calibration in intelligent and automated systems is crucial to effectively integrate the agent's support into the final decision while understanding their advantages and limitations.

The human decision-making process is mostly ignored by current agent designers since new technologies cannot offer the required human-decision making support in a user-friendly manner to enhance the information evaluation and the weighting process affecting the final decision. Adequate trust calibration in the agents is also missing, resulting in human operators ignoring the agents' recommendations and support. Finally, an effective collaboration enabler technology is also required to allow a trusted and efficient interaction between the agent and the human.

We propose that an effective human-agent decision-making collaboration framework can enhance human-agent communication by allowing the required transparency on the agent's rationale to enable a successful trust calibration. Furthermore, we propose that an effective framework can also enhance the human decision-making process making it easier for the operators to incorporate and use the agent's decisions. An effective interaction technology such as Augmented Reality (AR) will enable the interaction using interactive data displays.

4 Proposed Framework Details

This project will capitalize on existent resources across industry, academia and government to develop an effective framework for human-agent decision-making collaboration. Low-cost Augmented Reality (AR) technology such as the Microsoft HoloLens will be utilized as the main technology enabler for the human-agent interaction. Data visualization techniques and visual data analytic models will be employed to enhanced communication through effective user interface design techniques [14–16]. A well designed and elegant framework will improve the efficiency of creating software. It will improve developer productivity and importantly, improve the quality and reliability of the software.

The Agile Decision Computation Model (ADCM) and Agile SA Machine Model (ASAMM) previously developed at SSC Pacific will be adapted to this project. The ADCM specifies a standard decision format for agents to track the provenance, i.e. the who, what, when, where and why of the agent's decisions. The ASAMM will specify a standard SA format for agents to reflect and build rational explanations of why a decision was suggested. An Agent Communication Model (See Fig. 1) will be developed to integrate input from both the ADCM and ASAMM models and specifies how information from these models will be communicated back to the human operators. A Human Communication Model will also be developed to determine a standard format to allow humans to communicate with the agents at the different interaction modes. Finally, a Human-Agent Interaction Model will be developed to mediate the interaction between the human and the agent communication models. This model communicates to the AR capability to enable the interaction and visualizations. See Fig. 1.

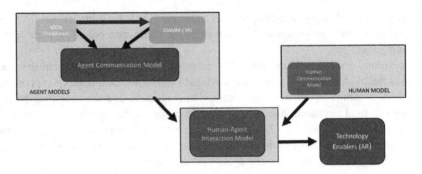

Fig. 1. Human-agent decision-making collaboration framework

4.1   Capturing Agents Decision Structure

The ASAMM will allow a situational understanding of an agent's current decision in terms of past context and the future impact of their decisions on mission goals through the machine-understandable representation of the intersection of processes. Situational Awareness has been defined as "...the *perception* of the elements in the environment within a volume of time and space, the *comprehension* of their meaning, and the *projection* of their status in the near future" [17]. Based on this definition, what is needed for machine situational awareness of an agent's decision is the perception of the decision (e.g. a machine representation) and its components, along with the decision's provenance providing the comprehension of the meaning of the decision, and the impact of the decision on relevant ongoing processes. The ASAMM model is designed to capture these components. For instance, the model captures processes that can be thought of as a series of "steps" for accomplishing a goal (decision goals) [18]. A "step" in this setting is a "task", or an "action", something the machine needs to do. See Fig. 2. For a task to be completed, something needs to have been accomplished, and that accomplishment can be considered an output "product" of the task. Each task may have one or more input or output products. We all execute processes in our daily lives and work; however, the processes are not always obvious or well defined. A well-defined machine task will have clearly defined tangible input and output products. A "process" can be represented as a sequence of steps where each "step" represents an action that has an input and an output "product". The products represent interim or final results and are instances of generic product types relevant for command and control such as agent's Observation, Course of Action, Request, Approval, Decision, and Metric. Utilizing this type of machine SA model will allow agents to communicate with humans on why and how a decision was made. To do this, a process needs to specify by the human operator in a machine understandable way. Once that done that information will be used to check on the agent status and provide feedback to the user that will allow adequate calibration of trust.

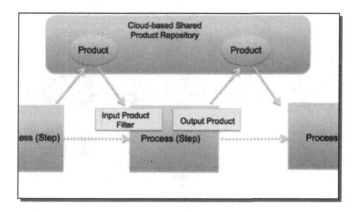

Fig. 2. The process step building block

4.2 Tracking Agent's Decision Provenance

Often, when information is passing from intelligent agents to human operators there is no information about the agent's confidence in the decision and the overall decision criteria used by the agent. This type of information is critical for military decision makers since decision criteria requirements can rapidly change in real time missions. Understanding information reliability, especially decision confidence and criteria, is key to effective decision performance [19].

To understand the agents' decision-making a standardized, machine-understandable representation of their decisions is required. The Agile Decision Computation Model (ADCM) being developed at SSC Pacific will allow us to capture agent's decision provenance [20]. It consists of 5 simple stages: (1) identify the need to make a decision; (2) gather information; (3) judge alternatives; (4) select an alternative; and (5) add the outcome of the decision following execution of the decision. Using the PROV representation of decisions, the ADCF can consider managing the agent's decision. The framework will provide an Application Programming Interface (API) and reusable software library in different programming languages enabling the management (e.g. creation, retrieval, update, deletion and query) of decisions. The framework will also provide a validator, a graphical visualization, a cloud repository and other common services to ease the burden on developers and users. The ADCF will allow us to capture the agent's decision rationale in detail (Fig. 3).

4.3 Enabling Human-Agent Interaction Technology

Choosing a technology that will effectively support the human-agent collaborative decision-making is key to the success of any framework. Through the process of considering interactive technologies some requirements were identified as critical to success in the type of military settings being considered. Those requirements include: (1) a user-friendly platform that allows different type of interaction and effective data visualization; (2) single or multiple decision-makers; (3) little or no modification of existing

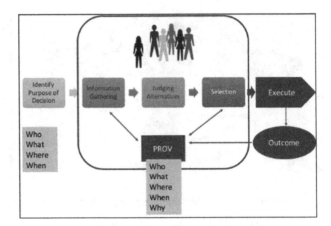

Fig. 3. Agile decision computation framework

military systems (separate platform); (4) lightweight capability for expeditionary types of missions; and (5) easy integration of information coming from different systems.

AR enables natural communication by displaying the visual cues necessary for a human and intelligent agent to collaborate in a decision-making situation. Augmented Reality (AR) technologies combine real and virtual objects while the real objects are still perceived in the real world. Furthermore, AR can enable task collaboration with multiple users or decision-makers at different locations. AR allows displays of information without modification of existing systems, and introduction of new displays and capabilities in otherwise constrained and limited environments. AR platforms such as Microsoft HoloLens provide a lightweight and easy to integrate capability. Finally, AR can easily integrate data found in different systems into one single display that will provide the required information for collaborative decision-making without modification of existing systems.

5   Proof of Concept with AR Capability Implementation

Once the models are adapted to this project, a proof of concept prototype implementation will be developed for a mine-hunting naval mission scenario. In this scenario, an ATR technology is used to support the human decision-making in finding underwater mines. With AR, a sonar operator could use AR glasses, such as the HoloLens, and see overlaid on top of the ATR target on the sonar display, as needed, a 3D rendering (derived from the ATR system) hovering in mid-air of the specific type of target detected, intelligence about that target or type of target, and then to further drill-down, the operator could see a pop-up graph of the metrics used by the ATR algorithm and the scores and confidence. Moreover, AR technology could support human decision-making by providing a step-by-step explanation of how the target was chosen by the agent and allowing a more informative decision while also learning about the agent's limitations and advantages. This type of interaction is expected to allow an effective trust calibration.

To the operator, the interaction will appear as if the operator is interacting with one system, a very helpful system which provides not simply an alert about a target, but a realistic visualization, intelligence, drill-down information and agent's confidence levels. The operator can "communicate" by indicating interest by gaze, or by touch, or by voice, or by input device, and with the system responding with the desired information. So, for this purpose, AR assists the operator by integration of disparate capabilities. AR assists system developers by not requiring separate, individual interfaces and not requiring onerous early integration limitations. For this project, AR allows significant flexibility in providing a lightweight but effective integration capability so that we can integrate capability directly on existing systems without impacting those systems directly. AR allows us to do our experiments and measures directly on top of the operator's existing systems.

6 Conclusions

This paper briefly discusses the details of a human-agent collaborative decision-making framework to be developed at SSC Pacific. Tracking an agent's decision-making information through a provenance model will help us uncover critical information that is required for effective collaborative decision-making and allow the user to better understand and trust the information. The framework will avoid a ripple effect on decisions caused by using unreliable information. Additionally, an agent SA model will allow the agent to track its decisions and offer feedback in terms of their past and future performance. The goal is to provide greater transparency and decision-support to the human operator's decision-making process. Performance data along with details on the decision-making used by agents can help human operators to effectively understand the reliability of informational sources provided by the agents. Moreover, AR data integration and visualizations will support a user-friendly interaction while supporting drill-down examination of the agent rationale. A proof of concept prototype will be developed for the mine countermeasures Navy scenario to demonstrate and evaluate the human-agent decision-making collaboration framework.

References

1. Barnes, M.J., Evans, A.W.: Soldier-robot teams in future battlefields: an overview. In: Barnes, M., Jentsch, F. (eds.) Human-Robot Interactions in Future Military Operations, pp. 9–29. Ashgate, Farnham (2010)
2. Parasuraman, R., Sheridan, T.B., Wickens, C.D.: A model for types and level of human interaction and automation. IEEE Trans. Syst. Man Cybern. Part A Syst. Hum. **30**(3), 286–297 (2000)
3. Office of the Under Secretary of Defense for Acquisition, Technology and Logistics. Washington, DC. 20301-3140. Department of Defense: Defense Science Board. Task Force Report: The Role of Autonomy in DoD Systems, July 2012. https://fas.org/irp/agency/dod/dsb/autonomy.pdf. Accessed 12 Jan 2018
4. Parasuraman, R., Riley, V.: Humans and automation: use, misuse, disuse, abuse. Hum. Factors J. **39**(2), 230–253 (1997)

5. Hancock, P.A., Billing, D.R., Shaefer, K.E., Chen, Y.C., DeVisser, E.J., Parasuraman, R.: A meta-analysis of factors affecting trust in human-robot interaction. Hum. Factors J. **53**(5), 517–527 (2016)

6. Hoff, K.A., Bashir, M.: Trust in automation: integrating empirical evidence on factors that influence trust. Hum. Factors J. **57**(3), 407–434 (2015)

7. Navy War College. Navy Planning, December 2013. https://www.usnwc.edu/getattachment/ 17afbf3-a1e2-46b3-ble9-d1fa4b0fec5a/5-01_(Dec_2013)_(NWP)-(Promulgated).aspx. Accessed 20 Jan 2018

8. Wagenhals, L.W., Levis, A.H.: Course of action development and evaluation. In: DTIC, Fairfax (2000)

9. Lee, J.D.: Trust, trustworthiness, and trustability. In: The Workshop on Human Machine Trust for Robust Autonomous Systems, Ocala, Florida (2012)

10. Chen, J.Y.C., Barnes, M.J.: Human–agent teaming for multirobot control: a review of human factors issues. IEEE Trans. Hum.-Mach. Syst. **44**(1), 13–29 (2014)

11. Mercado, J.E., Rupp, M.A., Barnes, M.J., Barber, D., Procci, K.: Intelligent agent transparency in human-agent teaming for multi-UxV management. Hum. Factors J. **58**(3), 401–415 (2016)

12. Wang, N., Pynadath, D.V., Hill, S.G., Merchant, C.: The dynamics of human-agent trust with POMDP-generated explanations. Intelligent Virtual Agents. LNCS (LNAI), vol. 10498, pp. 459–462. Springer, Cham (2017). https://doi.org/10.1007/978-3-319-67401-8_58

13. Wang, N., Pynadath, D.V., Hill, S.G.: The impact of POMDP-generated explanations on trust and performance in human-robot teams. In: Proceeding of the 15th International Conference on Autonomous Agents and Multiagent Systems, Singapore, pp. 997–1005 (2016)

14. Lim, K., Suresh, P., Schulze, J.P.: Oculus rift with stereo camera for augmented reality medical intubation training. In: Proceedings of IS&T the Engineering Reality of Virtual Reality, San Francisco, CA, 1–2 February 2017

15. Wiley, B., Schulze, J.P.: archAR: an archaeological augmented reality experience. In: Proceedings of IS&T/SPIE Electronic Imaging, the Engineering Reality of Virtual Reality, San Francisco, CA, 9–10 February 2015

16. McCarthy, D., Schulze, J.P.: Distributed VR rendering using NVIDIA OptiX. In: Proceedings of IS&T the Engineering Reality of Virtual Reality, San Francisco, CA, 1–2 February 2017

17. Endsley, M.R.: Toward a theory of situation awareness in dynamic systems. Hum. Factors: J. Hum. Factors Ergon. Soc. **37**(1), 32–64 (1995)

18. Jeff, W., Bruce, P., Pilcher, J., Odland, A., Jones, D.: A dynamic agile process model for situational awareness: a machine-understandable, fractal-based, data-driven approach. Presented at the Cognitive Methods in Situational Awareness and Decision Support (CogSIMA) Conference, San Diego, California (2016)

19. Langloz, C.: Fundamental measures of diagnostic examination performance: usefulness for clinical decision making and research. Radiol. J. **228**(1), 3–9 (2003)

20. Putman, C., Waters, J., Rodas, O.: A standard decision format using provenance. In: Proceedings of IEEE International Symposium on Signal Processing and Information Technology, Bilbao, Spain (2017)

360 Degree Mixed Reality Environment to Evaluate Interaction Design for Industrial Vehicles Including Head-Up and Head-Down Displays

Markus Wallmyr[1(✉)], Daniel Kade[1], and Tobias Holstein[1,2]

[1] Mälardalen University, Västerås, Sweden
{markus.wallmyr, tobias.holstein}@mdh.se,
d.kade@web.de
[2] University of Applied Sciences, Darmstadt, Germany

Abstract. Designing and testing new information and safety features for industrial vehicles do not need to involve the realization of high-fidelity and expensive simulators. We propose a low-cost mixed reality environment which allows for rapid development and rearrangement of a virtual and physical setup of a simulator for industrial vehicles.

Our mixed reality simulator allows for safe testing of controls, information, and safety features to support drivers of industrial vehicles. In this paper, we test the implications of showing extra digital information to excavator drivers through a virtual environment, an external head-up display as well as a head-down display. Through user tests we have seen first indications that projected information through our mixed reality system and content on a head-up display is perceived as more helpful and intuitive than using head-down displays, when controlling our industrial vehicle simulator. Moreover, we have seen that the fear of overseeing an obstacle or other important information is lower when using a head-up display, in comparison to other tested visualization options.

Keywords: Rapid prototyping environment · Head-up display
Mixed reality · Head-worn projection display · Design evaluation

1 Introduction

The use of digitally created content is increasing in many types of vehicular systems, ranging from cars to industrial vehicles such as excavators or tractors. One possible drawback of this evolution, is that the user will spend more focus on displays and digital information and thus has a reduced attention to the surrounding environment. Subsequently, this might lead to hazardous situations [1]. One way to mitigate this is to use mixed reality interaction technologies, using for example head-up displays [2, 3], which show information in the user's line of sight while he or she is looking through the windscreen. Although these types of technologies offer possibilities for enhanced efficiency, usefulness and experiences, the technology itself does not warrant these

© Springer International Publishing AG, part of Springer Nature 2018
J. Y. C. Chen and G. Fragomeni (Eds.): VAMR 2018, LNCS 10910, pp. 377–391, 2018.
https://doi.org/10.1007/978-3-319-91584-5_30

benefits [4]. Many interesting technologies have failed or taken time to reach a market breakthrough due to insufficient maturity, lack of a usefulness or subpar usability.

Simulators, provide a virtual environment to users and are nowadays available in different varieties and range from low-cost simulators in front of a normal screen to highly realistic industry simulators with 360-degree visualization and motion feedback. Generally, simulators provide advantages in terms of reproducibility, standardization, and controllability of scenarios and tests. A simulator replicates scenarios that might be difficult, expensive or even risky to reproduce in reality, such as a dangerous driving scenario, where a driver would be physically at risk. Furthermore, it allows for controlled simulation environments that are not affected by wind, weather and other external circumstances [5]. Additionally, the use of simulators and interactions with them can be evaluated without placing humans or physical objects in a real environment, or before the real environment is ready, for example when evaluating improved operator environments.

These benefits make simulators useful in areas such as understanding user behavior and evaluation of designs. However, despite the progress in hardware and software used for simulators, there are still limitations. Industrial simulators are often built with computer monitors or projection solutions that can be space consuming, require long setup times and pose high costs. Therefore, initial experiments, user evaluations or even trainings are often performed with simpler simulators. Fully featured simulation environments are used in later stages of a project, when previous stages indicated positive results. This way of working restricts early evaluation of interaction with the technology or interface and may lead to increased costs because possible issues get detected late in the development process [6].

A popular alternative when creating a simulation is to use virtual reality (VR) or mixed reality (MR) headsets. Simulating an immersive virtual environment in which the user can naturally look around by moving the head can be important in many scenarios, such as the simulation of complex industrial vehicles (cranes, excavators, forklifts, etc.) or even normal driving scenarios (e.g. overtaking, parking, etc.) [7, 8]. Nevertheless, a major limitation with virtual reality, is when physical artifacts like sliders, knobs and interior design of a real-world prototype have to be used while performing in the virtual environment. Mixed reality headsets will, on the other hand, let the user see the physical space, but will have limitations to show a fully immersive virtual environment.

This paper introduces a mixed reality simulator that allows for rapid prototyping within immersive virtual environments, using also physical artifacts and physical ways to visualize information, i.e. transparent screens. The purpose is to support testing new control concepts and design ideas in a fast and prototypical way. Our solution consists of off-the-shelf hardware and software. It is also low-cost, easy to install and scalable from smaller setups where virtual windows or screens are in front of a user up to larger CAVE-like installations.

We have evaluated the technical approach by building a rapid prototype excavator simulator. In such environments it is of higher importance, compared to ordinary on-road cars, to be able to look up and down and to see the environment around the vehicle. The user can look around in a projected virtual scenery while still being able to see the physical controls and physical displays, the latter in form of a head-down display and a head-up display. The simulator has been used to perform a user feasibility study. The aim of the study was twofold;

First, an evaluation of the approach of building rapid prototypes for mixed reality simulations, supporting a mix of physical and virtual content, and to what level of realism it is perceived by users.

Second, to make a pilot study evaluating how presentations of visual information in different places would benefit the information intake of operators driving excavator machines. More specifically, how users perceived the use of head-up displays and head-down displays for situational awareness information while driving.

The paper will first cover related work. It will thereafter present the technical approach and the simulator setup. Then it will describe the pilot study and its result with a final discussion and conclusion.

2 Related Work

The use of head-up displays and mixed reality interfaces for vehicles have been of long interest for researchers, such as its possibilities to increase safety and user experiences [9, 10]. According to Sojourner and Antin, a head-up display speedometer produced improved performance and shortened response time to hazardous situations [11]. Ablaßmeier et al. also observed that head-up displays can result in reduced workload, and increased driving comfort [12]. However, the design of a head-up display interface and information clutter can greatly affect performance [10, 13]. Moreover, the large body of work around head-up displays have mainly related to road vehicles and although head-up display solutions have been evaluated in industrial vehicles and shown potential benefits, there is still more work needed for it to be useful in daily life, both in terms of technology and potential benefits [14, 15].

Simulators, have been used in many vehicle research areas to evaluate user behavior and HMIs. These can range from specific replica simulators costing hundreds of thousands of euros [16] to low-cost simulators [17] and desk simulators [18]. Simplified or conceptual simulations are sufficient for many purposes, "as our ability to 'fill in the gaps' to create strong cognitive representations has clear potential as an alternative to modeling every last detail of the space" [19]. In, for example, an on-road driving simulation it may be enough to look at a PC monitor to display the simulated environment in front of a car and to use a gaming steering wheel as an input device. However, the PC monitor approach offers a very limited field-of-view (FOV), restricting simulations were operators need to move their head or body. This is especially a problem when interactions need to be tested were the user has to pay attention to the surrounding environment. The same goes for simulation of head-up displays. A head-up display is often constructed using a combiner glass or transparent retro-reflective film and some sort of projection device as image source [20–22]. Current head-up displays in vehicles have a relatively small view box that can be simulated via simple setups, for example using a combiner glass and a tablet as information source [23]. However, the pre-conditions for many industrial vehicles are very different, with bigger windscreens and a wider working area for the user to observe.

The interest to build virtual and mixed reality display systems [24–26] has increased as new products are introduced to the market. The above-mentioned limitations can be avoided by disconnecting the user from the real world using head-worn displays e.g. virtual reality headsets [27]. These naturally offer the possibility to freely look around in the virtual world. However, they also bring new challenges, as real-world content must be replicated into the virtual world [7, 28].

Most of the mixed reality see-through products offer a near-eye solution with a limited field of view, a constant focus, single eye usage (no stereoscopy) and limited depth. Many near-eye solutions come with a great deal of optical complexity in design, e.g., Meta's Meta 2 Glasses [29] or Microsoft's HoloLens [30]. Other alternatives, use special contact lenses or project directly on the retina to present the information [31, 32]. While near-eye solutions can be used to evaluate head-worn mixed reality, they lack the physical representation of a vehicle-mounted head-up display [33]. Moreover, they face the same problem with occlusion of real-world objects as the virtual reality headsets, if the surroundings shall be visualized via glasses.

Wearable laser projectors, as we use it in our research, offer an interesting alternative. Harrison et al. used a shoulder-mounted projector combined with a depth camera to project images to non-reflective surfaces and to allow gestural interactions [34]. In our approach, we have further developed the idea of using a laser projector as a head-worn mixed-reality device using a retro-reflective surface as a screen.

Laser scanning pico-projectors do not require any optical components to focus on the projection surface and the number of pixels displayed stays constant with the increasing distance between the projector and the screen. Additionally, they come with a coin size light engine [35] with further possibilities for miniaturization, thus making it even more wearable.

The image qualities, as well as the use of reflective material, has been investigated before [36, 37]. Image projections can also be made onto non-reflective surfaces [38, 39]. However, in our setup, we use a reflective material, as this enables mixing of physical controls with the virtual scenery without distortion as well as in different lighting conditions. This technology has also been used for motion capture acting support applications and for gaming tests [40, 41]. Unlike other systems like e.g. from CastAR [42] or from other research [43], this system does not require multiple projectors. Thus, problems originated from using multiple projectors, such as the keystone or image registration effect, are not an issue in our system.

3 Simulator Setup

A mixed reality simulator was built that allows controlling an excavator over an obstacle course by using a conventional joystick and wireless keyboard. The virtual world visualization consist of a head-worn projection system and a room coated with a reflective cloth. It also has physical information providers, in form of a head-up display and a head-down display, as well as software to drive and display the simulation. It was of importance that the real and virtual world can be controlled and seen at the same time and that the system was low-cost to allow testing of new control concepts and design ideas in a fast and prototypical way.

3.1   Cave Room

The simulator room was coated with a high-gain retro-reflective cloth no. 6101 from RB Reflektör. The cloth is used to reflect the projected light back to the source and has a high light gain. This effect allows users standing close to the projector to basically see a very bright image. We placed the reflective cloth in a 3.5 × 2.5-m room with a height of 3 meters and also covered the floor in front and around the user. In this room, we placed a rotatable chair and mounted a joystick and Bluetooth keyboard on the chair. The setup of the room and the chair can be seen in Fig. 1.

Fig. 1.   Left: picture of the cave room. Right: picture of the operators' position in the cave room.

3.2   Head-Worn Projection Display

Our head-worn projection display system, as shown in Fig. 2 consists of several off-the-shelf hardware components: (1) a stripped-down laser pico projector, SHOWWX + from Microvision Inc., with external battery pack (2) a Samsung S4+ smartphone, (3) a headband with 3D printed housing holding the equipment, and (4) retro-reflective cloth covering the walls of our simulator room (can be seen Fig. 1).

The pico projector acts as a light engine in our head-worn projection system. The maximum native resolution of the projector is 848 × 480 px @60 Hz v-sync in size. Its light emission is 15 lm. To increase the image size, a 180° fisheye lens is attached which allows for a field of view of roughly 83.6° × 47.5°. The optical abilities of the laser projector give the user an image that doesn't suffer from any key distortion effect, even when the reflective cloth used as a screen is distorted or not perfectly flat. This enables a faster screen or CAVE-like setup by allowing a clear and distortion free image without sensitive calibration of projection screens and projectors.

For our mixed reality application, we used the gyroscope sensor of the smartphone to look around in the digital environment.

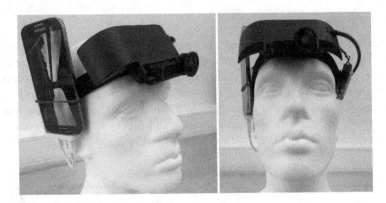

Fig. 2. Picture showing the head-worn projection system including a smartphone, laser projector with battery pack and 3D printed housing.

3.3   Head-Up Display

Our head-up display is built by using a projector as an image source and a combiner or screen in the form of a transparent projection film. The screen is based on an unbranded transparent holographic projection film attached to a metal frame of 0.6 × 0.9 m. This gives a screen that is transparent when looking through it and reflective when projected by light.

The projector used is a standard office projector, NEC VT 46, with 1200 lm and 800 × 600 pixel resolution. It is mounted on an adjustable stand and points up towards the head-up display. The projectors Key-Stone functionality is used to adjust for the otherwise distorted image. The picture presented by the projector is hosted by an additional computer, communicating with the mobile phone in the head-worn projection system.

The setup works because of the specific combination of projectors and reflective materials. The head-worn projection system worn by the user projects the virtual world but emits such a low level of light that it will not be enough to provide a noticeable picture on the head-up display, even when the operator is facing its screen. The highly reflective cloth, used for the cave's wall, will on the other hand provide a clear view of the projected image back to the user. The projector for the head-up display has a much higher brightness (80 times more than the head-worn projection system) which is enough to project a bright image on the head-up display. Since the projector is projecting from below it will not be reflected by the cave wall. A setup with these types of projectors works best in caves with dimmed lights, since the ambient light of normal lit up rooms will lead to faded or washed out projections.

3.4   Software Description

Figure 3 provides a general overview of the technical components and the implemented architecture of our industrial simulator setup. A smartphone holds the digital simulator environment, which is developed in the Unity game engine. The smartphone's built-in gyroscope sensor is used to detect movements of the users head, thus making it possible to look around in the digital environment using natural head movements. Moreover, the smartphone is used as a connection hub for the input devices and as a computation unit to show the digital environment through the head-worn projector.

A tablet PC is used as a head-down display which is also used to generate the graphics for the head-up display. The visuals presented are implemented using Unity and presented at each moment in time when received from the smartphone, sent via a network connection.

The excavator's boom is controlled using a joystick, a Thrustmaster T.16000M, that is connected to the tablet computer which is used as a head-down display. A software component was implemented converting joystick events into an XML format and sends those to the smartphone. The excavator tracks are controlled via a keyboard which is connected to the smartphone via Bluetooth.

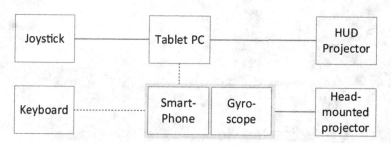

Fig. 3. An overview of the components in the mixed reality simulator

4 Simulating Excavator Driver Support

The implemented excavator simulator prototype allows a user to control a virtual excavator. Moving the lower excavator boom up and down was set to the vertical axis of the joystick, rotating the body of the excavator to the horizontal axis, moving the upper boom was controlled by twisting or turning the joystick around the Z axis and finally two buttons on the top of the joystick controlled the bucket movement of the excavator. Driving the excavator through the scenery was controlled via the 8, 4, 5, 6 keys on the keyboard.

To evaluate the use of our mixed reality projection system, three different variants of delivering visual information were used in the study: (I) via a virtual presentation (in the virtual environment), (II) via a physical head-up display, and (III) via a physical head-down display placed at the armrest of the chair, see Fig. 4. The virtual presentation used the head-worn projection to present the head-up display information in the virtual windscreen of the excavator. This simulation gives a fully virtual simulation without additional physical information sources in the real world.

The transparent screen gives a physical representation of a head-up display in the cabin windscreen. The information displayed will thus always be visible and enables detection from the peripheral vision. This in contrast to variant (I), where the information is not visible when the user is looking in a direction where the projected virtual world will not contain the virtual head-up display. The head-down display, variant (III), is a reference to traditional monitors used in today's vehicle cabins that present information aside the operational area, requiring the user to focus on the screen while neglecting primary tasks.

Fig. 4. Photo showing all three display solutions at once.

4.1 Scenario

A scenario was created in the virtual world. The task in this scenario was to navigate through a construction site while avoiding obstacles in form of vehicles, cones, and avatars, see Fig. 5. Additionally, the user had to locate three pillars of stacked cubes and use the excavator to tip the orange cubes over. Navigating in the virtual world required attention to the ground and surroundings of the machine. Arriving at a pillar and tipping them over required the user to look up to navigate the excavator boom towards the pillar. Thus, a wider visual area had to be covered than just looking straight ahead.

Fig. 5. Top-down view of the virtual scenario, with key elements colored.

A visual warning system was implemented to support the user in detecting obstacles, i.e., objects in close range. This system consisted of simple graphical figures, shown on the currently active display, i.e., one of the above-presented variants. When an obstacle was close to the excavator, a warning triangle was shown together with a numeric value that indicates the distance to the object. When the excavator was imminent to hitting an object, a hexagon shaped stop sign was shown. When an avatar, resembling a virtual human, was close to the excavator, an additional circular warning sign was shown.

The navigation towards the next task was supported by an arrow that pointed from the excavator bucket towards the next pillar, similar to an arrow shown in navigational systems.

4.2 Method

We invited seven users to test the scenario in order to assess the feasibility of our approach and to get a first impression from users about the usage of the head-up display. Users were informed of the purpose of the study and introduced to the equipment, the controls, as well at the task to perform in the scenario. Each user test was also recorded with an additional camera facing the user, to be able to evaluate the user reactions and comfort or discomfort while using the prototype. Any recording was only performed after acquiring consent from the user. Each user was also informed that he, or she, could abort the study at any time.

After a user was successfully equipped, he or she was asked to complete the given scenario. Users had to run the scenario three times. Each time using a different variant of presenting the assistive information, the head-down display, the physical head-up display or the virtual head-up display. The order was pre-determined and counterbalanced, so each user operated a different sequence of information assistance systems. Through this we aim at mitigating the risk of having the results influenced due to users getting familiar with the scenario.

After completing the test, users were asked to fill out a questionnaire to document their experiences with the prototype and the three different variants of displaying warning signs and navigation aid.

4.3 Results

The pilot tests were conducted with seven users (one female and six male users, N = 7). Due to the limited amount of test users, no firm conclusions can be drawn from the results. However, the results can be seen as indications to guide the shaping of future designs, prototypes and studies.

Four of the users were in the age of 26–35 years and three users were over 35 years old. Only one user had driven a real excavator before, but four users had prior experiences of vehicle or industrial simulators. Moreover, four testers had experienced a virtual reality headset or a head-worn projection system before.

A user test with three test runs took about 15 min to complete per user. The time for each run decreased, due to users getting familiar with the scenario.

All users completed the three test runs and filled in the questionnaire. In the questionnaire, the users were asked to grade the helpfulness of the support information as a navigation aid throughout the test track, see the left plot in Fig. 6. Here, users gave the two head-up display solutions positive ratings while the head-down display received lower ratings on its helpfulness.

Moreover, the users were asked to rate the risk of missing or overlooking presented information when using the different display options. Hereby, the head-down display was rated with a higher risk than the head-up displays. Also, the physical head-up display received slightly more consistent scores. This indicates that it would be interesting to further evaluate the use of head-up displays. It furthermore supports the assumption that physical representations, such as a physical head-up display that is always present to a user, could be beneficial when presenting information that should not be missed by the user.

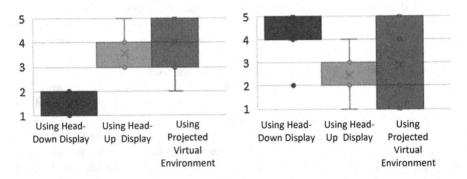

Fig. 6. To the left, questionnaire result for the question regarding the helpfulness of the different display systems, where 1 is low helpfulness and 5 is high helpfulness. To the right, questionnaire result for the question whether the user perceived that information could be missed using either display system, where 1 is low risk and 5 is high risk.

Furthermore, the users were asked to rate the readability of the presented content. Both head-up displays scored on the positive side for readability, as presented in Fig. 7. The head-down display was rated with a lower score than the head-up display in this respect. This was an unexpected result, since a head-down display was expected to be rated higher, due to it being a self-lighted display with high prerequisites for producing good readability.

The users were also asked what level of realism they felt when using the head-up display simulation. The results, shown in Fig. 8, indicate that the users experienced a good level of realism. This is also supported by earlier tests, evaluating the realism of mixed reality simulation using head-worn projection systems, versus a simulation in front of a static screen [44].

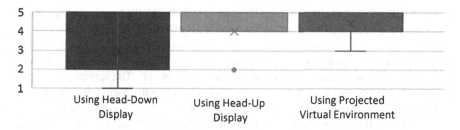

Fig. 7. Evaluation result for the question regarding the perceived readability of each display, where 1 is low readability and 5 high readability.

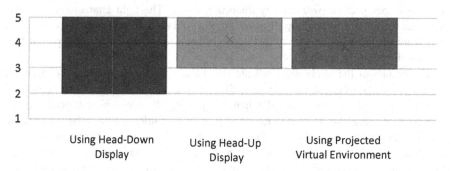

Fig. 8. Evaluation result for question regarding the perceived realism experienced, where 1 is un-realistic and 5 is realistic.

5 Discussion

Designing and developing vehicle interaction systems is a substantial project with high investments and long development times. The role of software with its increasing level of complexity and its interaction with the user is challenging, as also others mention [45]. Moreover, Sanches et al. state that for industrial vehicles "the need for research that informs the design of effective, intuitive, and efficient displays is a pressing one" [16].

Also, interaction design literature argues that possible designs shall be evaluated early, using swift methods, such as sketching, rapid prototyping, etc. [46, 47]. The argument is that good or bad designs can be identified early, through early evaluations and involvement of users. This opens up possibilities to elaborate on alternative designs and to avoid efforts being spent on less successful designs [48]. One method to evaluate a design is by using simulated environments. Simulated environments can range from desktop simulators, to virtual simulators, and to full-scale prototypes of vehicles. Nonetheless, the possible techniques for rapid prototyping are reduced, when physical artifacts need to be mixed together with virtual content, for example, physical controls or displays.

In this work we present an approach for rapid prototyping of mixed-reality simulations, using a head-worn projection display in a cave-like environment. This approach let the user look around freely in a virtual world, which is built quickly and supports a mix of virtual and physical artifacts. Building the cave together with the transparent screen and additional equipment was done within days, excluding the head-worn projection system, as well as the chair used as an excavator seat which was already existing. A simulation like this can be built in a few hours, with adequate planning, preparation of the virtual environment, and integration of different electrical components. The approach was tested in a pilot feasibility study, with seven users, indicating that the users felt a sensation of realism in the simulation and that presented content was visible and readable.

The key to this mixed reality simulation environment is the use of a pico laser projector with a low light emitting source, together with a highly reflective cloth to build the cave environment. Using the head-worn projection system, the user is able to look around in the virtual world. He or she, will always see the scenery from a first-person perspective, without key distortion effect. The light characteristic is also what enables the use of head-up displays in the simulation. The light emitted from the head-worn projector is too low to make a significant reflection on the transparent film used for the head-up display.

The results of the study also indicate that head-up displays may be preferred for information that is of interest to the user while working with an excavator. All users rated the head-up displays more helpful when completing the scenario, compared to the head-down display. All users also rated the risk to miss information to be lower when presented via the head-up displays. Spoken feedback from some of the users also indicated that the head-down display wasn't in attention while driving the excavator because it was outside the user's visible area. Moreover, that information on vehicle displays is missed by operators, is also indicated by real world studies [49]. The physical head-up display scored the lowest risk for information being lost, which was expected because the image presented is more inline of sight and always visible. This was also supported by comments from users, noting that something happened on the display while driving. It is also notable that the virtual head-up display scored a lower risk for information getting lost than the physical head-down display. Its responses were, however, more diverse and one user commented that information presented could be missed, because the information could be rendered outside the presented area by the head-worn projector.

5.1   Limitations and Future Work

This was a feasibility study to evaluate the use of mixed reality simulators using head-worn projection systems and head-up displays, which met the expectations in functionality and display characteristics. The number of participants in the study and their limited experience of real excavators reduces the possibility to draw general conclusions on the given feedback. However, making simple prototypes and taking in feedback early, is fruitful to guide the design, even though fidelity is far from final [50]. A limited amount of test users can still give valuable feedback for further and more detailed user evaluations, as well as for improvements in the design of the interaction [51].

One example, and also a possible limitation, was how the user got familiar with the task and could possibly learn how to use the presented information, or how to operate without it. A future work would, therefore, be to perform a bigger study with a task that requires the user to regularly check the information presented.

For this evaluation we only used simple figures for user presentation. The type of user support, its information, and how it is presented must be further evaluated to be able to understand how to use mixed reality interaction in industrial vehicles. A future work would also be to extend the environment with bigger head-up displays, with the support of presenting the information at the location where the user is looking and thus providing possibilities to evaluate augmented reality visualization.

6   Conclusion

In this paper, a prototype of a mixed reality simulation system for industrial machinery was presented to support designing interactions of, and with, information and safety features. Our system also enables rapid prototyping and evaluation of prototypes using virtual and physical artifacts simultaneously. The virtual environment is projected by a head-worn projection system that lets the user move and look around freely while still allowing for physical displays to be added to the environment. This includes support for transparent displays, which can be used to evaluate different variants of information presentation and placement, such as the use of head-up displays or head-down displays.

The approach was evaluated in a pilot study, where a scenario with an excavator was designed and implemented using three different display solutions: a traditional head-down display, a head-up display that was physically present, and a head-up display that was shown in the virtual world. The results of the study indicate that the simulation using head-up and head-down displays is realistic for prototyping. It also indicated that users felt the head-up display solutions to be more helpful while completing a given task, compared to the head-down display. Moreover, users rated the head-up display highest in reducing the risk of information being missed. Our result show that there are potential benefits with head-up displays and mixed reality interaction for industrial operators. However, more work is needed to understand how this can be used. An area that we can explore using rapid mixed reality prototyping.

References

1. Department for Transport: Incident at Llanbadarn Automatic Barrier Crossing (Locally Monitored), Near Aberystwyth, 19 June 2011 (2012)
2. Lagnel, O., Engstr, J.: Bättre arbetsmiljö med Head Up Display (2015)
3. Doshi, A., Cheng, S.Y., Trivedi, M.M.: A novel active heads-up display for driver assistance. IEEE Trans. Syst. Man Cybern. Part B **39**, 85–93 (2009)
4. He, J.: Head-up display for pilots and drivers. J. Ergon. **3**, e120 (2013)
5. Christodoulou, S., Michael, D., Gregoriades, A., Pampaka, M.: Design of a 3D interactive simulator for driver behavior analysis. In: Proceedings of the 2013 Summer Computer Simulation Conference. pp. 17:1–17:8. Society for Modeling & Simulation International, Vista (2013)
6. Donahue, G.M.: Usability and the bottom line. IEEE Softw. **18**, 31–37 (2001)
7. Ihemedu-Steinke, Q.C., Sirim, D., Erbach, R., Halady, P., Meixner, G.: Development and evaluation of a virtual reality driving simulator. Mensch und Comput. 2015–Workshopband (2015)

8. Kemeny, A.: From driving simulation to virtual reality. In: Proceedings of the 2014 Virtual Reality International Conference, pp. 32:1–32:5. ACM, New York (2014)

9. Kun, A.L.: ARV 2017: Workshop on Augmented Reality for Intelligent Vehicles (2017)

10. Gabbard, J.L., Fitch, G.M., Kim, H.: Behind the glass: driver challenges and opportunities for AR automotive applications. Proc. IEEE **102**, 124–136 (2014)

11. Sojourner, R.J., Antin, J.F.: The effects of a simulated head-up display speedometer on perceptual task performance. Hum. Factors **32**, 329–339 (1990)

12. Ablaßmeier, M., Poitschke, T., Wallhoff, F., Bengler, K., Rigoll, G.: Eye gaze studies comparing head-up and head-down displays in vehicles, pp. 2250–2252 (2007)

13. Silva, M.F., Barbosa, R.S., Castro, T.S.: The effects of interface design for head-up display on driver behavior. Life Sci. J. **10**, 14–17 (2013)

14. Wallmyr, M.: Reflections on augmented reality for Heavy machinery- practical usage and challenges. In: ARV 2017 Workshop on Augmented Reality for Intelligent Vehicles, Proceedings of the 9th International Conference on Automotive User Interfaces and Interactive Vehicular Applications Adjunct, Oldenburg (2017). http://doi.acm.org/10.1145/3131726.3131735

15. Lundin, M., Malmberg, A., Naeslund, C.: Head-up-display i engreppsskördare. Skogforsk (2005)

16. Ranta, P.: Added values of forestry machine simulator based training. In: International Conference on Multimedia and ICT Education, Linsbon, Portugal (2009)

17. Bretschneider-Hagemes, M.: Development of a new low cost driving simulation for assessing multidimensional task loads caused by mobile ICT at drivers' workplaces – *Objective-Fidelity Beats Equipment-Fidelity?* In: Yamamoto, S. (ed.) HCI 2015. LNCS, vol. 9173, pp. 173–179. Springer, Cham (2015). https://doi.org/10.1007/978-3-319-20618-9_17

18. Politis, I., Brewster, S., Pollick, F.: Evaluating multimodal driver displays of varying urgency. In: Proceedings of the 5th International Conference on Automotive User Interfaces and Interactive Vehicular Applications, pp. 92–99. ACM, New York (2013)

19. Turner, P., Turner, S., Burrows, L.: Creating a sense of place with a deliberately constrained virtual environment. Int. J. Cogn. Perform. Support **1**, 54–68 (2012)

20. Soomro, S.R., Urey, H.: Design, fabrication and characterization of transparent retro-reflective screen. Opt. Express **24**, 24232–24241 (2016). https://doi.org/10.1364/OE.24.024232

21. Head-up display. https://en.wikipedia.org/w/index.php?title=Head-up_display

22. Van Krevelen, R., Poelman, R.: A survey of augmented reality technologies, applications and limitations. Int. J. Virtual Real. **9**, 1–20 (2010)

23. Lauber, F., Follmann, A., Butz, A.: What you see is what you touch: visualizing touch screen interaction in the head-up display. In: Proceedings of the 2014 Conference on Designing Interactive Systems, pp. 171–180 (2014)

24. Cakmakci, O., Rolland, J.: Head-worn displays: a review. J. Disp. Technol. **2**, 199–216 (2006)

25. Rolland, J., Thompson, K.: See-through head worn displays for mobile augmented reality. In: Proceedings of the China National Computer Conference (2011)

26. Rolland, J.P., Thompson, K.P., Urey, H., Thomas, M.: See-through head worn display (HWD) architectures. In: Chen, J., Cranton, W., Fihn, M. (eds.) Handbook of Visual Display Technology, pp. 2145–2170. Springer, Heidelberg (2012). https://doi.org/10.1007/978-3-540-79567-4_134

27. Firth, N.: First wave of virtual reality games will let you live the dream. New Sci. **218**, 19–20 (2013)

28. McGill, M., Murray-Smith, R., Boland, D., Brewster, S.A.: A dose of reality: overcoming usability challenges in VR head-mounted displays. In: Proceedings of the 33rd Annual ACM Conference Extended Abstracts on Human Factors in Computing Systems, p. 177. ACM, New York (2015)

29. Meta - Augmented Reality. http://www.metavision.com/
30. Microsoft: HoloLens: a new way to see your world (2015)
31. Guillaumée, M., Vahdati, S.P., Tremblay, E., Mader, A., Bernasconi, G., Cadarso, V.J., Grossenbacher, J., Brugger, J., Sprague, R., Moser, C.: Curved holographic combiner for color head worn display. J. Disp. Technol. **10**, 444–449 (2014)
32. Bohn, D.: Intel made smart glasses that look normal. https://www.theverge.com/2018/2/5/16966530/intel-vaunt-smart-glasses-announced-ar-video
33. Kun, A.L., Janssen, C.P.: Calling while driving: an initial experiment with HoloLens, pp. 200–206 (2017)
34. Harrison, C., Benko, H., Wilson, A.D.: OmniTouch: wearable multitouch interaction everywhere. In: Proceedings of the 24th Annual ACM Symposium on User Interface Software and Technology, pp. 441–450 (2011)
35. Freeman, M., Champion, M., Madhavan, S.: Scanned laser pico-projectors: seeing the big picture (with a small device). Opt. Photonics News **20**, 28 (2009)
36. Hua, H., Gao, C., Rolland, J.P.: Imaging properties of retro-reflective materials used in head-mounted projective displays (HMPDs). In: AeroSense 2002, pp. 194–201 (2002)
37. Bolas, M., Krum, D.M.: Augmented reality applications and user interfaces using head-coupled near-axis personal projectors with novel retroreflective props and surfaces. In: Pervasive 2010 Ubiprojection Workshop (2010)
38. Mistry, P., Maes, P.: SixthSense: a wearable gestural interface. In: ACM SIGGRAPH ASIA 2009 Sketches, p. 11 (2009)
39. Mistry, P., Maes, P., Chang, L.: WUW-wear Ur world: a wearable gestural interface. In: CHI 2009 Extended Abstracts on Human Factors in Computing Systems, pp. 4111–4116 (2009)
40. Akşit, K., Kade, D., Özcan, O., Ürey, H.: Head-worn mixed reality projection display application. In: Proceedings of the 11th Conference on Advances in Computer Entertainment Technology, pp. 11:1–11:9. ACM, New York (2014)
41. Kade, D., Akşit, K., Ürey, H., Özcan, O.: Head-mounted mixed reality projection display for games production and entertainment. Pers. Ubiquit. Comput. **19**, 509–521 (2015)
42. Technical Illusions: CastAR (2014)
43. Sonoda, T., Endo, T., Kawakami, N., Tachi, S.: X'talVisor: full open type head-mounted projector. In: ACM SIGGRAPH 2005 Emerging Technologies, p. 32 (2005)
44. Kade, D., Wallmyr, M., Holstein, T., Lindell, R., Ürey, H., Özcan, O.: Low-cost mixed reality simulator for industrial vehicle environments. In: Lackey, S., Shumaker, R. (eds.) VAMR 2016. LNCS, vol. 9740, pp. 597–608. Springer, Cham (2016). https://doi.org/10.1007/978-3-319-39907-2_57
45. Holstein, T., Wallmyr, M., Wietzke, J., Land, R.: Current challenges in compositing heterogeneous user interfaces for automotive purposes. In: Kurosu, M. (ed.) HCI 2015. LNCS, vol. 9170, pp. 531–542. Springer, Cham (2015). https://doi.org/10.1007/978-3-319-20916-6_49
46. Garrett, J.J.: The Elements of User Experience: User-Centered Design for the Web and Beyond. Pearson Education, London (2010)
47. Benyon, D.: Designing Interactive Systems. Pearson, London (2014)
48. Buxton, B.: Sketching user Experiences. Morgan Kaufman, Burlington (2007)
49. Wallmyr, M.: Seeing through the eyes of heavy vehicle operators. In: Bernhaupt, R., Dalvi, G., Joshi, A., Balkrishan, D.K., O'Neill, J., Winckler, M. (eds.) INTERACT 2017. LNCS, vol. 10514, pp. 263–282. Springer, Cham (2017). https://doi.org/10.1007/978-3-319-67684-5_16
50. Nudelman, G.: One Dollar Prototype. DesignCaffeine Publications, San Francisco (2014)
51. Rozanski, E.P., Karn, K.S., Haake, A.R., Vigliotti, A.M., Pelz, J.B.: Simplified eye tracking enhances problem understanding and solution discovery in usability testing. In: 49th Human Factors and Ergonomics Society Annual Meeting, HFES 2005, pp. 2090–2094 (2005)

Author Index

Printed in the United States
By Bookmasters